OMNIVM
LVX
CIVIVM
MDCCCLII
MDCCC
LXXVIII

BLACK ON RED

My 44 Years Inside the SOVIET UNION

Leningrad
Stalingrad
Finland
Baltic Sea
Gulf of Finland
Gulf of Riga
The United States Government has not recognized the incorporation of Estonia, Latvia, and Lithuania into the Soviet Union
Bornholm (Denmark)
Öland
Gotland (Sweden)
Saaremaa
Hiiumaa
Turku
Tampere
Helsinki
Kotka
Imatra
Vyborg
Tallinn
Haapsalu
Pärnu
Tartu
Narva
Ventspils
Liepāja
Klaipeda
Riga
Jūrmala
Jelgava
Kaliningrad
Sovetsk
Chernyakovsk
Siauliai
Panevežys
Kaunas
Vilnius
Gdańsk
Baltiysk
Olsztyn
Warsaw
Bialystok
Grodno
Lida
Brest
Lublin
Minsk
Borisov
Vitebsk
Polotsk
Orsha
Mogilev
Bobruysk
Smolensk
Pskov
Luga
Kolpino
Novgorod
Staraya Russa
Velikiye Luki
VALDAI
Bologoye
Vyshniy Volochek
Torzhok
Rzhev
Kalinin
Klin
Moscow
Noginsk
Zagorsk
Serpukhov
Kaluga
Tula
Kolomna
Ryazan'
Vladimir
Kovrov
Dzerzhinsk
Gor'kiy
Arzamas
Murom
Yaroslavl'
Kostroma
Ivanovo
Kineshma
Andropov
Vologda
Cherepovets
Petrozavodsk
Lake Ladoga
Lake Onega
Tikhvin
Volkhov
Kirishi
Belomorsk
NORTHERN
CENTRAL RUSSIAN UPLAND
OKA DON PLAIN
Bryansk
Orel
Kursk
Yelets
Lipetsk
Voronezh
Michurinsk
Tambov
Penza
Saransk
Cheboksary
Yoshkar-Ola
Kazan'
Ul'yanovsk
Syzran'
Tol'yatti
Kuybyshev
Novokuybyshevsk
Saratov
Engel's
Balakovo
Kamyshin
Volgograd
Krasnoarmeysk
VOLGA UPLAND
Chernigov
Kiev
Zhitomir
Vinnitsa
Cherkassy
Kirovograd
Kremenchug
Poltava
Sumy
Khar'kov
Belgorod
Dnepropetrovsk
Zaporozh'ye
Nikopol'
Krivoy Rog
Donetsk
Gorlovka
Makeyevka
Voroshilovgrad
Melitopol'
Berdyansk
Zhdanov
Simferopol'
Kerch'
Sea of Azov
Taganrog
Rostov
Novocherkassk
Novoshakhtinsk
Shakhty
Volgodonsk
Novorossiysk
Krasnodar
Tikhoretsk
Armavir
Stavropol'
Elista
Maykop
Sochi
Nevinnomyssk
Kislovodsk
Pyatigorsk
Nal'chik
Sukhumi
Kutaisi
Batumi
Poti
Ordzhonikidze
Groznyy
Tbilisi
Rustavi
Makhachkala
Astrakhan'
CASPIAN LOWLAND
Below sea level
Gur'yev
Ural'sk
Fort Shevchenko
CAUCASUS MTS

BLACK ON RED

My 44 Years Inside the SOVIET UNION

An Autobiography by
Black American

Robert Robinson

with Jonathan Slevin

ACROPOLIS BOOKS LTD.
WASHINGTON, D.C.

ACROPOLIS BOOKS, LTD.
Alphons J. Hackl, Publisher
Colortone Building, 2400 17th St., N.W.
Washington, D.C. 20009

Printed in the United States of America by COLORTONE PRESS
Creative Graphics, Inc.
Washington, D.C. 20009

Cover photo, courtesy of Photri, Inc.

Cover design by Pamela Moore

Library of Congress Cataloging-in-Publication Data

Robinson, Robert, ca. 1902-
Black on Red : a Black American's 44 years inside the Soviet Union /
by Robert Robinson with Jonathan Slevin
p. cm.
Includes index.
ISBN 0-87491-885-5
1. Robinson, Robert, ca. 1902- .
2. Americans—Soviet Union—Biography.
Slevin, Jonathan.
II. Title.
DK34.B53R63 1988 87-26120
947.084—dc19 CIP

"Robert Robinson stood outside Ford Motor Company's Dearborn Assembly Plant Thursday morning, an 80-year-old man returning to the place where his incredible odyssey began.

"It was 57 years ago that Robinson, then a tool and die maker at Ford's Rouge complex, went to the Soviet Union to help the Soviets."

THE DETROIT FREE PRESS
June 26, 1987

Acknowledgments

I WOULD LIKE TO MENTION just a few of the many people to whom I am grateful. I first met William Worthy, an American journalist, in Moscow in early 1955. Accompanied by the associate editor of *Pravda*, he came to my factory to interview me. Although I could not speak frankly with him at the time, a few days later I visited him at his hotel and told him about my plight and my decade-long effort to get out of the Soviet Union and regain my freedom.

Worthy first advised me to see the British consul in Moscow, because I still had my old British passport. While he was in Moscow he did his utmost to help me, and when he returned to London he arranged for me to be granted an entry visa to England. Unfortunately, the KGB prevented me from using it.

Worthy arranged for me to meet Daniel Schorr and Clifton Daniel, the only two white American journalists I ever met in Moscow. I wish to thank these two men for their sympathy and support.

I also wish to express my gratitude to Mathias Lubega, who was the Ugandan ambassador to the Soviet Union from 1971 to 73, and to his successor in that post, Michael Ondoga, and their wives Pat and Mary. They arranged my escape in 1974. Ibrahim Mukibi, who currently serves as Uganda's minister of foreign affairs, provided me with my first link to the Ugandan embassy in Moscow, after we met on a bus during his student years. He and Mr. Oseku, who was Idi Amin's personal secretary when I first arrived in Uganda, helped me immeasurably. I am grateful to both of them.

I first met William B. Davis, an American diplomat, at the American Exhibition in Moscow in 1959, and then encountered him again in 1971. I am greatly indebted to him for his untiring efforts to help me finally return to the United States after my hasty escape from Uganda in 1978, during its war with Tanzania. It was he who first suggested that I write this book.

I also wish to express my appreciation to my wife, Zylpha Mapp-Robinson, for her patience, dedication, and support during the lengthy ordeal of typing a manuscript from my handwritten draft.

I wish finally to tip my hat to the US Immigration and Naturalization Service. Because of the generosity of Uncle Sam, I am able to live out my latter years in freedom.

RNR
Washington, D.C.

Table of Contents

PART I
The Stalin Era

PART II

The War Years and Their Aftermath

PART III

The Khrushchev Era

PART IV
Brezhnev to Gorbachev

Prologue

FORTY-FOUR YEARS is a large chunk of life. That's how long I lived in the Soviet Union. I never intended to stay very long. How could I, a black American from Detroit, have endured in a culture that was alien to almost everything I believed in or viewed sacred? Now that I'm out of the Soviet Union, I often marvel that I ever survived.

Maybe it was my mother's values, my unwavering belief in God, or my natural stubbornness that kept me from becoming Sovietized. There were a few other blacks in Russia when I was there, but they arrived as pilgrims reaching paradise. I understood how they felt, because what they left behind in the United States—besides relatives and close friends—was nothing to grieve over. Trying to survive in a society where dark-skinned people feel anxious, despised, and unwanted, and are considered inherently inferior by many whites, is an undertaking filled with agony. The handful of blacks who emigrated to the Soviet Union were serious, independent minded, sensitive, and usually well-educated. They all viewed Lenin as their Moses. So deep was their belief—and their need to believe—that they refused to notice the Bolsheviks' shortcomings.

Every single black I knew in the early 1930s who became a Soviet citizen disappeared from Moscow within seven years. The fortunate ones were exiled to Siberian labor camps. Those less fortunate were shot. It is strange that I, who never embraced Communism—even though I eventually became a Soviet citizen—was the only one who survived.

I never intended to stay for long. I always planned, and then hoped, and prayed, to come home. At times my chances seemed bleak. I might have starved, or frozen to death, or been blown away by a Nazi bomb during the war years in Moscow. I might have been sent to a labor camp, or a psychiatric hospital, or simply taken away and shot.

Many nights I fell asleep depressed. During the purges I never undressed until 4:00 A.M., fearing the awful pounding of the secret police on my door. Every night I waited my turn. One night in 1943 they came. I woke up with a start and said to myself, "God have mercy on my soul!"

I opened the door. When they saw my black face they seemed surprised, saying, "Oh, excuse us. There is some mistake." The odds were against my ever getting out. The pressure was constant, because I knew the secret police were always watching me. I learned to be on guard whenever I left my one-room flat, a state of mind which, fortunately, I had mastered while a young adult in the unfriendly climate of the United States. After many, many years I came to understand the Russian mind. I learned the Byzantine workings of the Soviet system, and I disciplined myself not to slip up. I can honestly say that I don't believe I ever allowed myself a careless moment.

I lived in the Soviet Union for seven years before I first won the trust of a single Russian. During all my years there, although I had many friends, I never dared to trust anyone. There were eighteen units in my apartment building, each one containing two or three families. There were informers throughout the complex, spying on Robert Robinson; watching, listening, and then reporting my every move and every sound, every day of every year.

No matter what my Russian neighbors told me, regardless of how much Communist officials bragged about their system of social justice and the equality of people, I was never really accepted as an equal. I was valued for my professional abilities; nevertheless I was an oddity and a potential asset to the Soviet propaganda apparatus. I somehow adapted to all of this, even to a life without marrying, with no woman by my side warming my bed and no children at home to hug me and call me

"Daddy." I dealt with all of this, and I learned to deal with almost everything else, with one big exception.

I could never, ever get used to the racism in the Soviet Union. It continually tested my patience and assaulted my sense of self-worth. Because the Russians pride themselves on being free of prejudice, their racism is more virulent than any I encountered in the United States as a young man. I rarely met a Russian who thought blacks—or for that matter Orientals or any non-whites—were equal to him. Trying to deal with their prejudice was like trying to catch a phantom. I could feel their racism singeing my flesh, but how do you deal with something that officially doesn't exist? I was the target of racism even though I had gained national recognition as a mechanical engineer by inventing machinery that dramatically increased industrial productivity. I even have my share of Soviet medals and certificates of honor.

This book is written to tell the story of my experiences in the Soviet Union. I am not writing out of bitterness, nor out of desire for fortune and fame, or vengeance. I am by nature a fair person, not a vindictive one. I can say, for example, that in some respects I benefited from my stay in Moscow. In the United States of the 1930s I never would have been allowed to become a mechanical engineer, because of my race. I never would have won the respect of my professional peers. I never would have been offered a job that challenged my creative urges. I never would have been honored professionally. In Moscow I was given the opportunity to achieve all of these things.

I wrote this book because I feel deeply that the way a black person was treated in a society that is supposed to be free of racial prejudice is a story that should be told. For forty-four years I observed the Russians and their political system, not as a white idealist but as a black man who had been well-trained by racism in America to judge the sincerity of a person's words and deeds. I can say as an expert that one of the greatest myths ever launched by the Kremlin's propaganda apparatus is that Soviet society is free of racism. This message has been hammered home both to the Russian people and abroad.

The fact is that all non-Russians are considered inferior. On the unofficial scale of inferiority, the Armenians, Georgians, and Ukrainians are more acceptable than other non-Russians. The eastern Soviet citizens—those with yellow skin and almond-shaped eyes—are considered to be at the bottom of society. They think of blacks as even worse. The reality of racism contrasts with the picture of social perfection painted by the authorities. It is maddening that Russians pride themselves on being free of racial prejudice. It is difficult for them to understand how thoroughly bigoted they are.

But I survived their racism too. Now I am back in the United States, an American citizen once again. What a journey it has been! My days are filled now with the joy of my present freedom and the memory of my past, as I relate this account of the Soviet system and the people it controls.

I have been dwelling upon matters that otherwise would be better left untouched. If I allowed myself the choice, it would be to enjoy the winter beauty of Washington, D.C., rather than relive life on the other side of reality. However, I feel compelled to talk about what people can only dimly imagine and may not even want to hear.

My story will begin where it ended, on a December day in 1986, in Washington, D.C. I will then take you through my journey, step by step, from such an innocent beginning, when Robert Robinson was a young man, in 1930, working for the Ford Motor Company in Detroit, as a toolmaker.

PART I

The Stalin Era

CHAPTER 1

An American Once Again

TODAY IS DECEMBER 9, 1986. I escaped from the Soviet Union thirteen years ago. It took at least two years for me to stop pinching myself to see if my freedom was real. It was another year before I stopped waking up in the middle of the night, jumping out of bed, dashing to the window, and peering outside. I was afraid that I would find myself in the midst of a Moscow winter, that I would learn that my escape had been a cruel dream.

Life has taught me that there is no predicting what the next day will bring. Eight decades have chiseled me into a realist. I lived for so long physically distant and spiritually apart from everything that was familiar to me. Now I am no longer on Soviet soil, no longer subject to constant surveillance, no longer dependent on the Soviet state for my food and the whims of Soviet justice for my life.

Yet I've only enjoyed partial freedom since 1974, when Uganda's Idi Amin helped spring me from my long captivity. It has been a long, long journey, and today is a special day. It is a day of reverence, because I am about to become an American citizen once again, after forty-nine years. Since 1974 I have still needed to be cautious. I have not talked or given interviews.

"Why alert the KGB?" I reasoned. Although I'm no longer on Soviet soil, I can't feel wholly safe. If you had seen as many people purged as I have, you would understand how I have to consider the possibility of a pellet through my head as realistic. Even though I renounced my Soviet citizenship six years ago, the Soviets might still consider me one of them. They might decide to exercize their claim on me. Soviet agents could kidnap me and cart me back to Russia. It may be unlikely, but it is far from being unheard of. I am just a little guy, after all, an unknown who has been living nearly anonymously. I have no government, no organization, and no ethnic group to come to my defense.

My concern for my physical safety has been a factor in my silence. But there is another, bigger reason. The Soviets won't like my book. I am writing as an outsider, who lived and worked inside Soviet society for forty-four years. Mine is not a story of labor camps and exile, but of living nose-to-nose with Soviet workers. There has never been anybody else like me—never in the history of the Soviet Union. This is not a boast. It is nothing so grand, and certainly not what I meant to do with my life. I state this simply, as a fact.

The Soviets would prefer that my experiences die with me. They may seek to discredit me and my account. I would prefer to deal with this as an American citizen, reattached in some sense to my spiritual roots. Facing a campaign of lies, distortion, and hatred will be no fun. I have not been ready for that, until now.

Neither am I a campaigner or an outspoken advocate for a cause. Although circumstances have forced me to fight all my life, I am by nature a reserved person and my battles have been quiet affairs. Until now, my knowledge, my memories, and my secrets have kept themselves company in the privacy of my mind.

Years ago the United States stopped calling me one of its own. Without ever asking me about it, the State Department decided I had become a witting instrument for Soviet propaganda. They gave me an ultimatum which in effect cut me loose and put my fate in the hands of Joseph Stalin. Faced with an impossible choice in 1937, I relinquished my US citizenship. I intended to get it back, but I couldn't.

Ever since that time, I have thirsted for even the partial freedom of being a black American. Even in America before *Brown* v. *Board of*

Education, before the NAACP, before the activism of Martin Luther King, Jr., blacks had a partial taste of freedom. I have always known that a little bit of freedom in America was better than the Russian reality of none at all.

You know, then, that this is a special day. I am sitting in a government building in Washington, D.C. A hundred or more other people are milling around, some standing in line waiting to be called, others sitting in assigned places along the rows of chairs. All of us are here to become naturalized US citizens.

''Robinson, Robert,'' a woman calls out my name. Clutching my card in my right hand, I wave it in the air and walk over to her. She examines it, checks my identification, tells me that everything is in order, and directs me to sit in a different row. We are arranged in alphabetical order. As the clerk continues through the R's and into the S's, I return to my thousand thoughts.

I know that life after today will feel different. But even as an American citizen, I will probably be wise, not paranoid, to continue taking simple precautions, like not going out alone at night. There is no reason to be foolish just because I am free. I do not think I will feel tempted to stand alone on a deserted beach, romanced into carelessness by a brilliant sunset or an enchanting spell of solitude. I have come too far to be carried to my Maker as the victim of an unsolved homicide.

I am thirteen years out of Russia, away from the heaviness of a life that holds little joy. In the Soviet Union, grey gloom searches out any who would dare to have hope. It takes its cruel pleasure by snuffing out their spark, with awful certainty, sooner or later.

''Zulkovsky,'' the clerk calls. Her voice jars me back into the present. The last name has been read.

"Everybody rise," call another woman. We stand up. In walks the judge.

"Raise your right hand."

CHAPTER 2

The Formative Years

NEWS TRAVELED QUICKLY through the grapevine. In 1923, five dollars a day was like riches for the average worker. The word in Harlem for the adventurous was, "Go to the Ford Motor Company. Go to Detroit."

Leaving Harlem wasn't easy. It was a place where a black man could at least feel fairly secure. You didn't have to pretend or play anyone else's games. It was a place where a person could feel relaxed. But the Midwest! It was as foreign to me as China. In spite of my apprehension, two things lured me there. There was the hope of financial security and my dream that I could somehow be in a position to invent something mechanical. I knew the chances of that happening in New York City were practically nil.

Even as a child I yearned to build things. I was always able to figure out how to fix things around the house. When others thought I was daydreaming, I was actually designing new machines in my mind.

Mathematics and science thrilled me just as much as political theory and current politics bored me. Beginning with an idea in my mind and turning it into something tangible and useful was simply a fantastic thing to do.

I thought about Detroit and weighed the risks. I was no fool. I knew that the Ford Motor Company belonged to the white man's world. It would be tough for any black man to land a skilled job there. I would never make it unless I could show more skill and knowledge than the white workers, and there was no guarantee I would even be given that chance. I already knew this from personal experience.

Before I came to New York I had studied toolmaking for four years in Cuba, where I grew up. I graduated as a universal toolmaker. Cuba at that time was two-thirds black and one-third white. I never experienced racial prejudice and did not know what it was until I arrived in New York. After I got settled in the United States, I sent out a batch of resumes. I got a reply from each one of them, asking me to report to work. I was very excited.

But I never got near a machine. When I reported to each company, the personnel manager who had seemed so eager to hire me, looked at my black skin and explained to me lamely why the job was no longer available. I went to Detroit knowing there were obstacles to being hired in a skilled position, even though I was qualified. But I went determined to try.

Once settled, I began going to Ford's employment office at 6:30 in the morning, so I could be near the hiring point when they opened up at 8 A.M. The first time I told the hiring officer I was a toolmaker, his reaction was, "What, you a toolmaker! Run along, boy."

Tenacious by nature, I kept going back twice a week. Soon the two different employment officers knew me so well that they would not even say a word, but instead signaled me to move on with a wave of their hands. On one occasion one of them said to me, "Boy, why don't you go back to school."

I continued with my twice-weekly exercise until it began to seem almost ridiculous. Then one Sunday an older man who worshipped at the same church took me aside and said, "Son, to the best of my knowledge toolmaking is a white man's job. You just can't break into that kind of work in the usual way."

He had been working at Ford's for more than ten years. "First you've got to get a job as a floor sweeper," he said. "The most important thing is getting hired. Once you're in, you can show what you know and enroll in the factory's trade school. When you pass the exams there's a chance they might start you as a toolmaker."

The next day I was back in the employment line, with a renewed sense of expectation. Fortunately, there was a new hiring officer. When he asked me what kind of work I was looking for, I told him floor sweeping, and he told me to go into the factory. In the seventh week, on my thirteenth try, I was finally hired.

I worked eight hours a day, sweeping a large machine shop floor without stopping, except to go to the bathroom. Four months later I was able to enroll in the factory's technical school. Fourteen months later I graduated as a toolmaker, the only black toolmaker in the entire company.

The next step after a student completed his theoretical training was to send him to a special instructor. He would then receive hands-on instruction in a machine shop for four weeks. In my case, they skipped this part of my training and sent me directly to the foreman of the same shop where I had recently been a sweeper.

When I reported to work, the foreman took me to a vacant shaper. He told me where to obtain the tools, gave me a job with its accompanying drawing, then left me standing there without even showing me how to turn the machine on or off, or what the different levers and handles were for, or even how to hold the job in the vise. As he walked away I glanced around and saw that all the toolmakers, more than twenty of them, had stopped their machines and were watching this spectacle with great amusement.

The next part of their game was to see what the colored boy sweeper would do, whether I would try to use the shaper and break it, or give up in despair, collapse in tears, get angry, or whatever. I knew I should not give away the fact that I knew how to operate a shaper. I pretended to study the machine from every angle. Throughout the rest of the afternoon, I inspected every part of it.

The next day I brought my machine shop handbook and opened it to the page describing the shaper. I continued to study every lever and handle, all day long. I did the same thing the following day. Then I finally turned it on, and by the end of the day had the shaper running to the required stroke needed for machining the job. By the morning of the fourth day, always referring to my handbook, I went to the grinding wheel and ground the cutting tool and came back to the shaper and set up the cutting. Then I took the drawing and pretended to be studying it with great concentration for some time before actually machining the job. When I had finished it, I took it to the foreman who brought it to the inspector right away for checking.

He came up to me a short time later and said very seriously, "Boy, you must have had some experience before in toolmaking." Of course, I denied it. He shook his head in disbelief. Then he gave me another job and left. I stole a glance at the other toolmakers around me. They were looking rather astonished. It was a great victory.

As I had produced no scrap after six months of working on the shaper (used to shape pieces to designer specifications), I was transferred to the surface grinder. Again, I was given no guidance on how to use this machine, which I supposedly had never operated before. I went through the same routine as I had with the shaper and did just fine.

At that time Ford had 270,000 people working around the clock in three shifts of 90,000 each. There were 700 toolmakers in my department: 699 whites and one black. I really had status, although it was not something I thought about much. I considered toolmaking just a way station on my way to greater heights. I was confident that I had the ability, and I felt a strong drive urging me from within to reach higher and to excel.

In 1930 I was twenty-three years old and I had been at Ford for three years. Although the stock market had crashed and the depression was underway, my future seemed bright. I was making a good wage, enjoying my work, and I was able to save money with the goal of bringing my mother over from Cuba.

Then in April 1930, it happened. The Russians arrived. One pleasant spring day four men dressed in suits came into the department where I worked, the grinding section where we produced huge forming dies. They stopped near my machine. Even with my head down, concentrating on my work, I sensed they were looking at me. I glanced up and noticed an older, stout man motion to one of his younger companions to speak to me.

As a rule, I avoided talking to anyone while I was working. Although I believe the quality of my work was excellent, that still did not mean that the foreman and other supervisors wanted me there. I was extremely cautious about doing anything that would give them an excuse to fire me. But I thought this situation was probably different. It looked like an official delegation, which would have been sanctioned by the front office.

The young man approached and began speaking to me in very thickly accented English. His sentence structure was mixed up and at first I could not understand what he was saying. Then I gathered that he was asking me how long I had been a toolmaker, where I had learned the skill, and how old I was. I answered him, and he translated for his boss.

I did not know why they were speaking to me, and I felt uncomfortable. I wished they would go away and leave me to my work. When the young man asked me if I was willing to go to Russia to teach young apprentices the toolmaking trade, I said, "Sure," thinking they would then go away and stop bothering me. They did leave then, and I soon forgot about our encounter.

A week later I had a horrible shock. My foreman walked over to me at my machine. He had never done that before, and I sensed trouble.

"The employment chief at the main office wants to see you," he said. "You'd better get over there right away."

I froze with fear. "They're going to fire me," I thought. I left my machine right away but could not bring myself to go to the office and face the firing squad. Things had been going so well. Despite the depression, I had a well-paying job and a chance to advance. I could see myself in the street selling apples, hustling to scrape up enough money to buy a loaf of bread. It took me ten minutes to reach the office area, but for most of the next hour I delayed going in, fearing my fate, thinking that I was ruined. It was as if there was a firing squad behind the door that had been given the order to shoot me.

Finally I opened the door and entered. I told the man behind the desk that I was Robert Robinson and I had been instructed by my shop foreman to report to the office. He erupted.

"You black monkey, you were supposed to be here half an hour ago. Couldn't you get your face over here any quicker than that?"

He kept snarling and cursing. He just wouldn't stop, until I did not think I could stand it any longer. I was shocked and humiliated. I forgot my preoccupation of the last hour, that I was about to be fired, and just stood there trying to keep from exploding. I wanted to strike back, but I knew that would bring the police. Better to be out of work than in the city jail. But I could not take his barrage of verbal abuse any longer. To survive, I turned myself half-numb and half-conscious, almost going into a trance so that I would not hear the venomous words coming out of this man's mouth.

Then the storm subsided. He swiveled back in his chair, looked directly at me, and said with disdain, "Your friends want to see you."

He handed me a slip of paper and added, "Here is the name and address of the people you have to see." He even told me what streetcar would get me to the place. It was clear that he knew he would be held responsible if I failed to find my way there. I thanked him and walked out.

Outside the office, I was still in a state of shock. The fact that the man did not fire me still had not dawned on me. Much like a robot, I got on the streetcar and went to the address on the piece of paper. It was a short, easy ride, and I found the office building with no trouble.

When I opened the door to the office, I first noticed a number of Americans, all whites, who seemed to be taking an exam. Some were looking over blueprints and others had pencil and paper and were absorbed in calculations. I introduced myself to the receptionist and handed her the slip of paper the Ford official had given me. She asked me to wait while she went into the office behind her. I noticed the other applicants in the room had all stopped what they were doing and seemed surprised at what was happening. Soon the door opened and the stout man who had been in my department the previous week offered his hand and warmly invited me inside.

I must say I was bewildered. I still had not recovered from the scare of being fired. The man asked me to sit down; I settled in a nearby chair. Again he asked me if I wanted to go to Russia, and he continued talking without letting me answer his question. Then he began to flatter me, which sounded awfully good, especially after my morning ordeal and the general lack of acceptance I was experiencing at Ford.

He said, "During the past week I have checked your work, background, and character. Everyone I have talked to is favorably impressed with you."

Then he told me that he was so confident of my ability that he had decided to waive my taking the mathematical and mechanical drawing test that applicants were required to take. He was willing to have me sign a one-year contract right away.

"Of course, the contract will be renewable, subject to your performance," he said.

By this time I had come to my senses. "This man is serious," I thought. "What a contract!"

I was making $140 a month, which I figured was hard to beat anywhere. He offered me $250 a month, rent free living quarters, a maid, thirty days paid vacation a year, a car, free passage to and from Russia, and they would deposit $150 out of each month's paycheck in an American bank. With that I should be able to bring my mother to New York in a year or two, which was a driving goal for my brother and me, since she was alone in Cuba without any family.

I was impressed. I thought to myself, "America is in the grip of a serious depression and I could be laid off any day at Ford. Judging by all the applicants in the outer room, white Americans are lining up for this chance. Why not me too?"

That whites were competing for the same job made it easier for me to sign the contract. To get something that they wanted was appealing; it also helped to ease my doubts about actually going to the Soviet Union, because I was aware of media accounts criticizing the Soviet system. But to think about the obstacles I was facing, trying to advance within the insitutionalized racism in America—and recalling that the cousin of a friend of mine had just been lynched three months earlier—I made up my mind on the spot. I read the contract and signed it.

I was scheduled to leave from New York in six weeks, on May 28. I would have enough time to visit my mother in Cuba. I could not think of leaving without seeing her, especially since it had been several years since I had kissed her good-by and left as an ambitious seventeen-year-old to seek a better way of life in America. My mother was someone very special, and now I could save more money and bring her to America sooner than my salary at Ford would allow.

The best way to get to Cuba was on a boat from Key West. So at 7:00 P.M. on April 30, I hopped on a Greyhound bus in Detroit. I was carrying a sack of cakes, some bread, three bottles of Coca-Cola, and a suitcase. I had prepared myself against the likelihood that restaurants on the way would not serve me. By the time the bus pulled into Richmond, I was tired of my own provisions and felt a need for something hot. A cup of coffee and a sandwich would do. But as soon as I stepped into the restaurant at the bus terminal, I was motioned around to the back door by a startled waitress. Entering by the back door was something I would not do, so I returned to the bus.

In Atlanta I found a restaurant for blacks near the terminal, and ate my first real meal since leaving Detroit two days earlier. I reboarded the bus and sat down in the window seat in the last row on the left. I chose the worst seats in the bus—you could feel every bump and there was barely any leg room—because I figured they would be the safest. White folks would not want to sit here.

But in Macon a number of passengers got on, the seats up front filled up, and a young white couple sat down next to me, with the man closest. I stiffened a little and scrunched up closer to the window in an effort not to touch him. But for three days I had been forcing myself to stay awake, and I was very tired. My guard slipped and I began to doze off. I tried to fight my body's agonizing need to sleep, tried to fight it, tried to fight it . . .

Suddenly I was wide awake! My head was spinning; it had crashed against the bus wall. I was trying to figure out what was going on. The man from the next seat was standing over me. His eyes were blazing, his fists clenched. His face was distorted, with a look that said he wanted to kill me.

What could I do? If I hit him back, pushed him away, or even protested, the other passengers would probably turn into an angry mob. I could not run away; I was cornered. I might be murdered. In that moment of hopelessness and near panic, Claude McKay's poem, "If We Must Die," suddenly and strangely came to mind. I don't know if it came as a special source of inspiration, but I did something I never would have done if I had thought it out.

I stood up and began beating on my chest and crying out in Spanish, "Yo no deseo de ser linchado! Porque yo soy Cubano! Yo soy Cubano! Yo soy Cubano!"

I was hysterical. I shouted over and over, "I'm not prepared to be lynched. I am a Cuban. I am a Cuban."

By the grace of God I struck a humane cord in the heart of the man's wife—or sweetheart. "Leave him alone!" she cried out to him. "He's not an American. Can't you hear him? He's a Cuban; leave him alone."

Someone up front yelled, "Throw him out. Throw the nigger out!"

But the woman won the day, and the man relaxed and sat down. By now the bus driver had pulled over, stopped the bus, and was walking toward us to find out what was going on. I had sat back down in my seat and was weeping uncontrollably. The woman came to my rescue again by telling the driver everything was all right. He went back to the front and off we went.

By the time we got to Key West I was tired beyond belief, hungry, but glad to be alive. I boarded the boat for Havana and then rode the train fourteen hours to reach St. German, the small settlement where my mother lived, which was near a huge sugar processing plant. I had not told her I was coming, and she was stunned to see me. We were both overwhelmed, and she wept tears of joy. I had left nearly seven years before.

On the night of my arrival, after enjoying the elaborate supper my mother prepared, we talked late into the night. After going to bed, I found it difficult to fall asleep, and lay awake thinking of my mother's demanding life, full of sacrifices and toil. She was from Dominica in the West Indies, which had been colonized first by the French and then by the British. At a young age she began working for a British doctor, and when he went to Jamaica he took her with him. She met my father in Jamaica, where I was born. We later moved to Cuba, where I grew up and where, when I was six-and-a-half, my father deserted the family. He left my mother without any money or source of income, in a land, language, and culture that were strange to her.

Somehow we made it, but until this visit I did not fully comprehend how difficult it was for her. A few hours earlier she told me something I had never known before, and which I can never, ever forget. She explained that a month after my father left us she had no money to buy food. She had not eaten in two days, had barely been able to feed me, and the rent was due in two days. In addition, I would ask her where my father was, and why I no longer had a father like the other kids in the neighborhood. These questions were like a dagger stabbing her heart.

My mother told me how on that bleak night seventeen years ago she gave me the last small piece of dried bread and was then without hope that she would be able to get any more food for me. She decided she could no longer bear my hungry cries, her loneliness, her sense of hopelessness, and it would be best to end it all. At eleven that night, she muffled my mouth, held me tight, and headed straight for the sea, about five blocks away.

She walked onto the beach and headed straight for the water. Tears were flowing down her cheeks and I was crying out in hunger. The waves were lapping at her ankles and she kept walking, praying to God for forgiveness, and asking Him to have mercy on her soul.

Suddenly she stopped! In the darkness she saw the silhouette of a tall man standing just a few feet in front of us. He cried out to her, "Where are you going?"

My mother started, and then began walking backward, out of the water and up onto the beach. He looked at her sternly and commanded, "Don't you ever do that again!"

Later that night back in her room, as my mother slept, she dreamed of her grandmother for the first time in her life. She looked very sad as she said, "Why don't you move from this house? You must leave right away."

My mother responded, "How can I move when I have no money?"

Her grandmother told her to go ask Alphrenize, a woman in her church, for a room. The next day my mother did just that, and Alphrenize gave her a room and helped her find a job ironing washable cotton pants, so that in time she could get back on her feet.

My mother raised me with inexhaustible dedication. She never screamed at me, and strange though it may seem, I remember always feeling her warmth and sincerity, though I cannot remember her even hugging or kissing me when I was a child. She was very strict, and had a passion for teaching the need for self-discipline and self-reliance. She ingrained that into me, and made sure that I grew up knowing how to do everything for myself. I would not only wash the dishes, clean the floor, and wash and iron my clothes, I would wash and iron and mend her clothes as well. She was my first teacher, from the time I was two. By the time I was six I could spell and read from the Bible. She taught me to respect all people, regardless of race, status, or religious belief, and instructed me that my most important possession was my word. As a result of my environment, I grew up trilingual. I learned English at home and Spanish as well as French in school. There were many Haitians in Cuba at that time, and French was encouraged as a second language.

As overjoyed as my mother was to see me, she did not think much of my plan to go to Russia. She felt intuitively that it was not right. I assured her that it was only a one-year project, and in the end she gave me her blessing.

CHAPTER 3

My Journey Begins

MY VISIT WITH MY MOTHER was short, and in six days I returned to Havana and took the first boat back to Florida. The ninety-mile trip passed by quickly, and fortunately, the 1,800-mile bus ride to New York went by without incident. Two days before departure, I reported to Armtorg, the Soviet agency that was coordinating our venture. I picked up one hundred dollars in expense money and my second-class ticket for my trans-Atlantic trip on the steampship, *Majestic*.

Several days later we steamed into Southampton. From there, the forty-five of us bound for the Soviet Union traveled by train to London, where we spent four-and-a-half days.

During our stay in London, the hotel where the group stayed was for whites only, so I ended up in quarters about a twenty-minute walk away. As a result, I never learned until later that the group had been treated to four days of sightseeing. Whereas I sought out the London sights by myself, they had the benefit of buses and tour guides.

Next we boarded the *Rykov*, a Soviet ship that would transport us to Leningrad, where I gained my first fascinating insight into the workings of the Soviet system. On the second day out, the captain invited all of the passengers on a tour of the ship. The cleanliness and orderliness impressed me. Even the engine room, which is usually the dirtiest place on a ship, was sparkling. Nothing was out of place in the crew's quarters.

And by watching the crew at work, I could see that their morale was high. The sailors approached their work with the enthusiasm of new religious converts. Most of them were young, from their early twenties to late thirties. I wondered how the crew could be so high-spirited, whether it was a national characteristic, or if something else was at work. To discover the answer, I decided to do some snooping around.

I soon found a young English-speaking Russian sailor who told me he could answer my question. He also said that he was aware of the discrimination against blacks in the United States, and assured me that I would find racial equality in Russia. There had been an incident in the dining hall the day before, when two white Americans got up from my table and walked away in protest as soon as I sat down. At breakfast the next day, after the incident was repeated, the captain stood up and said firmly to our group, "Comrade specialists, you are all invited to work in the Soviet Union. Under the Soviet system there is no discrimination based on nationality or the color of a man's skin. Everyone in Soviet Russia is equal. I am not authorized to segregate anyone on this ship. I am asking that everybody—all of the passengers—obey Soviet law."

This incident had impressed the young sailor who was now going to answer my question. He told me that each day at 5:30 P.M. the captain assembled all crew members who were not on duty for a meeting in the dining hall. Attendance was mandatory and a sign-in sheet was maintained. At the sailor's invitation I attended the meeting later that day, and then afterward listened to his explanation of what had gone on. First the crew heard reports of the social and economic progress in the Soviet Union. This information came from radio broadcasts out of Moscow. The sailors cheered at the announcement of certain factories surpassing their production goals. When individuals were recognized for outstanding work either in a factory or on a farm, the sailors expressed their admiration. I could sense that they wanted to be honored in the same way. During the next part of the meeting, each crew member's work was evaluated. Minutes were kept. At the end of each month a ship newspaper was posted, citing which sailors excelled and admonishing those whose work was substandard to follow the example of the model crew members. Promotions were always promised to those who did well. In this way the crew developed into an efficient force.

The young sailor also explained to me that at these meetings, the crew was reminded that news of the world outside the Soviet Union must come from a Soviet source to be considered reliable. They were constantly warned that political forces throughout the world were determined to destroy the Soviet Union. These meetings, I later discovered while living in Russia, were held regularly for workers in every professional and vocational area and for students and faculty throughout the educational system. Artists, dancers, writers, factory workers—noboby was exempt. I am convinced that these indoctrination methods were a major factor in turning the Soviet Union into a superpower in such a short period of time.

It was a gorgeous spring day in 1930 when the *Rykov* steamed into Leningrad and maneuvered gently alongside a pier. The sun was shining brightly in a dazzling blue sky. My spirits were high, and I felt like the weather was a good omen, telling me that my hasty decision had been a good one. I was twenty-three years old.

I stood at the railing watching the Russian men tie the ship's lines to the piers, and then eagerly disembarked with the other members of our group. "Perhaps this really will be a rewarding year," I thought.

We were escorted to a stately hotel, called the Europa, where we were to spend the next four-and-a-half days. Once we were inside the lobby our names were called and we were shown to our rooms. When we got to a large room with four beds inside, it became clear to three of the whites in the group that they were to share it with me. They wanted nothing of it. They picked up their bags and headed back down the hall to the hotel clerk. Not sure what to do, I at first waited for them to return. I finally thought, "Why wait?" Lunch was not for an hour, and in that time I could treat myself to a little tour of the city.

What I first saw of Leningrad intrigued me. It was unlike any city I had ever seen. I saw no buildings made of wood. Everything was either stone or brick—no steel or glass—and all were about three or four stories tall. Leningrad was an old, carefully groomed city. I was surprised that the cobblestone streets were spotless. The city felt like it had a rich heritage, and I could tell that its citizens were proud of their home and the way they kept it up.

Other things startled me on my first view of a Russian city. The streetcars were huge. They strung three coaches together and each one I saw was packed with people. It was shocking to notice that all the drivers were women. You would never see a woman in that sort of profession back home. At first it seemed peculiar—even wrong—but as I thought about it, I came to think that maybe this kind of progressiveness was what distinguished the Soviet Union from the West, and maybe I would come to appreciate it.

I noticed something else that I could immediately respect. Whenever a streetcar came close to a school, it slowed down and the driver started ringing the bell so long and so loud that I figured even the deaf would be warned.

As I strolled back to the hotel I studied the people in the street. Most of the women had long black hair, strung in single or double braids. Some had powdered their faces, but I only saw one or two with lipstick. None of them wore earrings, bracelets, necklaces, rings, or watches; I didn't see any jewelry at all.

The clothing was so ill-fitting, they could hardly have looked worse in potato sacks. Most of the women looked like blocks, stocky and stout, and colorless, wearing mostly blues, browns, and grays, with an occasional white blouse. The men were even less fashionable. Their suit jackets were so short and small they barely covered their waists. They gave the impression of penguins with their bottoms sticking out. And the seats of their pants were thin and glazed from constant wear. Some even had patches. They all wore heavy, square-toed shoes that squeaked when they walked.

Every man needed a haircut, at least by Western standards. The slicked-down Rudolph Valentino look so popular in the United States clearly had not reached as far as Leningrad. As I looked around, during my walk and in the hotel, I noticed quite a few men who were so covered with dandruff that it looked from a distance as if their hair was turning white and the shoulders of their jackets were growing white manes. I learned later that there were no consumer goods in Russia because of Stalin's Five-Year Plan.

Previously, Lenin's War Communism, a policy in effect from 1918 to 1920, caused great deprivation in Russia because of the speed with which the country was converted to a socialist state and the continuing civil war between Lenin's forces and the supporters of the czar.

To revive the country's depressed economy, Lenin introduced his New Economic Policy in 1921. This policy, which reduced peasant taxes and permitted small private stores and manufacturing in the cities, was continued under Stalin until 1928. It was at that time that the Five-Year Plan was implemented, mandating the closing of private stores and workshops and the forcible collectivization of peasant-owned farms. Shortages of food and consumer goods were an immediate result. Those who resisted selling their property to the state at a greatly reduced value saw it taken from them by force, and were themselves—and their families—sent in boxcars to Siberia. Approximately seventeen million people lost their lives during implementation of Stalin's Five Year Plan.[1]

After lunch came a wonderful surprise; we were to be given a tour of the city and I was included. Here in Russia, they were not running a "white's only" tour. I was not being left behind. "Russia seems different from the West," I thought. "Maybe here I'll really find freedom."

We were taken to the Hermitage, an enormous art museum which at the time I had never heard of. For two-and-a-half hours we looked at some of the most inspiring paintings in the history of mankind: Rembrandt, Rubens, van Gogh, Renoir, Raphael, da Vinci, Michelangelo, Cézanne, and Giorgione. They were all there. The experience overwhelmed me. We were in a wonderland, a magical place detached from the tumult of the world, where we could soak in the brilliance of history's greatest artistic geniuses. There was so much more to see, I would have gladly spent the next week there, had our guide allowed it.

The next stop was the Soviet mint, where we watched money being printed and stamped, and then on to the Tomb of the Czars. Our guide seemed particularly impressed with Peter the Great, czar of Russia for forty-three years, from 1682 to 1725. I vaguely remembered being taught in school that Peter the Great had tried to westernize Russia, often with brutal force. On the way back to the hotel, our guide told us an eerie story about this czar which is part of Russian folklore, though I do not know if it actually is true.

It seems that months after Peter the Great's funeral, a mask—an exact replica of Peter's face—had been fashioned to be placed on his skull. To do so, the maskmaker and his helpers carefully lifted the lid of the czar's coffin. They discovered with a great shock that Peter the Great's face was still intact, looking as fresh as the day he was buried. But then in a flash, as they gazed at the body, because of its exposure to fresh oxygen, the face flattened to ashes.

When we returned to the hotel we all went upstairs to rest. I had the big room all to myself, since my roommates had not returned. Perhaps they had succeeded in making separate arrangements, or maybe they were loitering in the lobby. Dinner was scheduled in an hour. I

[1]*Stalin told Churchill that the "great bulk" of ten million peasants were "wiped out." Winston Churchill,* The Second World War, *Vol. 4 (London: Cassell, 1951) 447-448. Solzhenitsyn estimates that fifteen million died. See Alexander Solzhenitsyn,* The Gulag Archipelago Three *(New York: Perennial Library, 1976), 350. A number of Communist Party sources told the author that seventeen to nineteen million people died.*

thought how foolish they were to insist on segregation in a country that rejects making distinctions among people because of their skin color.

"It's all they know," I thought. "They are victims of the racism in the United States."

At dinnertime I sat down at the same table where I had eaten lunch. Again I ate alone. No member of my group joined me, nor did any tourist.

"If I were to go to a restaurant that catered only to Russians," I thought, "I would not have to eat alone."

For the enjoyment of our group, the hotel orchestra attempted to play American jazz while we ate. The musicians were not very good, yet the guests remained at their tables, relishing the familiar tunes. But I was not moved. Rather than reminisce about my recent past, I preferred to dive into my future. I wanted to go out and see what Leningrad was like at night.

I hurried upstairs to wash before going exploring. But when I peered out the window, I was surprised to see that there was no night. At 9:30 P.M. it was like high noon in Harlem in the middle of June. I just stood at the window for the longest time, looking out in fascination. I was still there an hour-and-a-half later, and the sun was still brightly shining.

"What is going on?" I kept wondering. Finally I dashed downstairs to find out from someone why there was no nightfall. The hotel clerk laughed at me. He explained that in Leningrad the sun never sets during the summer. The people in northern Russia call it "white nights," he said.

When I returned to my room there was still no one else there, so I figured the three whites had found another place to stay. Though I knew I should be tired, I did not like the idea of going to sleep while the sun was still blazing. I went back to my vigil at the window as something to do. I noticed that there were double window panes, which I figured might be there as added protection against thieves. We had been warned that because the Europa catered to Western tourists, and mostly Americans—who were thought to have lots of money—there were robberies and burglaries in the hotel and the surrounding area.

Before going to bed I fastened the windows and door as securely as possible. Because it seemed like daytime, which to me always meant

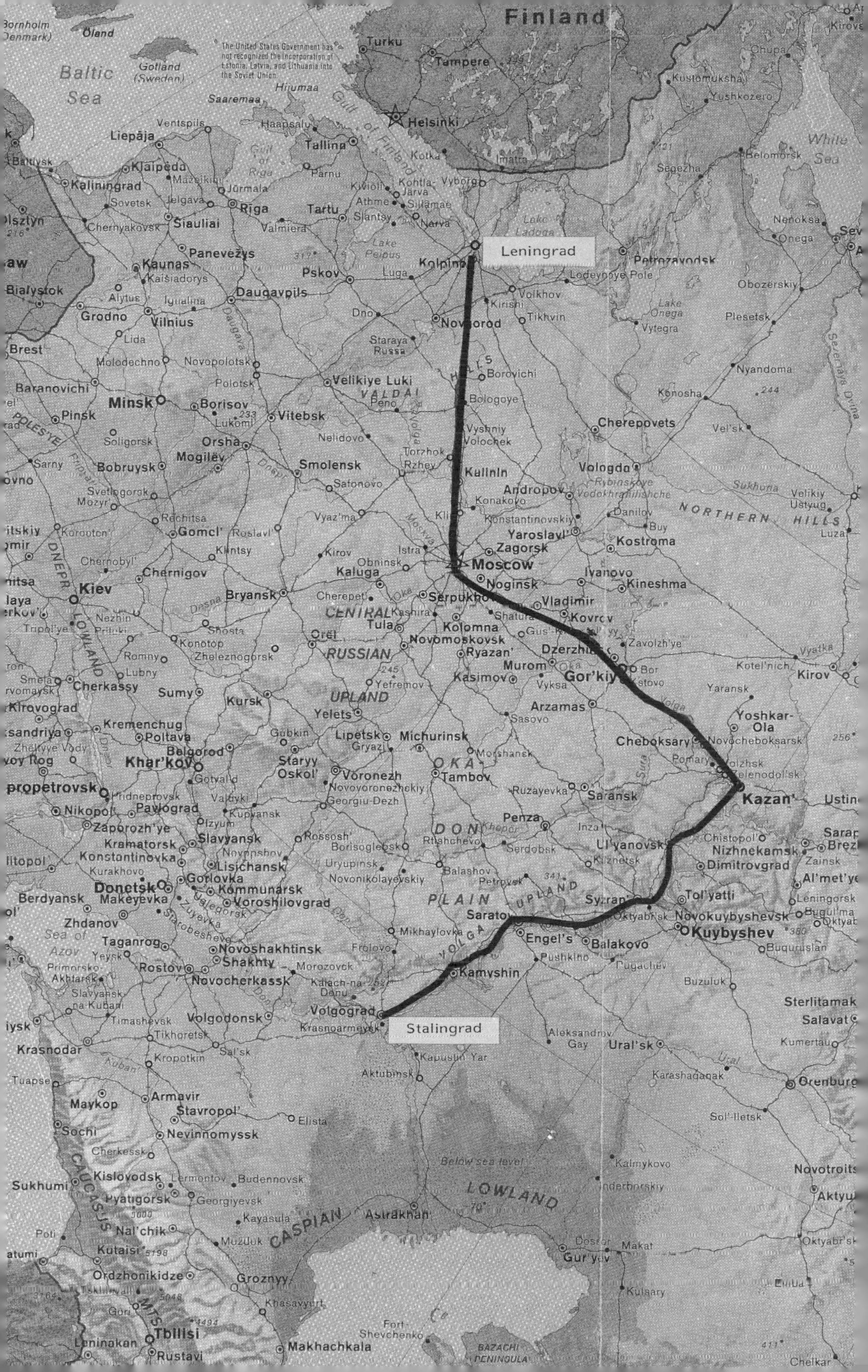

Finland
Leningrad
Stalingrad
The United States Government has not recognized the incorporation of Estonia, Latvia, and Lithuania into the Soviet Union
Baltic Sea
Gulf of Finland
Helsinki
Tallinn
Riga
Minsk
Kiev
Moscow
Kalinin
Novgorod
Gor'kiy
Kazan'
Ul'yanovsk
Syzran'
Saratov
Kamyshin
Volgograd
Kuybyshev
Astrakhan
Tbilisi
White Sea
Lake Ladoga
Lake Onega
Lake Peipus
VALDAI HILLS
CENTRAL RUSSIAN UPLAND
OKA DON PLAIN
VOLGA UPLAND
NORTHERN HILLS
CASPIAN LOWLAND
CAUCASUS MTS
DNEPR LOWLAND
POLES'YE
Sea of Azov
Below sea level

work, activity, action, it took me a long time to doze off. Soon I was stirred from my sleep by a desperate pounding on my door.

"Thieves!" I thought. "What a fix!"

I wondered, "Were there police in the hotel? But how can I contact them, since there is no phone in the room?"

The pounding continued. I tried to holler but because of my fright, no sound came out. More pounding. I started to pray. The door shook violently. Then I suddenly realized, "This couldn't be a thief. Thieves wouldn't make this much noise."

I tried to speak again, and this time the words made it past my lips, "What do you want?"

"Open the door," a man demanded in English.

"Who is it," I countered.

Two men answered at once, saying that they had been in the room that morning and were returning for the night. When I opened the door, the three white segregationists walked in, carrying their suitcases. They did not say a word to me. Even though they could not get another room, and had to stay with me, they were going to make the best of it by acting as if I was not there.

One of them walked over and unfastened the windows and raised them halfway. I turned my back to them, trying to fall asleep. We never did say a word to each other. I was glad to be alive and not to have been robbed of my few meager possessions.

I awoke before my roommates, around 6:30 A.M. The sun was still blazing. I looked around the room and saw that all three of them were still sleeping, one fully clothed and still wearing his shoes. I wondered if he did that because he thought he might suddenly have to escape from me in the middle of the night, horrible monster that I was.

I dressed quickly and slipped out of the room. Downstairs the hotel clerk told me that the three white men had waited all day to try and get a separate room. They had taken their appeal all the way to the hotel manager. But none of the guests had checked out by midnight, so they reluctantly returned. There they remained for the next four days, never saying a word to me.

As I walked out of the hotel and into the street, I felt at peace. I sensed deep down that my Soviet adventure was going to be exciting.

Even though I was in a foreign land, I felt calm as I strolled the streets. I did not feel uneasy or anxious or like an outcast.

I was reflecting on my sense of well-being when I found myself in front of the Leningrad railway station. I went in.

What an unbelievable sight! The place was choked with people. There were hundreds, maybe even a couple of thousand people sitting on the hard marble floor. There were men, women, and children, and some of the women were nursing their babies. It seemed as if these people had been there for days waiting to get on a train.

A moment before I had enjoyed such a strong feeling of warmth and sense of possibility in Leningrad. But the atmosphere in here reeked of gloom and resignation. The people as a whole looked hopeless and resigned. I stayed for awhile wondering what could be done to help them out or lift their spirits. I was moved by what I saw and did not understand why it was this way or what it all meant.

When I returned to the hotel the guests were gathered in the dining hall for breakfast. We had the choice of a large quantity of food—beef, ham, tomatoes, hard-boiled eggs, cheese, a yellowish bread, butter, and coffee. Everything but the coffee was served cold. Accustomed to eating hot meals, especially at breakfast, I couldn't take the thought of cold eggs, so I filled up on bread and butter, cheese, and coffee. Some other Americans demanded that the Russians heat their hard-boiled eggs, and others made a fuss about wanting fried eggs, which they finally got. Watching this scene, I thought back to those wretched souls in the railway station. I was sure that if they had this meal put before them, rather than fussing about it, they would have been grateful.

After breakfast we were off again for more sightseeing. The architectural glory of the czarist years was apparent as we visited Alexander's Column, St. Isaac's Cathedral, and Prince Yusupov's Yellow Palace. Our guide even took us to the basement where the mystic Rasputin was assassinated. At the czarist Duma—or parliament building—we were told how from July to November 1917, the government of Alexander Kerensky and the Bolshevik leadership had struggled for control of Russia. At the Smolny, which had been a fashionable school for the daughters of wealthy parents, we were shown where Lenin and Trotsky plotted the October Revolution. The ornate building now served as the headquarters for Leningrad's top Communist party officials. From what we were seeing it was obvious that Leningrad was a city where kings once ruled. It had a fairy tale quality about it. Its magnificence probably so dazzled those who lived here when it was known as St. Petersburg, that they paid scant attention to the poverty and misery of their countrymen living elsewhere in such a vast and harsh land.

By the end of the morning I had grown tired of exploring Russia's past. After lunch at the hotel I set out on my own tour, in search of present-day Russia. I discovered a contrast. I walked along the streets and peered into many shops. Without exception they were clean, but they also were nearly empty. The shelves were bare. No sugar, no eggs, no ham, no cheese—none of the common items we had just been served at that morning's breakfast. In fact, the only goods I saw in abundance were matches and jars of mustard. There were also a few loaves of black bread for sale, here and there. In a clothing store—which carried merchandise worse than what you might find at a consignment shop on skid row in Manhattan, the fabric was so incredibly shoddy that the threads were unraveling and the colors had faded. The designs were also very primitive. I got the sense that Russia was a poor, struggling country. Fortunately the people on the streets seemed well-enough fed, and no one was begging.

The next morning we were taken on another guided tour. On the way to the statue of Peter the Great I learned something more about my new home. On the streetcar, a lady in her mid-sixties or so came down the aisle carrying a large bundle. Every seat was taken so she leaned against a seat and tried to keep her balance as the steetcar pitched and rolled.

I was stunned to notice that a young man in a seat right next to where she was standing made no attempt to offer her his seat. I asked the tour guide, who was sitting across from me, why the youth—or anyone else for that matter—did not give up his seat for the old lady.

The guide smiled self-assuredly and said, "In Soviet Russia everyone is equal. Because of our glorious Communist system no one is required to give up his seat."

"But certainly," I replied, "that young man has a mother, and in the same situation he would surely get up for her."

"That, my friend," said the guide, "is bourgeois thinking. That kind of thinking has no place in the Soviet Union."

"Well, I have a mother," I thought, "and I was raised to be courteous." With that I got up, walked over to the woman, and while pointing to my seat, spoke English very slowly, hoping that she could understand at least the spirit of what I was trying to convey to her.

To my astonishment she answered in perfect English, "Thank you, sir, but I'm getting off at the next stop."

I was perplexed. Because she spoke English, she had understood my entire conversation with the guide. I wondered if she really planned to get off at the next stop, or if she did so in order to avoid trouble. Or on the other hand, she may have believed wholeheartedly in the Soviet concept of equality and been insulted by my gentlemanly efforts.

I did not know what to do. I was embarrassed by what the other passengers were probably thinking about my so-called bourgeois behavior. I was usually pretty good at doing as the natives do when I found myself in a strange situation. But there were times like this, when my own set of values would conflict strongly with those of the culture where I was living, which I was trying to understand.

Two days later, on June 19, our group boarded a fast-moving train and was on its way to Moscow. Through the night we traveled, racing over the vast prairie that separates Russia's two leading cities. Around 9:30 in the morning the train slowed down and then stopped, in the middle of nowhere with nothing but fields as far as one could see in every direction. I looked out the window and noticed the engineer and fireman gathered around the locomotive. They were talking and pointing at the wheels. In a few minutes more people, mainly passengers, joined them. Curious, I joined the crowd to see what the trouble was.

By watching the gestures of the highly animated engineer and fireman, I came to understand what was wrong: the nut fastening a connecting rod to the crank pin on one of the wheels was missing. The connecting rod was resting on less than half the pin.

"Incredible," I thought. "If the engineer hadn't been alert, and sensitive to the flow and rhythm of the train, we would have had a disastrous accident and probably scores of passengers would have been killed. This could have been the abrupt end of my adventure, whether I survived or not.''

Now we needed to find the missing nut; without it we could go no farther. The engineer and fireman began backtracking through the cinders along the track. Good fortune was with us because in about an hour they found it, tightened it securely in place, and we continued on our way.

We arrived in Moscow only ninety minutes late. But the expected welcoming committee which was supposed to take us to our hotel was not there. Fortunately the group's interpreter, a Russian-American named Novikov, had lived in Moscow and knew the city. He led us to the Metropole Hotel, in the center of the city. It was a massive building, at that time probably the largest hotel in the country, though only six stories high.

This time my room arrangements worked out well. My three white roommates—one of them was Novikov—did not complain about having to sleep in the same room with a black man. What a relief! Without the hostility I had experienced in Leningrad, my lunch was truly enjoyable.

After lunch we went off to tour again. Our guide took us to St. Basil Cathedral. In Red Square, which is considered the heart of modern Moscow because that is where the Kremlin is located, the cathedral was built in 1560 at the order of Ivan the Terrible to commemorate the conquest of Kazan from the Tatars. With its bright colors and onion-shaped domes, St. Basil's was truly magnificent.

On the other side of the Kremlin, on the banks of the Moscow River, we watched the beginning of the dismantling of the Church of the Savior, one of the largest churches in Russia. It was to be replaced by a six-story apartment building which would house many of the top leaders of the Soviet Union. We were told that the church's domes were covered with pure gold.

The next morning we returned to Red Square—which was spotless—to visit Lenin's Tomb. The tomb is akin to a holy place to many Russians, and functions as the most important shrine of the Communist regime. Many people were waiting to see the founder of the Soviet Union, and we had to wait in line for more than an hour. Once inside we saw people staring in awe at Lenin's stretched out body encased in glass.

Though dead for about six years, he appeared as if asleep. There was an air of reverence in the place, much as one experiences in a great cathedral.

We then viewed the artifacts and memorabilia at Lenin's Museum. I got the feeling that Lenin was a genuine patriot, a hero, a man who placed his countrymen ahead of himself. The display explained how Lenin had evaded the czar's police, how he smuggled messages to his followers, and how he slept on the floor of humble peasants' houses while hiding out and plotting the revolution. We saw his old crumpled suit, a pair of black shoes, a pot he ate from, and a long wooden spoon he had used. There was a worn out coat he wore after the revolution, with patches sewn on by his wife, Nadya.

After lunch we were escorted to another museum, where the revolution was glorified in pictures showing ragtag Bolsheviks defeating the czar's army, and ecstatic peasants and workers welcoming the new regime.

The next morning we were shown some of the accomplishments since the revolution. On Gorky Street, one of Moscow's main thoroughfares, our guide showed us the new post office building, the Moscow Soviet building, the Marxist-Leninist Institute, and the railway station. We turned back on Gorky Street until we reached Pushkin Square. Here we were told about how the nineteenth century poet had suffered through poverty. He was only thirty-eight years old when he died, yet now he is considered the father of the Russian language. They did not explain—and I only learned years later from one of my black acquaintances in Moscow—that the fair-skinned, nappy-haired Pushkin was black. We did learn that his works have been an inspiration to many Russian composers, dramatists, and poets.

Walking on to Nikitsky Gate and Gertsena Street, we reached the Moscow Tchaikovsky Conservatoire, the most prestigious music school in Russia. We went inside and saw two rows of pictures of the leading European and Russian composers. Our guide explained with pride that the auditorium had the best acoustics in the world.

As our group returned to the hotel for lunch, I started thinking about how much more graceful a city Leningrad was than Moscow. Moscow was grey, dull, and coarse. There were only four paved streets. The rest were narrow, winding, cobblestoned alleyways in between rows and rows of one-story log houses. For transportation there were only the streetcars with their three long coaches connected together, and now and then one would see a horse-drawn carriage. The seat of political power was a rugged, primitive place.

As in Leningrad, when I saw grown women and teenage girls sweeping the Moscow streets and directing traffic, I felt that philosophically I could support the Soviet Union's attempt at advancing women's rights, but I did not feel right about seeing women as sanitation workers.

In the afternoon our group was taken to the Gorky Central Park, seven hundred acres of recreational and athletic facilities designed for people of all ages. I thought the park was a fine example of the government's concern for its citizens. Activities ranged from checkers to soccer, and there were even coaches on hand to help aspiring sportsmen. We were told that symphony, jazz, and pop groups performed on weekends. The people I saw in the park seemed healthy and happy.

We took a detour on our way back to the hotel so that we could see GUM, which was being renovated at the time and destined to be the largest department store in the Soviet Union. We were taken through what was then the largest store—TSUM—which only demonstrated how far Russia's standard of living was behind that of the US, Britain, or France. The merchandise—what there was of it—was shoddy and drab. There were bare shelves throughout the food section, except for the jars of mustard, which I had figured by now were the only thing in regular supply anywhere, and loaves of black bread.

For the next three days we were taken to more of Moscow's famous sights. We saw the Pushkin Museum of Fine Arts, with its rich collection of renaissance and nineteenth century impressionist paintings, we went to the Planetarium, and to the Anthropological and Archaeological Museum, which attempted to explain the origin of the human species and the development of its different races. In keeping with Communist doctrine, man's spirtual nature was debunked. According to the museum exhibit, a human being was entirely an animal creature, though the highest on the evolutionary scale. My upbringing and experience would not allow me to agree with this point of view. I believed that human beings are distinguished from animals because we have a spirit, an inherent need to commune with someone, or something, greater than ourselves.

Next we were dazzled by the royal jewels at the State Armory of Wealth. We toured a watch factory which was bought and transported lock, stock, and barrel from the United States, and set up in Moscow by an American firm. Americans were in the factory running the machines and training Russians to take over from them. About a third of the Russian workers were women, and I wondered if these Americans were experiencing the same kind of culture shock I felt at seeing women sanitation workers and streetcar operators.

At the Stalin Automobile Works, which we visited next, women wearing overalls and lifting heavy machine parts were working alongside men on the assembly line. The only thing that distinguished the two sexes was the head cloth the women wore tied around their heads. I was becoming more and more convinced that the Soviets were truly making headway toward their goal of equality of the sexes.

After dinner I went upstairs to my room to rest, too tired to dance or listen to the jazz band in the dining hall. When I entered the room, two of my roommates were there, still dressed but looking about as weary as I felt. But then Novikov, the translator, abruptly entered the room, full of enthusiasm, and said that he wanted the three of us to go with him to visit his brother's family in their Moscow home. I immediately forgot about going to bed early, and the four of us left.

''What a relief,'' I thought, ''to be in a Russian home and to meet Russians face-to-face in a natural situation.'' I still had only seen the country and its people from a distance, and I could not get a sense of what Russia was like. Thus far my experience in the Soviet Union was more like watching a documentary film than seeing real life. I was being educated, but it was all from the outside. I wanted to break through the invisible barrier between the people and me.

Novikov's brother lived in one of a long row of single-story log buildings, the only kind of house in the neighborhood. Novikov's sister-in-law greeted us at the front door, delighted to see us. She had a round face, with large brown eyes. Her black hair was showing streaks of gray, and I guessed she was about forty-five. She appeared less dumpy than the Russian women her age whom I had seen on Moscow's streets. Her daughter, in her early twenties and wearing a flower-patterned dress like her mother, approached us. She was slender, shy, with eyes that appeared sad. Mother and daughter greeted us in Russian.

''You are welcome,'' they said, and right away I felt welcomed. The house, with no more than three rooms, was clean. Everything seemed to be in the right place. The main room had one large window with spotless white lace curtains. The dining table in the middle of the room was covered with a white lace tablecloth and had a pot of fresh flowers in the center. Around the table were six wooden chairs.

A small sofa, with three beautifully designed cushions, sat against the far wall. In a corner was a small table with a variety of silver and brass utensils on top. There were many pictures on the walls, mainly of family, including a handsome wedding shot of the husband and wife. There was a picture of the daughter as a child, the couple's parents, and possibly their grandparents. It was as if their heritage was on display, which undoubtedly meant they were aware of their roots and proud of them. I noticed two other pictures: one of Lenin addressing a group of people, the other of Stalin serenely smoking his pipe.

Novikov's sister-in-law came out carrying a large silvery object. One of my roommates asked Novikov what it was. He laughed and said it was a samovar, which was used to make tea for a fairly large group of people. Our hostess heated it by lighting charcoal. She then left, and came back with a saucer piled with hard sugar squares and a tweezer. I was anxious to try out this new and strange custom, wanting to watch them and do everything correctly.

Next came a plate of hard cookies, and then from the cupboard came seven glasses, glass holders, and teaspoons. A small spoon was placed in each glass, which I later learned was to keep the glass from cracking when the boiling water was poured in.

When all the ingredients were in their proper place for the tea party, our host urged us to take a seat around the table. What happened next is something I will never forget. It was their custom to place the small sugar cube in their mouths and suck on it while sipping the tea. This seemed reasonable enough. But our host did not sip; he drank the tea thirstily. Before we had taken three or four sips, which was no easy matter because the tea was so hot, he had finished his glass and filled it up again.

He quickly drank a second glass, then said something to his daughter. She went and got him a towel, which he placed around his neck.

I wondered what the towel was for, and then I noticed that the other two Americans looked just as puzzled. Halfway through his third glass it became clear what it was for. The man's face had turned beet red and the sweat was rolling off his face like water overflowing a dam. I had never seen anything like it. After the fifth glass the towel was completely soaked.

Even as his daughter began playing the guitar and singing, he kept drinking tea, sucking on the cube of sugar, glowing redder and drenched in sweat. This was in a sense so comical, and I almost laughed at the sight, until I thought more seriously that he might burst apart at any moment. I wondered, though, if this was a traditional Russian cure for some kind of illness. I could not imagine that he was putting himself through this ordeal for pleasure.

At 11:30 P.M., when we got up to take our leave, our host was still drinking tea. I lost count of how much tea he had guzzled during the last three hours, but I was sure it was at least fifteen glasses. When we said good-by, he was still as red as a sizzling coal.

The next day, our next-to-last in Moscow, my roommates and I took a casual tour of the city. It was a pleasant day, with a brilliant blue sky, the kind of day when nature pulls you outdoors. My spirit was in harmony with the weather. There was so much to be grateful for. Novikov's family had showed genuine friendship the night before; in fact, most of the Russians I had met seemed to be sincere people. My roommates seemed to be reconciled to my presence, and there was no tension among us. We walked a long while. I do not know how many miles we covered, but I was unconcerned, for my heart was lighter than usual.

It was far more interesting to study the people we passed than it had been to trek around Moscow's drab buildings. All the faces were white, but it was a different look than on New York's Fifth Avenue or in downtown Detroit. Many of the Moscovites had a slant to their eyes with high, prominent cheekbones. It was interesting to note that even some of the blond, blue-eyed natives had this same look. No doubt the Mongols and Tatars who had conquered and ruled European Russia for more than 240 years had spread their seed across the vast land. Moscow, I sensed, was a place where the Orient and Occident overlapped.

The city certainly was not a center of high fashion. The people were even more poorly dressed than in Leningrad. Many women wore shoes that had an unusual fit to them, giving them an awkward gait. I discovered later the reason for this. It was impossible to buy shoes and clothing as we did in the West. The government allotted coupons to the people for these goods, but they were hardly ever available. When they were, word would travel quickly that shoes were in the shop. The women would then begin standing in line around midnight so that they could get a pair when the store opened at 9:00 A.M. But getting inside did not guarantee success. There would likely be only one, two, or three sizes. Then there was no choice except to buy whatever they had. The women I saw on the street had bought shoes that were way too small and stacked up soft heel pads inside the shoe until the heels of their feet were high enough to get the shoes on.

To buy a well-fitting suit was practically impossible. That is why so many of the taller men who passed by looked like teenagers who had spurted up six inches in a year. I wondered at the time if wearing suit pants well above the ankles and jackets only to the middle of the forearms was the latest style in Moscow. Of course, it was not, and I later learned that the government taught that carefully tailored garments and a well-kept appearance were considered a sign of capitalist decadence. Some super patriots even cultivated a plain and disheveled look. Rumpled suits and dresses and clashing colors came to symbolize devotion and deep commitment to the Marxist-Leninist ideology.

On our way back to the hotel we learned that we were not the only ones who were watching passers-by with curiosity. We too were being watched. Three children ran toward us, chattering excitedly in Russian, eyes open wide with wonder, staring at me.

"Uncle," a girl of about six exclaimed, "how did you ever manage to get such a sunburn?" After Novikov told me what they were asking, he explained to them that I was a member of the black race. That answer, of course, had no impact on the children. Fascinated, the girl ran to me, took hold of my hand and rubbed it with her little one. She was startled when my color did not rub off.

"Are you so dark because you don't wash?" she asked innocently.

"No," Novikov explained. He seemed embarrassed for me. "That is the natural color of his skin."

I am sure the children still could not grasp what Novikov was telling them; it was outside the realm of their experience. To them, I was a strange creature. I was not bothered a bit, because they were so innocent, following us all the way back to the hotel, chattering, laughing, and looking at me with affection and curiosity.

CHAPTER 4

A Boat Trip on the Volga

OUR GROUP OF AMERICAN SPECIALISTS was taken next to the city of Gorky, where we boarded the boat that would carry us down the Volga River to Stalingrad. Gorky was a smaller, cruder version of Moscow, with the same kind of winding, cobblestone streets and row after row of two-story log houses. On almost every corner stood a church. They were no longer used for worship, but served as offices for government officials, schools, or museums, or simply were boarded up. The faces and dress of the people in Gorky seemed the same as in Moscow. They walked with purpose and vitality. They carried a sense of optimism, believing that the promise of Communism soon would be fulfilled. This was especially true of the younger people.

The boat that was to be our home for the next seven days was fairly large, with two decks. On the bottom were the third-class passengers—mostly peasants—with their cloth bundles of pans, utensils, and jars of food. They carried securely fastened wooden suitcases containing their more prized possessions. The quarters down below seemed cramped. But these people—some of them practically in rags—wearing crude sandals and needing a bath—did not complain.

Their situation reminded me of all those peasants in the waiting room at the Leningrad train station, huddled on the floor waiting patiently for their turn to board. The passengers on the lower deck were not served any meals, not even tea. But they seemed to manage, pulling black bread, salted dried fish, and cucumbers from their bags and enjoying the little they had to eat.

I wondered if they knew what accommodations were like on the top deck. We were with a group of intellectuals and professionals, including some teachers on vacation. We all had separate berths, were served three hearty meals a day, and had access to a game room with billiards, chess, and checkers. The top deck was fairly spacious, mainly because the third-class passengers weren't allowed upstairs.

The first-class passengers spent most of their time outside, in chairs or leaning against the railing, chatting with one another. I stood alone against the railing watching the land go by that only three months earlier had not even been a part of my fantasies. Russia had meant nothing to me then. My roots were in Africa and the Caribbean. When I thought of faraway places it was the Congo, or Jamaica, with its warm green-blue water lapping gently onto smooth beige beaches and its lush flora.

The Volga was muddy in color and its beaches were rocky. To the Russians it is as mighty as the Mississippi is to Americans. The Volga is not only an important north-south transportation artery, it is also the lifeblood of the country, its aorta. And it is the great repository of Russia's tears. No Russian could imagine the country without the Volga.

During our boat trip on the Volga I learned that Russians love the sun. At first glance they appear to be a society of sun-worshippers by the way they sit with their eyes closed and their faces positioned toward the sun. From the expression on their faces, I sensed that some were even talking to the sun, imploring it to keep showering its warmth on them, praising the sun for providing them with pleasure. Now and then some would let out a sigh of gratitude. When the boat stopped at towns along the way to pick up and discharge passengers and cargo, many people would take the opportunity to strip off their clothes, swim around in the Volga, and then sunbathe naked on the rocky beach, inviting the rays to seep into their pores. I thought it was curious. It seemed as if they were trying to store up the sun's energy. After living through my first Russian winter, I could understand the Russian love and longing for the summer sun.

There were other unusual experiences on the boat trip, like food, for instance. We were exposed to *borscht* and *accroshka* at our first lunch. *Borscht,* which was served hot, I liked. It is made of slivers of meat, potatoes, cabbage, onions, a dash of sugar, and is topped with a tablespoon of sour cream. Eaten with a thick piece of black bread, it is a delight. *Accroshka,* on the other hand, was an abomination. Most of the Americans did not like it. *Accroshka* is a thick green blend of juices from a special leaf, tomatoes, cucumbers, vinegar, and salt, with sliced hard-boiled eggs plopped into the middle. After my first spoonful, I never ordered *accroshka* again during my forty-four years in Russia.

On the second evening aboard ship, I was trying to detect signs of life in the dark countryside. About all I could see was the light from the dimly flickering oil lamps in the log houses along the river. I wondered what life was like in those places. I imagined it was crude: no indoor plumbing, no central heating. As I was considering whether people could be happy in those primitive dwellings, I heard the sound of live music coming from the dining hall. I had heard earlier that there was to be a dance, and a chance for the Americans to dance with Russian girls. I wanted to be there, for the sound of the music was appealing, and I was lonely for some companionship, for a human touch.

As if my silent prayer had been answered, two Russians approached me. One was a woman with a friendly round face. The other, a man, introduced himself as Tolstoy. I learned later that he was indeed a close relative of the revered Russian author and humanitarian. They urged me to come to the dance. In fact Tolstoy—he also was a writer in his own right—went to fetch his niece. It was terribly embarrassing. These good folks were sincere about their wish to have me join in the fun. But I had never been at a dance where there were only white people, and I had never danced with a white woman before.

In a few minutes Tolstoy came back with his niece, whose name was Vera. He asked, "Why don't you invite Mr. Robinson to dance?"

I was torn between fear and a desire to be with Vera. I did not know what to do, but Vera solved my problem. Without any shyness, she took hold of my forearm. I then took hold of hers. She explained that holding one another's arms was a Russian custom. In that manner we reached the dining hall.

We then began dancing to the tune, "I Can't Give You Anything But Love, Baby." Vera's strength kept me going; she was so sure of herself. But not me. I was the product of my upbringing in a racist society that had beaten into me the need to be leery of white folks, to be always suspicious that when given the chance they would want to destroy a black man like me.

As we moved around the dance floor I could sense what the white Americans were thinking. Soon their thoughts gave way to taunts. I am sure Vera knew what was happening, but we kept on dancing. She wrapped an arm around my shoulder and her grip on my hand grew firmer. When the band began the next song, the Americans escorted their Russian partners back to their seats. They were protesting the presence of a black man on the dance floor with them. Here was Jim Crow on a boat steaming down the Volga. There were only two other couples dancing. I searched Vera's face for a reaction to the Americans' boycott. She was aware of what was happening and sensed my uneasiness.

Calmly, in her Russian-accented English, she said, "Don't pay attention to them, you are on Russian soil dancing with a Russian girl." She smiled and added, "Don't you see, we have more space to dance."

The Americans did not dance again that evening. But they did remain, and saw other Russian women ask me to dance, including some who had been their partners. The Russian women had helped to smash the social barrier that the white Americans had put up. This was a great lesson for my fellow countrymen, and by the next day their desire to dance with Russian girls overcame their need to hold me in contempt because of my dark skin. The next night they were foxtrotting alongside me on the dance floor, no longer making snide comments.

It was on this boat trip that I gained my first insight into the Russian's passionate attachment to "the motherland." It is a fierce nationalism, so strong that even Russians who emigrate to other countries usually yearn to return one day so that when they die their bones can rest in Russian soil. On the sixth night of our journey we were dancing in the dining hall when the music stopped and a violinist in the orchestra asked for everyone's attention. He announced that several men who had emigrated to America and were returning to Russia as contracted technical specialists were going to sing Russian songs. People applauded wildly.

Six men appeared, dressed in black suits, with white shirts and ties. Though they were not trained singers, they sang with deep feeling. The first song was about the Volga, a familiar tune, which the great Russian singer Chaliapin had immortalized in concerts around the world. I did not have to be a Russian to be moved by the haunting melody, sung with deep feeling by the six men. When they started singing ''Mother Russia,'' even the Americans stopped talking and moving about. The singers had captured their audience. These returning Russians seemed to expose the soul of their country with their tender, heartfelt singing. The struggle of the Russian people throughout their history, their battle to survive against the harshness of nature and the many foreign invasions—from the east and from the west—was expressed through their music. This was a different kind of love song. It touched rarely reached emotions, such as when a parent dies or a child is born. I felt goose bumps all over. On stage, the singers were lost in a love of land that I had never witnessed. I had never seen Americans so stirred by the ''Star-Spangled Banner'' or an Independence Day parade. Three of the singers had their eyes closed, the eyes of two others were moist with tears, and the last had a longing and faraway look.

When the song ended, there was a moment of silence. Suddenly one of the singers, with tears streaming down his cheeks, reached into his inside jacket pocket, pulled out his American passport, ran to the railing, and flung it into the river. Then he broke into a wild dance.

We reached Stalingrad, where I was to spend the next year, on July 4, 1930. The other Americans let the day slip by without celebration. No one from the factory where we were to work was on the dock to greet our ship, even though we had wired the chief engineer when we were in Gorky. Novikov took charge and led us to a streetcar station, where a crowd of peasants weighed down with bundles were waiting for their ride. Many of them stared at me, some pointing and shaking their heads in astonishment.

The leading officials of the industrial complex were waiting for us at the factory. I spotted Melamed, the man who recruited me in Detroit; he was the factory's chief engineer.

We were directed to our living quarters, which were about a mile and a half away. I counted twelve four-story brick buildings. The white Americans shared one entire building and two floors of another one. The nine returning Russians were assigned to a six-room apartment. Novikov and I were given three adequately furnished rooms in a separate building. It was obvious why I was segregated from my fellow countrymen, for as soon as I set foot in the living quarters center, several Americans who had already been there several months noticed me. As they stared at me and muttered something I could not hear, looks of disgust and contempt disfigured their faces. It was clear they were not pleased to see this particular fellow American.

Later in the day Novikov and I went to the restaurant for a snack. He noticed someone he had met in the United States a year before, and introduced me. The man—his name was Mamin—insisted that we go to his apartment for refreshments. He lived in our building, and his quarters were elegantly furnished. He even had a new copper-colored piano. Mamin's wife was as well-adorned as the living quarters. She wore a new white dress, silk stockings, and well-fitting black high heel shoes, which were probably imported from America or France.

She was an attractive woman with raven black hair worn in the usual Russian style, parted in the middle and drawn tightly into a bun on the back of her head. Unlike most Russian women, however, she was rather slender and had a sophisticated air about her. She could not have been older than twenty-six.

Her husband was perhaps five years older, and seemed like an ambitious and bright young man. He had a thick shock of dark brown hair that needed combing. His eyes sparkled with energy when he told us about his trips to Germany, Sweden, Britain, and the United States, where he had studied the way tractors were made in those countries. He openly admitted his respect for technological achievements of those countries. Although he did not say it, I sensed he believed that the Soviet Union would advance beyond them technologically and that he would have a part in reaching this glorious goal. It was obvious that he was highly regarded by the government, because at such a young age he was already assistant chief engineer of a gigantic industrial complex. His comfortable lifestyle was not only a reward for his achievements but also served as an incentive to accomplish more.

There was another guest in the apartment, a man who didn't say much. He struck me as a naturally quiet sort of person. Dressed in a pilot's uniform, he stood up when he was introduced to Novikov and me. Even while he greeted me, his eyes were focused on the floor. In fact, the few times he spoke he did not look at anybody. I sensed something sinister about the man that made me feel uncomfortable. I never saw him again in Stalingrad but we were destined to meet in a different place, years later.

Despite my discomfort around Comrade V. M., Mamin and his wife made the afternoon delightful. I basked in the couple's generosity. We enjoyed a delicious cake with marmalade and the usual glasses of tea. Everyone sucked on squares of sugar while sipping the tea, just like the Soviet family I had visited in Moscow. This time our host drank only two glasses. Late in the afternoon Mamin asked his wife to entertain us with some music. She gladly agreed, and played Beethoven's "Rhondo" followed by Schubert's "Ave Maria." She performed with feeling and delicacy. When we took our leave they invited us to come again after we were settled in.

It had been such a splendid afternoon, one of several occasions I had enjoyed thus far in Russia when I was free from other people's hatred. At dinner that evening among the Americans, the tension returned. A cluster of them stood at the entrance to the dining hall when I arrived. They muttered all sorts of insulting remarks at me as I passed. I ignored them, and I sat down to eat trying to keep my eyes on the food in front of me. When I did glance up I saw angry people everywhere, staring at me. They began cursing me as they ate. Novikov had joined me and he, too, sensed the hostility and heard the swearing. He also pretended to be unaffected. But he gobbled his food quickly and said he was returning to our apartment. The hatred was more than he wanted to bear. I was determined to stay in that dining hall until I had finished the last crumb on my plate. Nothing those racists could do was going to keep me from what I wanted to do.

It was 8:30 when I finished dinner. As in Leningrad, the sun was shining brightly, and I thought a walk along the river would do me good. I was surprised to see that the beach was crowded, mainly with sunbathers, including some Americans from my group. One of them noticed me and told his friends. They all began looking at me with hostile stares, so I turned my back on them and began walking down the beach. After about a quarter of a mile I sat down on a large rock, practically alone, trying to absorb the beauty of the landscape. Thoughts of past experiences, of my mother, of friends in Detroit came to mind. But more than that, I began thinking how I was in a place I had never heard of three months ago, halfway around the world from my home.

"Why am I really here in Stalingrad?" I asked myself. "It can't just be to earn a decent wage doing the kind of work I enjoy." But as I sat there thinking, no other reason came to mind. Time passed, and the sun moved much farther to the west. My surroundings were cast in a scarlet glow and directly above me were the first signs of nightfall. To the east was a crescent moon. The hour there had passed so quickly.

As I returned to the dining hall I could heard the sounds of music, but not dance music. It was dark inside and a film was being shown. Although I did not yet understand much Russian I decided to watch anyway, and as it turned out I was glad I did. I could grasp the message without knowing the language.

The film was a documentary illustrating some of the good the government was doing for its citizens. Efforts were being made to find and rehabilitate children who had lost their parents during the October Revolution, and a program was established to help transform delinquent boys and girls into useful citizens. I was moved to see how lice-infested youngsters in rags were being fed, clothed, and taught a trade. A compound on eighteen square acres had been built at a place called Bolshevo, for these youngsters. I learned later that nearly all the youngsters from the restoration camp ended up fitting smoothly into society and were spared any stigma that might have resulted from their having been there. By the end of 1935, a number of them were holding high positions in several professions.

I left the dining hall impressed by the commitment of the Soviet government to help its people live a better life. The film made the government's actions seem genuine. Sure, I knew there were many things the people did not have. I had already seen how the country was primitive compared to the United States. The point was that the Soviet system represented a goal that seemed attainable. Even if the goal was not reached, I felt comfortable here, less pressured than in the United States, more accepted for what I was, a human being whose skin happened to be dark.

In the days that followed I began integrating myself into the working pattern of the Soviet plant. Everything went fairly smoothly, unlike the trauma of my breaking-in period at Ford. There I learned to inspect my machine very carefully each morning, before turning it on. During my first week at the Ford plant I found my machine had been tampered with every day before I arrived. Undoubtedly there were other toolmakers in the shop who would do just about anything to try and get rid of me. If only I would break the machine, lose a finger or an eye, or fracture my arm, they would rejoice. One Monday morning while inspecting my machine carefully, I noticed it had been rewired in such a way so that I would have been electrocuted if I had turned it on. It took six months before the toolmakers at Ford began to tolerate my presence. I am sure none of them wept when I left for Russia.

CHAPTER 5

The Stalingrad Incident

MY THIRD DAY of work was a good one. I was getting into a comfortable routine, there was no harassment, and my productivity was increasing. However, my feelings of satisfaction were short-lived. On my way home from work, a strapping American was walking toward me. He began to slow down and I sensed trouble. As we drew closer to each other my muscles tensed. We both stopped and he said, "Robinson, be careful when you go to the Volga. On the night you arrived all the Americans got together and decided to drown you in the river."

That was all he said before continuing on. I returned to my apartment to try and sort things out. My custom had been to go to the Volga every day. I relished my time by the river and was loathe to give it up. "Would the pressure ever let up?" I wondered.

Perhaps they were only trying to scare me into leaving Stalingrad. Part of me refused to believe that one hundred people would all agree to murder me. Surely there had to be some dissenters, some decent people who would protest such a criminal act. Another part of me—the part that had been conditioned all my life not to trust white people—accepted that a group of one hundred white Americans could carry out their plot to kill me. Had not whites done that very thing hundreds, no thousands of times, during the three hundred years that blacks have lived in America?

"But this is Russia," I thought. "The chances of a black man being murdered in Stalingrad because of the color of his skin are a lot less than back home."

I decided not to forgo one of my few pleasures because of this threat. So, as was my usual custom, at 4:00 that afternoon I went down to the beach, determined not to go near the water and to stay close to whatever Russians were there. Several Americans walked by where I was sitting, stopped about ten yards from me, and sat down. From time to time I would catch them staring at me. For the next five days the same group did the same thing, except that every time they sat down they were a few yards closer to me, so I drew a few yards closer to the Russians. Whenever the Russians would leave, I would tag behind them too closely for the Americans to seize me.

On the tenth day after my arrival in Stalingrad I discovered that the Americans' decision to murder me had changed. Evidently I had thwarted their beach campaign. After dinner that night I noticed two men following me. They were Americans, walking quickly, obviously trying to catch up with me.

I refused to quicken my pace and in a few moments they were beside me. I learned later that their names were Louis and Brown. "Nigger," said Louis, "where are you from? How did you get here?"

"I got here the same way you did," I said, continuing to walk.

"You have twenty-four hours to leave this place," said Brown, "or you'll be sorry."

Suddenly Louis leapt in front of me and began beating me with his fists. Brown tried to grab my arms to prevent me from hitting back, but I broke loose and struck back at Louis. No way was I going to let Louis, or anyone else, beat me. No way.

Both men then jumped on me and tried to wrestle me to the ground. Brown was able to pin down my arms. I had to strike back somehow, but I couldn't get my arms free.

Then something inside me exploded—the rage that had been building for years. My every fiber screamed for revenge, against every racist remark and every hating white person I had encountered throughout my life. Louis lunged at me. My teeth caught his neck. I dug them deeper and deeper into his flesh. Brown was pummeling me but I was determined not to let go. I even felt his blood trickling into my mouth, but I was not going to let go.

I was biting into him for all the humiliation I had suffered, for the pain I had quietly endured. All of my years of suppressed anger spewed out. A wild drive that I had never felt before possessed me, as if some demon caged within me had sprung free. My teeth stayed fastened on Louis' neck, while Louis screamed and Brown tore at my shirt.

Louis' cries for help apparently were heard, because a group of Americans and Russian-Americans rushed to his rescue and began tugging at me, pleading with me to let go. I wouldn't, but their strength overwhelmed me, they forced me off, and Louis was led away, whimpering, blood running down his neck. His friend Brown, who was visibly shaken, followed him.

I walked slowly back to my apartment. I walked alone, shaking inside, but not hysterical. I think I felt like someone must feel who has just achieved some marvelous physical feat. As I walked, I did not notice anyone. I was alone in the world with my thoughts.

"Did I do a bad thing?" I wondered. "That wasn't a Christian thing for me to do, to hurt another human being. But is there any justice if I do nothing and let them destroy me? Surely not. God is just and merciful."

Soon after I returned to my apartment, I was sure I had done the right thing. Never again, I vowed, would I run away from racist attackers. I fell on my bed exhausted, but overcome by the sweet sensation of liberation, which I was feeling for the first time in my life.

A knock on my door punctured my self-satisfied feeling. Were these cronies of Louis and Brown coming to complete what the other two had failed to do? I hesitated, and there was another knock. It was as gentle as the first one, so I decided it was probably someone who was either friendly or neutral. I opened the door. A policeman and two detectives were standing there. They looked like decent fellows, and they politely asked me to come with them to the police station. Their superior wanted to hear my version of what had happened with Louis and Brown.

Now, I had already learned as a child that the police station was obviously a place to avoid. For a black man especially it could well be the first step to jail, beatings, and oblivion. I was very wary. But a few minutes after arriving at the station I felt at ease. The station chief asked me to explain what had happened, listened sympathetically, and then told me to go home. At that time I was still new to the country and thus politically naive. I had no idea the possibilities that this incident offered to the local Communist party apparatus. I did not know what opportunity I, a black man, represented to them.

The Stalingrad newspaper ran an editorial denouncing American racial prejudice and warned the American specialists not to export their ''social poison'' to Russia. Our nation's laws forbid racism, declared the newspaper. At the factory everyone—from floor sweepers to the administrative staff—was talking about the incident. They all deplored the attack on me. Many viewed me as a hero, which was something I really could not understand. I was dazzled by the adulation and attention showered on me. I had never been a celebrity before, and it was difficult to cope with. By nature I am a retiring person. I cherish my privacy and enjoy my solitude. For three days I was the center of attention, with everyone in the complex engrossed in how I was being treated by my fellow countrymen.

On the fourth day after the incident there was a massive rally in the square in front of the administrative building. Workers of every rank—men, women, even children—thousands of people gathered to hear twelve passionate speeches on the evils of racism. The crowd cheered enthusiastically whenever the orators reminded them of their government's enlightened position on racial prejudice. A resolution was proposed calling for the punishment of the two Americans who attacked me, and the crowd roared its approval. A copy of the resolution was wired to Moscow and to the local press. ''Strange,'' I thought, ''I merely act to preserve myself and they hail me as a hero.''

The day after the rally a reporter came to interview me. Her name was Anna Louise Strong, an American working for the *Moscow News,* Russia's only English-language newspaper. (She was later expelled from the Soviet Union in 1949.) Before our interview, I had been led to believe that she had talked to Louis and Brown, heard their side of the story, and now wanted to listen to mine.

That is not what happened. It was, in fact, the strangest interview I have ever had. She never asked me a single question. She did not even ask if I was from the United States, or how I came to Russia. I learned that she wrote an extensive article, but I never read it. "How could she write accurately without even questioning me?" I wondered. Perhaps the local government was her source, and she felt that was enough. If so, I reasoned, what a peculiar way for a journalist to seek to uncover the truth.

Now that I was prominent I experienced another kind of pressure. Even in the factory, where I thought I could lose myself in my work, Russian workers would come up to me throughout the day to express their sympathy. They often communicated warmly by use of a few English words and a lot of gestures. The people were so sincere, I did not have the heart to complain to the foreman. My only relief from their attention was during my trips to the river after supper, where I usually could find some solitude by walking a little distance from the beach entrance.

These solitary walks were short-lived, because I struck up an acquaintance with a Russian woman, Liubov, and her sixteen- and eighteen-year-old daughters, Zoya and Lydia. For two weeks we met after supper and they would teach me Russian until it was too dark to read or write. It warmed my heart to have people do something for me just because they liked me. I believe I cheered their hearts as well, especially when my mispronunciation of a Russian word would make the girls giggle. Liubov (or Suda, as she was called), invited me to their two-room apartment in one of the buildings in our complex. The apartment was like the others, whitewashed walls and green woodwork. It was well-furnished, very orderly, with a fairly new sewing machine standing in the corner of the room that was used as a combination parlor, dining room, and bedroom. White lace curtains hung on the windows.

It was here that I received more training in the art of Russian tea drinking. I learned that placing a towel around one's neck is not a part of the ceremony. The tea was served in cups, with two lumps of sugar placed on each saucer. I naturally placed the sugar in my tea and began stirring. My companions not only placed a square of sugar in their mouths, they also poured some tea out of their cups and into their saucers. They used their left hand to position the saucers on the fingertips of their right hand, and then drew the saucer to their lips. They would take a sip, talk a bit—while still balancing the saucer—and then take another sip. After they drank a saucerful, they would repeat the whole process. I never learned to master drinking tea that way but I did adopt their custom of sucking on sugar cubes.I learned that it was more economical. With one cube I could drink two cups of tea and have as much of a sweet taste as I would usually get by dropping two cubes into one cup.

The daily meetings with the Russian family were a pleasant diversion from the hectic aftermath of my encounter with Louis and Brown. Our friendship helped to refresh my spirit, for I was feeling beset by the pressures and duties of my new status as a celebrity. I frankly wanted to forget the whole incident and get on with what I had been hired to do. But that was not to be.

One week after the two Americans attacked me, the factory authorities asked me to go to the police station at once. When I arrived, I was introduced to a lawyer, his assistant, a secretary, and the prosecutor.

"Why do I need a lawyer?" I asked. "Because those two Americans who assaulted you must be prosecuted," I was told. "They violated Soviet law."

I had no desire to take part in a trial, but I felt I had better cooperate with the Soviet justice system. If I did not they could ship me back home. At the time, in the midst of the Great Depression, I knew I probably would be unlikely to find a decent job.

The trial began the next day, after work, at 6 P.M. A wooden building served as the makeshift courthouse. I arrived about fifteen minutes before the proceedings were scheduled to begin. As I walked toward the building, people pointed me out and talked about me, as if I were a famous actor or politician or war hero. A teacher with an interpreter approached me and urged me to meet with a group of five- to seven-year-olds standing nearby. The interpreter explained that the children wanted to register their protest against American racism. So I had to walk along the row of children like some potentate, shaking the hand of each student, about fifty of them in all.

As I stepped into the building, enthusiastic young people stretched out their hands to touch me. I had to shake each hand before I could get to my seat in the first row. Perhaps the most ardent youth was an attractive nineteen- or twenty-year-old woman, who pumped my hand twice with both of her hands and then followed me, sitting down beside me. From time to time during the proceedings, she would lean toward me, her eyes flashing in admiration of me, and whisper something unintelligible in Russian. She kept on speaking to me even though I tried to explain that I could not understand her. Finally a sensitive interpreter came over and asked her what she was saying to me. Then he told me that she was trying to reassure me that I was among friends, that I should feel at home, and that there was no need to fear the white racists.

The young lady sat beside me the first three evenings but did not show up for the fourth or the fifth, and final, night. I later learned from an acquaintance that the girl's father, a foreman at the factory and a Communist party member, did not want her sitting next to me. She defied his orders twice, so he shipped her back to her mother in Kharkov.

When the defendants' lawyer had me testify, I thought he might try to trick me, to twist the truth, and force me to say something I did not believe or admit to something I had not done. But I was pleasantly surprised. He put straightforward questions to me and he did not challenge my answers.

The prosecutor, on the other hand, was extremely forceful in questioning Louis and Brown. The courtroom crowd approved of his hard-hitting tactics; I sensed they wanted him to be even tougher. He asked the court to sentence Louis and Brown to five years in prison. The defense attorney begged for clemency.

There was no jury. The judge found the defendants guilty and ordered them deported from the Soviet Union immediately. Neither of the Americans wanted to leave the Soviet Union for, like me, they knew jobs were hard to come by at home. They both appealed their sentence to a higher court. Louis' appeal was rejected, but they allowed Brown to finish out his one-year contract. His request to stay another year was turned down.

I was now an even greater hero to the Russians. I represented good conquering evil. Letters of support and sympathy poured in from all over the country. I even got other job offers from Soviet industrial centers. The trial had a bit of a positive effect on the American community. A few of the Americans began to greet me when they passed, though I could not tell whether their hellos were genuine, since they never said anything else.

Several weeks later I gained some insight into why Americans harbored such negative feelings toward me in particular and blacks in general. I went to a Sunday afternoon party given by the factory's chief electrical engineer. When I stepped into the large, tastefully furnished living room of his apartment, I noticed three white Americans seated with their Russian interpreter girlfriends. My presence became a great test of their self-control. The urbane host, who spoke English well, began introducing me to his other guests. As I got closer to the Americans I could see their faces turning red. The closer I came the more desperate they appeared. But there was no way they could escape being civil to me that would not prove embarrassing to the chief electrical engineer. And if they offended him they might jeopardize their jobs in Stalingrad. So they offered their hands to me, and in that way we greeted each other. Their faces then seemed to relax. As the evening wore on we all became more at ease, especially after our charming hostess played compositions from Mendelssohn, Brahms, Chopin, and Offenbach's "Tales of Hoffman" on the large mahogany piano, and then served us tea with jam followed by homemade cakes and sweet wine.

Conversation gradually flowed easily between the Americans and me; we even shared genuine laughter. After a delightful three hours I believed that I understood better why so many white Americans feel the way they do about blacks. They never really get to know us, true feelings are never shared, and myths about blacks come to be accepted as true. By the time I left the party, I believed that the three white Americans now saw me in a favorable light, whereas before they had viewed me with suspicion and dislike from afar. Our progress was not monumental, but at least it was something. I felt that now there was a chance that one day I would be accepted by Stalingrad's American community.

Later that same evening, while strolling down the beach, I realized that I was not checking out the landscape for potentially dangerous areas or suspicious-looking people. Everything looked the same, but I felt different. Breathing seemed easier, my heart felt lighter, and the tension that was always a part of me was gone. I was floating. "This must be what freedom feels like," I thought. Every part of me was so calm. When I returned to my apartment I immediately went to bed, earlier than usual, and fell into a deep, restful sleep. When I awoke I felt as tranquil as I had the night before. As I was putting my clothes on, I even tried to think of things to worry about, so unnatural was this feeling of peacefulness. But the true me sensed that whatever worries I had were not worth dwelling on. I picked up my Bible, as I have done every morning of my adult life, and opened it. This passage from Isaiah sprung at me:

> Be strong and of good courage, be not afraid, neither be thou dismayed, for the Lord thy God is with thee whithersoever thou goest!

The message was clear and I took it to heart. Never fear a group of people, large or small, anymore. Go and circulate wherever I must. Fear no one, only God.

I was never attacked again during the remainder of my stay in Stalingrad. But my faith in my new awareness was tested a short time later. A fairly large number of American diehards never gave up trying to drive me out of Stalingrad. They knew from the experience of Louis and Brown that they could not risk trying to injure me physically. They had a job, were making good money, and did not want to be deported. Worse yet, they might have to serve time in a Russian prison. So they used other means to antagonize me. One clever trick was to train their non-English-speaking Russian girlfriends to parrot a few English phrases.

One afternoon I was walking by four of these couples as I approached the dining hall. The Russian girls started chanting, "I don't like dirty nigger! I don't like dirty nigger!"

Then the group burst out laughing. I was not irritated by their childish prank, and just walked into the dining hall and ate my supper without dwelling on the insult. As I left the hall I said to myself, "Never fear anymore, for the Lord was and is with me."

During the rest of my years in the Soviet Union, no day passed without my uttering those words at least once.

CHAPTER 6

Contract Renewal

ABOUT NINE MONTHS after I started work at the Stalingrad Tractor Plant, I was urged to stay another year. I could not believe how quickly time had passed, and that my contract would expire in three months. My decision was easy. I knew that times were difficult for everybody in the US, and especially for blacks. Stories of businessmen jumping off skyscrapers and people with college degrees selling apples on street corners had reached us in Stalingrad.

My mother had already moved from Cuba to Harlem, and I was able to send her $150 a month, which was more than enough for her to live on in those days. I enthusiastically signed a contract for another year in Stalingrad. After all, I was making good money, had the respect of my peers at work, and was appreciated by management.

I looked forward eagerly to my next year in Russia. I channeled most of my energy into my work, doing everything I could to become the most productive worker possible. I wanted to be productive, and it was also the best way to avoid getting trapped by social and political problems. Working in a Soviet factory was different from working in an American one. The Ford Motor Company was a place to work. Of course, there were forces of socialization at work, but these were natural, and not overt. In my Stalingrad factory, work was defined as a political statement, and the political indoctrination was constant. To be undisciplined, to lack dedication, to fall short of one's production goals—all were considered unpatriotic acts by the Communist party officials who held key administrative positions in the factory.

These party officials wanted everybody to live and die for the cause of Marxism-Leninism. But not everyone was a wholehearted believer. In fact, many of the Americans working there knew a great deal more about communism than the average Russian worker. What mattered most to the Russians was whether the present leaders cared more about meeting their basic needs than the czarist regime these leaders had overthrown. Of course, the political insiders knew this. They also knew how much the Russian workers treasured their jobs, as their source of food and shelter, something no Russian coming out of the czarist era took for granted.

In this kind of environment, the Soviet Ministry of Industry devised ways of exploiting the average worker's fear of losing his job and his source of security, for the sake of greater productivity. Force was never used; that was considered fascist. The Council of Ministers and the local plant leadership used emotional and ideological approaches instead. Lecturers were sent from Moscow, who painted the ideal Communist state as heaven on earth. This helped the officials tackle absenteeism, tardiness, and reporting to work drunk, all of which were serious problems during these early days, especially among the older peasants, who had little or no experience working in an industrial setting. The techniques were similar to what I had witnessed on the *Rykov,* except on a much grander scale. Every shop had a blackboard hung in plain view, on which each worker's name was listed. Next to the name was the percentage of shop production for which that person was responsible. The idea was that by everyone monitoring everyone, the entire shop would produce more.

Each shop had a quota, which was printed in the factory newspaper that was posted daily on each bulletin board. Each shop in the factory also published a bimonthly newspaper, which featured production successes and failures. It was all very personal. For example, if a shop or a worker exceeded a quota, praise and sometimes bonuses were given. An unusual success story would be fed to *Pravda* and a chosen worker would gain national recognition. Because many workers would strive for this great honor, overall production was kept high.

Those workers who failed to meet their quotas also would find their pictures in the newspapers, along with an article chastising them, in a teasing, nonmalicious way. Disorderly conduct, excessive tardiness, and drunkenness also were reported in amusing caricature.

It was during my second year in Stalingrad that we received a new management team whose job it was to put these measures into place. In about three months, production of tractors increased from twenty-five or thirty a day to one hundred. Most conscientious workers respected the new factory leadership for its ability to triple or quadruple productivity. We Americans soon learned that they were politically astute also.

A few months after they took over, members of the new administration called a meeting for all of the American specialists. Even the factory's Communist party secretary was in attendance. The place was jammed with Americans, all of us wondering why the meeting was called. News of the Great Depression back home had reached us in Stalingrad. In fact, Radio Moscow reported that plants were closing daily in the United States, while, in contrast, the USSR was opening new ones. We were told that the new tractor manufacturing plant in Kharkov was the largest in the world, producing fifty thousand tractors annually. We Americans were worried that the party secretary would announce that we had trained our apprentices sufficiently, and that they could take over our jobs and we could be sent home.

As the meeting began, many anxiously tried to guess what was to come. We were uncertain whether this new administration would honor our contracts until their expiration date or not. To our relief, the party secretary said, "My countrymen and I are grateful for the contribution you have all made to our nation's economic leap forward. You are all setting an outstanding example for the Russian worker."

He pointed out that committees had been established to collect data on the extent of the American contribution to the industrialization of the Soviet Union. The results were very impressive, he said, and would soon be published and distributed throughout the land.

It was nice to be patted on the back, but we really wanted to know whether we still had our jobs. Then the party secretary announced a new set of goals, which made it clear that we were still wanted. These goals had nothing to do with industrial production. They were:

1. All American specialists should belong to the trade union.
2. As many American specialists as possible should sign the Socialist Competition either with Russians or with other American specialists.
3. A few good American specialists should join the Communist party.
4. Young American specialists should join Komsomol, and a few children should join the Pioneers (a party indoctrination organization for elementary school age children).
5. Americans would participate in a campaign to keep the living quarters and commercial section of the compound clean.

It was clear that they were turning up the throttle. We were not now merely to be workers. They wanted us Sovietized. To join the party, or to place your children in the Pioneers, were serious steps. And by joining the Socialist Competition, workers would be moving away from their separate, foreign specialist status, and into the mainstream of Soviet factory life. The competition was designed to motivate workers by offering recognition and financial rewards for superior performance. It helped to assimilate people into the socialist system.

However, many of the Americans were already sympathetic to socialism, so no one protested these goals. Many of us were selected to come to the Soviet Union not only because of our technical skills, but also because we were considered ripe candidates for conversion to communism. Those who chose me probably felt that any American black would easily substitute Karl Marx's *Das Kapital* for the Bible, and that once I lived in a land that was free of racial prejudice I would gladly embrace communism. Only an insane person, they felt, would fail to take such a logical step.

Nevertheless, I was just such a person; I wanted no part of the party. Something they did not know, because I kept my religious views private, was that I would rather be killed than renounce my belief in God. These new goals concerned me, because having been in the limelight so often, I knew I was a likely candidate to be asked to join the party. After all, I had been hailed as a hero, and was praised time and again in the factory newspaper for my workmanship.

A short time later, I was one of two Americans chosen from our group of over one hundred specialists to represent our factory at the opening of the Rostov Great Combine Factory. We went there with twenty Russian delegates from our factory. I sensed even then that I was being specially cultivated, perhaps with the hope that I would help the Communist party in the United States to recruit blacks.

Fortunately for me, we had until the October Revolution celebration in 1932 to achieve our goals. I reasoned that by that time I would be home in the United States, since my contract expired in June. If necessary I could stall them by saying I needed more time to consider such an important decision. I thought that even if I rejected party membership, they would not send me back home for fear that the Soviet Union would then be accused of being a racist nation. I decided the best thing to do was just keep working to the best of my ability and avoid attracting attention. At the end of June 1932, my contract expired, and I left for Moscow to obtain my return ticket to the United States.

When I arrived in Moscow my first task was to report to an organization called VATO, where I was to receive my ticket home. Because my last months in Stalingrad had been free from political pressure and professionally satisfying, my resolve to leave had weakened. For two days I struggled over the question of whether to remain, or leave, and I was still undecided as I made my way to the VATO office. Should I stay among people who might never be able to trust me—a foreigner—and also risk getting trapped within the workings of the Soviet system, or should I head home and face the uncertain prospect of finding a job in depression-ridden America? I had come to Russia for one year and had stayed two. I had seen much that had impressed me and broadened me. I was ready to go home.

After arriving at VATO, I sat across from a man who studied my file for a few minutes and then told me that the First State Ball Bearing Plant had opened in Moscow just three months earlier, and there was an urgent need for a person with my qualifications. He recommended that I go there and see the director of the factory, a M. Bodrov. A car and driver were outside at my disposal. I areed to look into it, and in about fifteen minutes we had driven the seven miles to the factory entrance.

I was able to see the director right away. He was a man of medium height, with pleasant features. He received me warmly, saying that he had just been told that I would be coming and was impressed by what he had learned of my qualifications in the gauge grinding field. He said he needed such a man there, and offered me a one-year contract. I accepted his offer on the spot. The foreign specialists at the First State Ball Bearing Plant were housed in one of two five-story brick buildings. When I arrived, these two buildings were filled with Germans, British, Americans, Swedes, French, Rumanians, Austrians, Hungarians, Slovaks, Poles, and Italians. In all there were about three hundred foreign workers, most of them with their families. Because I was unmarried, I had to share a two-room apartment with a Russian-American. I settled into my new quarters and began work the next day.

On my second day at work I was shown the flat gauge department, with its three surface grinders and one rotary grinder. There were more than thirty people in the gauge department, and more than 750 in the entire machine shop. No one knew how to grind the flat gauges on the machine. This meant that the final 0.015 inches of metal were left to lap (polish to a high degree of accuracy) by hand instead of mechanically. They were wasting an enormous amount of time, because of their inexperience.

I drew up a list of seventeen different devices that were needed before any grinding could be started. My first task, while on the job and at home, was to start designing the devices, with all the dimensions included, so that they could be manufactured. After I had finished about half of them, I turned my designs over to the superintendent. After looking at the drawings, he asked me if I was an engineer. I said no, and that I had finished Ford Motors' technical school in the United States. He shook his head in amazement at what I had been able to do.

Two weeks later some of the metal devices had been machined, in a soft state, and were hardened. By this time I had been given six apprentices, three for the morning shift and three for the afternoon. With these trainees we began our next task, which was to grind the parts for the devices to specification. The apprentices would rough them out, then I would finish them to the required dimensions. In six weeks' time we were able to start grinding the gauges, leaving only .02 millimeters—almost .001 inches— on all dimensions for lapping. Before they were leaving between .2 to .3 millimeters of metal for lapping.

Thus on the first gauge we ground, after leaving .02 millimeters, it took the worker twenty-five minutes to lap it all over to the finished sizes, whereas before it had taken him five to six hours to remove .2 to .3 millimeters. Within the space of two months, 80 percent of all gauges were being ground. Production had increased seven-fold.

By this time the factory had received an optical grinder. It was placed under my supervision, and I was given two women as apprentices, one for the morning shift and another for the afternoon. I now had eight apprentices to look after. To cope with this situation I began to work nearly two shifts a day. I had to do this because the apprentices lacked experience and my being there was the only way to prevent them from making too much spoilage.

From the end of 1932 until 1936 my work schedule would start with the day shift at 7:30 A.M. and go until 4:00 P.M., then immediately begin again with the second shift and go until 10:00 or 11:00 P.M. My only extra reward for four years of sixteen hour days instead of seven-and-a-half hour days was a twenty-four-day pass to a vacation spot in the Crimea, valued at eight hundred rubles. I was never paid anything for the 1,250 extra days I put in. Nineteen thirty-two and the first half of 1933 was a good period for me, a time of professional productivity. The workers in my factory became increasingly aware of the mood of German militarism that followed Hitler's rise to the office of chancellor of Germany on January 30, 1933. The Nazi party's rise to power greatly disturbed many of my friends and co-workers, who felt that the world in general and Russia in particular were endangered.

However, I just kept putting in my sixteen-hour days, improving my toolmaking skills, and remained as apolitical as I had always been. The shop was my laboratory, where I was free to design and construct devices that turned our department into one of the most efficient at the plant. I enjoyed our accomplishments, and the respect of my peers, especially the foreigners. Yet my greatest joy was simply having the freedom to detect a problem and create a mechanical solution. In some respects, working at the First State Ball Bearing Plant in Moscow was like being able to play my favorite game, and getting paid for it.

Because of my record, the factory's administration approved my request to visit my mother in the United States during the summer of 1933. Before leaving, they urged me to sign another one-year contract, which I did. They knew I enjoyed my work, and with my contract in their hands, they trusted that I would return. They imagined correctly that I would find depression-ridden America an undesirable place to be.

As I prepared to leave for the US, the only thing that concerned me was that a few fellow workers had suddenly left the factory without saying a word or even hinting that they would be leaving. This had started happening a few weeks before I left on vacation, and resulted in ugly rumors circulating in the shop that they had been arrested as enemies of the people. I could not believe it, however, because I knew them to be competent men who, if not dedicated to socialism, were certainly sympathetic to its philosophy. Besides, some of those who had suddenly left were not even Russians.

Getting out of Russia and back into the United States was easy. American immigration whisked me right through. My American passport was valid and I had a clean record. Although I had been the central figure in the Stalingrad trial, which was publicized around the world and shed unfavorable light on American life, US authorities in Moscow and New York never mentioned the incident.

I was glad to be home, but strolling down 125th Street in Harlem left me with a chill, as I watched grown men dressed in shabby, dirty clothes rummage through garbage bins for food. It was disturbing to see defeated, drunken men staggering through alleys and huddling on sidewalks waiting to die. Here was the face of the depression. I had lived in Harlem before, and it was nothing new to see its residents struggle to make ends meet. But the level of poverty and suffering I was seeing now was so much greater.

The best part of my six-week vacation was seeing my mother. Second best was eating her cooking. *Borscht* was good, but fried plantains, yams, and peppery-hot chicken stew were better. Here was the food I had grown up on; it generated happy memories that would later be a source of comfort during the long, frigid Moscow winters. My mother's apartment was comfortably furnished. I felt good to know that the fruits of my labor were helping to provide her with a home she felt proud of.

On my first day back my mother and I sat up most of the night talking. She asked me everything. She sat before me, her eyes bright with curiosity, her face alternately reflecting approval, surprise, shock, and dismay, at each of my revelations about my life in Russia. I noted that Mama was aging with grace and dignity, and that she was still as independent in her thinking and her mind was just as agile as it had always been. When she asked what Russians thought of black people, I told her that while racism was illegal and rarely shown openly, it did exist.

"Most Russians not only have never seen a black person before," I told her, "many of them never even knew that we existed."

Her verdict on the Louis and Brown incident was a feisty one: "Those two got what they deserved. But if I had been the judge, I'd have given them a taste of Siberia."

When I told her that I had signed up for another year she asked me pointblank, "Are you a Communist?"

"No, Mama," I assured her.

"Then are you married to one of those white girls?" she asked, almost holding her breath for my answer.

"Not at all," I answered quickly.

"Then why do you want to go back?"

"Mama," I explained, "you know there's a depression in this country. Just look at those men on the steets outside. I don't want to be one of them."

"But why don't you go back to Detroit?" she insisted. "Since you finished the technical school and worked there I'm sure they'd consider your case and give you a job."

"Mama, a friend wrote me and told me that I've been blacklisted because of the incident with Louis and Brown. There isn't a plant in Detroit that would hire me. Besides, I can still send you money from Russia. And remember how I wanted to study at Tuskegee Institute to become an engineer? Now I am getting the same kind of training in Russia, a lot cheaper."

She accepted my reasoning. Before she left me to go to her room for the night, she asked me to join her as she said a prayer of thanks for my safe return and asked for my continuing health and success.

Word somehow got out to the black press that I had returned from Russia. When reporters asked me about my impressions of the United States after being away for three years, I told them the only way

I knew how—honestly. One newspaper account, quoting me accurately, surely did not win me any friends among white readers.

It said:

> The minute I arrived at 125th Street all the desire to be back in America vanished. Everyone looked so listless and discontent, that a pall of gloom descended over and enshrouded me. It was so contrary to the lively spirit manifested by the Russian workers going happily about their daily tasks with no thought of tomorrow's loss of job or eviction.

With my arrival, my mother's apartment became a kind of magnet, drawing old friends from the neighborhood and even from Detroit. They bombarded me with questions about life in the Soviet Union. From afternoon until late evening, the sound of our voices filled the living room. I told everyone about the Soviet system of employment, under which workers do not receive a fixed salary but rather are paid by the piecework system, earning according to their output. When some heard of the absence of Jim Crow and unemployment, they were eager to journey to the USSR as I had. But I cautioned them that the standard of living was much lower than in the US, and that if they had to live like ordinary Russians they could not count on having running water or indoor plumbing. But one young doctor, obviously enthusiastic, pressed me about how he could get a job in a Soviet hospital. I gave him the name of an organization that recruited professionals in a variety of fields to work in Russia.

At the end of six weeks I said good-by to my family and friends. I was physically rested, spiritually replenished, yet eager to get back to what I enjoyed most—my work.

CHAPTER 7

The First Purges

UPON RETURNING TO MOSCOW everything seemed the same, except that the people who were missing shortly before I left for home were still gone. I did not ask about them and nobody volunteered any information. I tried to forget about them and concentrate on my work. It did not pay to be inquisitive at the factory, because all the administrators were party officials.

However, a few weeks after my return, I learned that in early spring, 1933, a Russian electrical engineer named Ramzin was arrested and tried for sabotaging a factory. He had been working with an Englishman who represented an electrical factory in Britain. Ramzin was part of the old czarist intelligentsia, did not like being used by the new regime, and said that the idea to commit sabotage came from the Englishman.

Until 1935 all of the engineers in the Soviet Union were either from the czarist intelligentsia or foreigners. The Soviet regime had not yet produced its own technical personnel. The Russian engineers had experienced the benefits of a market-driven economy in the preSoviet era. In addition, through their association with foreign engineers in the early thirties, they were reminded how greatly their standard of living had suffered. Ramzin disclosed the existence of a network of saboteurs in many industrial provinces throughout the country.

Stalin set in motion a countermeasure—the purge. Between 1933 and 1935 most of the czarist engineers were rounded up. There were large-scale transfers of people to different provinces, so they could not communicate with each other. There were arrests, show trials, and secret trials. Many innocents were executed immediately; others were banished to Siberia.

Many from my factory were sent away. They would be given a few hours notice so they could not contact anyone else, then they were whisked away. Husbands and wives were often sent to different places. Workers would appear in the factory who had been sent from other, often distant provinces. Most of these people were later arrested again, and shot. Men, women, and children throughout the country were uprooted and forced to start a new life in some distant place.

Near the end of 1933, a number of qualified men came to my Moscow plant from the Stalingrad Tractor Factory, under the regime's transfer plan. I knew several of them well. Melamed, for example, was a chief engineer in one of the shops in Stalingrad and also had served as the interpreter of the delegation which came to Detroit in 1930 and invited me to the Soviet Union. He was named chief engineer in Moscow. Gross, who had been my superintendent in Stalingrad, again became my superintendent in Moscow. He was born in California of Hungarian parents and was a party member. He spoke Russian fluently, his wife was Russian, and they had two young daughters.

I later learned from Gross, under a pledge of secrecy, what had really happened at the tractor plant and in the city of Stalingrad. Thousands of men and women, party and non-party members alike, were arrested, secretly tried, and either sent to Siberia or summarily shot. Among those shot was a good friend of mine, named Kudinov. He was the factory's party secretary and had been sent from Moscow a few months after I arrived in Stalingrad. Kudinov and his wife Marusya shared a medium-sized room in a two-room apartment in my building. He was an honest man and devoted to the party. He normally left home before eight in the morning and did not return home until eleven o'clock at night. His wife protested his long hours, but Kudinov was too deeply involved in his work to pay heed.

Kudinov was arrested, secretly tried, and found guilty of lacking vigilance over the so-called enemies of the people. He was shot. Marusya had to give up the room they were living in.

The men transferred to Moscow from Stalingrad, whether by accident or design, maneuvered their way out of the show trials in Stalingrad. Each one probably thought he would be free from prosecution in the capital. But one day in 1934, Melamed, the chief engineer of the entire factory, did not show up for work. This bold sign that the GPU (the secret police, forerunners to today's KGB) were now operating in our factory too alarmed all of us.

A few weeks later, Gross, the machine shop superintendent, also failed to show up for work. The secret police confiscated his Order of Lenin medal, given for his outstanding service to the state, evicted his wife and two daughters from their apartment, and banished them from Moscow.

Within a few months all of the other men from Stalingrad disappeared. A year later we heard that both Melamed and Gross had been shot. Immediately after Kirov was assassinated, on December 1, 1934, the purge that had been building up steam gradually became an avalanche. Sergei Vironovich Kirov was the Leningrad party boss and the man everyone assumed would eventually become Stalin's successor. At his death, the preferred status of foreign specialists ended overnight. Contracts were cancelled, and party and non-party workers alike were arrested. Every day people failed to show up for work, not only in my factory but in other factories in Moscow and throughout the country.

The factories were not the only targets. People in the city also were disappearing daily. Lena and her husband Petya were friends of mine. He was an electrical engineer at the power station in Moscow. One day he failed to come home from work, and he did not show up the following day either. His wife found out on the third day that he had not been reporting for work. She went to the police, but they had no knowledge of his whereabouts. Finally, in desperation, she went to the GPU. There she learned that he was in custody, but they would not tell her more than that. At three A.M. the next day she was arrested, too.

This happened at the end of 1934. The next I heard of her was in 1946. Her life had been spared because she was a nurse and her services were needed at hospitals in Siberia. Her husband was never heard from again.

Evdokia Filipovna was another city acquaintance of mine, a specialist in chemistry who had been working for the ministry of agriculture for more than fifteen years. She was taken away one day at 4 A.M. Knowing how dangerous the situation was, her husband did not go to find out about her but instead sent their sixteen-year-old daughter. When the girl reached the imposing Lubyanka prison building, she became afraid of what they might do to her if she went in. She returned home to her father; her mother never returned.

Eight acquaintances of mine from the city disappeared, and only one ever returned. The Moscow purges were so terrifying and dangerous that I had to stop visiting my friends in the city. As soon as they would open their doors and see me standing in the hall, they would say courteously but in a pleading and cautious tone, ''Please, I beg of you, do not come and visit us again.''

My American passport most likely saved my life, at a time when thousands of innocent people were disappearing daily in a state-sanctioned witch hunt. Because of my American citizenship, I was not afraid of being arrested. I just kept doing what I could do, which was to put in sixteen-hour workdays. I had no time during the week to do anything but go home and rest, but on the weekends I would go out. I never sat around with the other foreign workers drinking vodka, but usually ventured out among the Russian people, until it became too dangerous for them to see me, a foreigner.

I had become acquainted with a number of the families still remaining from the czarist intelligentsia. At that time there was not yet a Soviet intelligentsia, nor a Soviet social elite of any significant number. I was a constant guest at one of five apartments, for Saturday and Sunday late afternoon and evening entertainment, until the second purges started in 1937 and our meetings stopped.

My introduction to this group of people came through Coretta Arle-Titzs, a black American I met while she was on tour in Stalingrad. Coretta was married to a Russian music professor and had been living in Russia since before the revolution, in 1912.

Among this rare group of people were artists, writers, dancers, singers, musicians, sculptors, poets, and physicians. Many of them were famous performers. To survive after the revolution they had to appear to assimilate into the new Bolshevik environment. They therefore displayed conspicuous portraits of Lenin and Stalin in their apartments for the benefit of any government official who might drop in.

I never would have met these beautiful people if I had not gotten sick. In 1933 I developed pain around my heart. The doctors at the clinic could not help me, so I contacted Coretta. She referred me to a Dr. Bermin, who diagnosed my illness as pleurisy and treated me. In three weeks I was back at work.

Several months later I received a formally written invitation from Dr. Bermin and his wife to attend a party at their apartment. In those days Russians were warmly disposed to foreigners. I had never been to the Sabachi Pereulok section of Moscow where the party was to be held, so I arranged with Coretta and her husband to go with them. When we reached this section of town I felt as if I had been transported entirely out of Russia. Instead of the usual one-story log row houses, here were four- and five-story houses made of stone and brick. These were elegant buildings, obviously the homes of nobility. During czarist times one family would occupy the entire house, but in 1934 a different family lived on each floor. Like Dr. Bermin, most of those families were part of the Russian aristocracy prior to the Bolshevik revolution. Upon entering the apartments, you could sense it.

Dr. Bermin, who greeted us at the door, was a man of noble bearing, about six feet tall, erect, with sparkling blue eyes. He kissed Coretta's hand, a gesture I had never seen before in Russia. I soon saw that all of the men greeted the women in this manner, and the women responded with a bow.

We walked through a large entryway. Paintings by nineteenth century Russian artists decorated the walls. On the shining hardwood floors were several thick scatter rugs. In the huge living room—about twenty-eight square meters or three hundred square feet—stood a beautiful Steinway grand piano. From the twelve- to fourteen-foot-high ceiling hung a large crystal chandelier. Adorning one wall was a large tapestry.

I had never in my life experienced such refined luxury. Nothing about Dr. Bermin's apartment was pretentious. It was truly a home where I was made to feel completely at ease. It did not have a museum-like feel, which would have made me uncomfortable. The sofas, chairs, lamps, vases, and drapes were part of an era that most Russians, even during the time of the czar, never knew existed. During this first visit, I was so overwhelmed by the elegance and beauty of the place that I never even wondered how the Bermins could maintain such a home in a nation that frowned on wealth and privilege. Soaking in the splendor of their home, I suddenly realized that during my stay in Russia I had become starved for beauty.

The people were as dazzling as the home. The women dressed in lovely evening gowns, displayed gold and diamond jewelry, wore lipstick and rouge, and smelled of sweet perfume. The women would arrive at the Bermins' wearing their drab Russian clothing, with their gowns and jewelry concealed in a bag. They did not dare alert the authorities that they would be dressing and behaving in a manner that would have been considered counter-revolutionary. Coretta told me later that, soon after the revolution, Lenin issued a decree that all gold be turned over to the government and no gold be displayed in public. The government opened a store where gold could be exchanged for food. Therefore, the women wearing gold jewelry had to be careful not to be seen in public. The men were not as well-dressed. But what a sight; how different from the women at work! This was a fairy tale unfolding before my eyes. Only the people were real. They did not talk about quotas, tractors, party solidarity, and enemies of the people, but of opera, dance, literature, art, and drama. And there was more than discussion.

We feasted: boiled ham, sausage, salmon, veal, sardines, cheese, pickled cucumbers, tomatoes, red and black caviar. We drank champagne, red and white wines, vodka, and assorted soft drinks. There were also cakes and candy and tea from a samovar. We ate and drank all we wanted, yet there still was plenty left. Until this evening I could only have imagined such a meal. And to top it off, there was singing, piano playing, and poetry recitations. The performers were professionals, and they shared their talent freely and willingly. I soaked in every note and every word, like a thirsty desert traveler sipping water from an oasis stream.

Attending a formal concert in central Moscow in the best opera house could not have been better. The intimacy, and the affection and respect these twenty people had for one another, is what made it so special. I was impressed with how the entertainment got under way. It was both gracious and informal. After we finished our tea, Mrs. Bermin approached a beautiful woman in her early thirties and said, ''Elena Dmitrievna, please, be so kind and sing for us.''

''With pleasure,'' said the woman. As she rose, her husband went to the piano to accompany her. She announced each piece before she performed—songs by Pushkin, Glinka, and Borodin.

Next a famous actor in the group, Victor Vasilevich, was asked to recite something. He read a few stanzas from Pushkin's, ''I Remember a Marvelously Fleeting Moment,'' recited part one of Chekhov's *Three Sisters,* and ended with ''The Flea'' by Korsakov. Although I had been assigned a translator for my first year in Stalingrad, who had also served as a Russian language tutor—and I had been studying the language diligently ever since, trying to understand the verse strained my Russian language skills past their limit.

Next came a baritone who sang two songs by Rimsky-Korsakov. Then my friend Coretta stepped up to the piano with her husband. I could tell she was a favorite among the people at the party; they applauded before she even sang a note. After performing two Russian songs, she took me back to the America I knew best —black America—by singing ''Malindi Brown'' by Paul Lawrence Dunbar. I suspect she included that song for my benefit.

Without a doubt this was the most pleasurable evening I had spent in the Soviet Union. I had studied music at the Detroit Conservatory for three years, had read the biographies of many composers, and was always enchanted by classical music. I was in my element here. I had arrived at 3:30 P.M. The first time I checked my watch, it was 12:30 A.M. I went up to Dr. Bermin and told him that I had to leave, because the last streetcar to my section of the city was at 12:55. He and his wife urged me to come to the next party the following month. I assured them I would be there. The others came over to bid me an affectionate farewell. I learned a few days later that the party lasted until 4:00 A.M.

During the time of my visits to the Bermins, in June 1934, I received a pass from the Trade Union Committee to take a twenty-four-day vacation at a home of rest (a vacation home run by the government) in the Crimea. I was still recovering from my bout with pleurisy under Dr. Bermin's supervision. Workers were not free to decide when and where we might take a vacation. Instead, we were assigned to a home of rest and told when we could go and how long we could stay.

In Moscow I boarded a train heading for the Mis-Mor Home of Rest. Forty-four hours later, at 9:30 A.M., we reached Sevastopol. A number of agents from surrounding sanatoria and homes of rest had come to meet the train. When I heard one of the agents call out, "Mis-Mor," I raised my hand and he pointed me toward a yellow bus standing nearby.

As soon as the small group of us who had climbed into the bus to Mis-Mor arrived, our documents and our passes to the home of rest were checked, recorded, and taken. The passports would not be returned until after they were registered with the local militia. Everyone was given a bath towel, pointed to the male and female bathhouses, and told to wash. We were then taken in pairs to our rooms. Two or three to a room was the rule. It was our good fortune to arrive on the first day of admission, because we all received rooms for two. After settling in, it was nearly 1:30 P.M., so we went downstairs for our first meal. We were served a small piece of meat and about eight tablespoonfuls of buckwheat, with a dab of gravy on top. Halfway through the meal we were given a glass of stewed fruit. Then after lunch, while most of the others napped, I ventured outside to inspect our surroundings.

Over the next few days I went with the group on a number of excursions into the surrounding area. These were all planned for us, and we were expected to participate. One of our trips was to the famous Voronsov Museum, which contains a large collection of paintings by the old masters. While outside the museum, I noticed three young women walking toward us and recognized one of them as an acquaintance of mine from Moscow. She introduced me to her two friends, and invited me to meet with them that evening outside the museum, which was about a thirty-minute walk from where I was staying.

That evening I met the women and we sat for awhile and chatted in the park surrounding the museum. Then we went to another part of the park to listen to some gramophone music we had heard in the distance. As we approached, we could see that couples were dancing. By their clothing I could tell that they had come from Moscow or Leningrad. As it turned out, they were part of the Leningrad Ballet and Opera Company, and the two women I had just met with my Moscow acquaintance were a part of the company.

We stood listening to the music and watching the couples dance. Then one of the women invited me to dance with her. As soon as we began, the man operating the record player stopped the music. The people dancing looked up at him, a bit surprised. In a little while he began playing the music again and the couples resumed their dancing. I decided to wait a bit, to see whether he was objecting to my presence. After two more records had played, one of the girls asked me, "Why don't you dance with us? Must we always be the ones to invite you?"

I smiled and said that I thought they did not like to dance to such music, since they were used to classical.

"Not at all," they said in unison.

Then one of them stretched out her arms to me, saying, "Let's not argue; let's just dance," and we began dancing.

The music stopped. Another couple went up to the man playing the records and said something to him. The man said something in response and pointed toward us. I told the women that I was not welcome there and that we should go and sit somewhere else where we could listen to the music.

Instead of agreeing, one of the women said in an angry voice, "What makes you think so? You are not in America, you are in the Soviet Union!"

Then one of the others suggested that we go behind a couple of trees near the dance ring. We all agreed, and once there she said, "Now let's see who was right." We began to dance, and the first song shortly came to its natural finish. The first woman told me that I was wrong to think that the man stopped the music because he was prejudiced against me. When the next record started I invited her to dance, but by this time the man must have caught sight of us. He stopped the music abruptly.

We all looked at one another without speaking. After awhile the man started playing the record again and I invited the third woman to dance. But no sooner had we started than the music was stopped again. We tested the man again by letting three records go by without dancing, then we started to dance to the fourth. The music stopped.

The women were finally convinced, so we found a bench and sat down. After a bit of conversation, I said that it was time for me to return to where I was staying. They walked me back until I was within five minutes of Mis-Mor. As we parted, one of them said under her breath, "There are security guards all around here, because Molotov [the prime minister] and Kuybishev [also a member of the Central Committee] live nearby."

Then my Moscow friend said, "Don't forget, we are expecting you to let us show you the beach tomorrow morning."

The next morning, on my way to meet them, I saw two men on horseback coming toward me. As they got closer, I recognized Kuybyshev. As we were about to pass each other, he bowed to me, and I did the same. I soon passed his home and shortly after reached the park, where the three women were waiting for me, in their bathing suits.

As we walked to the beach, it became clear to me that the one who had acted most spirited the day before, insisting that we dance because we were in the Soviet Union and not in America, was very quiet and appeared somewhat disturbed. As soon as we reached the beach she went right into the water. I asked my friend from Moscow what was troubling her.

After some hesitation she said, "After we walked you home last night, we returned to the park and she got into an angry dispute with the man who was playing the records."

"What was the cause of the dispute?" I asked.

"It was on account of you," she said. "My friend asked the man why he stopped the music each time we attempted to dance. His answer was, 'I did not bring my music from Leningrad for the pleasure of any baboon.' Of course, this caused further quarreling."

I told her that we would be foolish to let this one man's bigotry spoil our time together, though I appreciated her friend's intercession on my behalf. My remaining time in the Crimea was enjoyable. I was able to visit many interesting places, including Goursouf, where Pushkin wrote his famous poem, "Bakhchisaraisky Fountain," which has since been made into a ballet, and Livadia, formerly the czars' summer palace, which is now a sanatorium. After my twenty-four days of rest I returned to Moscow feeling like a new person.

But when I arrived back at work, even after such a short absence, I immediately sensed a different mood in my fellow workers. Then on December 1, Kirov was assassinated. The purges switched into high gear. People were disappearing from the factory daily.

CHAPTER 8

My Election to the Moscow Soviet

DECEMBER 10, 1934, is a day I shall never forget. I was walking down the long, tunnel-like corridor at 7:30 A.M., heading toward my workshop, when it suddenly struck me that something was different. Then I realized what it was: everything was silent. Normally at this hour the air would already be alive with the sounds of machines whirring and grinding and the pounding of presses.

"Was it a holiday?" I wondered. There seemed to be nobody at work.

As I continued walking I began to hear some sounds. Somcone was speaking. Then there was loud applause. I quickened my pace and came to my workplace. But nobody was at the workbenches and machines. Instead, all the workers—about 750 in all—were gathered at the end of the shop. I walked over and stood at the far edge of the crowd. Because of the people in front of me I was not able to see the speaker, but I could hear him through the loudspeakers.

A fellow worker motioned me over to him, and explained to me that I was witnessing grassroots democracy at work. In factories throughout the district, candidates were being nominated to serve on the city council of Moscow, called the Moscow Soviet. He explained that out of hundreds of thousands of workers, 112 people would be elected.

One speaker followed another, giving nominating speeches. Each speaker used the same dramatic style, first describing the candidate's virtues and then finally at the end revealing the person's name. Then the chairman would ask the workers to raise their hands in approval. This process went on and on.

At about 10 A.M. yet another speaker rose. In a rich, deep voice he spoke eloquently about his candidate's unselfish contributions to the First State Ball Bearing Plant. The candidate's inventiveness was emphasized. Raising his voice in a crescendo, the speaker exhorted, "This candidate cannot be ignored."

He paused slightly, for dramatic effect, and then said, "Comrades, I nominate none other than Robert Robinson!"

The workers applauded wildly. Hundreds of people turned to me, smiling, clapping, and cheering. People close to me reached for my hand; others slapped me on the back. But I was far from jubilant—shocked, perplexed, and anxious, but not jubilant. I stood in stunned disbelief, my thoughts racing.

"What have they done to me?" I thought. "What have I gotten myself into? I'm not a political person. And besides, I'm an American citizen, and not even a Communist party member. My very fundamental beliefs are in complete opposition to the party and the Soviet regime. I'm not an atheist, not even an agnostic. I believe in God, I pray to Him, and my first allegiance is to Him."

I wondered if what was happening was real. Nobody had asked me. It was without my consent, and against my will. Why hadn't anyone asked me first, before nominating me? I would have talked him out of it. I worried, "What will the American government think? Will they force me to leave my job and return to depression-ridden America?"

Needless to say, I didn't accomplish much that day at work. At 4:30 that afternoon everyone was ordered to stop working and gather at a vacant lot next to the factory. Thousands of people were there, from more than twenty shops. Those of us chosen for the Moscow Soviet—twenty in all—were asked to come forward and stand before the cheering crowd. A few party members read short biographies of us. When mine was read, the Stalingrad assault and trial were emphasized. After we were all introduced, the chairman asked the crowd for another show of approval. Thousands of hands were raised. Then the crowd of workers was asked if there were any objections to any candidate. No one came forward.

My heart kept pounding throughout the meeting. I was furious. They are treating me like a man without a will. I felt torn apart. Here was a system that offered me the opportunity to work and earn a respectable living, but that was also demanding from me an allegiance I did not wish to give.

"Perhaps I should quit and go home," I thought. "But then what about my mother?" She needed my support. The $150 a month I was able to send her allowed her to live with some dignity, after a life of much hardship. "How could I rob her of that?" I thought. I decided that I couldn't.

I was elected to a four-year term. I feared I would lose my contract if I rejected the position, but to accept it would make me vulnerable to charges in the US that I was a Communist or Communist sympathizer. This might place my status as a naturalized American citizen in danger.

Finally I reached a decision. I would not protest the election, but I would go home after my current, one-year contract expired. I would put in as little time as possible as a member of the Moscow Soviet, I would continue to work sixteen-hour days, and the time would pass quickly.

At 6:30 P.M. everyone except the candidates was dismissed. We were told to march to the Moscow Soviet building, which was six-and-a-half miles away. So we marched. But when we reached the building, in the center of the city, it was closed. No one was around to cheer or greet us, so we all went home by streetcar.

I entered my apartment about 11:00, too tired to fix a meal, so I had some tea and went to bed. But shortly after midnight I awoke to the sound of someone pounding on my door and calling my name. I refused to budge, not wanting to see anyone or go anywhere. When I heard someone on the other side of the door say, "We don't need such people in our ranks," I realized this was most likely a group of my fellow candidates. I rolled over and went back to sleep.

The next day my shop foreman and other party members acted cool toward me. In their zeal, they had gone to hear Comrade

ПОРТРЕТЫ ДЕПУТАТОВ

МАНДАТ ДЕПУТАТА РОБИНСОНА

ВТОРОЙ РАЗ в жизни, второй раз после того события в Сталинграде окружают Робинсона журналисты. Снова имя этого скромного человека встречается на страницах наших газет.

... Робинсон приехал в Советский союз в 1930 году из Америки. Сам он негр из Ямайки. Мать его до самых последних лет гнула спину на сахарных плантациях. Отец Робинсона был бедняком. Товарищи Робинсона — рабочие-негры — до сих пор ведут жизнь черных парией в нью-йоркском негритянском гетто — в Гарлеме.

Робинсон исколесил все западное полушарие. Он работал в Бразилии, служил в Детройте у Форда, причем был единственным негром среди семисот белых инструментальщиков.

Талантливому инструментальщику приходилось до этого работать носильщиком, катать болванки, штамповать железо, потому что никто не хотел давать квалифицированную работу черному.

Америка разговаривала с молодыми эмигрантами из Ямайки на грубом диалекте заводских боссов. Молодого человека, только-что приехавшего в Америку, попросили выйти вон из ресторана, потому что в Америке для негров есть особые харчевни так же, как и особые гостиницы для негров. В театр его пускали только на галерку. Америка, увлекающаяся танцами первобытных негров, негритянской музыкой, не подпускает негров даже в смокингах на расстояние ближе, чем первый ряд галлереи шестого яруса.

Робинсон изъездил весь мир в поисках страны, где темный цвет кожи не мешал жить и работать. С места на место его толкала тоска по настоящей родине. Вместе с большой группой американских рабочих он прибыл на Сталинградский тракторный.

Еще по дороге к заводу Робинсона удивляло многое. Летом 1930 года, когда пароход подвозил его по Волге к Сталинграду, русская девушка подошла к негру и пригласила его на танец. Этот казалось бы незначительный факт произвел на Робинсона потрясающее впечатление. Он сам пишет об этом в книге «Люди Сталинградского тракторного»:

«Мне казалось, что я нашел причину того, почему иностранные капиталисты так боятся русских, почему так поддерживается представление о большевиках как о мужиках в грязных сапогах с нечесаными бородами. Заграничная пресса не любит и боится русских потому, что русские сумели уничтожить у себя расовое различие и национальную нетерпимость. Они сумели создать у себя другие законы и другие отношения, одинаковые для всех, кто умеет работать» («Люди СТЗ», стр. 132).

Вскоре после прибытия Робинсона в СССР и произошло событие, приковавшее к этому скромному человеку внимание миллионов. Американцы на Сталинградском тракторном жили в изолированном Нижнем поселке. Там образовалось нечто вроде «кусочка Америки»: патефон, фокстроты, дансинги в американской столовке. Здесь вновь возникли некоторые «зарубежные традиции». На негра стали посматривать косо его американские товарищи. Они не хотели, чтобы негр обедал с ними в одной столовой. Однажды Люис и Браун, двое американцев, напали на Робинсона, возвращавшегося из столовки. Они пытались его избить. Робинсон никогда не забудет той волны негодования, которая охватила тогда всю нашу страну. Суд осудил и выслал из нашей страны Люиса и Брауна, пытавшихся перенести традиции рабовладельческой Южной Америки на почву советского завода. Во всех газетах нашей страны тогда впервые появились портреты Робинсона. Он получил десятки писем от организаций и одиночек-рабочих. Особенно тронуло тогда Робинсона письмо рабочих Электрозавода, пригласивших рабочего-негра приехать на их завод.

Из Сталинградского тракторного Робинсон перевелся в Москву в инструментальный цех 1-го господшипникового завода им. Кагановича. Говорят, что в инструментальном нет более старательного и знающего работника, чем Робинсон. Он уже обучил десять человек тонкому искусству шлифовщиков. Его ученики — Другов, Пинкевич, Кокель — сейчас уже сами высококвалифицированные шлифовщики и могут обучать других. Робинсон очень часто задерживался позже положенного времени, занимаясь со своими учениками. Этот худощавый, очень подвижный парень в очках, обладающий незаурядными способностями конструктора, сумел не только обучить десяток рабочих, но и дать около пятидесяти ценных рационализаторских предложений. Собственными руками Робинсон изготовил синусную линейку и призму для точных угловых работ.

Когда износились привезенные Робинсоном из Америки индикаторы, он лично изготовил первый советский индикатор.

Робинсон — беспартийный. Он приехал в СССР человеком, мало интересующимся политикой. Но вот уже серьезные перемены происходят в самом Робинсоне:

«... и еще осталась у меня привычка необщительности. Вам это будет понятно, если я расскажу вам следующее: за все время работы у Форда я был окружен молчанием. Я работал в цехе среди сот людей, но со мной не говорили слова». («Люди СТЗ», стр. 163).

Вокруг Робинсона на «Шари[...] подшипнике» — большой кружок д[...]зей, его учеников. Инструмента[...]щики с «Шарикоподшипника» л[...]бят этого знающего, молчаливого [...]ловека. Они уважают его умение [...]ботать над собой. Робинсон хоро[...] научился говорить по-русски. [...]бинсон перестал быть необщител[...]ным. Он читает наши газеты, [...] изучает **Ленина и Сталина**.

Получилось совершенно есте[...]венно, что рабочие инструментал[...]ного цеха выдвинули кандидатом [...] Моссовет именно Роберта Робинс[...]на. Он — лучший ударник це[...] общественник, рационализатор.

Робинсон внимательно присматр[...]вается ко всему происходящему в[...]круг. Он многое критикует:

«Я замечаю в России неумен[...] организовывать мелочи, какую[...] непонятную неряшливость в ва[...]ных мелочах. Еще по пути на Ст[...]линградский завод на пароходе б[...]ло человек пятьдесят обслужива[...]щего персонала, но кормили нас [...] во-время — то через каждый ч[...]то с громадными промежутками. [...] Америке с таким делом справили[...] бы два буфетчика». («Люди СТ[...] стр. 163).

Он разоблачает беспорядки [...] производстве, борется с браком.

Сердит Робинсон и на наш тра[...]вай, не умеющий еще как следу[...] организовать работу.

Теперь Робинсон непосредствен[...] сам включится в работу Моссове[...] по организации этих «мелочей».

Черный человек будет заседа[...] впервые в Белом зале Моссове[...] Он займет свое место по праву к[...] депутат рабочих передового сов[...]ского завода, как представитель [...]мой угнетенной в капиталисти[...]ском мире национальности, наше[...]шей родину в стране советов.

Евг. МАР[...]

Moscow Eve. News

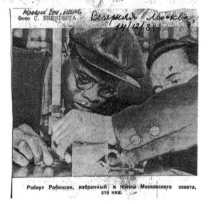

Фото С. ВЕЙНБЕРГА

Вечерняя Москва 14/12/34

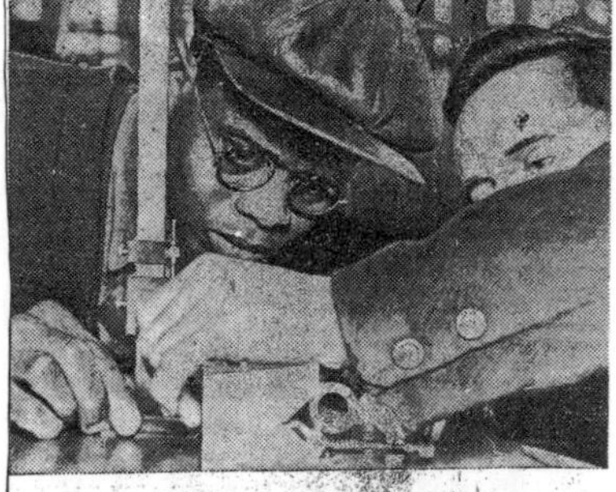

Роберт Робинсон, избранный в члены Московского совета, ста нка.

A profile of Robinson appeared in the Moscow Evening News *on December 14, 1934, following his forced election as a deputy to the Moscow Soviet. Under the headline, "The Mandate for Deputy Robinson," the article begins: "For the second time in his life, after that event in Stalingrad, journalists surround Robinson. Again the name of that modest person gets into the pages of our papers." The accompanying photo shows Robinson at work instructing one of his apprentices.*

Kaganovich, a member of the Politburo of the Communist party, speak for about three hours the night before. They resented my unwillingness to join them.

I regretted that I was now becoming even more of a celebrity than I had been as a result of the Stalingrad incident. Almost everywhere I went I would see a large picture of myself and the other members of the Moscow Soviet displayed. My picture was on the front page of all of Moscow's newspapers. I was now part of an elite group.

The only other member of the Moscow Soviet whom I knew was Ottolinger, a German socialist who was thrilled beyond measure that he had been selected. He asked me how I felt about being elected. He was puzzled at my noncommittal, unemotional response, because to him, being elected to the Soviet Union's largest city legislature was an honor he could never even have dreamed of.

One week after the election I was summoned to a meeting with the factory's top administrator, who was also the leading Communist party official. He told me that I was to meet with Comrade Nikolai Bulganin, chairman of the Moscow Soviet, at 10:00 the next morning. The factory official was curt and gave no clue as to the reason for the meeting.

The next morning promptly at 10:00 I entered Bulganin's office. He stood up, smiled, and reached out to shake my hand. Then he invited me to sit down in the chair in front of his desk.

"Here is a pretty decent fellow," I thought. He had a jovial manner, and unlike most other high-ranking members of the party I had met, he did not look as if he was carrying the world's troubles on his back. In Bulganin's presence I quickly felt at ease.

He looked at me like a father talking to his favorite son. "The reports I have received on the quality of your work have impressed me," he said. "I want to thank you personally for what you are doing."

I really didn't know what to say, except thank you.

Bulganin went on to ask me how I liked Moscow, where I lived, and whether I was satisfied with my living accommodations. Before I could answer, he said that he could get me a better apartment outside of the industrial complex area, in the center of Moscow. When I told him that I was satisfied with where I lived, he asked me what I did with my free time during the week. He seemed surprised when I answered that I

ЛУЧШИХ ЛЮДЕЙ ПАРТИИ И СТРАНЫ ИЗБИРАЮТ ПРОЛЕТАРИИ И ТРУДЯЩИЕСЯ В МОСКОВСКИЙ СОВЕТ

РАБОЧАЯ МОСКВА

11 1934 г. № 287

С первых дней революции на всех выборах в советы рабочие и работницы Трехгорки первый мандат депутата в Московский совет отдают бессмертному вождю мирового пролетариата В. И. Ленину. Трехгорцы по праву гордятся своей славной традицией. Вчера рабочие и работницы Трехгорки на выборах в Моссовет первый мандат отдали В. И. Ленину.

МОСКВА ВЫБИРАЕТ

ПЕРВЫЙ ДЕНЬ

ДА ЗДРАВСТВУЕТ ВКП(б)

ДА ЗДРАВСТВУЕТ СОВЕТСКАЯ ВЛАСТЬ

Robinson's photo is displayed in the December 11, 1934, issue of the Moscow Worker, *(left column, six down from the top) in an article about members of the Moscow Soviet. The headline above the masthead reads: "The Best People of the Party and Country Voted to Moscow Soviet by the Laboring Proletariats." Robinson is pictured along with (from top left) Kossior, Kuybishev, Voroshilov, Kaganovich (large photo in center), Stalin, Molotov, Ordjhonikidze, Kalinin, and Andreev. A photo of Nikita Khrushchev, a fellow member of the Moscow Soviet, is at the top of the left column.*

Robinson is holding a scrapbook with the headline (above) from the Negro Liberator, *a left-wing New York weekly newspaper, which carried an article about his attendance in 1935 as an elected deputy to the first session of the Moscow Soviet. The headline reads: "U.S. Negro is Elected to City Council in Moscow, U.S.S.R." Robinson's brother sent him the article. Below, the English-language* Moscow News *carried a photo of Robinson's attendance at the first session of the Moscow Soviet.*

often stayed home during my day off and that I sometimes went to the theater or to the cinema at night.

Bulganin then moved forward in his chair, so that he was closer to me. He peered at me kindly. "Would you like to have a dacha in the country outside Moscow?" he asked. "I can secure one for you, and you will not have to pay for it right away. To get there, arrangements can be made for you to rent an automobile at a reasonable rate."

I thought it strange that I was being offered such luxuries, which were unavailable to the average Soviet citizen. As attractive as they sounded, they obviously would not come without strings attached. I knew there would be a price to pay if I accepted. I would refuse his temptations, but how to do that without insulting him was the dilemma I felt.

As politely as possible, I said: "Comrade Bulganin, I deeply appreciate your offer of assistance. It is very, very kind of you. However, I am perfectly satisfied with my present work and living situations."

Bulganin looked at me for a moment, without saying a word. Then he said, "You are the first person who has ever refused every offer I made."

I thanked him again for his thoughtfulness and assured him that when the time came and I needed help, I would certainly call on him. He then stood up and wished me well: our meeting was over.

As I left the Moscow Soviet building I felt relieved and even a little bit proud of myself that I had not been seduced by his offers. For a moment or two I felt myself weakening. But I knew that if I had accepted, I would have become more entangled in the Soviet system, making it more difficult to leave when my contract expired. I would have grown accustomed to the new comforts and I would have felt indebteded to the Soviet Union for the advantages I was enjoying.

Three months later I was again notified to report the next morning at 10:00 to Bulganin's office. Expecting more offers of help, I prepared a few polite ways to tell him no. I felt secure as I entered the office of this powerful yet kindly man. But almost immediately I realized that the man sitting behind the desk reading a report was not the father-like person I had met before. This time he didn't stand up. Instead he ignored my greeting and raised his head slowly and stared at me. In a cold, stony voice, he demanded, "What do you want?"

Looking glum, Robinson is congratulated by his shop colleagues after his election as a deputy to the Moscow Soviet, representing his factory.

I was stunned. Standing speechless in front of him, I felt like an idiot. I was afraid of saying the wrong thing and tried quickly to collect my thoughts.

"I've been trapped!" I thought.

I decided I had better ask him for a favor, or else he might erupt on the spot, accuse me of disrupting his day, and send me back to the United States immediately. I had to come up with some kind of request—and quickly.

"Comrade Bulganin," I said. "Since my election to the Moscow Soviet, I have had no assignments. Is it possible for you to secure me some?"

"In a few days some work will be found for you," he answered.

He never looked up from his report, and after speaking to me he continued reading it. I took this as my dismissal. I said good-by to him, but he didn't utter a word. Feeling relieved, I slipped out of his office.

Bulganin kept his promise. In two weeks I was asked to report to the headquarters of the Moscow Soviet, where a bureaucrat gave me my assignments. I was to inspect two small factories. One of them manufactured pencils, the other one produced women's powder boxes. I was to file a monthly report with the Moscow Soviet, describing the quality of workmanship, the morale of the workers, and whether the factories were meeting their quotas. If the plants were not meeting their goals, I was expected to recommend ways for them to improve production.

These reports were due on the fifteenth of each month, and I would often be asked to read my findings to the Soviet. Members of the city legislature would then vote on whether my recommendations should be adopted, which they always were. I thought at the time that if I had been a dishonest or vindictive person, I could have made the lives of the workers in these two factories miserable. No one in the plants, not even the director or chief engineer, had the power to appeal my findings.

My inspection trips to the factories were awkward at first. I could feel the tension of the workers as I moved about from machine to machine. The leadership was terrified because they knew I had the power to help them or break them. They could be promoted, demoted, or fired as a result of my reports. But after about six visits they came to understand that my recommendations were designed to help them, and they came to trust me. For example, the pencil factory was using hard wood in its pencils. Consumers were complaining that it was practically impossible to sharpen the pencils. So I suggested the obvious: that they use cedar or pine and create a balanced mix of clay and graphite to help produce a smoother pencil.

My work for the Moscow Soviet was considered so important that I was excused from my regular job whenever I went on an inspection mission. I always carried my Moscow Soviet mandate with me. The mandate was a special leather folder containing my picture and the seal of the Moscow Soviet with the words, "Member of the Moscow Soviet, 1935-1939" stamped inside. The mandate not only got me inside the factories, it was also good for free rides on the streetcars.

CHAPTER 9

A Fateful Decision

AS I HAD SUSPECTED, MY ELECTION to the Moscow Soviet soon began to haunt me. My older brother, who had a small tailoring business in New York, sent me clippings from the American press. All the reports were unfavorable. The establishment press was particularly harsh. Although I was quoted as saying I was not a Communist, the articles implied that I was lying, and that in my heart I was a Marxist and a traitor. An article in the December 24, 1934, issue of *Time* magazine was typical.

> Last week that coal-black protege of Joseph Stalin, Robert Robinson, was elected, somewhat to his surprise, to the Moscow Soviet . . .
>
> In Russia, Perfect Gentleman Robert Robinson is famed because of the Communist propaganda trial put on in his honor in 1930 at Stalingrad where he was working as a machinist. Two white U.S. machinists objected violently to being lumped with a "nigger" at meals. They were solemnly tried, convicted of "race prejudice," and one was banished from the Soviet Union . . .

> [Robinson's] election last week was elegant propaganda among US Negroes.

What could I do against such misinformation? I was defenseless against the press.

As it turned out, I did not fare any better with the State Department. Six months after my election to the Moscow Soviet, I received an official notice to visit the vice-consul at the US embassy in Moscow. He ordered me to leave Russia immediately and return to the United States. When I asked why, he said, "This order is based on a law which states that a naturalized citizen can remain abroad for a maximum of five years without returning to the United States."

He said the law had been in effect since 1861. Since I had brought my passport with me, I took it out and showed him that in fact I had returned to the United States in 1933, for six weeks. However, he refused to yield before this evidence and insisted that I heed the State Department's order.

What an injustice! I was incensed, but I knew I had to act swiftly and rationally, and that it was no time for open outrage. I just could not face the bleak prospect of returning to the United States at that time. By now I had decided that I would probably renew my contract when it expired in six months, despite the political dangers of being on the Moscow Soviet. I kept returning to the thought that going back to the United States at that time would be like committing suicide. There was the difficulty of a black man getting a job based on experience and ability during a crippling depression. I had an elderly mother to support. And by this time I had also been blacklisted in my professional field. My brother had written me that I should not expect to get my job back with the Ford Motor Company, or with anyone else for that matter. The bad publicity had branded me a "Red," a "Bolshevik," a "coal-black protégé of Joseph Stalin." I knew that even under the best of circumstances, I would be unemployable.

This meant that if I had to return to the United States, I would become a scavenger, existing on the edge of civilization, unable to meet even my most basic needs. I was determined instead to stand up for my rights as a US citizen. I began an investigation to locate naturalized Americans working in Russia whose passports had been extended. It was not difficult to find them. There was Herzog, who worked as an engineer at the Magnitogorsk plant, whose passport was extended after he was in the Soviet Union for seven years. I found others who had extended their stay, without having to face any obstacle from the US. There was even one fellow named Ivanov, a Russian-born naturalized US citizen who had returned to Russia and taken out Soviet citizenship. He was allowed to regain his American citizenship, get a US passport, and return to the States. I brought this evidence to the embassy, but the State Department denied my appeal and again ordered me back to America. The only difference between me and the people who received a passport extension was that they were white and I was black.

I then decided to approach the American ambassador. I hoped he would understand and intervene with the State Department on my behalf. I wrote to him and, to my surprise, within a few days I received notice that an appointment had been arranged. Because this meeting would be so important, I asked a black American journalist, Homer Smith, to come with me and help plead my case. Smith was bright, distinguished looking, articulate, and had spent considerable time in Russia. I had never spoken with a diplomat. The only way I knew how to communicate was in a straightforward manner. The ambassador had once been a journalist, and I thought that Smith would be a useful ally.

On the day of my appointment, Smith and I arrived at the embassy on time, and were made to wait a half-hour before being introduced to Ambassador William Bullitt. I began explaining my situation, pointing out the strange events that led to my election to the Moscow Soviet and the reasons why I needed my job in Russia. The ambassador seemed pleasant, listened earnestly, and appeared to be concerned with my plight. But as soon as I finished talking, he said, "I cannot do anything in your case, because the State Department order is for you to leave the Soviet Union immediately. This order is final."

I was taken back by his abrupt, absolute statement. I could not think of what next to say. But Smith came right to my defense. "Comrade Bullitt," he said, "must this man go back to the States where both he and his mother would have to stand on a soup line while. . . "

The ambassador cut Smith off in mid-sentence. "I am no comrade of yours or anyone else! Do not address me as 'comrade'," said an outraged Bullitt.

Smith quickly shot back, "You must know by now that in this country there is no 'mister.' Surely you recall the maxim, 'When in Rome, do as the Romans do.' I'm simply applying what I learned in school in the United States. There is only comrade in this country."

This made Bullitt even angrier. He was furious, his face a crimson red. He stood up abruptly. Glaring at us, he said, "I will not hear any more of this."

He pressed a button, and in a few seconds an aide appeared. "Conduct these two men out," he ordered.

As we were leaving, I politely bid the ambassador farewell. But Smith, who was lagging behind, stopped, smiled at the ambassador, and said with derision, "Good-bye, comrade ambassador."

My heart sank. If for any reason my fate had not been sealed a moment earlier, it certainly was then. I was angry at Smith, and upset at myself for having asked him to help. I should have gone alone to the appointment.

My visit to Ambassador Bullitt left me even more troubled about what to do. Then a few weeks later it got even worse. I was honored by the Soviet government for inventing a mechanical device that would save 15,500 rubles annually in production costs at my factory. I accepted the award gratefully. I had earned it by doing something worthwhile, and I enjoyed the gesture of appreciation. I was given a medallion engraved with Stalin's profile, with a gold, green, and red ribbon flowing from it. Russian newspapers carried articles about me and unfortunately, so did American ones. The way they reported it, and the reaction generated by these reports, compounded the mistaken impression of me that had already begun taking shape back home.

Congressman Knutson from Minnesota became very upset. He introduced a bill making it "unlawful for any American citizen to accept from a king, prince, or foreign government, save for military service rendered, any present, emolument, office or title of any kind whatever."

An editorial in the *New York Evening Journal* supported the bill, and urged that

> . . . the bill might go even further. It might well prohibit the acceptance of any decoration from any foreign power. . . . [A] five and ten cent medal or a yard of red

> ribbon can turn too many so-called citizens as soulful rooters for anything across the Atlantic, and equally soulful booers of anything at home.
>
> It [the bill] will remind a section of our people that their duty to their country comes first, and is not to be bartered away for some tin-horn title or rubbishy rosette.

Had I not been in enough trouble with the State Department before, I was now. And I could now add members of Congress to the list of powerful people in the US who saw me as a traitor, as one who was submitting himself willingly to Soviet propaganda. I do not suppose Congressman Knutson or any editorial writers considered that I actually might have earned the award.

How could I go back to the States at this time? How could I not? By disobeying the State Department order I was beginning to feel like a man without a country. My contract expiration date grew nearer. In desperation I contacted the British embassy in Moscow to see whether I could become a British citizen, since I was born in Jamaica, a British colony. I was politely turned down.

With just a few days remaining on my contract, I decided to renew it again, and wait to see what would happen. Almost every day I expected a letter from the State Department saying that my citizenship was revoked. That letter never came. But a little while later I was given another reason for not returning home. The Evening Institute of Mechanical Engineering in Moscow accepted me into a degree program in mechanical engineering. Ever since I was a child in Cuba I had dreamed of going to Tuskegee Institute in Alabama to become a mechanical engineer. Now I would be able to get the theoretical training I had always wanted, and at a much lower cost. It would take me at least four more years in Russia to earn a degree. Along with my practical experience gained through years of working and inventing in the field, I could now fulfill my ambition of becoming a first-class engineer.

I believed that as long as I was a member of the Moscow Soviet, I enjoyed a degree of security and would have no problem continuing to renew my one-year contracts. But I wondered about my future.

The depression in America seemed like a chronic, unending

affliction. There were no signs of a let-up. Perhaps the Soviet prediction that the capitalist system was dying was correct.

I decided to take a critical step. I asked the Soviet authorities if I could become a Soviet citizen for now, but then return to the United States when I wanted to and have the Soviets consider me an American. They assured me that this was possible, citing examples of two Americans—and an Englishman who, together with his Russian wife and two children—had done just that. I knew one of the Americans, a woman named Rosa who had been living in the Soviet Union for seven years. I visited her while I was making up my mind, and she confirmed what the Soviets had told me. With these apparent safeguards, I filed for Soviet citizenship.

The day I became a Soviet citizen, I felt no different. I was the same Robert Robinson: toolmaker, inventor, aspiring mechanical engineer, trying to survive in an alien culture, within a political system that viewed foreigners with distrust. I did have to give up the foreign specialist card that admitted me into the elite shops that carried western-style goods. Now I had to eat at a smaller, plainer-looking restaurant that catered only to Russian technical personnel, and served meager portions of dull, plain food. I had accepted a less comfortable lifestyle for a greater sense of security. I figured that I had not lost much since I never had the time to indulge in the luxuries offered to the foreign specialists. I considered being with Russians even more at work, in the dining hall, and at school, an advantage because I could improve my language skills.

At times I wondered about the trade I had made. ''How really secure am I?'' I thought. Russians and foreigners at the factory—including some in my own shop—were disappearing. Were they transferred to different factories? Were the ugly rumors of exile and shootings true? At that time, I didn't know.

CHAPTER 10

Social Engineering and the Second Purge

I HAD MADE my fateful decision at a time when disappearances were increasing but could not yet be considered epidemic. That soon changed. The massive government scheme to reorder society, which had begun in 1933, was picking up steam. Although there was no way at the time to understand fully whether there was an overall plan and pattern to the first purges, one later became clear.

By the spring of 1936 almost all of the young people trained as engineers and in technical fields during the years 1927 to 1932 had disappeared. The authorities first created an entire class of technocrats, and then destroyed it because they came to view this class as a threat to their power. Before they could eliminate these skilled industrial leaders, the party and government prepared their replacements so that the country's industrial progress would not come to a grinding halt.

A new group was trained in technical institutes called Industrial Academies, or Prom-Akademia for short. Thousands of carefully selected students from the party and the Komsomols—in the twenty- to thirty-five-year-old age range—were moved through these institutes before the first purges could begin. The Prom-Akademia provided a two-year, crash engineering program. Those chosen for the program had no choice but to go; if they didn't they faced severe punishment. About 75 percent of those recruited were little more than one generation removed from the countryside. The other 25 percent were born in Leningrad or Moscow, of parents who were among the poorer peasants.

These students were placed in groups for the duration of their two-year course of study. They did not have to do any laboratory work or conduct tests or analyses. They were not required to experiment in their fields of study, such as chemistry, physics, or electrical or hydraulic observations. To hasten them through the curriculum, one student from each group who was considered the brightest was chosen to take the exams for his entire group. Based on this one student's performance, everyone in the group received a certified diploma as a mechanical, chemical, or electrical engineer.

After graduation these two-year wonders—as they were called by more experienced hands in the factory—were channeled into supervisory positions as soon as the previous job holder disappeared. This novel approach was planned obviously and carefully and carried out boldly and ruthlessly over a period of several years. From the point of view of social planning, this scheme appeared on the surface to work well. The immediate goal of creating, as the government's slogans proclaimed, "an untainted, truly Soviet" class of technicians was achieved. However, these new supervisors had no front-line industrial experience, and due to their crash two-year study program, had a poor theoretical understanding as well. Their presence had a devastating effect on the average worker, and they were the object of much silent resentment.

Once enough of what the party considered to be new, true socialist technicians were in place throughout the industrial sector—with thousands more enrolled in the Prom-Akademias—the large-scale purge against the current industrial leaders began. Especially vulnerable were those the government had sent abroad to study and who then took over from the old czarist class and the foreign specialists. They were now considered hopelessly tainted, especially condemned by the bourgeois influence of their association with foreign specialists. The foundation upon which the technical development of the country depended began to disappear rapidly.

It became practically impossible to ignore the government-orchestrated purges as they began to sweep the country. Not only was the industrial sector affected, but all other segments of society as well. By 1936, nine of the fifteen members of the Politburo of the Central Committee, headed by Stalin, had been purged. More than half of the best brains in the country were purged, from the factories to the ministries to the military. Particularly targeted were the administrative ranks: mid- through upper-level management, those who actually ran the country on a day-to-day basis. Slogans appeared in the factories, and the state-controlled radio and newspapers constantly reminded everyone of the need "to rid the Soviet system of technocrats who were being poisoned by foreign ideologies."

Another factory slogan expressed the grandiose purpose behind the purge:

> Clean out all suspicious elements, especially those who were educated during the time of Czar Nicholas, regardless of their sincere conversion to Bolshevism.
>
> Replace them with the pure-hearted young peasant men and women who haven't been tainted by urban sophistication.

The purpose was to mold a new kind of human being, whose only experience, only thought was of socialism; whose reason for living was to advance the socialist cause, according to how the party and the government defined it. As a result, many talented, loyal, nationalistic young people were shut out of the system. They were not allowed to attend desirable schools, they were not allowed to have responsible jobs. Their family background made them suspect and unwelcome.

A toolmaker in our shop, a bright man with an insatiable yearning for knowledge, was denied entrance into the night engineering institute because his father had been a Russian Orthodox priest. It made no difference that the young man was a dedicated believer in communism. Ten Russian engineers who lived in my apartment complex were removed from their jobs and exiled. Because the government had sent them to Germany a few years earlier for training, they were now considered hopelessly influenced by bourgeois thinking. These policies and purges of the thirties later came back to haunt the Soviet Union, especially at a time of great stress during World War II. Middle management in industry, education, and the military caved in because of a lack of experience and talent.

The purges caused morale to plummet and indifference to set in. The slogans that had exhorted the workers to overtake and surpass the United States in fifteen years now proclaimed, "We shall destroy the enemies of the people, comrades!" We were warned: "Always be vigilant, among you are enemies of the people!"

People were disappearing daily. They were never tried, never convicted of any crime. They were simply sent to Siberia, the Taigas, or the Arctic region, and were rarely ever heard from again. In one day, in my shop of 750 people, nine people did not report for work. Three foremen were missing, four toolmakers, a technologist, and the shop *nachalnik,* or superintendent. The *nachalnik* was a Jewish mechanical engineer who had received his diploma in Germany. He and the chief engineer were arrested and, two months later, executed.

From 1934 to 1936, more than twenty people in our shop suddenly disappeared. They were engineers, toolmakers, foremen, even party members. After awhile rumors stopped circulating because everyone was afraid to talk. There was a constant fear that the secret police (the NKVD, forerunner to today's KGB) would come knocking on the door in the middle of the night. No one could feel safe. Since I was now a Soviet citizen, I knew I was as vulnerable as the next person. I did not think being a member of the Moscow Soviet afforded me any protection.

Being from another country became a mark of suspicion. With the rise of Hitler and Mussolini, the German and Italian workers in my factory came to the end of their road. The fascist nations were the most despised enemies of the Soviet Union. To the average Russian, Hitler was Satan and Mussolini was his chief deputy. Nearly every day the Soviet press reported stories of atrocities committed by the Nazis. Hitler's public proclamation against Bolshevism was well-known in Moscow.

In my factory, toward the end of the 1930s, a group of Austrian workers known as *Schuschbundtsevs* arrived. They were named after Schuschnigg, the chancellor of Austria in 1938 when Germany annexed Austria to the German Reich. Schuschnigg protested the German move, called for a referendum on the annexation, and rallied thousands of young

Austrians behind him. Schuschnigg was arrested and imprisoned. Although thousands of his sympathizers met a similar fate, some managed to escape and find refuge in the Soviet Union. In Russia their name *Schuschbundtsevs* meant followers of Schuschnigg.

These Austrians were given work and a place to live in one of the buildings reserved for foreigners. The factory administration placed them four to a room. A huge brawl erupted among them a few weeks after they arrived. A lot of blood was spilled, many were hurt, and most of them wound up in the factory's first aid clinic. The administration and the local NKVD investigated the incident. They discovered that a number of Nazi spies had infiltrated this group of anti-Nazis. A few days later all of them were transferred out of our factory. No one was ever able to learn where they went: out of the country, to other factories, into exile, or to their graves.

As a result of this incident, the NKVD launched a campaign to arrest all German workers, regardless of their innocence or membership in the party. The wives of some of these men appealed to me for help in finding out what had happened to their husbands. At that time I was still a member of the Moscow Soviet, and they mistakenly thought my membership meant more than it did. I was helpless and could do nothing. I could not tell them what I really thought, that their husbands were dead. When the women left my apartment, I cried. Two weeks later, they vanished too.

In 1936 the man who had launched the 1934 purge was arrested and put on trial. Yagoda, the head of the NKVD, was charged with lacking communist consciousness and vigilance and maintaining a low level of Marxist-Leninist militancy. Ironically, he was also charged with the December 1, 1934, assassination of Kirov, the Leningrad party boss, the event that served as the catalyst for the first purges. What he was not charged with was the murder of thousands of innocent men and women whom he had ordered executed.

His trial was held in the House of Trade Unions, amid a great deal of publicity. Workers in my factory who followed the details of the trial somehow began to develop a sense of foreboding about the future. During the trial I could sense that the already low morale in my factory was falling even lower. The earlier Bolshevik idealism, of molding a new nation, had faded. During the trial it eroded even more. Many young idealists had been buoyed by the toppling of the czarist regime in 1917 and Lenin's promise of an egalitarian society. But these hopes, which had been discouraged by the purges, were dashed during Yagoda's trial. It soon became apparent that the Russians were in for more of the same under Yagoda's successor, a small, scrawny-looking man named Yezhov, who rose out of obscurity to become the new head of the NKVD, the People's Commissariat of Internal Affairs.

Yagoda was found guilty and executed. The day after his execution, the entire factory was gloomy. I learned during my forty-four years in the Soviet Union, that along with their mammoth capacity for brooding, the Russian people have an uncanny ability to sense the presence of danger. This was one of those times. No one really worked. Some stood before their machines like zombies. Others paced back and forth with their shoulders hunched and their hands in their pockets. It was a far sadder scene than a Soviet funeral. Not even the usual idle chatter about food and the weather could be heard. There was only the sound of the machines.

It was not that the workers mourned the passing of the head of the secret police; he had certainly been no friend of theirs. I think instead they were girding themselves for the next onslaught of suffering they all sensed was on the horizon. Suffering was something they knew well; it was as natural a part of Russian life as eating and sleeping.

As for me, a day did not go by that I did not ask myself what kind of hell I had gotten into. No longer a US citizen, I could not go home.

Bullitt, a man not inclined to do me any favors, was still the US ambassador. If by some miracle I could get home, the problems were still the same. I was branded a Red, I was black, there was a severe depression, and I needed skilled work to be satisfied. Furthermore, in Russia I was becoming an engineer. The thought of sacrificing this dream was too painful. I just kept on going, one day at a time. I was too afraid to be depressed and too intent on my survival to think about much else.

From 1936 on, a day never passed without my thinking that the NKVD would drag me out of bed and send me off to some remote part of Siberia or shoot me. Most nights I could hear the foreboding sounds of the NKVD cars prowling the streets or the ominous echo of a knock on the door of a nearby apartment.

"When would my turn come? Would it be now?" I wondered,

as I lay awake until dawn. "In an hour, or perhaps not until tomorrow?" So great was my fear during the purges, that I never undressed until after four A.M. I later learned from other workers that many of them shared my custom.

During these years before the war, one thing became quite obvious. I now knew that while America was far from perfect, the Soviet Union was no promised land either. The so-called haven for oppressed people was in a constant state of incredible oppression, especially when contrasted with the idealistic vision that was presented to the outside world.

I knew many idealists who came to Russia from other countries, filled with good intentions and believing with all their hearts that they would be helping to create the paradise on earth depicted by Marx and Lenin. Dr. and Mrs. Rosenblitz were such idealists. They left behind in California the material benefits of his successful dental practice—an elegant home, two cars, attractive clothes. Friends and relatives tried to dissuade them from leaving, but the Rosenblitzes were insistent. I met them soon after they arrived in the Soviet Union, filled with enthusiasm and ready for adventure. Dr. Rosenblitz brought his modern, state-of-the-art dental equipment with him and gave it to the Soviet government as a gift. The equipment was installed in a clinic in Moscow, and he was assigned there to instruct Russian dental students in the profession.

Less than a year later, Yezhov's NKVD arrested the Rosenblitzes and shipped them to separate labor camps in the far north, where temperatures of fifty degrees below zero are not uncommon. They never returned.

The First State Ball Bearing plant benefited from the idealism of a group of six Russian-born Americans, who had returned to their native land to help build the ideal socialist state. They were all ordinary workers who, before coming in 1930 and 1931, had pooled together their savings and purchased the modern electrical equipment that was installed in the factory's four-story, thousand-seat dining hall. They had planned and installed the equipment themselves, then instructed the local people on how to operate it. From the time the factory opened in March 1932, most workers ate their lunch in the dining hall, and were well-satisfied with the meals they were served.

One day in 1937, five of them failed to report for work. They had disappeared the night before. The remaining one of the group eventually committed suicide later that year.

Another group of Russian-Americans also met a tragic end. They had returned to Russia, full of revolutionary zeal, bearing equipment for a modern laundry in the factory. This group also helped to install, mount, and test the new equipment, and then later taught the local people how to operate the machines. They all disappeared during the purges of 1936-1938. To the best of my knowledge, none of them was ever seen again.

As the purges intensified, it became clear that rule by law simply did not exist. Any sense of justice was swept away by the midnight knock of the NKVD. In my factory, a person no longer dared seek redress of grievances. If you reported that someone had cheated you, or if you tried to correct an injustice yourself, you were likely to find yourself in a boxcar headed for Siberia. One toolmaker I admired was a twenty-four-year-old man of exceptional ability hired in 1934. Bogatov was normally quiet, softspoken, and very bright. Although he was definitely of leadership caliber, he was not a party member. I suspect he was either indifferent to or disenchanted with communism, because normally a person with his abilities and potential would have been swept into the party if he had showed enthusiasm for the Soviet system.

One spring morning in 1936 Bogatov's troubles began. When he came to work and picked up his assignment from the foreman, he noticed that he was given a job that he had done two months earlier. It should be understood that most categories of people in the Soviet Union were working under the piecework system. Streetsweepers, bus drivers, salespeople, harvesters, barbers, tailors, people milking cows, factory workers—everyone got a "technological card" listing his work category, from one to eight, and also indicating the time required to do the task and the amount of money the task was worth. Bogatov approached the shop's norm setter, who assigned the time needed to complete the job and how much it was worth. He thought a mistake had been made in his assignment.

The norm setter was adamant. He said there had been no mistake, that there was no record of the job having been done before, and then, in a loud voice, he accused Bogatov of making a false charge and ordered him to leave immediately.

Bogatov looked at the norm setter and said, quietly, "It is people like you who make life so difficult for us."

The next day Bogatov came to work, still looking unhappy about the incident. That night the NKVD knocked on his door and whisked him away to a Siberian labor camp. Although his sister, as assistant secretary of the factory's party committee, had some influence, she did not try to intercede on his behalf, fearing that if she did they would implicate her and make things even worse for her brother.

One night during the summer of 1936, someone knocked on the door of my apartment. It was eleven o'clock and the purges were gaining momentum. After 10 P.M. people did not open their doors on the first knock. (Some time after the purges had slackened, one couple told me that whenever there was more than a series of two knocks on their apartment door, after 11:30 P.M., they would hug and kiss each other and then hug and kiss their two children before opening the door. Twice in 1937 the NKVD had come for someone else in their apartment.) The person continued knocking and then loudly called out my name to assure me that he was an acquaintance and not the NKVD. When I opened the door, I saw V. M., the man I had met in Stalingrad in the summer of 1930. He was wearing the same pilot's suit and cap as he had then. I felt the same wariness I had felt then, and I was on my guard immediately.

As I greeted him I wondered how he had found me. He came in without invitation, but I kept him standing just inside the door. He quickly said, "Comrade Robinson, I have come to ask you to do me a great favor. I hope you will help me."

"What is it?" I asked.

"Please don't refuse me," he continued. "You see, I am greatly in need of two small ball bearings for my bicycle. I live ten miles from Moscow and I always use my bicycle instead of having to walk two-and-a-half miles to catch the train. Please help me. I shall always be grateful to you."

"I am working in the machine tool shop," I told him. "I have nothing to do directly with the actual output of bearings."

V. M. persisted. He continued to try every angle he could think of, but I knew what the game was about. He was trying to trap me. If I were to help him by bringing the ball bearings to him, I would be charged with sabotage, or with theft of state goods, then exiled or shot.

After about twenty minutes of fending off his arguments, I told him we were disturbing the neighbors and said, "Listen. It's useless to try to convince me. I cannot do what you want me to do. Go tomorrow to the administration of the factory and put your case before them. I'm sure they will help you. Good night."

That was the last I saw of him until almost a year later, when he came back again. Although Yezhov was still rounding up so-called enemies of the people, when I heard a knock on my door a little before midnight, I remembered V. M. and opened the door without hesitation. There he stood again, in the same clothing and wearing a wry smile on his face.

I said in an abrupt, businesslike manner, "What can I do for you?"

"I feel very awkward," he replied, "to have to seek help again for my bicycle."

"Well, did you go to see the factory administration as I recommended?" I asked.

"Yes," he said. "I was successful in getting two bearings which were not new but good enough to serve up until a week ago. But now almost all of the balls have fallen out, so I've come to ask you to get me about a dozen balls."

Concealing my disgust, I told him, "Please, do not come to me for any assistance about ball bearings again. You are simply wasting your time. Please understand that."

I shook his hand and bade him good night. Then I cautiously nudged him out. That was the last I ever saw him. I expect that whoever sent him was convinced by then of the uselessness of trying to entrap me in this manner.

You never knew when the NKVD would strike. It was not always in the middle of the night. Informers were in practically every housing development, including ours, but it was difficult to tell who they were. It could be a kindly-appearing old lady, or it could be your best friend. Wise people kept all conversation on a superficial level. The terror was such that no one dared to speak, even to a relative on the street, without looking over his shoulder first, and then only in a whisper.

Only once did the police knock on my door. It was in 1943, at about 12:30 A.M. When I opened it and they saw my dark-skinned, non-Russian face, they excused themselves. I obviously was not the person they were looking for.

In mid-January 1937, a friend of mine did not show up for a meeting we had arranged. I had first met Kokiel in 1932, when he introduced himself to me as a member of the Shop's Trade Union Committee. He had helped me two years later when I was recovering from my bout with pleurisy. When Kokiel learned that I had been assigned to a home of rest for people stricken with sexual diseases, he got my pass changed to Mis-Mor, a far more desirable and appropriate vacation spot. Then on the day I was to leave, he came to my apartment and carried my suitcases all the way to the train station. Although I always had to be wary of him, because that was how one tried to survive in the Soviet Union, I also liked him.

After he failed to show up, I waited a couple of days and then went to his department and asked his comrades where he was. At first, no one answered my question. When I asked again in a louder voice, one of his colleagues looked up at me, his eyes filled with tears, and said: "I am sorry to tell you, Comrade Robinson, but we don't know. He hasn't come to work for almost a week now."

Without saying a word, I went back to my workplace feeling very disturbed. After work I went directly to his apartment. A woman tenant answered my knock.

"Please excuse me," I said. "Are the Kokiels in?"

She said, "No," and then moved to close the door.

I held onto the door and explained that we worked together and that I had not seen him for a little over a week.

"I am a foreigner," I said, "but you need not be afraid of me. If he is not home, may I speak to his wife?"

At the word wife, the woman raised her head, looked at me, and said, "She is not here either. Four days ago a truck came here at night with two policemen and told her that she must vacate the room immediately. They began moving out all their furniture, all their belongings at once. They ordered her to go with them. That was the last time we saw her. We do not know what has become of either of them."

She then invited me into the apartment and showed me that the Kokiels' room was sealed. I could do nothing else except thank her and leave. As I was on my way out she said, "I beg of you, please, do not tell anyone what I told and showed you."

I promised.

The reign of terror under Yezhov, from the end of 1936 to the beginning of 1939, was far broader and more ruthless than the earlier one under Yagoda. It was a time of inhumanity at its worst. The brooding Russians had been right to fear the passing of Yagoda.

CHAPTER 11

I Am Interrogated

ONE BRIGHT SPRING MORNING in 1937 I was summoned to the designing department. This was the NKVD's lair in our factory, the place where workers were summoned and somctimcs never returned. As I left, I was sure that the apprentices working with me believed that they were seeing the last of Robert Robinson. The thought that this was the end certainly passed through my mind, but for some reason I was not scared. My own reaction bothered me, because I knew I ought to be frightened.

As I approached the designing department, I saw three men seated at a table facing the entrance. None of them acknowledged my greeting; I was motioned to sit in the chair directly in front of them.

"Comrade Robinson," began one of them, "how did you happen to come to the Soviet Union?"

"I came to the Soviet Union through a one-year contract," I said, trying to emulate his tone and approach.

"By whom were you invited?"

"The Soviet Union invited me through its representative, Comrade Ivanov, who was recruiting technicians at the Ford Motor Company in Detroit, in the United States of America."

"Can you remember on what date you were employed?"

"The third week in April 1930."

"When did you leave the United States for the Soviet Union?"

"May 30, 1930."

"When did you arrive in the Soviet Union?"

I hesitated for a moment, wanting to give them accurate answers. I guessed that they already knew all the answers, and were checking to see if I was indeed the real Robert Robinson. Having already lived in Russia for seven years, I had grown accustomed to the Russian way of thinking. I understood that my interrogators most likely considered it possible that the real Robert Robinson was killed by a black American intelligence agent who took over his identity in order to spy for the US government. I answered the question correctly.

Then another asked, "Comrade Robinson, do you have your old contract?"

"Yes, but it is in my apartment," I said.

"After lunch bring it to us."

"Yes, of course." I thought to myself how tricky they were.

If I have no evidence that I really am Robert Robinson, I was as good as dead. Still, I was sure I could get my hands on the contract.

"Thank God," I thought, "that I'm a fastidious person who keeps everything important in neat files."

The next question was, "What organization invited you to work in this factory and when?"

"I was invited by VATO in July 1932."

"Were you under contract, also?"

"Yes, a one-year contract, which was renewed every year."

"Please also bring your contract with this factory after lunch."

"Yes, I will."

"That's all for now, Comrade Robinson."

I returned to my desk, unable to concentrate on the mathematical problem before me, waiting anxiously for the lunch bell to ring. I knew I had the contracts, but it had been a long time since I had gone through my files. Suddenly, a horrible thought paralyzed me! What if the NKVD agent entered my apartment while I was at work and took the contracts?

I tried to calm myself down by reasoning, "I'm not their

enemy. What would they want with me? I'm no threat to the Soviet system.''

As soon as the bell rang I wanted to dash to my apartment. I realized that I was being watched and that I most likely would be followed, so I knew I had to act naturally. Running would be taken as a sign of guilt. And under the Soviet system, if they can catch you appearing guilty, you are as good as in prison or six feet under the ground.

I entered my apartment and began looking through my files. To my relief both contracts were there. I then waited in my room for awhile, thinking that if I rushed back I would give the NKVD the impression that I was anxious or nervous. I wanted them to feel that I knew I had nothing to hide or fear.

When I gave them the contracts, I asked politely if they could return them to me. They assured me that I would get them back in a few days. I never did. After five attempts I stopped asking for them, lest I antagonize them. But not having the contracts struck me as a serious blow to my plan to leave the Soviet Union one day. They served as the only evidence that I had gone to Russia as a foreign specialist on contract, and not as a communist ideologue in search of a new nation, as the American press had accused me. Now that evidence was gone. The only thing left was my word, and I knew that would not be worth much back home.

I expect that the contracts were seized as a calculated means of making me more dependent on the Soviet Union, an attempt to cut my ties further and set up additional barriers to my returning to the United States. They certainly did not want to have a disenchanted Robert Robinson, who had been publicized internationally as a black American pilgrim to the promised land of the Soviet Union, returning to America and blowing the whistle on their communist paradise. That would do no good for the Kremlin's image as a refuge for the oppressed people of the world.

I knew that they had reason to be concerned about me. No matter how long I lived in the Soviet Union, I knew I could never call it home. There was not only the treachery of the political system, but also the official denial of the spiritual nature of man. As much or more than anything else, that denial created a deadly atmosphere that made life a daily test. All I could do was to pray for strength to survive life in such an amoral world.

I could never condone such savage disregard for the value of human life. I could never feel proud to be a Soviet citizen. In a sense, I now regretted taking that rash step. But at the time I had no other realistic choice. Now I wanted to leave, but I was a Soviet citizen and they could do with me whatever they pleased. If I tried to leave through official channels I would be branded a traitor and sent into exile. Getting help from the United States was out of the question. At least I soon had something to concentrate on that would leave me with even less time to think about my predicament.

In July 1937, I began my engineering education. No more working two shifts; I would now attend classes at night. It had taken me several months to obtain a recommendation from my shop and a letter of request from the factory's party secretary approving of my plan to study for a degree. He wrote:

> To the Principal of the Moscow Evening Technical Institute:
> This is to certify that the Negro Robert Robinson is a helpful member of our collective, and we ask you to assist him in any way possible to enlist him as one of your students.
>
> Secretary of Party Committee of
> the First State Ball Bearing Plant,
> Moscow

I took my entrance exams, passing physics with an A and chemistry with a C. The next exam was in math. There are two stages in the Soviet examination system, written and oral, with the written exam coming first.

After I had completed the math problems given me, an examiner looked them over and said, "The third problem is not correct. Will you sit down, please?"

He quickly wrote down a simple problem for me to solve. I did so. Then he gave me another one, which I solved, and then a third one. Each problem was tougher than the one before. When I was unable to solve correctly the fifth problem he gave me, he told me to go home and study the material again because I was weak in mathematics. During the following week I studied the entire mathematical program and then returned. The same examiner saw me this time, and told me to wait for him. I felt discouraged, because usually you can choose any examiner at all, rather than the examiner choosing you.

As soon as I sat down before him, he began to test me with one problem after another, in drill-like fashion. I was soon not only nervous but confused as well. I solved five problems and then told him that I was mentally exhausted.

"You've made good progress," he said, smiling at me. "But you'll have to come back again next week."

When I returned the following week I was determined to avoid him. But to my surprise, soon after I arrived a student came out of the examining room and asked, "Is Robinson present?"

When I answered, he said, "Examiner Ivan Petrovsky wants you to come to him."

No sooner had I gone in and sat down before him than my mind went totally blank. Sensing my confusion, he gave me only three simple problems to solve, as a starter. Then he moved to more complex problems. He kept me much longer than the usual twenty minutes, and then said, "You've done very much better. Give me your exam record book."

Inside the book he marked a C. At this point I finally asked him why he had examined me so much longer and more thoroughly than the other students.

He said, "I have never had the chance to examine anyone from the USA. I was interested in comparing the knowledge of its high school students, especially a black one, to that of ours. I did not mean any harm. I was simply curious."

I passed my entrance exams, and on September 1, 1937, I attended the first session of a series of lectures, in a large auditorium with more than two hundred other students. My examiner, Ivan Petrovsky, who as it turned out was also the dean of mathematics, provided the instruction. All lectures were of course delivered in Russian. Because I could not yet write quickly enough in Russian, I would translate the lectures in my head and write my notes in English. At examination time I studied my English-language lecture notes and then answered the questions in Russian. I frequently clashed with my teachers because I either misunderstood or mistranslated the original lectures.

Even with the intensity of my coursework, it was still difficult to avoid thinking about the possibility of being arrested. One evening in mid-summer, 1938, I was in downtown Moscow on my way to class when I noticed a large gathering of people standing before a large banner attached to the Military Academy building. As I drew closer to the crowd, I was struck by their silence. The banner proclaimed: These enemies of the people—General Goriev, General Grishin and General Uritsky, were found guilty of treason and dealt with accordingly.

The crowd of people just stood there, horrified. Three generals revered as national heroes the day before, now killed as enemies of the state. It underscored the awareness that no one was safe. That night in my classes, I could not concentrate. I began to question seriously whether it was worth pursuing an engineering degree in such a terror-filled society. Unfortunately, I had no choice. Where could I go? Like my classmates, I was a Soviet citizen.

I had to be very, very careful. This was during the height of Yezhov's campaign, and he was unpredictable. No one was safe. Two of Lenin's closest allies, Gregory Zinoviev and Lev Kamenev, had been liquidated. Likewise ten leading Red Army generals, and Mikhail Koltsov, perhaps the most admired journalist in Russia, who was reputed to have enjoyed a close relationship with Stalin. Fame and reputation obviously made no difference.

In 1938, when people said good-by to one another after work, it was with a very firm handshake and a penetrating look into each other's eyes. We were saying, "This will perhaps be the last time we shall ever see each other. If so, farewell."

No one knew whose turn was next. Almost all of the really experienced, truly talented people were liquidated. A number of times, in confidential discussions with one of the lucky Russians who survived the purges, I was told that Russia would never again have such an army of people devoted to the cause of socialism. By 1938, with the formation of the new Soviet elite—a process which has continued to the present—a new breed of rulers appeared, less well-trained and less devoted than those they replaced.

Yezhov's purge was far more insane that the one under Yagoda. In all its tragedy, the purge that Stalin had Yagoda carry out had a certain rationale. If you disregarded the value of human life over animal life, and believed that the state was more important than the people comprising it, then the state-organized terror, exile, and murder could seem reasonable, and even desirable. A new, privileged class was created, dependent on the government and the party for its favors—for the best apartments, food, and clothing; use of the resort centers; low cost automobiles; and so forth. Many years later I learned that at a meeting in the thirties of the executive committee of the Central Committee of the Politburo, Stalin said, "Had we not created a new social rank, we would have failed to accomplish our program."

The purges were hell in any case, but under Yezhov they became wild, unpredictable, frenzied: scientists, artists, politicians, engineers, teachers, physicians, factory workers, army officers, streetsweepers—no one was exempt, everyone was a potential target.

Only after Stalin's death did the government admit that mistakes were made. Six million people who were executed were exonerated posthumously. When the government cleaned their slates, it enabled their spouses or children to receive some monetary compensation and an official certificate stating that the victim had been innocent.

The Soviet government still denounces periodically the purges under Stalin. On November 1, 1987, at a party meeting celebrating the seventieth anniversary of the Russian Revolution, Soviet leader Mikhail Gorbachev issued a statement denouncing the crimes of Stalin as "enormous and unforgivable." In a lengthy speech, he said a new commission would renew the inquiry into the purges, and that he would accelerate the ongoing efforts to clear the records of those who had been falsely arrested and exiled or shot.

Of course, just because the government confessed to mistakes after Stalin's death did not mean that Soviet citizens were no longer terrorized. These practices continued until the day I fled. Only their tempo slowed down, while the methods for gathering intelligence and controlling and eliminating undesirable people grew more sophisticated.

The Yezhov purges continued into early 1939. On the final day of December 1938, I was unable to attend a New Year's Eve party given by the Wissers, an American couple, because I was home with the flu. The Wissers, who taught at the Foreign Language Institute, were allowed to celebrate the new year, like anyone else in Russia. However, it was unacceptable and dangerous to recognize Christmas, which was eliminated as an official holiday after the revolution. The party position was that no modern, thinking person could accept the idea of a God. Those who wished to celebrate Christmas had to do so quietly, and only with trusted friends. As it turned out, I was fortunate to be sick on this December 31. My illness spared me the ordeal of a visit by the NKVD. I learned later that just a moment or two before midnight, as the host was filling people's glasses with vodka, a loud pounding was heard at the front door. The host opened the door to four large men wearing heavy overcoats. They showed their NKVD badges, and then were led to the parlor, where a large table stood, heaped with exotic foods like caviar, a suckling pig, goose, pickled vegetables, cakes and pastries, and wines and vodka.

The agents wasted little time. They asked to see everyone's passport, which fortunately no one had forgotten. The books were checked thoroughly, even shaken, and then tossed to the floor. The partygoers were ordered to stand in a line with their hands at their sides. One of the agents watched over them while the other three began to ransack the apartment. They stripped the bed, flinging the linens, covers, and pillowcases on the floor, then looked under the mattress. Every cupboard was examined. They opened the wardrobe and checked out every suit, every pair of pants, and all of the shoes, dresses, and coats. The agents explored the apartment for more than four hours, while the guests stood practically at attention, some crying.

The NKVD found nothing worth taking with them. Around 4:00 A.M. they left without saying a word. Everyone was in a state of shock. At this point, no one was in a mood to continue the party. After helping the hosts put their apartment back in order, the guests left quietly. This event was an ill omen for 1939. Things eventually did get better, but first they got worse.

Moscow lived under a blanket of gloom. I do not believe I ever saw anyone with a bright face or a smile. Sadness was everywhere: in the streets, in the restaurants, in my shop, and in the factory at large. People were living under a state of seige. But soon we were to hear some startling news. I was in the factory when Stalin's arrest of Yezhov was announced over the radio. We all stopped and stared speechlessly at one another. It was difficult to believe that Yezhov had lost power. Clearly there was a sense of relief, but it was mingled with apprehension about what would come next. There was a renewed sense of faith in Stalin, for prevailing over Yezhov.

After Yezhov was arrested, he acted as if he were insane and was shipped off to a mental institution. The rumors all over Moscow were that he was being foxy and using this ploy to try to escape execution. But he did not succeed. A party member whose information was reliable told me that Yezhov had held out at first, but eventually a confession was forced out of him. He revealed that he had been planning to seize power from Stalin by purging members of the Politburo.

Yezhov, the murderer of millions, was taken before a firing squad and shot.

PART II

The War Years and Their Aftermath

CHAPTER 12

The Hitler-Stalin Pact

SOON AFTER YEZHOV'S FALL FROM POWER, in the summer of 1939, the Kremlin announced that it had signed a pact with Nazi Germany. Everyone in my shop was shocked and amazed. This was more than perplexing to the Russians; it hurt. To think that their country, which championed equality, fraternity, and world peace, had overnight become linked with Adolf Hitler. This was as incongruous to the Russians as an alliance between the Ku Klux Klan and the National Association for the Advancement of Colored People would have been to Americans. In my shop, some workers wept openly, while others were solemn.

Ever since Hitler had gained power in Germany, the official Soviet line had been that Nazism was the enemy of all peace-loving people in the world, and that it should be fought wherever it tried to spread. The Soviet people had been told that the reason leading Red Army generals and thousands of Soviet soldiers had gone off to help the Loyalist cause during the Spanish Civil War was to fight the threat of Nazism.

I did not know a Russian who did not hate the Nazis. Anti-Nazi propaganda was incessant, to the point where Nazism was portrayed as representing the greatest evil on the face of the earth. Word of battlefield deaths in Spain spread from family to family. Everybody knew it was the

Nazis who were killing and wounding Russian husbands and sons. Though the accord was distasteful to me as well, I kept my thoughts to myself. It seemed to me that for whatever reasons, it was a strategy carefully measured by Stalin. Party members in my factory were sullen throughout the day the pact was announced, until at the end of the day they were summoned to special meetings for party members only. The next day these same workers were upbeat, even cheerful, from what they had been told the evening before. Editorials began appearing in the papers, urging all citizens not to despair but to have faith in the Soviet system. Without explaining why, they assured the reader that the treaty with Germany would be in the best interests of the people.

In fact, an immediate result of the pact was increased hardship for the average Russian, because foods like meat, sugar, eggs, butter, and flour were now being shipped to Germany. This was difficult for people to take, especially considering that these foods had become available at the general food stores only recently after years of severe rationing. I even heard party members grumbling about sending the food off to the Nazis. We never learned what, if anything, Russia received from Germany, other than two years of peace.

There were of course the party diehards who accepted the pact without question. Among those who doubted, nobody dared openly question the pact. But in small clusters, people might express themselves by first praising the Kremlin leadership and then asking, innocently, "Isn't it possible that signing an accord with a fascist country will weaken our nation's ideological foundation?"

The question would be followed by something like, "But of course, Comrade Stalin and the Politburo know things we are not aware of."

After the treaty was signed, the message and emphasis of Soviet internal propaganda changed significantly. Ever since my arrival in 1930, the press and radio had trumpeted the need for the worldwide expansion of communism and that every Russian should work toward that end. The caption beneath every newspaper and magazine logo read, "Workers of the World Unite!"

Nationalism was the new emphasis. Huge banners, hung in every shop in the factory, read, "Love your country first and always." Large signs were posted at railroad stations. Along the railroad tracks colored flowers were arranged to spell out the new slogans. Russians were now implored, "Love your Mighty Motherland always!" The spirit of internationalism had departed. Because I obviously was not Russian, this had a direct effect on my well-being. People who had once been friendly now kept their distance. Strangers no longer greeted me warmly in the street, and I was now often treated with disdain.

German soldiers began to turn up in Moscow. As a group they appeared friendly to the Russians. Although the Soviet military adopted the Nazi goose-step, I noticed very little inclination among the Russians to fraternize with the Germans. Not only were their favorite foods now being shipped off to their former enemies, but this wave of propaganda was whipping up a nationalistic fervor that made all foreigners undesirable.

Those of us living inside Russia were never told the particulars of the alliance with Germany. But Soviet military actions to some extent soon made it clear. In 1939-40, Russian troops seized Estonia, Latvia, Lithuania, part of Poland, and Bessarabia and Chernovtsy in Rumania, without resistance from the Germans. Each mighty giant would gobble up defenseless nations knowing that the other was doing the same.

The Russian people were very proud. One evening at the cinema, newsreels were shown of Russian troops and armored vehicles blazing across Bessarabia. The entire audience rose clapping and cheering, shouting "bravo" while shaking their fists defiantly in the air. They were so callously proud of how their nation was overrunning defenseless people. I was astonished.

"So this is the way communism is going to establish peace and social justice in the world," I thought. I had been just as surprised at the Russian people's reaction after Soviet radio announced—on December 10, 1939— that Finland had provoked peace-loving Russia into a war. They felt indignant toward Finland—ignoring the obvious differences in the size and relative strength of the two nations. No one ever suggested that the Soviets, and not the Finns, might be the aggressors.

When I arrived at work the day after the invasion was announced over Soviet radio, I realized that the decision to invade Finland had probably been a hasty one. Scores of workers were ordered to report immediately to the district war office without even having time to go home to say good-by to their families. This kind of immediate conscription was possible because all Soviet males are considered in the military reserve until they reach age sixty.

From the war office the reservists were transported by truck to camps where military units were being formed. They were given new uniforms, a two-day crash program in military techniques, and then sent to the battlefront. Several months later a friend of mine named Mikhail returned from Finland and told me about his experiences. At first, he said, the new recruits were told that they would be going home very soon. However, the bitter Finnish winter was no ally to the Soviet cause. Many of the Russian reservists wore only the thin socks they had on when they reported to work, before being carted off to the war office. As a result, thousands suffered frostbite. Many cases were so bad that men had to have their feet amputated. Mikhail said that the only thing that saved his feet was the newspaper that he had stuffed in his boots and wrapped around his feet shortly before he was ordered to go on patrol and capture a Finnish soldier. His commander had become frustrated at the elusive Finns, and wanted one to interrogate.

In battle, the Finns were hard to locate because they dressed in white and moved about on white-painted skis. The brown-uniformed Russians were easy targets for the camouflaged Finnish sharpshooters. Furthermore, with everything covered in snow it was difficult to orient oneself, even with a map. Often entire Red Army battalions were decoyed by the cagey Finns into traps where the Russians were crushed. It was not uncommon for advancing Russian troops chasing Finns to be led to an ice-covered lake wired with explosives. When the dynamite was set off, the Russians would drown.

In the end, of course, the very size of the Soviet Union forced Finland to give in to the Kremlin's demands, and on March 12, 1940, a peace treaty was concluded. Russia got the Isthmus of Karelia, the naval base at Hango, and other concessions. The Finns were forced to allow the Soviet navy to operate a base in one of their ports. The short Russo-Finnish war cost the Soviet Union many casualties. However, their experience fighting the Finns taught them a great deal about how to fight in the winter. Immediately after the Finnish war, the Russian Army adopted white suits and white-painted skis, a practice which helped them a year later when they were fighting the Germans.

Although most of the Russians I knew would not admit that

little Finland had given their army a good spanking, deep down they knew the true story because friends and relatives who fought in the war shared their feelings and experiences with those closest to them. The unpleasant news of the Russian army's poor showing gradually became commonplace knowledge throughout Moscow.

While the Kremlin was preoccupied with military adventures along its western border, the purges continued, though with less intensity since the execution of Yezhov. Lavrenti Pavlovich Beria, the next MVD henchman, took over at the end of 1938. At thirty-nine, Beria was stocky, clean-shaven, and short—about five feet four inches. It was rumored that no one had ever seen him laugh.

One of Beria's victims was an Italian who worked at the factory. Guerra, an underground Communist in Fascist Italy, escaped the Italian authorities by fleeing to the Soviet Union in 1931. Because he was a blacksmith by profession, he worked in the forge shop. One day while he was inspecting a machine, someone switched on the motor. Guerra's left hand was crushed and had to be amputated. While in the hospital, the trade union and the department where he was employed sent various people to visit him and lift his spirits. After his discharge he married one of the nurses who had visited him in the hospital. They lived together on the floor above me, and by 1939 had three children. He continued working with one hand.

One morning in 1940, in the early hours, the MVD men came and took him away. No one in the factory ever saw him again. Even though he was a fervent Communist who had worked against fascism in Italy, in the pre-war frenzy against foreigners, he was suspected of being a Fascist. His Russian wife was allowed to continue working in the factory until July 1941. The MVD roused her and her three children in the middle of the night, and took them away in a motor wagon.

By mid-July 1941, the number of foreigners working in my factory had been reduced drastically. When I began in 1932 there were 362 of us. Now a Hungarian and I were the only ones left.

CHAPTER 13

Germany Attacks Russia

WHEN I AWOKE ON SUNDAY, June 22, 1941, I turned on the radio before getting out of bed, as was my usual custom. I usually would listen to the BBC (British Broadcasting Company) rather than to Radio Moscow, because the news reports on state radio were censored. But this morning I chose to listen to a German station instead.

Moments after I switched the dial, I heard the voice of Joseph Goebbels announcing that German troops had crossed the Soviet border. With Finland and Poland already fallen to the Nazis, Russia was now encircled. Although I was not that surprised that an agreement between Communists and Nazis had been violated, the news nevertheless devastated me. I was well aware of Hitler's racist policies. I knew that if Hitler succeeded in his invasion of Russia, I was as good as dead.

When I arrived at the factory that morning, everything appeared normal. The Germans had crossed the border at 4:10 A.M., yet no one knew a thing about it. Finally, the news broke. At 11:30 A.M., all workers were ordered to stop what they were doing and listen to an important announcement. Vyacheslav Molotov, Soviet foreign minister and one of the men closest to Stalin, announced in a somber voice that the Nazis had invaded Russia. He mentioned nothing about the Red Army repulsing the attack. This served as a signal to the workers—conditioned through the years to listen and read between the lines of official pronouncements—that the Nazis had penetrated deeply into Russian territory.

Throughout the factory there was nothing but gloom. No earthquake, no volcanic eruption could have been as devastating to the Russians as the news that the Germans had invaded their motherland. It came at a time when the Russian people had finally begun to accustom themselves to the idea of a Nazi-Soviet friendship. At first people did not want to believe the news—it was too bizarre.

Molotov exhorted, "Our cause is right; we shall win." But the workers remained in a stupor. Hardly anybody worked the rest of the day. In the days that followed, most of the Russians I knew felt betrayed, not only by the Germans but by their own leaders.

"How could the Politburo not see what treacherous people the Nazis are," was the sort of statement whispered among friends. "The Germans invaded Russia before. We should have known better than to trust them."

Late that afternoon a factory-wide meeting was called, with attendance mandatory. The factory director, his assistant, a representative of the Central Committee of Trade Unions, and a few model workers addressed the thousands of workers outside on the factory grounds. Finally, it was one of the workers who was able to rouse the crowd, when he said,

> Comrades, we have been grossly apathetic. This is not the time to feel pity and regret. Now is the time to work day and night and stop the invading hordes. With the will to fight and return blow for blow, the Germans cannot deal with us as they dealt with Holland and Norway. Let us resolve right now that these treacherous enemies must be defeated.

After prolonged cheers, the member of the Central Committee of Trade Unions announced that every worker would have to work twelve hours a day until the Nazis were brought to their knees. A show of hands was asked for and there was unanimous approval. Everyone was obligated to work an extra five hours. I also volunteered to work after the twelve-hour shift whenever a serious technical problem arose that needed correcting.

After work that day I witnessed something I thought I would never see in the Soviet Union. Thousands of people—men, women, and children, young and old, even party members—were flocking to church. I was on my way to classes at the engineering institute, but this was such an unprecedented sight, that I decided to follow the crowd into a church. Once inside, candles were distributed to everyone. People were crammed into every corner. There was no place left even to stand. One heard people crying, some asking God for forgiveness, others asking for His intercession during a time of such great national peril.

I noticed that the authorities on the streets did not try to stop these masses of people from entering the churches for spiritual comfort. People streamed past stunned policemen to enter Moscow's hundreds of churches. It did not matter that there were no priests to lead them in prayer; they prayed anyway. It became clear that twenty-four years of anti-religious propaganda had not extinguished from Russian hearts a sense of the reality of God. I thought it fitting that the German invasion was announced on a Sunday, and that it was therefore on a Sunday that the people flocked to their churches. The traditional Sabbath day was never a regular day off from work. The government varied people's days off as a means of control, to make it more difficult for any group of people to congregate regularly. Sunday especially was a work day, to try and eliminate the reactionary practice of going to church.

Needing the support of the Russian people at such a critical time, the authorities no doubt decided not to prevent people from flocking to the churches the day of the German invasion. Throughout the war period, the government tolerated the churchgoing, and even invited people to join the party who had been rejected previously because their relatives had been clergymen. I expect this was allowed as a way of boosting the nationalism now considered so essential. The term "Russian motherland" began to be used instead of "Soviet Union," a subtle admission that the great mass of people were not as committed to their form of government as they were to their country.

On June 22 and June 23, fearing that the government would freeze their assets or that some other calamity would befall them, thousands of Muscovites dashed to the district bank to withdraw their savings. I witnessed a number of lines more than a mile long, of people desperate to pull out all their rubles.

News from the battlefield was not good. The German forces were destroying the Red Army. Almost four months after they crossed the Soviet border, the Nazis were only about seventy kilometers (barely forty-four miles) from Moscow. Exactly one month after they invaded, the Germans began bombing Moscow. Raids were so frequent that the the scream of air raid warning sirens became a natural part of the sounds of the city. Air raid shelters near the factory—which we ran to constantly—consisted of long trenches about seven feet deep, boarded on both sides and on top and covered with sand.

During the first bombing raid a man dropped dead of a heart attack running to the shelter. The next day the old man who operated a government fruit and vegetable stand outside the factory never made it to the shelter. A demolition bomb dropped on top of him. When I emerged from the shelter, he and his stand were gone. The only things left were a few slivers of wood, some shreds of cabbage blowing down the street, and bloodstains on the concrete sidewalk.

The raids took their toll. It was not enough having to contend with the fear of being killed; those whose apartment buildings were demolished were faced with the difficult task of finding another place to live. Even before the war most Russians lived in extremely cramped quarters. Often a family of four or five would live in one fifteen-and-a-half- by seventeen-foot room, with a bathroom in the hallway that they shared with from twenty to fifty other people. Those whose buildings were bombed either would move in with relatives or try to live in a damaged, abandoned building.

Although the Kremlin's propaganda broadcasts tried to fire up the Russians, many began to think there was a chance the Germans might defeat them. Doubts began to surface throughout Moscow, sometimes even in the open. Foreign radio broadcasts, with their uncensored reports of fighting, greatly fueled the doubts. Concerned, the Kremlin ordered that Russians turn in their radios. The penalty for noncompliance was death. As a result, like hundreds of thousands of others, I gave up my radio. They were to be returned when the war was over, but most Russians doubted whether they would ever again see what many of them considered their one luxury item. There were some daring souls, like a fellow factory worker I knew, who had two radios and handed in only one. This man kept the other one hidden in a clothes closet and played it once a day between 3:00 and 4:00 A.M. Every day he gave me reports about what was happening on the battlefront. Fortunately, he was never caught.

But even without radios, there was a pervasive sense of defeat. There was Comrade Vit, for example, the party secretary of our shop, whom I had known for nearly ten years. This short, stocky, good-natured man had the weathered face of a peasant and long, wavy, gray hair. The Communist party was his life, as was the First State Ball Bearing Plant, which he had helped to build, sometimes working without pay. Vit was an idealist who believed that communism could liberate every human being in the world. As our shop's party secretary, he was privy to information that was not available to most workers and even some rank-and-file party members.

I knew the man genuinely liked me. He had helped me get into the engineering institute, and he would come by almost every day at work to see how I was doing and say something complimentary. One day, about two months after the German invasion, he approached me in the shop. This time he had no smile on his face. He asked me to leave my work area and follow him.

"Comrade Robinson," he said, as we walked out of the shop and into the corridor, "we have known each other for a long time and you must know by now how much I respect your opinion."

As someone approached, Vit stopped talking and just looked down at the concrete floor. When the man was out of earshot Vit continued, "Now between us only, what do you think about this great misfortune that has overtaken us—this war?"

Another person was walking our way. Vit again looked down at the floor and stood motionless until the man was a safe distance away. Then he looked at me and asked, "Well, what do you think?"

"What can I say?" I thought to myself. Although I liked the man, he was still an official of the Communist party. He could be testing me. I decided I had better play it safe, and parrot the party line.

"It is difficult to make an assessment," I said, "being so far away from the fighting. On the other hand, I cannot believe that the Red Army will be defeated."

Vit looked at me searchingly. Then he responded, ''I wish I could see the picture as you do.'' He paused then added, ''The Red Army has been retreating from the very first day of the war. I do understand, of course, that on the morning the Germans attacked us, all of our planes and tanks at the place of attack were grounded and destroyed. Two days before the attack an order was made to change the gasoline and oil in all planes and tanks, and for that reason we could put up no mechanized resistance. Moreover, besides our material loses, manpower losses were enormous. In fact, not a single soldier remained alive to tell the story of the first few days of the war. As far as I know, no one is aware so far of who gave the order to change the fuel in those planes and tanks.''

Vit shook his head and added, "That was in late June. Now it is September and we are still retreating." He stopped talking and waited for me to respond.

''You must know,'' I said, ''that even Napoleon's army made swift progress during the early months. He even captured Moscow. But look at what the Russian army was able to do. Eventually they chased the French out in defeat.''

''I know that,'' said Vit. ''But this time there is a difference. The German army is highly mechanized.''

Pausing, he looked carefully to his left and right to see if anyone was approaching. Then he continued, ''Comrade Robinson, I am not the only one feeling uncertain. Very many of my comrades, some of them holding higher positions in the party than I do, have the same opinions about the war as I have.''

Though he waited for a response, I chose not to say a thing. He then continued. ''Listen—please believe me—I feel much more at ease and secure talking with you than I could ever feel with many other people, even my fellow countrymen. Hence I will tell you what I really think about our situation. If we do not get the necessary moral support and material help that we need, nothing will stop the Germans from seizing Moscow. If that happens, it will be all over. The only thing that could save us then would be Russia's historical, reliable, and helpful ally, a cold winter.''

Since we had been talking for more than a half-hour, I felt I could now break away from him. ''We had better be getting back,'' I said.

Vit responded, ''I'll let you go, but first let me remind you that what we have been discussing should be kept in the strictest of confidence.''

I assured him that I would not share what he had told me with anyone.

A week later I was approached again, this time not by an official but by Comrade Dima, a twenty-eight-year-old apprentice and a party member. That morning I had noticed that he seemed sluggish, which was unusual because he was my most promising apprentice. After lunch he seemed more energetic, but still not quite up to par. As I had just finished helping an apprentice next to him, and was about to return to my desk, Dima said, ''Comrade Robinson, excuse me for asking you such a question, but please tell me your opinion about the war. Do you think the Red Army can ever stop the Germans?''

I was startled that he had asked me this within earshot of the other apprentices. I thought this could possibly be the party's way of testing me, that perhaps there was a connection between Vit's approach and Dima's. I chose the safe route in responding, ''You know, I am not a military expert, so it is beyond me to answer your question. But in the long run I feel confident that the Red Army will triumph.'' Then I asked, ''Tell me, Comrade Dima, why did you ask me the question?''

Dima, who was married to a twenty-one-year-old Komsomol and had a one-year old baby, looked at his machine a moment and then said, ''Last night while in bed my wife began to cry because the Germans were getting closer and closer to Moscow. She is Jewish and she's afraid that should the Nazis conquer the city they will hunt down and kill every Jew in Moscow and our child would be motherless.''

He paused, turned away from me, and then said almost in a whisper, ''I'll be honest with you. I would never tell anyone else what I'm about to share with you, but I tell it to you because I trust you. When my wife cried, I cried too and prayed that the western countries would come to our aid before it is too late.''

''Comrade Dima,'' I said, ''a Communist is not supposed to have doubts and fears, and accordingly you are supposed to be the master of your own fate. Is it not so?''

''Yes,'' he answered, still looking at his machine, "that is what we were all taught during our study of dialectical materialism, but during the past few months, besides my wife and me, there are very many party members who are beginning to have doubts also, although they will not say so openly."

"As I told you before," I said, "the Red Army will certainly show its true capabilities when we least expect it. Now it is important to be patient until that day of days arrives."

"Thank you so much for those words of encouragement, Comrade Robinson," he said. "My wife will be comforted by what you have shared with me when I tell her tonight."

A few days after our conversation, I learned from the foreman that Dima had called up the factory to say that he had been inducted into the army. I thought of his lovely wife, wondering how she had handled his departure, and of his child. As if in answer to my thoughts, Mrs. Dima came to the shop the following day. With tears in her eyes, she told me that her husband had received a card from the War Department. Nothing I said could comfort her. Because the Soviet military was desperate for manpower, many other Russian wives were in the same situation.

In fact, as a Soviet citizen I, too, was eligible for the draft. Shortly after the Nazi invasion I had been ordered to the War Department for a physical exam. It was more like torture than a medical checkup, and was all carried out under the watchful eyes of dozens of army officers, who nearly outnumbered the doctors and nurses in the large examination room. They were there to make sure no one tried to evade military service with a fake ailment.

I was in good health, except for my eyesight. My left eye was particularly weak. The Soviet physicians and nurses used every device imaginable in examining my left eye. They held up special cards, showed me different combinations of fingers, and asked me to distinguish among different facial expressions. What bothered me the most was the electric eye analyzer, which was trained on my eyes for what seemed like an eternity, and left them sore, teary, and tired. Because of the army officer standing next to the physicians, I did not dare complain.

Although I failed the physical, and my poor eyesight was recorded in my file, I had to return every three months to be rechecked, often by the same doctor. This continued until the end of the war. However, there were others with worse maladies who had to endure greater harassment than I. A kindly gentleman and fellow worker reported for his re-examination at the same time I did. Each time he was humiliated. He had a physical handicap, and as a result, instead of being able to walk, he waddled. It was obvious to anyone that this man could not be a soldier. Nevertheless, each time he was tested thoroughly, which meant he had to take off all his clothes and expose his deformity. He was ordered to walk, then to walk faster, then to trot, and finally they told him to run at top speed. Sweating, fighting back tears, he would waddle as fast as he could. People would at first start to laugh, but then try to restrain themselves. It was actually hard not to laugh, because it was such an absurd spectacle.

Another twenty-six-year-old man had to undergo the same kind of torture. As long as I had known him, he had needed crutches to get around because one of his legs was shorter than the other. The doctor would order him to walk without his crutches. All he could do was hop.

"Now walk on the other leg," the doctor would insist.

Terribly embarrassed, the young man took a step with his crippled leg, and fell down.

It was not that the physicians were sadists. They were under pressure to prove to the officers present why someone could not be inducted into the army or navy. The physicians knew that doctors were needed at the front, and that if they failed to please the officers and ruled people unfit who the officers thought should be inducted, they could find themselves on the next train out.

Those who were drafted and survived or captured were never assured of returning to civilian life. Even though the law stated that a draftee would serve only two years during peacetime, the Red Army and Navy adopted the czarist practice of keeping soldiers they wanted. Thousands of recruits between the ages of eighteen and twenty-four were inducted into the military and never saw their relatives or close friends again. Everyone inducted knew there was a good chance that even if he survived, he might never return home again.

As a result, the traditional going away party for the draftee was a sad affair. I first attended one in 1938 for a young friend, Misha, who was engaged to a young woman, Marina. The gathering started at 8:00 P.M. in Misha's parents' sixteen- by eighteen-foot room. All of the beds had been moved into the corridor outside the apartment to make room for dancing. The parents had been allowed to take off several days from work, without pay, after their son received his draft notice, so they could be near him and arrange for his farewell party. For such an event, money could be borrowed from their trade union at no interest, to buy party food and beverages.

Nineteen people, all close relatives and friends of Misha, crammed into the room. One of them was an accomplished accordionist. Two tables in the room were filled with food prepared by Misha's mother and aunts. There were delectable Russian hors d'oeuvres and bottles of vodka and wine, seemingly enough to satisfy the appetites of seventy-five people.

By 9:00 P.M., four hefty toasts had been made. Then the Russian music began. First there were folk dances. People danced in the room and spilled out into the corridor. Neighbors did not complain because they knew the reason for the party. Because the weather was balmy, the accordionist led a procession outside, where we all joined hands in a circle and danced almost to the point of exhaustion. Back in the room at eleven o'clock there were more toasts, and people started singing Russian war songs. Misha and Marina held hands and listened. One could easily imagine their somber thoughts.

After midnight there were more toasts, and then the soul of Russia was exposed, with all of its pain and tears, through the singing of ancient Russian folk songs. The sorrow of the wretched past and present poured out of every heart in the room. I would say that the sorrow was even deeper at times and more mournful than the blues sung by black people in America, with their heritage of slavery, and the agony of their deprivation and rejection. In their hearts they were lamenting, through song, over so much suffering.

They sang for hours, with deep passion, sometimes in unison and at times in natural harmony. I pictured the Russian soldier trudging through the snow, carrying his satchel of frozen black bread and water on his back, head bent, half-frozen, wandering somewhere, but knowing always that death hovers nearby ready to pounce before hope could be found.

Misha and Marina faced the singers, still holding hands, her head leaning on his shoulder. All eyes, including mine, were filled with tears. The soul-rending songs were too mournful. Around three in the morning the sad songs ended, and people started making up lyrics to familiar tunes, changing the atmosphere. They were little verses about Misha and his fiancée, designed to generate laughter and good cheer. One man sang a song about duty to one's country, another sang something about the need for discipline, and another sang a song about the two lovers being only separated by time and eventually marrying.

Applause broke out. Then a man raised his glass of vodka and cried out, "Here is to a quick and safe return."

Glasses were raised, the vodka was washed down, and the accordionist began playing a dance. It was a special number in which you dance before the person you wish to have as a partner. Everyone seemed to be dancing, even Misha's father and mother. But the guest of honor was outside in the stairwell, talking quietly with his fiancée. His moment of departure was nearing.

The morning sun had risen. It was 6:00 A.M. and soon Misha would have to go to the tram car stop with his satchel, which contained a few toilet articles, socks, and underwear. That was all he would need at the induction center; the army would supply the rest. The music stopped. When Misha's mother embraced and kissed him, the frolicking and talking ceased. Then Misha's father hugged and kissed him, followed by Marina. Then every man and woman at the party embraced Misha and wished him well. Misha's mother then asked everyone to sit down and observe a moment or two of silence. I prayed that Misha would come home alive.

Out on the street, amid people rushing off to work, we formed a procession. Misha and Marina arm-in-arm, and his parents also arm-in-arm, walked beside each other. Most of us from the party, including the accordionist, followed. Soon the women started singing another sad song. Other songs followed all along the fifteen-minute walk to the tram car stop. As the tram car appeared in the distance, Misha kissed his parents and then embraced Marina.

Although the first fifteen months of the war resulted in an astonishing number of casualties to the Red Army—about five million—Misha miraculously returned unhurt from the war seven years later. He and Marina were then married and she gave birth to a son.

CHAPTER 14

Evacuating Moscow

THE GERMANS CONTINUED THEIR ADVANCE on Moscow. The closer they came, the more difficult it was to find food. A supper of black bread, dried fish, and tea without sugar was considered a treat. Even with a minimal amount of food, however, the workers at the factory were keeping production up. With their country at war with the Germans, they were in a patriotic, sacrificing mood. They competed with each other to see who could put in the most extra time without pay. They wanted to do anything possible for the war effort.

Because of a manpower shortage, a number of changes took place in the factory. A man named Gromov was appointed chief engineer of our machine shop. Soon there was bad blood between us. It began with Zavatsky, an ambitious technologist who frequently pored through foreign technical journals in search of new ideas for increasing production. He became excited about a concept he uncovered in American and British publications and then spent weeks at the drafting table, and many more weeks trying to design the device. Zavatsky then gave the drawings to the shop to manufacture. All the fabricated parts of the die except one fit correctly. A great deal of effort was put into producing the final part. Three different devices were designed and manufactured but each one failed. At this point Gromov urged me to help solve the problem of Zavatsky's complex die. He said the Moscow Soviet was pressuring him to complete the project within ten days.

"Please don't say you can't," he pleaded with me. "I know you can do it where others have failed. Please do so for the honor of the whole shop, and I will always be indebted to you." I had never seen Gromov so solicitious. I told him I would try.

I studied Zavatsky's drawing, and in about four hours I designed the needed device. Gromov was thrilled when I handed him my suggested adjustments to Zavatsky's design along with my own drawing. He ordered all of the foremen in our shop to put everything else aside and work on the fixture I had designed until it was completed.

"Comrade Robinson will direct the operation," said Gromov. The next day Gromov had the finished product he wanted. The fixture I had designed made Zavatsky's scheme work. Because of it, production was increased seventy-two fold. A week later those of us who had significant roles in the project were rewarded. Zavatsky received 2,500 rubles. Others who played lesser roles than I got between 1,500 and 150 rubles. When a woman handed me 75 rubles, I felt insulted. I told her to take the money back to Gromov and tell him that I had not worked for the money but only to help the administration. Gromov was angry at me, of course, for refusing his reward. His initial reaction was to refuse to speak to me. I was gratified that the factory director approached me in the shop and in the presence of others, thanked me for saving the Zavatsky project.

Gromov was well-known for having clawed his way to the top. He was a schemer, and he wanted to protect his coveted position, which was rare for him, a non-party member, to hold. His hand-picked assistant, Beloousov, was considerably my junior in knowledge and experience. Whereas I was in my fourth year at the mechanical engineering institute, he had just begun.

Two or three months after the German invasion, Beloousov appeared in my section, inspecting the machines and looking over the apprentices. After awhile he turned and snapped at me, "I do not like the way these machines are set up."

I didn't respond.

On September 3, Gromov's secretary came to my desk armed with a stack of papers, which she fumbled through until she found the one she wanted. She read it to me in an official voice: "Comrade Robinson, beginning tomorrow, September 4, 1941, your services as an instructor in grinding are no longer required. You are to report and begin work on one of the cylindrical machines as a worker." She paused, and then added: "Signed, Gromov."

"Tell Comrade Gromov," I replied, "that I will not leave my present place of work until I answer his order in writing."

Appearing puzzled, she backed up a few steps and then turned and briskly walked away. Three days later I handed Gromov a letter of resignation. In it I explained why his decision to demote me was unjust. I concluded, "I cannot accept your suggestion as I have a technical education and wide experience in toolmaking. It is, therefore, much better not to use me simply as an ordinary worker."

I gave a copy of the letter to the factory's party committee. I soon received a letter from Gromov in response. He covered his tracks by denying he had ever given me an order to step down from my instructor's post and saying that he had actually suggested two other, more worthy positions.

He wrote, "The request in your statement to resign is rejected." I had figured correctly that in the midst of a war, when the factory was straining to support the military effort, cooler heads above Gromov's would not look kindly on the thought of losing me. Apart from my experience, I had the added usefulness of being unfit for military service.

One evening in mid-October, as I headed to the engineering institute, I noticed men and women hurriedly building barricades at all the street entrances. This was a clear and foreboding sign that the Kremlin expected the city to be taken within a few days. When I reported to the factory the next morning, workers were standing around in small clusters and the machines had been uprooted and were placed on iron pipes, ready to be crated. White electrical wire crisscrossed the concrete floor. Someone explained to me that the wire was attached to dynamite, and that if the Germans broke through Soviet defenses and entered the city, the factory would be blown up. I was told that every factory in Moscow had been wired, as well as office buildings and the subway.

At nine o'clock Gromov mounted a large box and began addressing those of us in the machine shop:

> Comrades, our factory does not exist anymore. All machine tools are being sent to Kuybyshev. All of you will have to travel to that city and start working anew. Each and every one of you will receive in advance three months' salary and three kilos of flour. We expect to receive these between noon and two o'clock today. By six o'clock tonight the train will come for you all.

There was no panic. Everything seemed to be in order. Though no one said so, I sensed that most of the workers were relieved to learn they would be evacuated to a safer part of the country.

We all milled around until noon, when we started forming a line near the paymaster's office. Around 12:30 P.M., we figured he probably would not show up until 2:00 P.M. When he hadn't arrived by 2:00, people strayed from the line but did not leave for home. When the paymaster still had not arrived at 4:00 P.M., workers began grumbling and cursing Gromov, some saying they would like to choke him. At this point I decided I would walk around and see what was happening in the other shops.

It was eerie. The great First State Ball Bearing Plant, open seven days a week with more than 16,000 people working night and day, was like a giant corpse. Having spent nine years there, I felt sad leaving, especially because we were forced to run by the Nazis. There was a chance I would never come back for who knew what was in store for all of us. Perhaps we would even have to evacuate Kuybyshev in a few months, if the Germans continued to advance. I was saddened to think that I would probably never receive my engineering degree, the thing I wanted most in the world.

I had walked through several shops when I heard someone calling my name. I turned and saw a friend running toward me, breathless, with tears in his eyes. I did not recognize him at first, he was in such a state. Gone was the broad smile I was accustomed to seeing.

"Do you have a moment?" he asked.

I told him I did, and then waited for him to draw a deep breath. Then he began: "Comrade Robinson, I have something important I must tell you. I've chosen you to share what's in my heart because I trust you."

He looked into my eyes, probably to sense whether I appeared

Uganda Embassy
Moscow City Council
KGB HQ
Church
Kremlin
Red Square
Rossiya Hotel
St. Basil's
Lenin Mausoleum
GUM
Bol'shoy Theater
Swimming Pool
State Art Gallery and Central House of Artists
Gor'kiy Park
Kotel'nicheskaya Apartments
Novospasskiy Monastery
Paveletskiy Station
Moskva-Tov. Station
Engineering Institute
Donskoy Monastery
Danilovskoye Cemetery
Simonov Monastery
First State Ball Bearing Plant
Residence of Robert Robinson
Rechnoy Vokzal Station
Kursk Station
Bauman Park
Mayakovskaya
Pushkinskaya
Kolkhoznaya
Turgenevskaya
Kirovskaya
Kurskaya
Arbatskaya
Kalininskaya
Kropotkinskaya
Polyanka
Novokuznetskaya
Taganskaya
Marksistskaya
Oktyabr'skaya
Dobryninskaya
Serpukhovskaya
Paveletskaya
Proletarskaya
Shabolovskaya
Tul'skaya
Avtozavodskaya
Likhachev

sympathetic. He must have sensed that I was, because he continued, ''At first we had lots of confidence in our party and government. We were promised that in fifteen years we would forge ahead of America. What's more, we were promised that no wars would be fought on Russian soil. We believed those promises with all our heart and soul. But now we know that our leaders have run away to safer places and have left us leaderless. Today Moscow has been abandoned and the great mass of people have been left to face the murderous Germans.''

He paused here, again searching my eyes, then added, ''Please, Comrade Robinson, if you should be fortunate enough to be able to reach the West, please tell your people there the whole truth about the Soviet system, that the Russian people have been grossly deceived, that there has never been such a betrayal in history. Let the world know how we have suffered and were deprived of the good things of life, thinking always that the policies of Lenin were being carried out.

''Now we see that everything promised us was a fraud. Since 1917, we have been asked to sacrifice for the better day that was sure to come. Now we know that our leaders fooled us into a pact with the Nazis that has become our gravestone. After so much sweat and toil, going without meat for months at a time, sometimes going to bed on an empty stomach, hoping that everything we had done would make life happier for the people, nothing has come true.''

He began to cry like a child, sobbing loudly and hiding his face in his hands. I reached out and squeezed his shoulder, hoping that would calm him down. When he regained his composure, I tried to assure him that even if Moscow was seized, all would not be lost, that more than three-quarters of Russia was still in Russian hands. I urged him to be patient, and said, ''Capturing Moscow may be a prestigious act, but it doesn't constitute complete victory.''

Apparently I said the right thing, because he calmed down. After awhile, he thanked me for the advice and went back to his shop. I knew that what this man had told me was genuine, that I was not being tested by an NKVD agent. With the Germans pounding Moscow day and night and about to push into the city, the NKVD was not busy hunting counter-revolutionaries. Along with everyone else, they were out seeking safety and food, preoccupied for the moment with their own survival.

When I returned to my shop, the workers were in an uglier mood. It was six o'clock, no paymaster in sight, and no word of when he might show up. I decided to go home, a ten-minute walk away. On the way I purchased my daily allotment of black bread—twenty-one ounces —and with that, three old hard candies, and tea, I had supper. Since I had been on my feet most of the day, I decided to stretch out on my bed. As I lay there I thought of the man who had dared to share his true feelings with me. I knew there were many other people who felt betrayed. I had watched the Russian people for eleven years stoically accept poor housing, inadequate food rations, and inferior clothing, believing that their leaders were going to create a better life for them. At this point, I clearly understood that not only had the average Russian's trust in the Soviet system been crushed, but many Communist party members were throwing away their party credentials, some tearing them up and stuffing the pieces down the toilet, others simply tossing their party tickets with their names and pictures rubbed out, into the street. I saw scores of these passes strewn along the sidewalks.

I did not expect the paymaster to show up at the factory that evening, so I waited until the next morning to return to work. I soon discovered that I had made a big mistake. The other workers had remained, and when at nine o'clock there was still no money, they had marched to see the finance manager in the main office. Some of the workers began smashing the office windows, bringing the finance manager outside with assurances that the money was on its way. The window smashing continued throughout the night until at 1:45 A.M., a van and several policemen arrived. They carried the bags of money inside the office, where it was then passed out.

When I showed up in the morning and handed the paymaster my pay slip, I noticed that Gromov was with him. They both looked at my slip and then Gromov said something to the paymaster that I could not hear. He then handed me one thousand rubles instead of the three thousand that everyone else in my rank was given. (In those days five rubles were equal to one American dollar.) I decided it was best not to protest. Gromov had gotten his revenge.

Although I was shortchanged what was owed me, I realized that I had learned an important lesson about life in Russia. The uncharacteristic reaction of the workers was caused by one blow too many. Their traditional fear of authority—a fear mixed with respect—had broken down. They knew that when a Russian in authority promises you something you really need, you had better not leave until he makes good on his word. This lesson was to help me quite a bit during the next twenty-three years.

With nothing to do, and with the evacuation train not due until 6:00 P.M., I decided to venture into the center of Moscow to see what was happening. I did not get very far. I encountered thousands of people looking like refugees, with their suitcases and bundles, waiting for streetcars in their first step to flee ahead of the fast-approaching Germans. Most of them were Jews. With the streetcars so jammed, I returned to the factory and went to the nearly deserted cafeteria. I ate the meatless soup, which consisted of little more than boiled cabbage leaves, and munched on some black bread. Then I walked home.

On my door was a note from Gromov, urging that I contact him at once. I ignored the message, but about thirty minutes later I heard a knock on the door. It was a group of four men from my shop, sent by Gromov to ask me to pick up my train ticket. They said that all I could take with me was one suitcase of belongings. I told them that I had a wardrobe trunk which I had brought from America and I was not about to give it up. When they sensed that I was going to stand my ground, one of them suggested getting a wheelbarrow to lug the trunk. They finally settled on a piece of sheet metal, placed it under the trunk, then dragged it off to the factory's administration office. On our way to the factory, two friends in a truck spotted us and said that Gromov had given them my train ticket. They said that I would not need the ticket anyway, since they were on their way to Gorky, where we would take a boat to Kuybyshev, and that I could have a ride. The four men loaded my trunk onto the truck, I squeezed into the cab and the truck headed east.

In the weeks before the evacuation of Moscow, countless rumors circulated about the approaching Germans. They were seen as monsters, bloodthirsty tyrants who raped women and used children for bayonet practice. However, it was not rumor but newspaper accounts of the Nazis' treatment of Jews in already conquered territory that set off a mass exodus of Jews from Moscow. As soon as word was out that Moscow's factories were being dismantled and shipped to the east, thousands of Jews began to flee. If the Kremlin was abandoning Moscow, they did not intend to be left unprotected in the path of the Germans. They walked away from their jobs and homes, leaving their apartment doors open.

Jews held a significant number of the professional jobs in Moscow. They occupied the very highest positions at my factory; in fact, at times both the chief engineer and the head administrator were Jewish. As far as I knew, only four Jews were regular workers in my factory while hundreds of others held managerial positions. Many of the leading journalists, numerous high-ranking officials at the Ministry of Foreign Affairs, and the majority of physicians, professors, teachers, jurists, economic planners, and finance managers were Jewish.

As we drove toward Gorky, we saw those thousands and thousands of Jews who had been unable to make rail connections flooding the roads. As a result of this exodus, the Jews quickly came to be resented by other Russians, who accused them of abandoning Moscow rather than staying behind and resisting the Germans. After the exodus of Moscow's Jews in 1941 I frequently heard anti-Semitic remarks, whereas in my previous eleven years in the Soviet Unon I had never heard even one.

During its czarist past, Russia had at times been virulently anti-Semitic, and it now became clear that the past may have been dormant, but it was not dead. Although the younger Jews, many of whom were loyal Communists, had learned about the pogroms that swept through Jewish communities in the Pale of Russia—the district where Jews were allowed to reside—during czarist times, they were confident that with the birth of communism, anti-Semitism in Russia had died. The proof seemed undeniable to them. Not only were they able to attend the best universities and pursue whatever professions they wished, they also occupied many important policy-making positions within the government and the military. Besides, it was well-known that Lenin had a Jewish grandfather and that he openly deplored anti-Semitism.

Their parents, however, were not as trusting. Evidently, what they and their families had endured prior to the revolution was something they could never forget. They remembered how the Cossacks had burned their homes. They had watched them slaughter their cattle, rape and kidnap their daughters, kill their friends and relatives, and desecrate their cemeteries and temples. They had heard their gloating Russian neighbors cheer and had watched them comb through the debris and loot whatever was salvageable.

So the older Jews, knowing what a pogrom was like, explained to their children what their fate would likely be at the hands of the Nazi army. But the average Russian, insensitive to the Jewish fears that they would be slaughtered, could not understand and accept that they would all just pick up and flee. To them, the Jewish exodus was an act of cowardice. The older Russians were quick to relate to their children so-called stories about what they had either personally witnessed or been told, of how frightened Jews were of battle and of what a quivering, scheming lot they were.

As far as our eyes could see, there were Jews trudging along the road to Gorky—thousands of Jews, carrying bundles or suitcases wrapped together with cord, with small children running after their parents and crying babies pressed against their mothers' breasts to protect them from the mid-October chill.

It was 1:30 A.M. when we reached Gorky's District Party Committee headquarters. Inside and outside the building were hundreds of Jews, all waiting for the quickest passage to southeastern Russia, to places like Tomsk, Tashkent, Alma-ata, and Samarkand. We had arrived so late that there were no more mattresses, pillows, or blankets available. So along with many others, we slept in chairs wearing our coats and shoes.

In the morning my two friends from Moscow—he was Jewish and his wife was half-Georgian and half-Russian—invited me to go with them to a place where they knew it was possible to obtain bread and butter with tea and sugar. By 7:30 A.M. we had finished our breakfast, and decided to go to the shipping office and exchange our train tickets for boat passage down the Volga.

However, when we reached the office, even at that early hour, we were far from being the first ones there. Thousands of people, mostly Jews with their bundles and satchels, were camped outside the ticket office waiting for it to open. Had we joined the crowd to await our turn, we might not have reached the clerk inside before the office closed for the day. Nevertheless, I was resigned to wait, but the woman I was with asked, "Comrade Robinson, do you still have your Moscow Soviet mandate?"

"Yes," I said, "but why do you ask? It expired two years ago."

She smiled and said, "Because by showing the police your mandate they will escort us through the crowd to the head of the line."

When she noticed that I was hesitant to do that, she said she would lead the way if I gave her the mandate. I did so, and she approached a policeman, told him who I was, and showed him my mandate. He looked at it, then looked at me. Without saying a word, he led us through the crowd, yelling, "Let us through, please. Let us through!"

People were moving aside slowly, so he began to blow his whistle and people hurriedly got out of the way. Some older men and women, and some little children who could not move fast enough, were falling and getting squeezed together. Some started crying in desperation. Although I felt sorry for these people, I could not do anything to help. I simply followed the policeman and my friends.

Once inside the building, the audacious woman showed the clerk my mandate and pointed to me. In a matter of minutes we got our tickets, which included passes for our luggage, including my monstrous trunk. Now we had to get out through the crowd again. Again the policeman, with his whistle, provided us with a special escort. Even so it took us about fifteen minutes to get through. Eight hours later, although we had to battle every inch of the way, we finally made it on board the boat and were headed out of Gorky, on the way to Kuybyshev.

CHAPTER 15

Four Months in Kuybyshev

THE EVENING OF OUR ARRIVAL IN KUYBYSHEV we searched the city for a bathhouse. I had never been to one during my eleven years in the Soviet Union. I would not have relished the thought of having astonished Russians who had never before seen a black man gawking at the sight of me, except that I was filthy after our trip from Moscow.

My friend bought tickets for the two of us, and when we opened the door to the bathhouse, a gust of steam hit us, nearly taking my breath away. The manager showed us where to hang our clothes. While explaining the rules and procedures, he looked at me as if I were an extraterrestrial who had just dropped out of the sky and landed in his bathhouse. Others in the bathhouse stopped dead in their tracks and stared at me.

Added to my embarrassment at being stared at was my innocence about what to do. My impulse was just to jump in the tub and soak. But I watched my friend instead and learned that there are particular customs that need to be observed. Mimicking him, I filled the tub with water, sat down on a bench, picked up the birch twig nearby and began scrubbing myself from head to toe. Soon my skin was tingling. While I was doing this, I noticed two pairs of feet near me. I looked up and saw two young men scrutinizing me, looking almost as if they wanted to touch me. They turned to my friend and asked if I spoke Russian, where I had come from, and how long I had lived in the Soviet Union. Satisfied that I was probably not dangerous, they asked if they could scrub me. When I told them that I preferred to do it myself, they backed away, still gawking at me in disbelief.

I filled a bucket with warm water and dumped it on my head, then scrubbed some more and threw even warmer water over my body. After another scrubbing, I drew hot water and poured it over me. The sensation was exquisite. Every pore seemed to open and I felt totally relaxed. After this procedure, we dried ourselves and went into the lounge. My friend stretched out on a board and suggested that I do the same. I lay down for five minutes, then jerked up as I heard the sound of men pouring hot water over the brick floor. I discovered this was what caused the room to be engulfed in steam.

After about forty minutes of relaxing in the steam, I was ready to leave. But my friend, like the other Russians there, was accustomed to spending at least half a day in the bathhouse. To them it was a rare form of relaxation. The adults drank beer and the children sipped lemonade. Tales were told and gossip flowed freely. The bathhouse, I came to understand, was one of the few places in the Soviet Union where a Russian could escape from his worries and troubles. The hot air and vapor all around helped one to fantasize away all of his troubles. For the moment, the Nazis, the NKVD, and the general wretchedness of life could be forgotten. I too might have chosen to remain in the bathhouse, had I known where we would be living for the next few weeks.

Kuybyshev was another grey, grimy provincial Russian city with street after street of one- and two-room log houses. The side streets were either unpaved or made of cobblestone. It was to here that not only my factory but much of the Kremlin administration chose to evacuate. We arrived early; thousands of others from Moscow and Leningrad came in second and third waves.

In normal times housing and space were in short supply. The shortage only intensified with the influx of refugee workers and others. When we first got off the boat we were taken by truck to the industrial complex where we would work and live. We found a shell of a factory. Stacked outside the abandoned buildings were mountains of machinery and fine tolerance equipment, full of rust because it had been left uncovered in the snow. But at least the dining hall was in operation, we discovered. And our first meal was a delight. Two large Russian cutlets, made of 85 percent black bread and 15 percent meat, were put before us, along with potatoes, brown bread, tea, and sugar. For the next week we had cutlets and cucumbers every day for dinner, along with porridge without milk that set off groans of pleasure throughout the dining hall. That first meal in Kuybyshev was devoured in record time, amid a chorus of smacking lips. The meals were such a rare treat, that some thought nothing of licking their plates.

Our new so-called industrial complex had in reality been a center for training horses. These stables were turned overnight into living quarters. Rather than a fifteen- by seventeen-foot apartment in Moscow, each family now was given a small stall. Single people like me had to make do in the hallway until rooms could be found. I am sure that the horses formerly in those stables had enjoyed a far better quality of life than we did. The women's valiant effort to keep them clean was defeated by the sheer number of people and the lack of sanitary facilities. More than seventy people had to share one toilet and one washbasin. Before long the stables reeked of urine and excrement. Fortunately, the administration soon found living quarters for me in a two-room log house, inhabited by an elderly couple whom I came to call Uncle Misha and Aunt Olga.

Like most of the log houses in the provinces, this one was built with a huge brick oven in the larger of the two rooms. The oven had a flat cast-iron top, which was big enough to hold at least two mattresses. This was where Uncle Misha and Aunt Olga slept. Although the winter was the coldest I had yet experienced in my years in Russia, and the couple invited me to join them on top of the stove, I politely refused. I am sure they found it difficult to understand my decision. To a Russian, survival takes precedence over modesty.

It took us about two months to assemble the factory. Although it was a far cry from the one we had left behind in Moscow, it was operational. I worked the first shift, reporting in the dark at 7:00 A.M. I had to steel myself every morning before leaving the house. To walk out of a fairly warm house into the bitter, bitter cold—with winds that cracked the skin on your face and caused nosebleeds within fifteen minutes—was a daily act of courage.

One morning when it was at least twenty-two degrees below zero, I trudged to the plant along with hundreds of other workers, anxious only to get in out of the cold. As usual, we flashed our picture I.D. cards at the front gate. The guard made little real effort to check our passes, since he was no more anxious than we were to spend any unnecessary time out in the cold. I was past the gate and about twenty-five feet from the factory entrance when I heard someone shouting, "Stop that foreign spy! Stop that foreign spy!"

I stopped walking, wondering whom the guard was referring to. I looked over my shoulder to see him approaching me, his bayonet fixed and his finger on the rifle's trigger. I did not dare move a muscle, sensing that the guard was so jittery, one false move and he would plunge his bayonet into my back.

Two Russians who knew me from Moscow quickly came to my rescue. One of them shouted at the guard, "Stop! Do you know what you are about to do? I saw the comrade when he passed your station. He showed you his pass like everyone else, and you looked at it and said nothing. Then a moment later you suddenly turn into a madman!"

The other Muscovite added, "This comrade has been working in our factory for over ten years and he has always proved himself to be a reliable person. I'm going to report your action."

Turning to me, he said, "Go ahead Comrade Robinson. We are going to report this matter."

Most people in Kuybyshev had never seen a black person, which is what probably caused the guard's sudden suspicion. I had not known, and never again saw, the two men who came to my rescue, but they did as they said, because by the following day the guard had been replaced.

During the next two months, going to and from work in the midst of a severe winter gave me some idea of how the German army must have felt. Although I tried not to open my mouth while walking in the cold, the frigid air still penetrated my lungs and I winced with each breath. One day I was in such pain that I returned home and sat next to the oven. The next day I woke up shivering with fever. Every deep breath brought a sharp chest pain. Aunt Olga sent for a local doctor, but after two days of a steadily rising fever, a doctor still had not come. Aunt Olga then walked to the factory in the biting cold and reported that I was ill and urgently needed medical care. She returned in a car with a staff member from the plant. They helped me dress warmly, and we drove to a hospital in the center of the city. Two husky orderlies lifted me gently onto a stretcher and took me to a small waiting room. Soon a nurse came to assure me that the doctor would see me in a few minutes.

I could hear the coughing, hacking, and moaning of other patients in adjoining rooms as I waited. My condition was worsening steadily, and by now I was extremely weak and had lost any appetite for food. My fever remained high. The nurse returned and helped me up. She put her arm around my waist and carefully guided me down the hall to the doctor's office.

The doctor looked at me and demanded belligerently, ''What are you doing here? Where are you from?"

''From Moscow,'' I whispered weakly.

''No,'' he said, shaking his head in irritation. ''Before Moscow, where were you?''

''In America.''

''How did you get to Russia?''

''Through the Russian government,'' I answered. My exasperation had now overtaken my pain. I was again amazed at how consistently every Russian who is given even a little authority starts acting like a member of the NKVD.

Pointing to a stool, the doctor commanded, ''Sit down!''

I did as he said, and then he ordered me to stick out my tongue. He examined my tongue with the light from a small lamp, and said, ''Cough.''

I forced a cough, which hurt. The doctor turned off his lamp and said, ''Seriously, if you don't leave this place in another ten or twelve days you'll never be able to chase zebras again.''

Had I had the strength, I would have stormed out of his office.

''Zebras,'' I thought to myself. ''The only place I've ever seen a zebra is in a book.''

The doctor told me to take off my clothes because he was going to examine me further. The nurse, visibly shaken by the doctor's rudeness, helped me get my clothes off. Then he barked at me, ''Stand!''

He put his stethoscope to my chest and back. Then he placed

one hand on my back, tapped it with his other hand, and told me to cough. I did.

''Harder, harder,'' he said. I coughed again, and then he said, "Take off your shoes and cross one leg over the other." I did. Then he took a rubber hammer from his pocket and struck me so hard on my knee that I involuntarily kicked him under the chin.

His face turned as red as a lobster. "So you want to hurt me, eh," he said. "All right, put the other leg across the first one. He walloped me again, this time keeping his chin out of the way. Again, my reflexes were fine. He had me stand up, cough again, then told the nurse to take me to the next room to dress. As we walked toward the room, the nurse said to me in a soft voice, "He does not mean any harm. He simply likes to harass sick people."

On my way out, he had a letter ready, to the factory administration, saying that my survival depended on my leaving Kuybyshev for a warmer climate as soon as possible. He also prescribed some tablets to be taken several times a day.

When Uncle Misha and I returned home, Aunt Olga was not there, so we assumed she had gone out shopping. However, it was fifty-five degrees below zero, and waiting in line outside a store five miles away was too much for a woman her age to endure. We both worried for her, until finally she came through the front door, half-frozen and whimpering like a child. Her face was white as the snow. Her skin had split and the oozing blood had frozen onto her face. Misha helped her get her coat off and guided her to the oven. When the old woman, who was shivering and racked with pain, asked me how I was doing, I was able for the moment to forget my sickness, the cold outside, and the insulting doctor.

The following day the local doctor finally arrived. She told me that I had pleurisy in my left lung. There was also pus oozing out of my left ear. She agreed with the hospital physician that I must leave Kuybyshev as soon as possible. She also wrote a letter to the factory administration recommending that I be transferred to a warmer climate. Now armed with two letters, I felt confident that I could leave. However, I did not want to go to Tashkent or some other place in southeastern Russia. I wanted to return to Moscow so I could continue my engineering studies. The combination of the severe winter, plus a Russian counteroffensive in December, had relieved some of the pressure on Moscow. I expected the problem would not be the Germans so much as it would be convincing the authorities that I should go to Moscow, whose climate was no warmer than Kuybyshev's.

But after several days of Aunt Olga's tender care, my fever had lowered. I was eager to go to Kuybyshev's city hall to apply for a pass to Moscow. In Russia one could not move to a different city or village without government authorization. When I arrived at city hall, it looked like the site of a riot or a natural disaster. Thousands of people stood outside the building, many of them coughing, bundled up against the sub-zero cold, stomping their feet on the snow-covered pavement, and clapping their hands together, hoping to stimulate the blood flow in their shivering bodies. I simply had to get inside the building, which meant somehow circumventing the line of people stretching nearly two miles.

I decided I would use my out-of-date Moscow Soviet mandate. I knew it would be risky, but I just could not remain in Kuybyshev. I felt there was a good chance I would die having to live and work in the severe weather if I remained. I looked around for the least unfriendly-looking policeman I could find. If I chose wrong I could end up in a Kuybyshev jail, and with my illness, that would surely be the end of me. My heart began to race. I selected my target, rehearsed my introduction in my mind, and then plunged ahead.

"Good day, comrade," I said to the man, "please excuse me a moment." I took out my Moscow Soviet mandate, opened it to show my picture, under which were the words, "Member of the Moscow Soviet and Main Instructor, First State Ball Bearing Plant."

The policeman looked at it carefully, then stared at me for a moment. "Comrade," I added, "I have two letters from local doctors to the superintendent giving out departure passes. Could you be so kind as to let me have a few words with his secretary and give her the letters? I shall be most grateful to you if you can accommodate me."

Without hesitation the policeman answered, "Come along with me."

My spirits soared. When we reached the line he called out, "Let us pass. Let us pass."

A few minutes later I was standing in front of the secretary. I showed her my Moscow Soviet mandate, the two physicians' letters, and my engineering institute pass book and said, ''Please give all of this to the superintendent and ask him when I can see him.''

She asked me to wait a moment while she got up from her chair and went into her boss' office. She came out smiling, and said, ''He will see you after he finishes interviewing the comrade he is with.''

In a few moments the superintendent, looking tired and harassed, greeted me warmly and beckoned me to sit in a chair across from his desk. He quickly read the letters and checked my mandate, but spent several minutes looking over the grades on my institute pass. Finally he said, ''Excellent! How could you do it? Passing all of these difficult courses in the Russian language with such good marks. You must be a bright man. I congratulate you.''

Then he added, ''At first I wanted to send you to Tashkent, but I am going to send you back to Moscow so you can continue your professional studies. Now that the Germans are retreating, more than likely the institute will be reopening.''

''Yes, I understand it will be reopening in April,'' I said.

''Fine. If you could bring me two photos of yourself by this afternoon, I will issue you a pass to Moscow by 6:30 P.M.''

My elation was so great that I wanted to run all the way home. Although I was just recovering from pleurisy, I did not even notice the cold. I walked the six miles home, humming happily all the way. When I walked inside the log house and saw Aunt Olga lying on the stove, I broke into a wide smile. I could never become accustomed to that sight; it always struck me as looking so ridiculous.

I was in and out of the house in record time, greeting Aunt Olga hurriedly while getting the photos I needed from my trunk. I went back outside, and as I came near a street corner one of the infrequently appearing tram cars came around the corner, slowed down, and stopped. It was my lucky day. I hopped on and rode to city hall in warmth and comfort. When I reached my destination, I noticed the line was every bit as long as it had been in the morning. I grew worried, wondering if I would be able to find the policeman who had helped me earlier in the day. But then something strange happened. As I approached the end of the line, people began stepping aside, allowing me to proceed to the door of the building. Evidently they remembered me from the morning and thought I was a high-ranking person. Once inside the secretary took my pictures and told me that I did not have to wait, as she would give them to her boss. She said I should return by 6:00 P.M. to pick up my pass.

Getting back in later on was just as easy. Many of the same people who had been waiting since morning were still there, coughing and stomping the ground to keep warm. The superintendent handed me my pass and said, "I am hoping to hear some good news about your studies. I wish you all the success in the world. With this pass, go to the railway station at 8 A.M. tomorrow and ask the stationmaster what time the Moscow-bound train will arrive."

I thanked him for all of his help, and we shook hands and parted. By the time I arrived home I was nearing collapse. I had used up the extra energy that I had summoned to carry me through the day. My head felt hot and I began to shiver. I was burning up with fever. Aunt Olga took my temperature, which was 102°.

"Come," she said. "I have some hot *borscht*. Eat it and it will help you."

I was not really hungry but I dutifully sat down at the table. I began to sip and then started gulping down the soup. It seemed to help. My landlady smiled, and then ordered me to take an aspirin and drink some hot tea that she had poured from the samovar. In about a half-hour I felt revived. Then I told Uncle Misha and Aunt Olga what had happened. They were amazed.

"I still don't understand how were you able to reach the superintendent so quickly," said Aunt Olga.

I smiled and said, "It must have been the will of God."

"Do you realize," said Uncle Misha, "that I know people sicker than you who have waited months to get to the superintendent, and after they do, they usually come away empty-handed? There was one man who had two physicians' letters, suffered a heart attack in line, and was still denied a pass."

"You must have charmed the man out of his reason," said Aunt Olga, looking at me in admiration.

That night I did not sleep at all well. I was probably anxious about my departure for Moscow the next day. I awoke at 5:30 A.M. and got out of bed at 7:00 A.M. I took my temperature and found that it was still 102°. But a little fever was not going to keep me from finding the stationmaster. Aunt Olga prepared a nice breakfast, and then I gave her some money and asked her to prepare a fruit basket for me, for my trip.

When I reached the station and showed the stationmaster my pass, he said, "I have no idea when the next train to Moscow will be organized. Most of the trains are for army use these days. But one never knows."

He shrugged his shoulders and added, "The best thing to do is to come to my office each day at 8:30 A.M. and 2:00 P.M."

From the railway station I rushed to the factory. I also needed clearance from the administration before I could leave. I went straight to the factory director, Comrade Yousin, and explained my situation. I showed him the two letters from doctors and the pass from the city council superintendent, but he refused me permission to leave.

"You are needed here," he said. "I cannot let you go at this time."

I pleaded with him that if I stayed in Kuybyshev I would die, but he was unmoved.

As I walked toward the factory gates, the infection I had been fighting for days now flared up. Feverish again, I wondered how I could change Comrade Yousin's mind. Then I thought of the physician who had diagnosed my pleurisy. She was at a small clinic not far from where I was living, so I went there right away. When I arrived I was burning with fever, and then I had to wait an hour before she could see me. When she greeted me, she seemed tired and overworked. After I told her my problem, she asked me to wait in her office. A few minutes later she returned. She told me she had phoned Yousin, told him that I was seriously ill, and that if I died in Kuybyshev he would have to assume responsibility. She told him that if I were to die, she would report the entire episode to the city council.

I returned to the factory. Yousin's secretary rushed toward me and said, "Go to the chief accountant. He has your money. After that, go to the hiring office and pick up your discharge papers."

Hurray! The phone call had worked.

During the next two days I went to the railway station twice a day. Each time I heard the same thing: "No train to Moscow."

Then on the afternoon of the third day came the good news. A train would be leaving in three hours. He told me to report to the ticket office an hour before departure. I started running toward home.

Uncle Misha and Aunt Olga helped me gather my things. Olga reminded me that I would need a truck or a horse-drawn wagon to carry my huge trunk to the railway station. Such a critical point had somehow escaped my mind. I bolted out of the house and into the middle of the road. I flagged down several passing trucks but none of the drivers could help me. I ran to the factory garage where I was able to persuade a young driver to transport my belongings. The fact that I told him I was ill and had been discharged from the factory may have affected him, but it was more likely that the twenty rubles I offered him had been the deciding factor.

By the time I returned to the house, everything was packed. We lifted the trunk onto the truck. As I said good-by to the elderly couple who had been so much help, treating me like their son, Aunt Olga handed me two bags of food that she had prepared. Inside was a roasted chicken, a few slices of bread, two bottles of melted butter, several pounds of sugar, boiled carrots, and eight soft rolls.

At the station I got a porter to handle my trunk, but when we reached the ticket office we found a long line. I asked the porter to find the stationmaster. He did, and the first thing he did was scold me for being late. But then he entered the ticket office through the back entrance and got me my tickets. Now I had only thirty minutes before the train was scheduled to leave, so I jumped aboard to see where I had been placed. I put the heavier bag of food on a hook above my seat and then looked around to see if I could slide my trunk down the aisle to where I would be sitting.

Clearly, the trunk would be too wide, so I opened it into two halves on the station platform. In a matter of seconds this great event attracted a crowd of people, who began gawking at the suits and coats. Most of them had never even seen western-style clothes like mine before, not even in Moscow. Quite a commotion developed, with about a hundred people soon gathered around. With such a manpower pool, I asked the strongest-looking man in the crowd if he would help the porter and me move the trunk into the coach and over to my seat.

He said he would, and we got the trunk onto the hard wooden

seat that would be my living quarters for the trip to Moscow. The trunk took up three-fourths of the space and I squeezed into the small area that remained. It was February 15, 1942, and I was heading gratefully for my Russian home, six hundred miles away.

It felt good to be leaving Kuybyshev. Now that I was safely in my seat and with the train about to pull out of the station, I could relax a little bit. I decided I would eat one of Aunt Olga's rolls, and only then did I notice that the bag I had placed on the hook was gone. I checked the floor, the seat across from me, and stood up and asked the people around me if they had seen it. No one had. It was gone, stolen.

Fortunately I still had the other bag, with the roasted chicken and sliced black bread. As I bit into the chicken, the train began to move toward Moscow. We crept out of the railroad yard. We proceeded at a normal pace for about twenty miles, and then we slowed down and stopped. This process continued for the entire trip. At times we spent half a day without moving. I was told this was because of army railroad traffic. But we would also stop for another reason. Often, when we would approach a heavily wooded area in the daytime, the train would halt and the inspector would order us out to cut down trees. Without the wood for the locomotive's furnace, we would never have made it to Moscow. I appreciated these interludes, because the physical exercise and fresh air helped to clear my head and make me alert. Another break in the monotony and discomfort of sitting on a hard wooden seat was the inspector's periodic checking of luggage. Twelve times during the journey he (a member of the NKVD) inspected my trunk; each time he was intrigued and amazed to see what to him was my exotic apparel.

After two days I had to throw out the uneaten portion of my chicken because it was spoiling. I rationed myself to a slice of bread in the morning, one at noon, and one at dusk. From time to time I would join some of the other passengers at scheduled stops and buy a few hard-boiled eggs and cucumbers from peasants who had set up unofficial markets on the railway platforms.

One morning after scraping away some frost from the window, I saw a familiar sight. It was one of the commuter trains that took people to the center of Moscow. I figured we were probably thirty-five to forty miles out. We had left Kuybyshev two weeks ago.

"One or two more stops," I thought, "and I'll be back."

But suddenly a large man in an NKVD uniform stepped into our coach and announced, ''Everyone must leave this train at once. This is as far as it will go. To make connections to Moscow you must walk to the railway station and buy a commuter train ticket.''

All the passengers got out of their seats—except me. They put on their coats, locked their satchels, and hurried out of the train. I did not budge. I knew no one would be willing to help me carry my trunk a mile in the cold to the station.

Fifteen minutes later an inspector arrived. He was surprised to find me still in the coach. ''Don't you know you are supposed to get off the train?'' he asked.

''I know,'' I replied, ''but I can't abandon my trunk.''

''That is no business of mine,'' said the inspector. ''You must get off the train immediately because it is being dispatched to a different place.''

''I'm sorry, Comrade Inspector,'' I said, ''but I'm ready to go wherever the coach is destined to go.''

He shook his head in disgust and said, ''I'm coming back with the police. Perhaps they'll change your mind.''

An hour later three policemen walked into the coach and ordered me off the train.

''No!'' I said, in defiance. ''You can shoot me dead if you feel like it, but I will not walk out and leave my trunk.''

One of the police officers ordered, ''Show me what you have inside that thing.''

I opened it into two halves. They all hunched forward and studied the contents. ''Interesting,'' one of them said.

I knew they were fascinated. To win them over, I opened a few drawers and showed them socks, shirts, suits, even my hat. One of them pointed to the bottom of the trunk and asked, ''What is that?''

''That's my phonograph player,'' I said, lifting it out.

''Play some records,'' one of them asked.

The three policemen sat down as I placed a record on the turntable. They liked what they heard, swayed a bit to the dance music and even began tapping their feet on the floor.

"Please play another,'' they asked.

I obliged. But as soon as the music stopped, the leader of the group stood up and said, ''Comrade, I am sorry but you have one hour to leave this coach. If you don't, you will find yourself hundreds of miles from Moscow, perhaps in some isolated area of the country.''

I said nothing, and they left. I locked the trunk, sat down, and waited. I really could not leave the trunk. It was not so much the stylish clothes and a few precious, material belongings. The trunk held my most cherished memories. It was my last link to the past, and as a result, represented my hope for the future, that I would one day return to the United States.

I closed my eyes and prayed. I prayed for a long time. When I opened my eyes and looked at my watch I noticed that an hour had passed, yet the train had not moved. Quite awhile later I heard noises. The coach jerked, moved back a few yards, then lurched forward and back again. Suddenly the noise and movement stopped. I ran to the outside platform of the train and noticed that the rest of the train was gone. We were uncoupled. I returned to my seat, wondering how this drama would end.

I just sat and waited, and the hours passed by. Suddenly I heard noise outside, much like before. We were being hooked up to a locomotive. In a few minutes the train started moving. I sat down and closed my eyes again, praying that I would not end up in Siberia.

About forty-five minutes or an hour later, we stopped. I opened my eyes and scratched furiously at the frosted windows to see where we were. The coach door opened and two uniformed NKVD men stepped in. One of them said, ''Comrade, we are in Moscow.''

CHAPTER 16

Back in Moscow

ON MARCH 1, 1942, my trunk and I landed on the platform of the Moscow railway station. Two husky policemen lent a hand getting the trunk off the train, and a friend whom I called from the station came a half-hour later with a truck. But when we reached my apartment I was in for a surprise. My key wouldn't open the lock, and then someone inside called out, "Who is that?"

"I am Robert Robinson," I said, "and this is my apartment. I lived here before I was evacuated and now I'm back. In fact, I paid six months rent in advance and I've only been gone for four months."

"My husband was given this apartment two months ago," she replied.

I knew I was not going to get into my apartment that day, that I would have to take my problem to some authority like my trade union. But I had to find a place to store my luggage.

"Could I leave my trunk here until tomorrow?" I asked.

"No!" she said emphatically.

I found a neighbor downstairs who agreed to look after my trunk for a few days. I headed over to the factory. As I entered the building I saw Gromov coming toward me. He had stayed behind to coordinate the evacuation of the plant. I greeted him warmly, but he responded with characteristic harshness: "How did you get here? You didn't run away, I hope?"

He was still carrying a grudge. It seemed as if the man would never forgive me. I took my papers from my coat pocket and said, "I was authorized to come back to Moscow. These papers make everything official."

Gromov examined the papers, and as he handed them back to me I said, "I have no place to stay. A family moved into my apartment even though I had paid for it in advance. I can't understand why that would happen when there are sixty empty apartments in our compound."

Gromov looked at me coldly and said, "You go to the house commandant and tell him I sent you to spend the night in his office. You can sleep in the club chair."

As it turned out, a friend heard of my plight and insisted that I stay in his one-story log house until things got sorted out. He had two tiny rooms which he shared with his mother and father, his sister, and her child. The next morning my friend's mother roasted some nuts and brewed some tea for breakfast, which she served without sugar. After the meal I rushed off to the factory to get my bread card, which entitled me to my daily ration of six hundred grams (21.1 ounces) of black bread a day. When I went to the store for bread, I was shocked to see that the only other food available was potatoes, and that a sack cost nine hundred rubles, the equivalent of $180. At the time I was making eleven hundred rubles a month. So for the next few days I lived only on black bread, eating half of it in the morning, the rest for my evening meal.

Every day for a week I called on the people in my apartment, urging them to move somewhere else in the compound. Finally my pestering paid off. Ten days later they moved, though unfortunately, they took some of my belongings with them. I was so happy to have my room that I did not make an issue of their larceny.

I was soon to learn that food shortages, which before the war were frequent enough, were now acute. During 1942, I was hungry all the time. Obtaining food dominated my thoughts. When I would hear even a rumor that food other than bread and potatoes was being sold at the market, I would stop whatever I was doing at home and run to get something. One morning on my day off from work I learned that milk was available for sale. I found an empty bottle and raced to the market. I noticed a policeman as I entered the store, though I did not pay any attention to him. As I reached the line in front of the milk counter I felt someone tapping me on the shoulder.

"Let me see your documents," the policeman demanded.

"Why should I show you my documents?" I said. "I haven't done anything wrong."

The man turned over the lapel of his coat. He was an NKVD agent. I said, "I'm sorry, comrade, but I don't have any documents with me. I live close by, and all I did was run from my room to purchase some milk, which I haven't had for months."

"You are coming with me to the police station," he said.

A few minutes later I was standing before the station superintendent, listening to the NKVD agent explain why he had arrested me. It was clear from his reaction that the superintendent had never seen a black man before. He asked me why I did not have my documents. When I told him that I simply did not think I needed them to go to the neighborhood market to buy some milk, I sensed that he doubted whether I even had Soviet credentials.

He demanded to know, "What are you doing in Moscow?"

"I've been living and working here for eleven years," I said.

The superintendent hunched forward, looked me straight in the eye, and said, "Tell me where you are working."

"At the First State Ball Bearing Plant," I replied.

He picked up his phone and started dialing. He asked whoever answered the phone if they had a Negro worker in the factory. I felt a little apprehensive, since I had only been back a short time and perhaps the administrative staff had not processed my papers yet. I hoped that no one told him I was supposed to be in Kuybyshev.

Apparently the person at the factory said that, yes, a Negro was there, because the superintendent looked over at me and asked how long I had worked at the factory and if I had ever broken the law. After I answered his questions he spoke more loudly to the person on the phone, so that I would also hear.

"I advise you to impress upon Comrade Robinson the necessity of possessing documents at all times," he said. "He thinks he is still in a bourgeois society. This is the Soviet Union and he, as everyone else, must carry his identification papers with him. That is why he has been arrested. The next time he is caught without his documents he will be heavily fined."

I took his lecture to heart, and from that time on always made sure I had my picture I.D. work pass with me, even when visiting a neighbor in my apartment building.

Back at the factory, I was re-assigned to resume my job teaching apprentices in toolmaking. The timing of my return had been excellent, because not only did I soon witness the first signs of spring, but also, in light of the retreat of the German army, the Central Government ordered that half of the First State Ball Bearing plant be returned to Moscow.

Because our shop needed to be restored, it was a month before I could begin teaching again. Most of the machines were rusty from exposure to snow and rain in Kuybyshev. Some were inoperable and had to be rebuilt. It was a physically demanding job, with a good deal of lifting of heavy machinery in an unheated shop. With food so scarce, we were only given one meal a day during our twelve-hour shifts at the factory. It consisted of seven or eight cabbage leaves in lukewarm water, less than an ounce of meat that had been boiled in the soup, two spoonfuls of mashed potatoes, a dab of melted butter, and our allotment of five grams (0.175 ounces) of black bread.

Once production started, and our diet remained the same, some workers complained that they needed more food. They were reminded of the sacrifices of the soldiers on the front. Despite the heroic efforts of the workers, conditions began to overwhelm them. I saw men with fingers and feet swollen from the frost, standing at their machines crying in pain. Some fainted from hunger and exhaustion. I knew of two workers who dropped dead in their shops within a two-week period.

Only when production began to lag did the foremen petition for an increase in food rations. A week after the plant director appealed directly to the Soviet Council of Ministers, the dining hall began dishing out four spoonfuls of mashed potatoes instead of two. The mood of those who received the extra food improved, along with their productivity. However, there were a few hundred of us who were not eligible for the ration increase. When we asked, we were turned down without explanation. But we all knew what we had in common: none of us was a party member.

As time went on, I grew weaker and weaker. I had never in my life felt so undernourished. My usual zest for life was gone. The machine shop, which I usually delighted in as a child would a playground, was now a place of torture where I dreaded going. I started watching the clock, waiting for the day to end. I developed headaches, felt listless, and experienced dizzy spells. I could think of nothing except food.

In the machine shop, men and women toiling at their machines grew too weak to control their bladders. People would often suddenly dart over to the toilet. They would usually find a line, and then either quickly try to find a corner where they could urinate, or just let it flow in their pants. It was common to see people simply urinate where they were working. No one, not even the foremen, made an issue of it. One could see the same kind of scene in the city, with people urinating in the street.

In the midst of this near-famine, the factory set up new restaurants open only to the elite: directors and their assistants, engineers, party officials, shop superintendents, and a select group of foremen and special guests were able to eat well. Though the workers were angered, they did not have enough energy to protest. My food situation, which was already perilous, got very much worse when the administration put a new eating arrangement into effect. For some reason dining halls were established adjacent to each shop, instead of having everyone eat in the one, large dining area. These dining halls became jungles, where the weak had trouble surviving.

To start with, the food was now prepared close to where we were working. The aroma teased us all morning. By lunchtime we were like an aroused pack of wild animals. Some of the workers would stop their machines fifteen minutes early and stake out a position in front of the lunchroom door. There was no regular line, but instead a mob formed. Everyone was taut, ready to spring into the hall. The moment the doors were flung open, people went dashing headlong toward the food, shoving, pushing, and cursing. They ran like desperate animals, trampling over others who had fallen.

I could not join the mob for two reasons: I did not have the energy, and I found the scene revolting. So I did without lunch. At noontime I remained at my desk and ate some black bread with a dash of salt on it.

I sensed my life ebbing. I had heat in the factory but none in my room and very little food. A week after the new meal arrangement had started, I met Gromov's secretary in the corridor outside my shop. She knew me well and I sensed she liked me. As we greeted each other she looked concerned and asked, "Comrade Robinson, why are you so thin? Are you sick?"

"For the past few weeks I have had a headache," I said. She suggested I go to the clinic, but I told her that I needed more than aspirin.

"What is it that you need?" she asked.

"More food," I said.

"But what about the new meal plan?" she asked. "You should be getting more from that."

"I don't have the strength to compete with the other workers," I said. "At noontime the shop turns into a madhouse, with everybody fighting to get to the food first."

The woman felt sympathetic and said, "Comrade Robinson, come to my office after work. Ordinarily Gromov refuses to see workers at night, but I'll try to get you an audience with him. Ask him to allow you to take home the amount of food from the restaurant that your card entitles you to. I'm sure he'll agree to such an arrangement."

Fortunately I did not have classes that night, so after work I ate a few slices of bread, drank some water, and walked to Gromov's office. The secretary smiled, pointed to his door, and told me to go right in. I knocked on the door, paused a few seconds, and then opened it.

"Good evening, Comrade Gromov," I said. He was at his desk reading some papers.

Without lifting his head or acknowledging my greeting, Gromov asked, "What do you want?"

I never thought I would be reduced to begging, especially not before a conniver and opportunist like Gromov, whom I strongly disliked. But my instinct to survive prevailed.

"Comrade Gromov," I said, "I have come to ask you for approval to take home my allotted food from the restaurant because I cannot sustain the pressure of fighting for position at mealtime. Please grant me this favor."

"No, I can't do that," he answered, without raising his head from the report.

The hungry part of me that was devoid of honor and pride wanted to plead with Gromov. But my sense of dignity was stronger, and it won out.

"Good-by," I said, leaving immediately. He never answered me. Knowing Gromov, he would have granted my request if I had groveled at his feet.

CHAPTER 17

On the Verge of Death

THE WINTER OF 1942-43 was extremely severe. It was a wonder that I survived. I welcomed the coming of warmer weather in the spring of 1943. I do not think I could have survived even one more month of freezing temperatures. I felt weak all the time. My chest felt fine, so I did not believe that pleurisy had returned, but at times, walking up even one flight of stairs took a major effort and left me exhausted.

One morning I woke up and had no energy at all. In desperation I went to the factory clinic. A doctor diagnosed my problem as having too much sugar in my blood and put me on an insulin injection program. The insulin helped, but soon the clinic ran out of its supply of the drug. The physician then wrote me out a prescription for insulin, which I could use at a drugstore, but after trying more than a dozen pharmacies I gave up. They all said that they were out of insulin, that it was not being manufactured during the war, and therefore they did not expect to receive anymore.

A little while later I happened to meet a man with diabetes who had worked at the plant before the war. He told me that because of his problem, he had been able to obtain extra food. Following his advice, I went to the clinic doctor and had her verify in writing that I had a high percentage of sugar in my blood. I took the letter to a public health center where I filled out an application for an extra ration card. I was told it would be processed in about two weeks.

After two weeks passed and I had not received notification, I decided to fill out a new application. It was not that I expected the unwieldy Soviet bureaucracy to respond that quickly. Instead, I thought it would be wise to assume that my first application was lost. And because I was still plagued by a lack of energy, I returned to the clinic for another checkup. There I was treated by a new doctor, a woman in her late thirties or early forties.

While washing her hands before examining me, Dr. Seplayeva asked me to take off my shirt and undershirt. After drying her hands, she turned around to look at me and exclaimed, "Oh my God!"

She then turned away from me and went behind a screen, where she stayed for several minutes.

At first I wondered whether she was shocked at seeing my blackness. But that seemed unlikely, since she had not flinched when she greeted me. When she came out from behind the screen I could tell that she had been crying. She had tears in her eyes as she checked my heart and lungs with a stethoscope.

She ran her fingers over my every rib, shaking her head in disbelief. I knew I had lost weight, but not until her reaction did I realize that I looked like a living skeleton. I could not remember the last time I had been on a scale or looked at myself naked in a full-length mirror. When you are hungry you do not think about such things.

After the examination she went to her desk and wrote out a prescription. "You are very, very undernourished," she said with alarm. "Something must be done about it right away. Are you getting the full food ration you are entitled to?" she asked.

I told her about my plight and also explained my application for an extra food ration.

"Have you heard from the organization?" she asked.

"Not yet," I said, hoping that she would volunteer to prod the agency on my behalf.

"Whether you hear from them or not," she said, "I want you to see me in three days between 3:00 and 3:30."

When I returned for my appointment, the first thing she asked me was whether I had received my extra ration card. When I told her I had not, she said, "Comrade Robinson, my husband and I have discussed your situation and we would like you to join us for dinner on Sundays."

I did not know what to say. Had I told her of my feelings at the moment, I would have wept. I was unused to such kindness. I am sure she noticed the tears in my eyes, because after looking into them she bowed her head.

The following Sunday I approached Dr. Seplayeva's old one-story log house. I was surprised at how decrepit and uninviting it was from the outside. I knocked on the door and a teen-age girl answered the door.

"Comrade Robinson, of course. Please come in."

The first thing I noticed as I entered was the ubiquitous picture of Lenin sitting on a bench with Stalin standing beside him.

"Please have a seat and feel at home," the girl told me as she left the room. I surveyed the small room with interest. It was no more than twelve feet by fourteen. The walls and ceiling were whitewashed, and the walls were covered with Russian landscapes, paintings of birds, and family pictures. Half of one wall had four hanging shelves, three containing books and the fourth holding an assortment of Russian artifacts. The upholstered chairs, once fashionable, showed signs of age, as did a worn, rose-colored sofa bed. The style of furniture and general decor were typical of the class of artists and intellectuals who were now living incognito.

Dr. Seplayeva walked into the room and said, "Comrade Robinson, greetings! I am happy that you have come as promised."

Her radiant smile warmed me as I rose to greet her.

"I am glad to see you too," I said. "I assume the young lady who let me in is your daughter. She looks so much like you."

"Yes, she is. Please excuse her for leaving you all alone. She is very shy," said my hostess. "Your coming gives me and my family great pleasure. It has been such a long time since we had a guest."

"Now, please meet my husband, Boris Vasilevich," she said, as he entered the room. Then the daughter, Ella, came in, and Dr. Seplayeva asked to be excused as Boris and I sat down on the couch.

"Comrade Robinson," he said, "my wife told me you have been in the Soviet Union for a few years. I suppose when you first arrived in our country you must have experienced some difficulties adjusting to our way of life?"

"Yes, you are right," I replied.

He asked how I was faring now, to which I answered, "Well, I don't have much time now to think about myself because of the war. But I really can't complain."

We were then called to dinner, which was in a five- by six-foot room barely large enough for the four of us to sit around the table. I admired the spread of food on the table; there was such a variety, none of it available in the Moscow stores, which were only selling black bread and mustard. They must have gone by commuter train twenty or so miles outside the city and bartered for the food on the black market. The country folks who ran the markets would not accept paper currency or coin, which was worthless because there was nothing in the stores to buy with it. You would have to barter with old clothing, old shoes, watches, clocks, and the like. One of my neighbors had traded in an old sewing machine for two large bags of potatoes and a sack of cabbage. Adding up the cost in terms of time, expense, and fatigue, one can get an idea of what my hosts went through in their effort to save my life.

As we ate the delicious meal, Dr. Seplayeva responded to my questions about her background. She explained that she had been born in Leningrad but had moved to Moscow in 1921.

"Up to the age of fifteen I was interested in the arts such as music, painting, and dancing," she said. "But by the time I was ready to enter college, most of my girlfriends and I decided to study medicine, thinking that an artist's life was too precarious."

She rose from the table and came back with a deep dish of thinly sliced potatoes which she announced had been fried in sunflower oil. After tasting the most delicious potato dish I had eaten in years, I asked her, "Tell me, please, have you kept in touch with your girlfriends since graduation?"

"Yes," she said, "there was a group of three of us, all doctors, who met at a nationwide conference eight years ago in Kiev. It was all so unexpected."

"Since you were all such good friends from high school days, I suppose the reunion was most happy and rewarding," I said.

"Well, when we first met on the opening day, I was very excited," she said. "But near the end of the three-day conference I was very affected by the way in which fate had dealt with each of us."

Dr. Seplayeva paused a moment, and then told me the story of her two friends, and herself. "After graduation each of us was assigned to work in a remote village hospital for two years. Following this assignment, anyone who had lived in Moscow previously was only allowed to return if she had adequate living space available, which was written into one's passport. Or, if you had a close relative with at least a six- by six-foot-square room who was willing to share it, then the police would allow you to live and work in Moscow.

"I was the luckiest of the three. Because my parents were living here, I returned home after completing my assignment at the village hospital in Sverdlovsky district, in Siberia. I soon married, and two years later had my daughter, Ella.

"The other two met a different fate. Olga was sent to a district hospital in Irkutsk, where she wrote me that life was monotonous and lonely. However, a year later she wrote again to tell me that she had met a nice young engineer and was deeply in love. They married six months later. Unfortunately, after an eight-year marriage and three children, her husband was killed in a car accident. She could not return to Moscow then because her parents' apartment was too small to accommodate her and the three children.

"Then there was Nadya. After graduation she was sent to a tiny village a hundred miles from the port city of Mogadan, near Japan. She did not return to Moscow after her assignment because she had married a local man there. When we met at the convention I could not believe my eyes. Her hair had turned completely grey, and although she was only thirty-five she looked more like fifty, and was wearing shabby clothes. Her story was very sad, indeed.

"The other nurses in the village hospital resented her because she had theoretical training and a doctor's degree. But what weighed on her the most was the isolation and loneliness. Here was a woman from Moscow who now found herself transported to a village of whitewashed log houses and a small church that was used as the district courthouse. The few volumes in the library were mainly for teenagers and the one cinema showed old, dated films and then only once a week. When it rained, the mud was knee deep. Because she was viewed as an outsider, she had difficulty making friends. She told me that at times she did not think she could go on.

"So when a prince charming appeared, in the person of the new calisthenics instructor, he won her heart. Although he was twenty years older than she, when he asked her to marry him, she said yes. Only after the marriage did she learn that he was a violent drunkard. He abused both her and the children, verbally and physically.

"Her husband Gregory's death after seven years ended a disastrous marriage. But there she was, a widow with four children and nowhere to go. Even if they could have, her parents would not help her move to Moscow because they had yet to forgive her for marrying without their approval. Even had they wanted to take her in, their apartment was too small to accommodate five more people.

"After Nadya told me her sorrowful tale on the last evening of the conference, I could hardly bear to look at her. Before my train left for Moscow we embraced and shed tears of joy at seeing one another again, and grief for the losses in our lives. That night as the train sped me home to Moscow I wept alone in my bunk for a long time.

"When I woke up the next morning my thoughts were still of Nadya. I wondered why fate had inflicted such tragedy upon her. But I also realized that her life was not yet lost or over. She had undoubtedly gained a special knowledge of life, and probably without her thinking much about it, she was using her medical skill to reduce the suffering in the village."

At this point, fighting back tears, Dr. Seplayeva excused herself. Not long after, Ella left the table as well. Boris then asked me how I thought the war would turn out.

"I have no doubt," I told him, "now that the Germans have lost the initiative, they will lose the war."

"No, that's not what I meant," he said. "I am not worried anymore about the Germans, but I am greatly disturbed that the West has not opened up a second front. I am beginning to think that they will leave us to fight the Germans alone, in order to leave us weakened and exhausted at the end. Then they could easily dictate terms to us."

"Excuse me, Boris Vasilevich," I replied. "I don't think this is the intention of the West. You must not forget the difficulties they face in having to invade the European mainland. They must have a well-coordinated, carefully laid out plan. The German army has fortified the entire shore on the French side of the channel."

"Yes, I understand," he responded, "but why must they take

so long?'' They promised an invasion in carly spring of 1942. Now it is the end of the summer of 1943. This means we will not get any help until next summer.''

Before I could respond, Dr. Seplayeva entered the tiny dining room and lamented, ''Oh this tragic war! Indeed we have experienced the most painful, difficult, and devastating period in our history. To be honest with you, until recently I was afraid that the Germans might win. Now I can say that they are being slowly pushed back, due to a great extent to the moral and material support we have been receiving from the United States. We don't feel alone now, like we did on October 15, 1941, when the German army was about forty-three miles from Moscow.

''Although many of my colleagues dispute the efficacy of America's aid to our cause,'' she continued, ''I believe that without American tanks, planes, locomotives, jeeps, heavy trucks, and other war material, we could not have withstood the awesome pressure of the German army. We would have lost Moscow. Believe me, there's not a family in this city of seven million people that hasn't eaten America's canned goods, thick slices of lard, and condensed milk. Without this support, who can say how long we could have survived on seven hundred grams of black bread a day since June 22, 1941.''

''Tell me, Doctor, in your opinion, what should be done to prevent another war like this?'' I asked.

''We must never again trust the Germans, treaty or no treaty,'' she said. They have destroyed our industries, ruined many of our cities, and killed hundreds of thousand of innocent women, children, and old people. I find it hard to believe that these barbarous invaders share a common heritage with the likes of Schiller, Bach, Goethe, Beethoven, Kant, Strauss, and other German geniuses.''

After a brief pause she concluded, ''I'm hoping that after the German army is defeated, all our allies will join with us to form a union that would prevent them from ever attacking and plundering us again. Don't you think such a plan would help us all?''

''Yes, I agree with you completely,'' I said. ''Such a plan is absolutely necessary.''

I continued having Sunday dinner with the Seplayevas, and greatly looked forward to their affection, conversation, and food. What a contrast from the noontime madness at the factory. Every meal I was served by these generous people was a feast. I rediscovered real beef cutlets, *borscht,* Russian-style fried potatoes, rice, and gelatin.

About four weeks after my first visit, my extra food ration card came, eight weeks after I had applied. What a victory this was, regardless of how long it took. I could now receive sixty eggs a month and an extra pound of butter. I felt certain that Dr. Seplayeva had prodded the agency on my behalf.

I had to go to central Moscow to pick up the extra food, about an hour and twenty minute trip by public transportion from the factory. I was told to come between the 10th and 25th of each month, and always to phone ahead of time to be sure that what I wanted was available. The day my card came, I asked for and received permission from the factory to go for my extra rations. I discovered the store in an ancient, terribly rundown one-story wooden building. Outside about 150 people were lined up. Though I felt certain that the store would close before my turn came, the day was sunny and pleasant, and I figured that spending five-and-a-half hours outside was better than going back to a stuffy shop.

To my surprise, my turn came and I was served after only a four-hour wait. I left the store at 6:40 P.M. and got home an hour and forty minutes later. Here I was, with the kind of food that had not graced my room for more than two years. But I was too tired and weak to cook a meal. Instead I took out the butter, spread it thickly over chunks of black bread, added some salt, and devoured it.

The next day I shared my good fortune with Dr. Seplayeva and thanked her for everything she had done for me. When I told her that because of my allotment of food I could not in good conscience continue having dinner with her, her face turned red.

"That is absurd," she said. "We want you to continue coming over on Sundays. Besides, we enjoy your company."

She smiled and added, "If you don't come, my husband will come and get you."

Eating two eggs a day, and bread and butter, helped to restore my strength. But the eggs lasted only twenty-one days. Eighteen of them spoiled, and on the twenty-fourth day the butter had become rancid. I did not know anyone who had a refrigerator. During the summer months I kept the butter and eggs in bowls of cool water to stave off spoilage.

Unfortunately, when winter came I could no longer pick up my extra food. Standing four or five hours in the cold would have killed me. At first I tried having some of my fellow workers collect the food, but I soon learned this was a foolhardy idea. The first person came back with only five eggs, claiming the others had broken when she fell. She said the butter was crushed in the fall also, and she had to throw it away. The second person I tried never brought me a thing. The first day she claimed she had left the packages at home. The next day she said her friend had taken most of the food and she was too embarrassed to bring me the pitifully few things that remained. Both people promised to return the money I had given them to purchase the food, but I never received back even a kopek.

One day in September 1943, someone brought the news that packages that had come from the United States were in the factory store. He said they were filled with condensed milk, sausages, lard, and Roosevelt's eggs. We all ran as fast as we could to the store, which was across the street from the factory. We found a crowd of workers already there, jockeying for position. A clerk said that the food was inside, but that none of it would be sold until the first shift ended. We all went back disappointed. For the rest of the day we kept our eyes glued to the clock and, I'm sure, wondered what in the world was meant by "Roosevelt's eggs."

After work I headed for the store, along with other workers from my shop. There was a large crowd, and three policemen there to keep order, but everything was strangely well-organized. All one had to do was enter the shore, show the policeman an I.D., then go to the cashier and pay the eight rubles and fifty kopeks. Next, one went to a counter and was handed the items already wrapped in a package. While I was in the store I heard several people ask what was meant by "Roosevelt's eggs." The woman dispensing the packages merely replied:, "Comrade, in every package there is written what is meant and how to prepare it. When you get home everything will become clear to you."

When I got home and opened the package, I found condensed milk, a small bag of powdered eggs, and five long, thin sausages. Directions for preparing the powdered eggs were written in Russian; when cooked they looked like normal, scrambled eggs. The next day those people who had been fortunate enough to obtain a package were talking about the eggs. Some liked them a lot, others were indifferent, but everyone ate them. The reason they were called "Roosevelt's eggs" was because the Soviet people had developed a warm feeling in their hearts for the American president, and they had a sense that he was personally concerned for their welfare.

However, the eggs carried with them a uniquely Russian joke. In the Russian language, the word for "eggs" and for "testicles" is the same, pronounced "ya-it-sa." The Russians enjoyed pretending that the powdered eggs had been ground up from Roosevelt's testicles. They delighted in saying, "Hey, Misha, you know what? The devil take it. I just had a nice dinner from Roosevelt's ya-it-sa with black bread."

Food was not the only thing America sent the Russians. There were rumors in the factory that large amounts of clothing—especially shoes, coats, and ladies garments—were arriving regularly. Although I never saw an ordinary worker wearing American-made clothes, it was common to see a shop superintendent or other members of the Soviet elite attired in smartly-tailored overcoats and wearing well-crafted shoes that didn't squeak.

Though the war years were without question difficult, they were less threatening than the purge years before and after. At least when the air raid sirens wailed you could run to the nearest underground shelter. But when the NKVD knocked on your door in the middle of the night, there was no place to run. The purges stopped during the war. Sins real or imagined committed against the government were forgiven more readily, because everybody was needed to support the war effort. Though the Germans were retreating, hardships in Moscow were far from over.

CHAPTER 18

The Remaining War Years

GERMAN PLANES WERE STILL POUNDING Moscow with bombs. Often when I was walking home after my engineering classes, shells from incendiary bombs would fall all around me. There were times when they dropped in such rapid succession that I would stand and up and just wait for the next one to fall on my head. At first I ran for protection—into alleys or doorways or around corners. But after awhile I could see that no place was any safer than another. Houses were crumbling everywhere.

Besides, waiting in a Moscow street in late autumn or winter for a bombing raid to end was risky business; there was always the possibility of freezing to death. After a few weeks I simply ignored the bombs and continued walking all the way home, praying all the while. But avoiding the rain of Nazi bombs was not the only problem I faced. There was a wartime curfew of 9:00 P.M., but my classes did not end until 9:45 P.M. As a result, policemen arrested me fourteen times, hauling me into the nearest station where I underwent the same routine. While the arresting officer would report to his superior, I was made to wait with thieves, molesters, assorted perverts, and the other curfew breakers.

Standing before the night supervising officer always humiliated me. Without fail the officer would stare at me as if I were some strange animal who most likely had just escaped from a zoo. The police would take down my name, my place of work, and then call the plant to verify my story. Then when the police learned of my record of service—and the awards and commendations I had received—they would congratulate me, sometimes even shaking my hand. They would then warn me not to break curfew again. One officer told me, "You see, Comrade Robinson, we haven't got many of your people here, hence you create a false impression at night since it is so dark. I'm sorry but I'm sure you understand. I have been given a very good report about you. I never knew that we had such highly skilled persons like you helping us to beat the Nazis. But I can't let you go now because you will meet the same trouble again before reaching home. You had better sit on that chair in the corner until 5:30 A.M., and then you may go."

One night during the winter of 1943-44, the thermometer registered 3°F when I entered the engineering college, but by the time classes were over the temperature had dropped to –18°F. Public transportation stopped running at 9:00 P.M. because of the curfew, so I always faced a six-mile walk home. When I stepped out of the building, the wind was razor sharp. I wrapped my woolen scarf around my head and placed my woolen cap on top, then wrapped the ends of the scarf around my neck, buttoned up, and raised my collar up around my ears and face. Only my eyes and nose were left exposed to the bitter cold. Usually when it was this cold I would run home, but this evening the snow had turned to ice and it was slippery and dangerous.

By the time I had walked about five miles I could feel my hands getting cold. I placed my briefcase under my arm and put my hands inside my overcoat. I kept walking as fast as I could, all the time trying to keep my balance. When I reached the door of my apartment I pulled out my hands, but there was absolutely no feeling in them. I kicked the door with my foot. The neighbors inside demanded, "Who is it?"

"Open the door, please," I shouted. "It is Robinson. Quick, let me in."

When one of my neighbors opened the door and saw me rubbing my hands, he guessed what had happened. He pulled my gloves off and, without saying a word, led me into the kitchen. He put both of my hands under the cold water, and rubbed them vigorously for a half-hour. Gradually the feeling began to return. Tremendous pain started shooting through my palms; I was in agony. My hands, which had been green, slowly became red again. At this point my neighbor said, "We've done it! You're lucky! Your hands are saved!"

Until the Germans surrendered, my routine was such that I rarely got enough sleep, between working as much overtime as possible, attending classes, studying at home, and trying to find enough to eat. After my six-mile walk—or run—home from classes, it would be 10:30 or 11:00 P.M. I would then study for two hours or more before going to sleep. To get to work on time I had to leave my room by 5:30 A.M., so there were times when I would only sleep for an hour or two. In the winter months my room would be so cold that I would usually sleep fully clothed. I would also place a basin of water on the gas stove to generate some warmth and moisture in the room. I would sleep for no more than an hour at a time, afraid that I might either freeze to death or be asphyxiated by the gas.

Many nights I would go to the heat treatment department of the plant to stay warm. I had learned that many factory workers went there to sleep. When I first decided to try it out, I found the department crowded with people, between those who went there seeking warmth and others who worked the night shift and were taking a break near the furnaces to keep warm. Some people brought potatoes from their private gardens and baked them in the ovens. They would break them in half and sprinkle salt over them, then eat them with warm slices of black bread and a fresh cucumber. Such a meal was a real treat.

Having discovered the heat treatment department, I would go there often during the day, to warm my hands and feet. One time I ventured too close to the furnace and my overcoat caught on fire. The workers quickly threw sand on me and put the fire out, but I was left with a three-inch hole in the front of my coat, making it almost useless for keeping out the extreme winter cold. Still, I had nothing else to wear for the next four-and-a-half months because it took the tool shop Trade Unions Committee three months to get me an order to go to the tailoring shop and have a new overcoat made, and then it took the tailor six weeks to finish the job. After awhile I decided to study and do my homework in the heat department, not only for the warmth but also because it was better lit. From mid-1942 houses were supplied with only 40-watt bulbs, which made it difficult to study for long periods of time without damaging one's eyesight.

Many times during the war the superintendent asked me to come back to work after my evening classes and help on some project. One was paid for overtime work—beyond twelve hours—and entitled to supplementary ration coupons as well, worth two hundred grams (seven ounces) of black bread, twenty-five grams (.088 ounces) of meat, a boiled potato, and five grams (0.175 ounces) of butter or vegetable oil. However, for all the overtime work I put in, I never received either form of compensation. I never asked for what was owed me, because I knew that would be a sure way to create resentment against me. Even though I had a Soviet passport, I would always be a foreigner. I had always to consider my actions carefully. I could readily imagine the banner headline in the factory newspaper: "Robinson refuses to help. Demands double pay and ration coupons." One such headline would be reason enough for the authorities to send me to the front or to a labor camp. Such injustices occurred regularly; why should I be exempt?

In the spring of 1944 the Council of Ministers ordered the factory to operate twenty-four hours a day to produce chisels for pneumatic hammers. These hammers were to be used in the bituminous coal basin near Moscow. All available machines were put to use grinding the upper parts of the chisels. The superintendent asked me to return after classes to grind more chisels, and I of course agreed. This meant that I was now working eleven hours, from early morning to nearly 6:00 P.M., after which I would run to catch the streetcar, and then transfer to another one, to get to my 6:50 class. When classes ended at 9:45 P.M. I would walk the six miles back to the factory, in the dark, and then begin work on a pile of forged chisels until 4:30 in the morning when I would be ready to drop. Then I would go to the heat treatment plant and nap for an hour, get up, eat the seven ounces of black bread I carried in my pocket, go wash my face, and then go back to work. Although I worked overtime grinding chisels from the beginning of March 1944, until the end of April 1945, only once did I receive an additional meal coupon, which I gave to a neighbor who, I felt, needed it more than I did. Unlike other workers, I never received a kopek for my labors.

Finally the curfew was lifted in 1944, and with the coming of spring, getting to and from classes was no longer a barely endurable ordeal. On a warm, sunny June day in 1944 I was riding the tram to the engineering institute with my friend Libshitz. We were both in our final course before taking the mechanical engineering qualifying examination. The tram was moving slowly, and my friend and I decided we had better jump off and hurry to class on foot.

We jumped off in the midst of heavy traffic and sped across a wide road, against a light that had just turned red. There was a policeman there directing traffic, but we did not think he had noticed us. As we hurried off to get to class on time, we heard a police whistle, but did not think it was intended for us. Then about a block from the college we saw two men dashing across the street toward us. We stopped, and they pounced on us. Alarmed, we demanded, "What do you think you're doing?"

One of them motioned with his head and said, "There's a policeman coming after you."

In the Soviet Union you are obligated by law to try to help a policeman if he is chasing someone. Failure to do so could result in a severe fine or a few days in jail. For this reason, the two men held us tightly until the policeman ran up, out of breath, and said to us, "Citizens, be kind enough to show me your documents."

Immediately I was gripped by fear. I was not certain that I had my documents. I felt my pants pocket and they were not there. Although I now knew that I had left them at home, I searched my briefcase for the benefit of the policeman. Libshitz was in the same predicament.

"After all the trouble I went through earlier for not carrying my documents, here I am, caught without them again," I thought. "How stupid."

The policeman told us, "Without your documents you are illegally walking the streets. For that, you are under arrest."

Libshitz and I looked at each other, both feeling like fools. I was irritated at the policeman for bothering to come after us for such a minor offense. As we were escorted to the station house, I realized that the two of us probably had looked a little strange, dashing across the street with our black briefcases. Libshitz, who was wearing large, dark glasses, was completely bald. He had a long, bushy black beard that was wider than his white face. And here I was beside him, a black man, with a large mound of dark hair. When we entered the station, the cluster of criminal suspects in handcuffs took one look at us and immediately stopped talking. They had probably never seen a stranger-looking pair of human beings in their lives. Nor, for that matter, had the police station superintendent, who was seated behind a high desk, peering down at us.

The arresting policeman told the superintendent what had happened. In desperation Libshitz showed the superintendent his college pass.

"These are not real documents," said the superintendent, without even looking at the pass. He then rang a bell and another policeman appeared. "Take this citizen and find out where his document is."

As Libshitz was escorted down the hallway, he turned back to me, his eyes silently pleading for help.

I was left at the superintendent's desk. I would look up at the officer and catch him staring curiously at my hair. Whenever our eyes met, his face would flush and we would quickly look down at the papers in front of him, or pretend to sweep away dust or crumbs from his desk.

Suddenly I heard a terrible, piercing scream. It was Libshitz. I glanced at the superintendent, who did not flinch. Another scream forced me to close my eyes and grit my teeth. Fifteen minutes later Libshitz appeared, sobbing, with a policeman at his side. The officer saluted the superintendent and declared, "Everything is all right."

Libshitz stood beside me, obviously in pain, crying softly.

The superintendent looked at us harshly and said, "I advise both of you to carry your documents always. It will save you from further arrests and unpleasantness."

A self-satisfied smile creased his face as he added, "You are both now free to go."

As soon as we were outside the police station, Libshitz burst into tears. There was nothing I could say to comfort him. I placed my hand on his shoulder and we walked in silence to the college entrance. Then he turned to me and with an anguished look made we swear never to tell anyone what had just happened. Classes that evening were a blur. All I could think of was the frightened, helpless, pleading look on Libshitz's face as he was led down the corridor of the police station, and his sobbing when he returned.

As soon as class was over, I ran to find my friend. He was standing with a group of his classmates, who were trying to persuade him to go someplace with them. I could tell he was relieved to see me, because it gave him an easy way to excuse himself from them. We left the building together and began walking silently along the tram car route. His anguish, coupled with my concern, kept us silent. But I wanted desperately to know what had happened. Finally, I asked him.

For a long moment Libshitz said nothing. Then he told me. "I was taken down the corridor. We stopped at a door, which was open, and the officer beside me asked the one inside that room to come with him. We continued to walk down the hallway until we reached a room with a padlock on it. The second officer unlocked it and we went inside. It was a small place. Ropes and belts hung from the walls. There was a tall post in one corner, with hooks on it. When I was told to remove my shirt and undershirt, I saw one of the officers take two belts from the wall. I was terrified because I thought they were going to whip me. Instead, they used the belts to strap me to the post. One of the policemen told me to look up at the ceiling. Then they grabbed my beard and yanked it repeatedly. Then one of them braced his foot against the wall and gave a mighty yank. I screamed for my life. They tried this a few more times, and then put some kind of contraption on my beard. The gadget produced pain that was unbearable. I screamed until I could bear it no more, and then I fainted.

"When I came to, I was lying on the floor and the two men were sponging my face with cold water. Finally, they sat me up. While I was unconscious, one of them had called our factory to verify what I had told them, about working there. He apologized for torturing me and said, "Since the war we have found spies wearing false beards, mustaches, and hair. Because you and your friend looked so different, we had no alternative but to check out your beard to see if it was real."

Not long after this unfortunate incident, in July 1944, after seven years of study at the Moscow Evening Institute, the all-important day arrived. I sat before a panel of seven professors, four from the institute and three from the State Ministry of Education. They examined me on my final mechanical engineering project. To my surprise, each one asked only three questions, which I answered readily. Then I had to wait outside the examination room while the professors deliberated. The final decision is based on all the grades during the entire course of study and an assessment of how the final project was completed and defended. In Russia, a fifteen-minute wait for something would be considered extraordinarily short, but on that day each minute seemed like an hour. This examination was now all that stood between me and a degree as a full-fledged mechanical engineer.

Finally I was summoned back into the examination room. I was too nervous to sit down. No one was smiling.

"Oh, no," I thought, "I have probably failed," even though I was certain that I had answered the questions correctly. Still, during seven years at the institute I had learned that doing something right was not always a guarantee that you would pass. I had failed the laboratory examination in electricity three times, even though I knew the subject matter inside and out. A teaching assistant was instructing us in the lab. When I told a friend of mine about my problem, he laughed and asked me, "Comrade Robinson, did the assistant ask you to consult with him about the examination every time he failed you?"

"Well, yes," I answered, somewhat puzzled.

"Let me explain. You have violated an unwritten rule of the institute. You see, the man asked you to consult with him, because every time a student comes to him for extra help he receives ten extra rubles from the institute for tutoring. He expects you to meet with him at least three times; that way he receives thirty rubles."

I took my friend's advice, met with the assistant three times, and asked to take the examination again. This time, with the same answers as before, I passed.

But now, standing before the panel of professors was an ordeal. I knew the Russian penchant for holding people in suspense. They seem to derive a certain pleasure from watching someone squirm. I knew I should have relaxed and let them play their game, but I was too tense, too emotionally involved to maintain an inner calm.

Each professor made a statement about me. Then the chairman of the group said. "Comrade Robinson, you have graduated with a grade of 'B'. They all rose and congratulated me. One of them said, "Your diploma will be ready in a month. Please come by for it then."

The next few days I moved about as if in a dream. For the first time since the food rationing, I thought little of eating. I kept thinking over and over, "Now I am a college-educated mechanical engineer."

I wrote my mother immediately, knowing how the good news would cheer her. She was getting older, and I had not seen her in eleven years. Now that I had my degree, I vowed to myself that as soon as the war was over I would find a way to get back home and see her. On the day I was to pick up my diploma, I rushed to the institute right after work, skipping supper. But when I reported to the registrar's office, instead of a diploma I was handed a slip of paper. It said that I was to report to a factory in Stalingrad, that I would be paid eight hundred rubles a month, and I was to live in a hostel with three other engineers. This would be a career setback, not an advancement! In Moscow I was making twelve hundred rubles a month and I had my own room.

I rejected the offer. As a result I was not given my diploma. During the next two years I made several protests to the institute's administration, but I got nowhere. I then wrote the director of my factory and asked him to intercede. He did, and a month later I received a postcard from the institute saying I could pick up my diploma. This time when I went to the registrar's office it was given to me. In the Soviet Union a diploma is much more than a piece of paper stating that a student has graduated; it is a folder containing your transcript of courses and grades, as well. It is signed by the dean and the party secretary of the institute and has the seal of the Ministry of Education. If an official asks to see your diploma you must show him the folder with all of its contents. A certificate or diploma alone does not suffice.

Other students were less fortunate. Those without influential connections, and who had passed all of their subjects but refused to take the assignment offered, were never allowed to practice engineering professionally. I knew one young woman who took a job in Moscow sweeping streets, and a young man who joined a road construction crew, rather than accept unappealing assignments. Beginning in 1938, night college students at the institute had to pay one hundred rubles a semester, so it was not that the government was paying for a student's education in return for a work commitment. Most students felt as I did, that a person paying for his education should have a say in where he works.

My education cost me twelve hundred rubles. In addition to the technical knowledge I gained, I learned quite a lot about the Soviet educational system. It has a much narrower focus than western systems. The only nontechnical courses taught during my seven years were the mandatory two-year courses, "The History of the Communist Party of the Soviet Union" and "Political Economy." Because most of the students had attended elementary school and high school in the Russian hinterland where instruction was extremely provincial, they left the institute as ignorant of the rest of the world as when they entered. They ended up well-grounded in their particular technical program, but did not know a thing about the humanities. Not only were most of them unaware of where Indonesia or Jamaica was, for example, but what was more shocking and disturbing was that they lacked the desire to learn more about the rest of the world with its many different people and cultures.

Since the October Revolution of 1917, millions of people have been educated through the Soviet system. From kindergarten to old age, everyone is exposed to a constant barrage of political indoctrination. Soviet students soon learn that they are not allowed to think freely or question dogma without running into trouble with the authorities. As a result, their viewpoints remain narrow. Whether they are in service to the advancement of the state is of primary importance. The point was to dedicate one's life to helping Mother Russia achieve what was taught as its so-called sacred mission—to achieve world domination even if achieving the goal took a hundred years. Developing individual intellectual potential is not a priority.

Soviet education does not stress the development of a well-rounded, developed mind. For this reason, the Soviet intelligentsia is different from the intellectual elite in the West. This is an important point which the West needs to understand.

The peasant students entering the institute, usually in their late twenties, still had a village frame of mind at graduation time. They were trained to perform a specific function, and they knew that by doing that well they were guaranteed housing, food, and a limited medical care plan. Why waste energy learning more about the world? It did not make any sense. They were by and large guided by the Russian street maxim: "Make the most of the safe situation you are in. To break with the norm is to invite trouble, or even death." The great majority of Russians were conditioned to accept their lot in life and be thankful for what they had. Stories of deprivation passed down through the generations, along with the specter of the NKVD knocking on the door in the middle of the night, sobered and haunted every home.

But now, in the summer of 1944, still in the midst of the war, I had finished with my college education at the institute. I faced a new problem: what to do with the extra time on my hands. I knew that when my mind was idle I became restless and irritable. Now that I no longer had my engineering studies, I decided I should channel my energies into solving technical challenges at work. The first project I had in mind was one that I had been wanting to do for several years. The shop desperately needed more indicators, which were used for checking varying types of precision gauges ground on the surface grinding machines. The Soviet Union could not import them during the war and no one in the factory knew how to make them. For every ten machines there was only one indicator. Workers were on the piecework system, and to wait for a fellow worker to finish using the checking tool was extremely frustrating. I knew the results of this project would be welcomed by the workers, since it would increase their productivity.

I knew I could make the indicators. One morning I went to the shop an hour early. I carefully measured an indicator and observed its movement. Then I went to my desk to design the measuring instrument. The indicator in use measured in 1/1000 of an inch, which caused the workers quite an inconvenience because they would then have to convert their calculations from fractions of an inch to 1/100 of a millimeter units of measurement. Therefore it was necessary to produce an indicator in the metric system that could be read and understood easily by the worker.

When I showed a section head what I had drawn, and explained why I thought it should be produced in the shop, he seemed interested in the plan though skeptical about whether I could produce it. Several designers assessed my plans and gave my idea the same lukewarm reception. Nonetheless, the section head picked up the phone and called the chief shop superintendent to see if he could show him my design. Ten minutes later I received a call from the chief superintendent asking me to see him at once. When I entered his office, the chief engineer was looking over my drawing with the chief superintendent, who looked up and said, "Comrade Robinson, I think you ought to know that it's not possible for us to make all these tiny parts in our shop. Yet, I'm curious, who do you think is capable of making what you have designed?"

"No one in our shop," I said, "but if given the chance I can do it."

Neither man said anything for a few seconds. They looked at each other, surprised by my self-confidence. Finally, the chief engineer asked, "Suppose we agree to let you do this project, how long will it take you to finish it?"

"In two or three months, providing I am given access to any machine whenever I need it."

"That's a promise we can't make," he said.

"What about allowing me to use the machines after my shift when many are usually idle?" I asked.

"In that case, go ahead with the project," he said.

Many of the other designers and instructors laughed in disbelief when word of my plan reached them. One fellow came up to me and said mockingly, "You are only a grinding instructor with two years as a designer; to make what you have designed would require an ability to operate every machine in this shop."

Fortunately, the day I decided to begin the project our shop received three medium-sized German lathes, brought home by Soviet troops as booty. I chose one of them to work on, since they were better than anything we had. I ended up doing 70 percent of my work on that lathe.

The first week of my project everything was going well. But then I encountered trouble. One afternoon during my lunch hour, I went back to the shop to check the work I had done the previous night. A specially ground cutting tool that I had left on the machine was missing. I looked everywhere but could not find it. I suspected sabotage.

Five weeks later trouble struck again. This time someone had broken the cutting edge of the tool while leaving it mounted on the machine. From that day on I always removed the cutting tool before leaving the plant. But this did not foil whomever was trying to sabotage my project because the person now started loosening the machine when I was not around. Several days later, when I turned on the machine, the part I was working on flew out and hit me in the face. From then on, I took both the cutting tool and whatever piece I was building along with me, even when I went to the bathroom. When I completed the indicator parts, I asked the shop superintendent if I could assemble them in my room, to avoid further sabotage. He gave me permission.

Three-and-a-half months later I arrived in the shop very early one morning, armed with thirteen completed indicators. Seven of them were at 1/100 of a millimeter for each line, and six were at 1/1000 of a millimeter for each line. I waited for either the shop superintendent or the chief engineer to arrive. The superintendent showed up first. When he saw me he said, somewhat sarcastically, "Well, Comrade Robinson, how is your tiny job coming along? I haven't seen you in ages."

At first I did not let on that I had finished the project. I simply said, "It's going along all right."

I then picked up the box at my feet, placed it on his table, and removed the thirteen finished indicators. The man looked at me in disbelief, then picked up one of the indicators as if it were a diamond, checking each side carefully, while stealing glances at me out of the corner of his eye.

Finally he asked, "Have you checked them?" and then before letting me answer he added, "What's the result?"

"If you wish," I said, "we could check them together."

Still holding one of the indicators and shaking his head with amazement, he said, "No, it can't be! How did you manage? I never thought you'd accomplish such an enormous task."

The superintendent called the chief of the design department to come to his office immediately. Upon entering this man looked at me and said, "You have made fools of us all. Only yesterday a senior designer and I were wondering how you were doing. This is certainly a major contribution to our production effort. You are to be congratulated."

News of what I had done spread swiftly through the shop and plant, even reaching Chief Engineer Gromov. I was pleased with my accomplishment, and was enjoying myself thoroughly. The following morning I received a message to report to the chief superintendent's office. When I arrived, Gromov was also inside the office. When he saw me, he reached out to shake my hand and said, "Congratulations, Comrade Robinson. Thank you for your contribution to the machine shop. I shall surely brief the factory's director about this notable deed."

But it was the congratulations from my co-workers that meant the most to me. With the new indicators, they were going to make more money. Almost every worker in the shop came up to me and offered thanks by putting an arm around my shoulder or grabbing my hand and vigorously pumping it.

Two weeks after completing the project I received a phone call from the factory's Trade Union Committee requesting that I meet with them. After work I walked briskly over to the union office, but I never met with the committee. I was intercepted by their secretary, who told me that the factory director had awarded me a twelve-day pass to a rest home along with four hundred rubles ($80).

Imagine, that this was my reward for spending 105 extra work-days creating instruments that were going to increase factory production significantly. The pass was worth 380 rubles, which meant a total of 780 rubles, which in 1945 was equal to $156 dollars. Of course, I had done the work on my own initiative because I wanted to, but if I were to receive financial recognition at all, it should have been commensurate with the task performed. What irked me was that others were given much more money for designing less meaningful devices. I calculated that I was paid $1.48 a day for my efforts.

As a black man and a foreigner, I only received grudging recognition for my contributions to the industrial development of the Soviet Union. Rewards given me were always more a spit in the eye than a pat on the back. Over the years I garnered more than twenty awards, medals, and citations for my inventions and my work. However, none of those awards and nothing I ever did gained me a promotion or a significant pay raise. While my colleagues who had graduated with me from the Moscow Evening Institute of Mechanical Engineering had been promoted to directors of factories, chief engineers of factories and the like.

Four months later I was shocked and saddened to learn from a worker that he and his colleagues were no longer allowed to use the new indicators. He came to ask if I knew what had happened. I checked with the woman in charge of the supply room, who said they were being rechecked for accuracy and she had delivered them to the man in charge of testing. This was preposterous, since the instruments were so new and there had been no report of inaccuracy. But the Soviet Union had an arcane system for rechecking all measuring instruments at regular intervals, whatever their condition. That time had arrived, so the workers would have to do without the indicators for the time being.

All that was needed to check them was a good set of Swedish measuring blocks. Instead, they were taken apart, washed in gasoline and dried. They became all mixed up, and to reassemble them correctly was a huge task. I went to the office of the man in charge of testing and was told that he was ill, and had not been to work in more than a week. I wondered whether this was another example of sabotage. Although I complained to the shop's chief engineer, the indicators were never returned. The chief engineer eventually questioned the man who was supposed to test them, who said that he had left the indicators in a drawer at his workbench and when he returned he could not find them. Several months later a clue to their whereabouts surfaced. A machinist from the ball bearing plant in Kuybyshev told someone in our shop that they had received two new indicators. At first I did not believe the story, but then another worker from that plant visited someone in our shop and confirmed what we had heard. I wondered if someone in the factory had laid claim to the work I had done and shared it with other plants. Certainly that kind of enterprise would impress the Ministry of Industry at the Kremlin and lead to a promotion for someone.

As far as I knew, the factory administration made no effort to find the culprit. About six months later I learned that the Calibri Factory in Moscow was producing vast numbers of indicators similar to the one I had produced.

CHAPTER 19

Rejoicing at War's End

WE HAD SKETCHY NEWS ABOUT the Red Army's advances, but what little we heard was good. By late April we knew that Russian troops were in Germany. A few weeks later they were approaching the gates of Berlin. It was rare to have news of the American and British forces on the western front, so to the average Russian it appeared that the Soviet Union was fighting the Germans alone. On May 2, 1945, Russian troops captured Berlin, but there were pockets of German military resistance elsewhere in Germany. The remaining German armed forces surrendered to the Western Allies on May 8, and to the Soviet Union on May 9, a day I shall never forget.

I was in my shop when we learned that the war was over. The factory's whistles started blowing full blast. Everybody stopped working and started crying and hugging everyone in sight. When the shop superintendent and chief engineer emerged from their offices, the workers hoisted them onto their shoulders and paraded them back and forth, singing patriotic Russian songs.

The shop was shut down and everyone—workers, the foremen, the superintendent and chief engineer—streamed into the street in front of the factory. Thousands of people were already there. Elderly people who had managed to survive the daily terror of Nazi bombings were crying like babies. Mothers with young children clinging to them cried without shame. Emotions that had been building up for four desperate years were being released. Muscovites had endured hunger, bitter winters without fuel, the loss of loved ones in battle, and constant Nazi shelling and bombing. The Soviet Union had vanquished the seemingly invincible Nazi juggernaut. Young men and women kissed each other and danced together, singing, "Russia, Russia" with deep emotion. Every soldier in the crowd was embraced, lifted up in the air and passed from one set of outstretched hands to another. Tears of joy and relief were in every eye.

The presence of so many people in the streets forced the tram cars and buses to stop running. The drivers abandoned them and joined in the celebration. I had endured the hardships along with everybody else, and I rejoiced along with them, without reservation. Around 1:30 P.M. the crowd began to disperse, many heading toward the center of Moscow six miles away. Tram car conductors were offering people free rides. Along with others, I decided to take the subway, thinking I stood a better chance going underground than through the impassable streets.

When I reached the subway station I encountered a huge throng of people all trying to enter the train, while those inside were pushing to get out. The two masses of people created a human knot, before which the five or six policemen who were present, were helpless. Men, women, and children were screaming. Somehow the passengers inside managed to push their way through and out and the swarm of people outside rushed to fill the vacuum. I never made it inside that train, nor did I get to the doors of the next one a few minutes later. Thirty-five minutes later another train arrived. This time I was in the middle of the throng, which surged forward as the doors opened. Because only a handful of people wanted to get off, the crowd I was in prevailed. I was literally swept into the coach by the onrushing crowd, my feet never touching the ground. We were all packed together like fish in a can. Still, somehow, a man began playing his accordion, and everyone joined in singing, one song after another, to the glory of Mother Russia.

We were all heading for Red Square. But only about halfway there, about a thousand feet from a station, the train stopped abruptly. The crowd on the platform ahead had spilled onto the tracks. Too impatient to wait, some people in our train pried loose the emergency valves and jumped out onto the tracks. I learned later that a number of them were electrocuted when they touched the high voltage rails. I stayed put, and an hour later the train started moving again. I got off a stop before Red Square, figuring that the Red Square station would be impassable.

When I emerged from the subway station and had walked a few blocks, I came upon Red Square, which, as I had expected, was swarming with people. The streets feeding into the square were just as densely packed. I squeezed my way along, finding my skin color an advantage, because when people saw me they let me pass, either because they thought I was a foreign dignitary or because they were afraid of me.

As the crowd began chanting for Joseph Stalin to appear, I sensed they were acting just like their forefathers had in decades and centuries past, when they came to shower affection upon and seek reassurance from the czars. To the hundreds of thousands of people massed in Red Square, Stalin was not viewed as the head of the Communist party. Instead, he was the leading Russian potentate. He was their modern-day czar who, instead of defending the crown defended the hammer and sickle. Hundreds of children, carrying small bouquets of flowers, stood in the crowd hoping by some miracle Stalin would come close to them and they could hand him their gift.

"We want to see Comrade Stalin," the people chanted. "Long live Comrade Stalin." People wept as they chanted, "We thank you for our victory."

After two hours the balcony above the Lenin Mausoleum remained empty. The people were becoming restless, and some began to pout. Before the disappointment turned to despair and possibly recklessness, something could be heard over the loudspeaker system. Everybody grew silent. People stood on their toes and strained for a clear view of the balcony. Those with children hoisted the little ones onto their shoulders. Nobody wanted to miss this rare appearance of Joseph Stalin, at such a triumphant moment.

But he was not there. No one was there. Instead the radio continued to blare over the loudspeakers, "Moscow is speaking, Moscow is speaking . . ." Suddenly the voice of Stalin came over the radio. He was expressive as usual but sparing of words. Although everybody listened attentively, the people in Red Square were extremely disappointed at not having seen Stalin in person. He rarely appeared in public, and whenever he did, he was surrounded by a battalion of guards. He kept the people over whom he ruled at a fearful distance. Crowd control on this day in Red Square would have been a desperate task, at best. The short radio speech over, the people started for home. From that year, May 9 became an official holiday in the Soviet Union. Each year it reminds the people that Russia alone defeated Nazi Germany and won the war.

The war was over now. Many families with husbands, sons, or brothers at the front waited expectantly, not only to find out for certain that they were alive and safe, but also to see if they would be allowed to return to their prewar civilian life or if they would be kept in the military. I am sure that everybody also wondered, as I did, if the purges would begin again. In late July 1945, a strange-looking man showed up in the machine shop, to remind us of the recent past.

He had sunken jaws, and was shabbily dressed, wearing coarse, high boots that had not been cleaned for ages. Yet somehow he looked familiar. Curious, I went to the foreman of the group of lathe operators and asked who the man was. Looking in the registration book, the foreman said, ''D. Bogatov.''

Bogatov! It seemed impossible. But the foreman repeated the name, and I believed him. I wanted desperately to go over and talk to the man who had disappeared from our shop in 1936, but I knew to do so would cause both of us to be viewed with suspicion. Exercising discretion, I gradually pieced his story together, bit by bit as it unfolded later. From snatches of conversation with him I learned that after his arrest—for commenting under his breath about an unreasonable norm setter—Bogatov was taken to Lefortovo prison. There he was interrogated constantly for three days and then convicted to ten years imprisonment at hard labor. He was packed in a boxcar with thirty or so others and shipped off to a labor camp in Siberia.

''During the entire period traveling to the camps, especially at night,'' Bogatov told me, ''I kept on thinking about the unbelievably displeasing situation I was in, trying to find a reason for their having done this to me. I wondered if I would survive, and if I would ever see my mother and other relatives again.

''One moment, after infinite hours of soul-searching, I suddenly felt a sense of dread as I thought about the disagreement with the norm setter, Gerasimov, two days before I was arrested. It was as if an inner voice were talking to me, saying, "Do you remember what you said to Gerasimov as he walked away? Do you remember telling him that it is people like him who make life so difficult?' Yes, I remembered. And then I realized it was Gerasimov who had turned me into the NKVD in the secret department of our factory."

Some weeks later Bogatov continued his story. "At the first camp, we were told to cut wood with the daily norm set to a certain number of cubic meters. Anyone cutting less than the required norm would have his ration of black bread and buckwheat reduced. Perhaps one could say I was lucky, for after my fourth year at camp I answered an announcement on the blackboard for an experienced toolmaker. The commandant accepted my services. As a toolmaker, I not only made parts for an outdated lumber mill some four miles from the camp, but in time I was assigned two inmate helpers, whom I gradually taught how to file and work on machines.

"Four-and-a-half years later, one night after I had just gone to bed, a casual thought about my mother first crossed my mind, then another and another, until the thought became too strong to ignore. My heart was racing as I repeated to myself, over and over again: Why not ask the commandant permission to write your mother?

"When I awoke the next morning, the thought was still there. I took courage, and went straight to the commandant. After the usual greeting he praised me for my work and then asked what he could do for me. 'Please, I have come to ask your permission to write to my dear old mother in Moscow', I said.

"Do you know, Robinson, his whole demeanor changed. After a moment he said, 'Get in touch with my assistant, Petrov, in three days for an answer'.

"Permission was granted and seven months later I received her reply. I would read and reread her letter, and each time my eyes filled with tears. For many months afterward I felt like an entirely new person inside. But a year later I became ill with a high temperature. This began my bout with tuberculosis.

"In June of that year the commandant went to Moscow, but no one knew exactly when he would return. As the weather began to grow cool in late August, I began to worry again about my health, which had improved considerably during the summer months."

I ventured to ask, "But how did you become free?"

Bogatov answered simply, "Through the help of my sister's party friends.

"And confidentially," he said, "I have been told that Gerasimov was responsible for, at the least, the arrest and deportation of three other people, also on trumped-up charges."

When I left the Soviet Union twenty nine years later, in 1974, this same norm setter was still there. A number of people had told me that they were just waiting for an opportunity to get even with him for all his past treachery. I wonder if they ever got their revenge.

At the end of August, a month after Bogatov returned, I used the vacation pass I was given for my work on the indicators. I had not had a vacation in more than four years. Needless to say, I welcomed the opportunity to retreat to a country setting, where I could lose myself in nature and refresh my spirit. Before the war, my summer trips to the Crimea or the Caucasus Mountains were a welcome respite from the intrigue and anxiety of life in Moscow. Not that a citizen was free of the snooping of the internal security system while on vacation. The NKVD and its informers were at rest homes as well. But the trees, clear sky, and sea breezes made things more tolerable.

A regular vacation was usually twelve work days (plus two Sundays) for ordinary people and a total of twenty-eight days for those high up in the bureaucracy. My twelve-day holiday was scheduled for a rest home sixty-five kilometers from Moscow. When I got there, the long line at the registration desk immediately reminded me of Moscow. I took my place in the line, which moved slowly, because the policeman checking credentials was being excessively thorough. Upon registering, I was required to hand over my passport and pay a three-ruble registration fee. Then I was given a booklet, which had my room number and the number of the table where I would be eating written on the cover. The booklet also included a list of items I could borrow and use in my spare time, things such as a balalaika, an accordion, chess pieces or checkers, a tennis racquet and ball, books, a volleyball and net, and other sporting equipment. A rest home nurse took me and the other guests to our rooms.

There were no private rooms. Only the vacation places catering to the highest stratum of Soviet elite had private facilities. In the place I was staying the best you could get was one roommate, though I was not that lucky. Those rooms usually went to guests who registered the night before they were supposed to arrive. I was placed in a room with three other men, and the guests who arrived several hours after me found themselves in a dormitory room with five to seven roommates. There were precisely the number of chairs in a room as there were occupants. Regardless of the number of guests in the room, there was one decanter filled with water and two glasses turned upside down. The beds were narrow; two towels hung on a hook above the head of each bed. There was a bathroom on each floor of the wooden two-story building, which was shared by two hundred people. Hot water was available every other day, in the morning for men, in the afternoon for the women. Every room had at least one window. Ours had two, with white curtains. There was no maid service. Everyone had to change his own bed. Clean bedsheets and pillowcases were provided every twelve days.

On the first floor was a large sitting room, which could hold more than a hundred people comfortably. In the far corner was a library, open for two hours in the morning and two hours in the late afternoon. On rainy days and cool nights people would relax in the sitting room, playing cards, chess, or checkers and gossiping. An accordionist might play Russian folk songs, and the more energetic would dance. There was also a radio in the room, but it did not work.

The two most important people at rest homes were the gymnasts and the accordionist. The gymnasts were generally women, trained at a special sports institute, majoring in recreation studies. The gymnast would plan the daily activities, announcing a fifteen-minute session of morning calisthenics, which started promptly at 7:45 A.M. Calisthenics were optional, but I nevertheless felt compelled to attend for fear of being considered a deviationist and facing social ostracism during my stay. Breakfast was served at 8:30 A.M., in a first-floor room with fifty tables and four chairs to a table. A vase with freshly picked wild flowers rested on each table. The meal was identical each morning: herring, a slice of black bread with a quarter-ounce of butter, porridge, and a glass of tea.

After breakfast on the first morning came a twenty-minute hike led by the gymnast and the accordionist. While we walked, the accordionist played popular Soviet tunes and the gymnast led us in song until we reached a spot where we were divided into groups of four or five. Some searched for mushrooms, others picked berries. Some rolled up their pants and waded into a nearby pond. A soccer ball was brought along for those who wanted to do something athletic.

At 12:45 P.M. the gymnast blew her whistle as a signal to reassemble for another fifteen-minute session of calisthenics. We tried to touch our toes and do pushups to the rhythm of the accordionist's tunes, and then, singing, we hiked back to the rest home. We were given about ten minutes to get ready for lunch, one of the three most important events of the day. Living in hunger during the war years had created in most people an obsession with food. This was clearly noticeable when we sat down to eat. Most of the men in the dining hall gulped down their food, unaware or uncaring about their primitive behavior. The three men at my table tested me dearly. They devoured their food, and since I am always a slow eater, they spent the next ten to fifteen minutes watching me eat. I ate my *borscht,* I ate my four tablespoons of buckwheat, my three ounces of meat, and my glass of dried fruit. All three of them sat there, staring. The saliva would drip out of the mouth of one of them. Oblivious, he would suck it back in and swallow it, without ever taking his eyes off my food. I could feel them studying my spoon, as it went from my food to my mouth, and back to my plate for more. I felt as if three ravenous bloodhounds were waiting to pounce. During my stay, on the occasions when I left a few scraps on my plate, I would hear them arguing over who should get what as I was on my way out. Second helpings were given, but never of meat or dried fruit. Usually, after considerable pleading, the kitchen would dish out more buckwheat or potatoes.

After lunch, we were encouraged to take a two-hour nap. It was not mandatory, but those who did not were not allowed to loiter in or around the rest home. They usually took walks in the woods or down a country lane. At 5:00 P.M. we had the choice of playing some athletic game like volleyball, listening to a propaganda lecture about the international Communist movement, or taking a walk. Most of the women went for a stroll, and a few men with romance on their minds followed. Afterward, it was time for supper, and people filed into the dining hall as they had at lunch, as if they were starving. I was also hungry, but I did not relish the idea of having three sets of eyes riveted on my food. For supper, we were given four spoonfuls of mashed potatoes, and a cutlet which consisted of 85 percent black breadcrumbs and 15 percent meat, and weighed about seventy grams (3.15 ounces). We were also served a small dish of porridge and, of course, a glass of tea.

I soon learned that the more creative and determined guests found ways to secure food outside of the dining hall. Each morning the same group of men skipped the after-breakfast excursion and headed five miles down the road to a pavilion to check out what was being sold there. Curious about what they might be purchasing, I followed them one morning. When I reached the little pavilion I noticed that most of the men at the counter were buying vodka, and a flat dried bony fish less than five inches long called *vobla,* that had been saturated in salt. I observed one guest from the rest home sitting by himself, sipping vodka and devouring fish. In a matter of minutes he had eaten ten fish. Another man was seated on the ground, his pockets bulging with cucumbers. About a dozen more were piled between his legs. He was greedily chomping on one cucumber after another, eating them without condiments or bread. Before eating a fresh one, he would wipe it with his handkerchief and then plop it in his mouth. I counted; after the eleventh cucumber, he got up, satisfied, and headed back to the home. Many of the other men had cucumbers stuffed in their pockets and a bottle of vodka hidden inside their shirts. I wondered where they got the vegetables, because I did not see them being sold at the pavilion. The shelves were stocked only with the ever present jars of mustard, black pepper, vodka, black bread, hard tasteless biscuits, and ordinary candies stuck to one another. I learned later from a waitress in the dining hall that peasants arrived at nine every morning with sacks full of cucumbers, which they sold to the rest home guests.

Every evening there were activities coordinated by the gymnast, designed to create a family-like atmosphere and help the guests get to know one other. There was usually dancing and games; nearly everyone would show up for the dancing. On the day before departure there would be skits and concerts performed by staff members and guests. On this occasion I missed the performance. I decided that my tablemates had become too much to bear. When their usual argument over my food erupted into a fight, I returned to Moscow, three days early.

CHAPTER 20

A Touch of Romance

BY EARLY 1947, the Kremlin's campaign to discredit the United States—its wartime ally—in the eyes of Soviet citizens, was in full force. The theater, cinema, and radio were useful media for the anti-American message. Ever since my arrival in 1930, I had seen and experienced how the Soviet authorities made effective propaganda out of America's history of racial inequality. After all, the reasoning went, America was a bourgeois country where the rich white capitalists crushed the poor black proletariat underclass, a vivid example and useful reminder of the overall failure of capitalist economics and so-called democracy.

The American play, *Deep Are the Roots,* was ideal for Kremlin propaganda purposes, so the state-controlled theaters were ordered to perform it in Moscow and throughout the country. The play was successful in meeting the Kremlin's propaganda objectives. Russian audiences became incensed over its portrait of the life of blacks in the American South, who were portrayed as subservient, groveling, serf-like people. Many Russians wondered how Americans could tolerate such racism, after fighting the Nazis with their philosophy of Aryan superiority and their efforts to eliminate the Jews. Unfortunately, the Russian feeling of moral indignation toward the United States covered over their own deep-rooted racial and ethnic prejudice.

Behind the scenes of the Russian production of *Deep Are the Roots* lay a tale of Russian racial prejudice. Bret, a black boy, the leading character in the play, was reared as a young boy alongside two small white girls of a well-to-do family in the South, where his mother had served as the family's cook. After he returned from fighting the Nazis in the war, Bret was welcomed home warmly by one of the now grown-up white women. The resulting conflict set the stage for the rest of the play. White Russian actors with their faces, necks, and hands painted with soot were bad enough in some of the minor roles. As they perspired, the soot wore off their white skin and they ended up looking more like Dalmatians than anything else. But it was far worse to have a white actor playing the leading role, especially since a very qualified black American actor in Moscow named Wayland Rudd, whom I knew, had sought the leading role. Although Rudd tried several times to get the part of Bret in the play, he was never even allowed to audition. The comments of an American theater producer who was invited to attend a performance of the play in Moscow were printed in one of Moscow's English-language newspapers. After the performance he asked, "Was it not possible to have a black actor perform the part of Bret?"

The Intourist interpreter answered him: "We would have liked to, but you must remember, there are no black artists in our country."

Rudd had obtained his diploma as an actor/director from one of Moscow's best drama institutes, and was well known by the authorities to be living in Moscow.

Shortly after *Deep Are the Roots* played in Moscow theaters and was broadcast over the radio, the Kremlin decided to make a film based on the life of Myklujo Maklai, a nineteenth century Russian anthropologist. This was another effort to discredit the American way of life, while at the same time emphasizing the humaneness of the Soviet system. Maklai had believed that all races were potentially equal in ability and that environment was the key factor in determining whether people reached their potential. He had spent several years studying the Papuans in New Guinea. The czarist aristocracy, who ruled Russia at the time, ridiculed Maklai. They called him a misfit and declared his theories the thinking of a madman. But when the Bolsheviks seized power they hailed him as a great hero of science.

There were scenes with black Americans in the film, and the producer said he needed black people to play those roles. The Kremlin found him the people he needed, and I happened to be one of the recruits. One day my shop superintendent, accompanied by two men from

Mosfilm, the production unit for the film, said he wanted to talk to me. They explained the project.

"Me an actor," I thought. "Never!"

But the three men were very persuasive. The superintendent said that as a loyal citizen I could not refuse to cooperate. I perked up at the use of the word "loyal" since people were beginning to disappear from Moscow again. With the war over, Stalin and the MVD no longer had the Nazis to worry about and could channel more of their energy into domestic security. When one of the Mosfilm men pulled out a contract with my name on it, I knew I had better sign it. It called for a three- to four-month stint in an Odessa movie studio, for which I would be paid ten thousand rubles.

"Not bad," I thought. It was a lot more than I was making at the ball bearing plant.

Odessa was the major port in the Ukraine, bordering the Black Sea. It was an old city in the southern part of the Soviet Union, with a much milder climate than Moscow. I opted to live in a sanitarium, which was only a ten-minute walk from the film studio, even though it was primarily for people recovering from surgery or illness. I expected to find a quieter atmosphere there and to receive a bit of pampering in the dining hall and the dormitories, which I did.

Following my first night in the sanitarium, I arrived for work the following morning at 8:00 A.M. sharp, as scheduled. Also reporting to the studio were six other blacks recruited for the film, including Wayland Rudd. One of the other six black actors was an American and the remaining three were born in Russia, in the Caucasus. I had known from Arle-Titzs that there were native-born blacks in the Soviet Union, but neither the media nor any Russian magazines or books I had come across ever mentioned them. Blacks have lived in the Caucasus since the mid-1700s, when they were brought out of Africa to Russia by Catherine the Great. I do not know of any foreigners ever being allowed to visit the colony of blacks living in the heart of the Caucasus Mountains.

Of the three native Russians, the two younger ones spoke Russian and were light-skinned. The other man was ninety-two years old. He was tall and dark-skinned, and the only language he spoke was the African language his ancestors had spoken at the time they were brought to Russia.

The six of us waited, along with others, but the director was not there. After four hours someone with Mosfilm told us that he was ill and would not be back to work for two days. That was not such good news for me, because I was anxious about making a fool of myself in my new found role as an actor. I would have preferred to get things underway as quickly as possible.

When we began two days later, my illusions of life as a film actor were quickly shattered. I was expecting to have to memorize a script and deliver lines. That did not happen with any of us. We were all told what to say and how to say it, moment by moment, on the spot. For the most part all we did was emulate the director. The white actors—all professionals—followed the same routine, trying to do as the director showed them and told them to.

The situation with the three black Americans was really gro tesque. Here was a white Russian film director telling three black Americans how blacks in the American South were supposed to act. Every scene, large or small, had to be done over and over again. When we did not do what the director felt was right, he would curse. It was not that he was swearing at us, it was more as if he was denouncing his fate. The only one who caught his wrath regularly was his wife, whose job it was to run his errands. He would usually call out to her by saying, "Hey, stupid, lazy woman, go get such and such." She never dared answer him but bowed her head—obviously humiliated—and carried out his commands. The Russian actors, who were more rational than the director, also loved to swear. Away from the camera, in restaurants or in any public place, they would lace their conversations with the most vulgar expressions. I was frankly embarrassed to be around them, and after awhile I tried to avoid their company. What amazed me, though, was their ability to assume a role the instant the camera starting rolling. That was one trait that separated the professionals from the amateurs like me.

However, it was what happened away from the studio that I remember most about my time in Odessa. After ten weeks of living in the sanitarium, the director said I would have to leave. After two unpleasant days in a hotel, I worked out an agreement with a couple I knew who lived in a two-room beach house. With all my moving about, the MVD people who had been assigned to watch me lost track of me for more than a week, a bit of information I learned when I ran into the sanitarium's assistant director.

She asked, "Where have you been for the past week?"

When I told her she said, "The police came by, asking for you. The sanitarium director referred them to the hotel, but when they couldn't find you there they came back, alarmed."

It was not long before they were snooping around the beach house, something I first learned from the couple's eight-year-old daughter. She had what to her was a pleasant encounter with them. She told me all about it one afternoon when she spotted me approaching her home. The sweet, precocious child ran up to me, clasping my hand with her little one and grinned.

"Comrade Robinson," she said, "there were some nice people who came by to see you today—two men and a lady. The lady was so sweet, she gave me chocolate candies."

"What did they want to know?" I asked.

"The lady asked me how long you have been living with my mother and father, and she wanted to know who came to visit you," said the child.

"What else did she ask you?" I inquired.

"She wanted to know if you went out after dark and if you did, if you stayed away a long time. I told her I didn't know."

"Were there any other questions?" I continued.

"Yes. One of the men asked if you got along well with my mother and father. Then the other man said that they would return to see you soon," she said. But they never did.

The local police soon got to know me also. My encounter with the Odessa police began when I reported that my watch was stolen from the locker I was using in a room next to the studio. It was a precious possession because my brother had given it to me as a gift in 1926, and it was the most reliable watch I had ever owned.

The film director wasted no time in calling the police. In a matter of minutes, three officers arrived. They questioned every crew member and actor, black and white, and ordered them to remain in the studio area. They questioned me thoroughly, after which I signed a document verifying that what I hold told them was the truth. The director also made a statement, in which he said that he had seen the watch around my wrist numerous times.

About thirty minutes after the first policemen arrived, another officer appeared with a large dog, which sniffed every inch of the locker room floor. When the dog arrived, everyone knew that the situation was potentially dangerous. For such a theft, a person could end up with three years' imprisonment at hard labor. Every member of the production crew was interrogated a second time. We were kept four hours after our normal quitting time, but not a clue was discovered.

When I returned to work the next morning, there were three policemen with two dogs in the studio. They had already combed the area outside the studio, including every bush on the grounds. When the actors left at the end of the day, the policemen and dogs were still there. The next day another batch showed up, but they too were unable to find my watch. Three days later I received a phone call from central police headquarters, asking me to come down there and to bring my passport along.

I showed up as requested on the following day. When I mentioned who I was, the officer on duty greeted me warmly and escorted me to the assistant chief of police, who also seemed very gracious. He asked me to have a seat and said, "I'm sorry that we haven't been able to find your watch, which I understand you value very much. Be assured that we will continue our investigation. We will find the culprit and you will get your watch back."

I thanked him for his concern, all the while wondering why I was being treated with such care. I soon found out.

"Please," said the assistant police chief, "may I have your passport? I need the number on it so that should my men find your watch after you leave Odessa, they will have a means of contacting you."

I handed it to him, yet when he noticed that it was a Soviet passport, his entire demeanor immediately changed. One moment he was cordial; the next moment indifferent.

"Oh, I see you have a Soviet passport," he said, unable to conceal his surprise.

He handed it back to me, and did not even bother to write the number on an official form but merely scribbled it onto a piece of scrap paper, which was obviously destined for the trash can as soon as I left. Now that he knew I was a Soviet citizen, my stolen watch no longer mattered. They had all assumed that I was a foreign actor. But now, since they knew I would not be going to a foreign country, where I could criticize the Soviet Union and its police force, I no longer mattered. I was certain that he would call off the investigation and that I would never see my watch again. My hunch turned out to be correct.

During my stay in Odessa I relished the opportunity to read and go for walks along the beautiful beach. While walking one morning with book in my hand, I heard a woman's voice calling out from behind me, "Good morning, citizen."

I turned around and said, "Good day, citizen," and waited for her to catch up with me.

"Isn't it a lovely day," she asked.

"Yes, it surely is," I replied.

We had met at an ideal spot. There was a large rock under a broad shade tree. I asked the woman, whom I had seen before working as a sanitarium registrar, to sit with me. Before doing so, she called to two female friends to join her. I stood up to greet the other women, who were introduced to me as Nyura and Bellah. The woman beside me then said her name was Julia, and that she was from Leningrad, where she taught school before the war. Later I discovered that she was a scholar. Though she did not say she had been married, I figured that she must have been at one time. There were streaks of gray in her hair, and for all I knew she might have been a young grandmother. Bellah was plump, rather short, and had black hair, an olive complexion, and intense brown eyes. She said she was a chemist from Astrakhan. From her bearing I sensed that she was a dedicated party member, who had most likely been a model Komsomol. Unlike Julia and Nyura, she appeared suspicious and aggressive. I doubted whether we could be friends.

A special sparkle shone in Nyura's large, hazel eyes. In them I saw signs of someone who thought and felt deeply, a person accepting of others and capable of showing compassion. Nyura was tall for a Russian woman, about five feet six, and slender, with rather broad shoulders and a beautiful face. With her kind of figure, I guessed she was no more than thirty years old. Well-mannered and reserved, she did not volunteer any information about her profession or her background. Only by asking her did I learn that she was from Moscow.

None of the three women asked about my past, which I greatly appreciated, because such inquiries would lead inevitably to questions and comments about the race issue in the US I had long since become irritated at serving as the object of a discussion on the evils of American racism and capitalism. It was as if every time an Australian met someone in a foreign country, they asked him about kangaroos and boomerangs. Toward me, Russians usually would assume or affect a sympathetic attitude. This not only bored me, but when people pity you they do not respect you.

On that warm, sunny day in May I simply wanted to be me. I sensed that Nyura and Julia felt as I did, and their presence, I'm sure, kept Bellah in check. The women suggested that we go down to the beach, which I agreed to without hesitation. As soon as we reached the sand, they removed their cotton dresses, which they wore over their one-piece, tight-fitting bathing suits. All three of them dashed into the sea, swimming at least three hundred feet away from the shore and then returning. They emerged dripping from the water and ran toward me.

"Come with us," urged Julia, breathlessly.

"It's so refreshing," Bellah added enthusiastically.

"Not today," I said. "I think the water is too cold for me."

"Once you are in it," Bellah said, "you'll get used to it and won't notice the coldness."

"I'm sure that's true," I said, "but my doctor in Moscow told me I should avoid swimming in cold water, because I've come down with pleurisy four times.

Although the Kremlin's decade-long campaign to warn Russians against mixing with foreigners was still in full swing, my morning acquaintance with these three women was to develop into a genuine friendship, although much more so with Nyura and Julia than with Bellah. Evidently, the further one was from Moscow the less one heeded the Kremlin's admonitions, because a few days after our meeting I encountered Nyura and Bellah waiting for me outside the film studio after work. I was especially surprised to see Nyura there, since she tended to be shy. I hoped that it was Nyura's idea to meet me, and that she might have persuaded Bellah to join her. When I reached them, they told me that a man and woman were looking for me at the sanitarium. We missed the tram car and had to walk to the sanitarium. I noticed we had an escort of three men, all guests whom I had seen at the sanitarium. They were lounging across the street, and they began tailing us from a short distance once we started walking. As we strolled along, Bellah pointed to a couple walking toward us, on the same side of the street, and said, "There is the couple who wish to see you."

As soon as the man and woman introduced themselves to me, Nyura and Bellah left, with the three men following at a distance. The man spoke first. "Comrade Robinson, we have been asked by our theatrical director to request that you meet with him this coming Saturday."

"Why does he want to meet with me?" I asked. I was irritated at these people because I wanted to continue walking with Nyura. But not knowing who they were, to act rude or leave abruptly would have been not only discourteous, but dangerous as well.

"We are involved in an important government project and we need your help," the man said. He handed me an envelope and added, "Please read this. It is from our director."

Inside the envelope was a letter from the director of the dramatic theater of Odessa. He had been ordered to produce *Deep Are the Roots* as soon as possible and he wanted my advice on the behavior of southern whites and their black servants. For the next hour I stood on the street corner with those two people, trying to persuade them that I was not qualified to advise the director on these matters, since I had never lived in the South. All I knew about the South was what I had read, or what I had heard from southern blacks after they migrated north. But they were on a mission from their director and they obviously were not authorized to let me off the hook. Besides, I was a lot closer to being the real thing than anyone else they were likely to find in Odessa, and they knew that.

Therefore the next Saturday—my day off—I showed up at the director's office as agreed, at 10:00 A.M. The secretary ushered me into his office, where I met a tall, slender man standing behind a mahogany desk. He stepped back, bowed toward me, and said, "Glad to see you. Peter Alexandrovich is my name."

Then he came over to me, put his arm around my waist, and guided me to the sofa, where we sat down. Needless to say, this unnatural intimacy made me uncomfortable.

"Comrade Robinson," he said, "you know about our *Deep Are the Roots* project. We have ten days of rehearsal time left, and there are some scenes in the manuscript that trouble me because they seem inconsistent. For example, in some places the playwright has the rich white mistress asking her black cook and maid for advice. They talk to each other as if they were equals."

He looked at me, paused, and added: "Now that can't be! The blacks are treated like dirt in America."

He sat back and waited for me to agree with his reasoning. But I felt I should be honest with the man.

"I'm in no position to pass judgment on your play," I said, "because I'm not a theatrical person. However, I can say something about the race situation in America. It is true there is real animosity between whites and blacks in America. Nevertheless, it is more virulent in some parts of the country than in others. Also, it is a fact that there has always been a close relationship between the rich white mistress and her black cook and maid. In fact, several reliable and well-informed black people who were born and grew up in the southern part of America have told me that they knew of cases where white mistresses would have their infant babies breast-fed by their black maids, cooks, or other black servants who were already breast-feeding their own babies."

Peter Alexandrovich turned red, stood up, and exclaimed, "What! That is impossible! How can I believe such a preposterous story?"

I said nothing, but just looked at him, without showing any emotion.

"Do you realize," he went on to say, "that by having their children breast-fed by blacks, the white mother is saying that whites and blacks are equal. But the whites in America believe they are superior to those with black skin. Breast-feeding is such an intimate act. It is practically as sacred as the sexual act."

The director paused, calmer now, looking puzzled but thoughtful. "Believe me," he said, "what you have said to me is totally new. I never thought such a situation could be possible in America, let alone an actual fact."

I looked him straight in the eye and said, "You should also know that black maids advise white ladies on what they should wear and at times suggest how to win a beau or treat a particular suitor."

"Well, I have never heard or read about such things," he said. "Now I have to think the whole matter over. It might necessitate my flying to Moscow to consult with my supervisors there."

He stood up and said, "Let's watch the rehearsal. I would

deeply appreciate it if you would criticize the performance, checking of course for inaccuracies in the way we portray black-white relationships."

The play was as I anticipated: a piece of blatant propaganda, a stiff, inaccurate caricature. Blacks were portrayed as sniveling, mindless creatures who spent more time on their knees than on their feet. Their white masters were depicted as ruthless, heartless monsters. After watching six scenes and writing down my observations on the more grotesque parts of the performance, the director asked me if I had seen enough to give an opinion. He stopped the actors and told everyone to listen to my critique.

I explained that they had an absolutely false notion of black-white relationships and attitudes in the South. As I sought to provide the actors and actresses a realistic understanding, I was surprised to find them inattentive and rather passive. I thought that they might have been so steeped in the propagandistic view of the United States that they would be unable to digest my opposing account. I think they looked on me as an impostor, as one who did not really know what he was talking about.

I finished my critique, said good-by, and was on my way out when Alexandrovich caught up with me and asked me into his office. Although I had no desire to join him I did not know how I could refuse. As we entered his office he thanked me for my time and comments, saying that my remarks were valuable. He shook my hand warmly and said, "Comrade Robinson, if you want to see the play when it opens, please come as my welcome guest. Just go to the ticket office and pick up as many as six tickets, which will be set aside for you. Just tell the ticket-seller your name and that I sent you."

I thanked him for his generosity and was about to leave when he handed me an open envelope. "This is for your time and trouble," he said.

When I saw the rubles inside the envelope I handed it back to him, thanked him for his thoughtfulness, and walked out the door. He called after me but I quickened my pace.

The next day, after Sunday dinner—usually the best meal of the week—I decided to read at a favorite spot on the grounds of the sanitarium. There was a bench encircled by large shade trees about three hundred feet from the guest house. Others liked that spot too, but there was little chance I would have to share it, since Russians normally take a nap after the big afternoon meal. I was enjoying both the solitude and my book, when I thought I heard footsteps. I looked around and, not seeing anyone, I turned back to my book. But then someone said, "May I disturb you?"

I stood up, trying to see who it was, but still I saw no one.

"Sure, sure, you may disturb me," I said, wondering if someone was playing games. Then Bellah jumped out from behind a bush. I wondered if she had been there all along. Of the three women I had befriended, she was the one I least cared to be with. I suspected her motives, and thought she might well be connected to the MVD. As I sat back down, she sat beside me, without invitation from me. Although this invasion of my privacy was unwelcome, I did not want to risk alienating the secret police so I acted as pleasant as possible.

"Bellah," I said, "I'm surprised to see you here this afternoon. Don't you usually take a nap after dinner?"

"Yes, that is true," she said, "but today I couldn't sleep. I was not feeling too well, so I thought a walk in the fresh air might clear my head. I remembered this lovely place, so here I am."

"So you have been here before?" I asked.

"Oh yes, with Nyura, We found this place one day while walking back from the sea. We liked it so much that we have been here several times."

I wanted to ask her where Nyura was, but did not. Bellah leaned toward me and asked, "What are you reading?"

"Oh, these are biographies of some of the great western music composers," I said.

"I'm sure you have read and heard about some of our great composers," she said, and then added, "Tell me, whose composers do you prefer, theirs or ours?"

If I had been in the West I would have given my honest opinion. But in the Soviet Union, especially with a possible MVD agent or informer on your hands, you have to be careful. I said what was most safe: "Bellah, generally musical tastes differ in different cultures . . ."

But before I could continue, she interrupted to say, sharply, "I asked for your opinion, not a general one."

"I'll tell you, my real opinion is that the Russian composers are far greater than the western ones. I think they have made more of a constructive contribution to music than those of Germany, France, and Italy."

I thought that this would satisfy her. I was in perfect sync with the Kremlin's campaign to develop nationalistic pride. Wherever Soviet citizens went they were reminded of the great accomplishments of the Russian people, past and present. Newspapers, radio, posters, and banners hailed the unique greatness of their native land, and boasted that Russians had invented almost every meaningful device in the world, from the straight pin to the airplane.

I had seen a curious drama in a Moscow theater that portrayed the story of how Russians had discovered electricity. The play showed how after much experimentation they added a solution of sodium chloride to some other mixture and produced a very dim light inside a specially designed oval glass. The play went on to show how soon after the Russian discovery, the American inventor Thomas Edison sent a high-level delegation to czarist Russia with an offer to buy the discovery. Even though the Russians agreed, through the worst kind of treachery the bourgeois delegation robbed them of their discovery anyway.

The play was strongly promoted in Moscow, so it was only in the seventh week of the performance that I was able to buy a ticket to *Let There Be Light* at four times its value. When the aroused Russian audience saw the dim light appear on the table, they rose to their feet in the darkened theater and applauded for more than five minutes. Of course, I was careful to clap just as vigorously as the next person. The play was a smash hit wherever it was shown.

In any case, after sitting and chatting with me for about an hour, Bellah said she was going to the guest house but would be right back. I wondered what she was up to. There was no way to prove, or know for sure, that she was serving the secret police in some capacity, but an inner voice kept warning me, "Be on guard!"

In a few minutes Bellah was back, but this time with Nyura. I was delighted to see her, but also anxious, since I was becoming particularly fond of her. Nyura smiled and said playfully, "Oh, here is our loner."

"What do you mean?" I asked.

"Well, we have not seen you for almost two days," she said. "I concluded that you were hiding from us."

"Oh, no, I wasn't hiding," I said. "In fact, all yesterday I was busy consulting at the dramatic theater."

"Do tell us what you did," asked Nyura. "And let's go back to the beach where the air is fresher."

"Fine," I said, as I stood and stretched a bit. I noticed Nyura watching me, interested in whatever I said and did, even in how I moved. I was enjoying her attention as we walked to the beach, with Nyura on one side and Bellah on the other. As soon as we sat down, Nyura glanced at Bellah, looked me straight in the eye and then said with a chuckle, "You know, Bellah, I think that when our friend returns to Moscow he will not only be a film actor but a performer on the theatrical stage as well. I hope you will not forget to send me a ticket to a front row seat on the night of your debut."

"Of course, I won't forget," I said, and we all laughed.

For a moment we were all silent, and I thought wistfully how the scene reminded me of the early 1930s, when I was free to associate with Russian women. But now things were different. Foreigners—and most particularly black foreigners—were discouraged by the Soviet system from becoming emotionally involved with Russian women.

"What were you doing at Odessa's City Theater?" asked Nyura.

"Some passages in *Deep Are the Roots,* which they will perform soon for the public, baffled the director, and he asked me to interpret them for him.

Nyura seemed excited. *"Deep Are the Roots!"* she exclaimed. "I tried to see it in Moscow but couldn't get tickets. It was always sold out. Oh how I would love to see it here in Odessa."

She paused, appearing embarrassed, no doubt wondering how aggressive she ought to be. Finally she managed to say, "Comrade Robinson, could you get me a ticket?"

Of course I would get her a ticket. I had already been guaranteed free access to the play from its director. Yet in case something were to go wrong, I only told her that I would try.

"I too would like to see the drama," piped in Bellah. "From it I should be able to learn more about the plight of your people in America. Tell me, is it really as bad as we've been told?"

But before I could answer, she asked, "What about you? How did you manage to come to the Soviet Union? And when? My history teacher used to tell us that blacks weren't allowed to go to school in America. Is that true?"

I knew I had to watch what I said to Bellah. I answered with a brief history lesson and likened the American slaves to the Russian serfs. I mentioned the abolitionist movement, and the effect of the Civil War on American whites and blacks. I acknowledged that there was racism in America, but Bellah's eyes grew larger when I told her that blacks could become lawyers, doctors, and dentists, and that they served the black community. When I told her how I got to her country, she rose on her knees and pointed at me with excitement and surprise. She asked, "Are you the one who was attacked by two white Americans in Stalingrad?"

"Yes, I was the one," I said.

Bellah moved toward me—now a genuine hero—clasped both of my hands in hers, and said with deep admiration, "I congratulate you for your courage and your decision to stay in our country. You know, it was after what happened to you in Stalingrad that our history teacher explained how your people were treated in America. I remember how upset our Komsomol unit was. In fact, we unanimously approved a resolution condemning those two Americans for what they did to you."

Bellah stood up, her arms outstretched like a Baptist minister welcoming a convert to his flock, and said, "Goodness me, I have met you. I must tell my husband and my son and daughter."

Nyura stood up, smoothed out the wrinkles in her skirt, and said, "It's nearing supper time. Let's go."

The following day Julia was waiting for me in the lounge when I returned from the studio. "Here," she said. "A man came by with this envelope and said I should give it to you."

It was from the director—250 rubles. Noticing I was upset, Julia asked what was bothering me. When I explained she counseled me, "Listen, there is an old Russian saying, and it's one I believe. 'When being given, take; when being beaten, run.' My friendly advice to you is to take it. If you don't, it will go into someone else's pocket."

I accepted her advice.

On my way back from work the following day I ran into Nyura and Bellah. I think they purposely walked toward the studio so they could meet me. As soon as I saw Nyura, all my tension from eight hours of the director's ranting and raving evaporated. The women said they had seen posters advertising that night's opening of *Deep Are the Roots,* and wanted to know whether I still planned to take them. I assured them I had not forgotten.

When we returned to the sanitarium, I excused myself so that I could find Julia. I wanted to invite her to the theater as well. Although the four of us arrived at the theater an hour before show time, there was already a long line of people waiting to buy tickets. I walked up to the ticket booth, hoping the man inside would notice me. But he acted as if I were invisible. After a few minutes I finally said, "I'm Comrade Robinson. Director Peter Alexandrovich has left some tickets for me. May I have them, please?"

The man responded with disdain, "There is nothing for you here. If you want tickets go to the end of the line. No one, whether you are from Odessa or abroad, receives special privileges here."

The chances were that the tickets were there, but the man had not even looked for them. I went looking for Alexandrovitch. Neither he nor his secretary was in his office, so I decided to wait outside in the hall. Ten minutes passed and no one came by. I figured they must all be backstage, and was about to go there myself, when a woman appeared. She was surprised to see me standing there. She evidently recognized me and said, "I'm Olga Vasilevna, the assistant director of the theater."

After I returned her greeting, she asked, "Shouldn't you be inside? The play begins in about twenty minutes."

Yes, I know," I said. "But I have a problem. The man in the ticket booth wouldn't give me the tickets Comrade Alexandrovich promised me."

"Oh, well, come with me," she said.

I followed her to the ticket booth, where she sternly ordered the man to give me four tickets. Before I left, she thanked me for my advice on the play, and said she hoped I would enjoy it. Bellah, Nyura, and Julia were beaming as they watched the man hand me the four tickets.

Everybody, my companions included, enjoyed the play. The cast received five curtain calls. Only a few of my recommendations were adopted by the director. I suspect it would have been politically imprudent for him to make many of the changes I had suggested. As we stood waiting for the tram car, Nyura asked, "When were your people brought to America?"

"In 1619," I answered.

"And the whites?"

"A white settlement in Virginia, called Jamestown, was founded in 1607," I said.

"So you arrived virtually around the same time," said Nyura.

She wanted to understand the root causes of white antipathy toward blacks.

"In the play," she said, "the black servants' children and the white landowner's children played together, learning to trust and love one another, but when they became youth they would gravitate to the superior and inferior roles that society expected of them." She shook her head and added, "How sad. I can't understand how that could happen."

Julia and Bellah were quiet, waiting for my response. In fact, they were quiet all the way back to the sanitarium, as I tried to explain what caused the sudden rift between black and white youth after years of close friendship. To do that I had to trace the cause of racism in America. I explained that many white men had sexual relations with black slave women, producing racially mixed offspring. They were startled when I told them that I believed that more than one-third of America's blacks had at least one white ancestor in their family. It was hard for them to accept the fact that even white immigrants were viewed by white Americans as superior to blacks whose ancestors came to America at practically the same time as the first white settlers.

I do not think I was able to explain adequately how race prejudice came to be so prevalent in America. Every explanation I gave seemed irrational to them. They found it difficult to understand how such a technologically advanced nation as the United States could be plagued by racism. They could accept that an underdeveloped country might have race prejudice, but they thought that the more materially developed a country was, the more socially liberated it would be.

Later that week I had a day off from the filming. It was ideal weather for the beach, the air warm and the sky a bright blue. As I stood outside the sanitarium's guest house, gazing at the blue sky streaked with gold, I wished there was a way to take my feeling of contentment and the warm, gentle climate back to Moscow in a bottle. Then on an icy winter night with howling, freezing winds I could remove the cork and take a whiff.

I walked alone to the beach and found a quiet spot. I found several sticks, planted them upright in the sand fairly close to the water, and placed my white undershirt and dress shirt over them, creating a miniature tent. With only my swimsuit on, I lay under it, closed my eyes and breathed in the fresh salt air. I built the tent on the advice of one of the doctors at the sanitarium, who told me to avoid too much direct exposure to the sun.

What a pleasure it was to lie there in the sun! I dozed off for a few minutes, awoke and crawled out of my covering, and sat there enjoying the panorama of sand, sea, and sky before me. I leaned back on my elbows and closed my eyes, then tried to replay in my mind the tranquil scene before me. I wanted to be able to recall this moment on some cold night when the Moscow winter wrapped me in its grayness. When I opened my eyes, I noticed something dark in the water, about a hundred feet out, that seemed to be moving toward me. I stood up to see what it was. It was a person swimming. Having satisfied my curiosity, I crawled back into my tent, stretched out with my arms folded over my chest, and closed my eyes. In a matter of moments I heard a woman's voice asking, "You are not sleeping, are you?"

I raised my head. It was Nyura, shining wet from the sea, her large hazel eyes dancing with mischief, a slight smile on her bronze-colored face. Seeing her there, I realized that in going to the beach that day, I had nurtured a hidden desire that I would find Nyura there.

"This is no dream," I thought excitedly, for Nyura was standing before me, vibrant and full of life.

"No, I wasn't sleeping," I told her.

"Well then, good morning," she said, still smiling. "How are you?"

I was still in my little tent, trying to recover from the surprise of Nyura's unexpected appearance. I never answered her question, but crawled out of the tent instead and stood up.

"All I have for a sand covering in this old newspaper," I said, pointing to the paper. "Would you care to sit with me?"

"Of course," she responded, kneeling on the newspaper and then turning to lie on one side, watching me all the while. I lay next to her, hardly caring about the powerful sun overhead.

"Tell me," I asked, "did you know I was here before you started swimming?"

Nyura looked away from me, staring at the sand. "Yes," she said. I was thrilled, and did not know what to say. She added: "I hope my presence hasn't disturbed your peace and isolation."

"Oh no, not at all," I told her.

Something electric was happening between us. Frankly, I was without words. I did not want to try speaking, with clumsy words that would only get in the way of feelings springing from the soul. Whenever our eyes met I longed to reach over and touch her. Lying side by side, essentially alone, surrounded only by nature's handiwork, I felt a burning desire welling up inside of me. This was the first time since I had come to Russia that I had felt this way about a woman. I knew I never wanted to marry a Russian woman, so I tried hard not to feel aroused. To marry would be to create another barrier to my quest to leave the country for good. I had learned to guard against falling in love. I could point to seventeen years of success, but now my control was slipping. I wanted to embrace Nyura.

"It's such a natural yearning," I thought, "why stop from doing what every man needs?"

Just then Nyura began asking personal questions, breaking the spell. I did not mind answering. She wanted to know where I had lived in the United States, how I managed to come to the Soviet Union, what I thought about Russia and its people, where I lived in Moscow, and what kind of work I did. She also wanted to know if I was married. Hearing my answer to this last question seemed to matter the most to her. She was clearly pleased with my answer.

"Nyura," I said, "let's go for a swim."

We both ran into the water, and for fifteen minutes or more we swam and frolicked, laughed and splashed, thoroughly enjoying our childlike play in the water. After awhile she suggested we return to the beach. When we reached our spot we lay side by side again on the ground, only this time we were a bit closer to each other. I was hardly in the mood for talk. All I could think about was the beautiful woman beside me. If I were to talk, I would ask her about her life, learn about her likes and dislikes. I imagined that she must love Tchaikovsky's music and Pushkin's poetry. I wanted to believe that we liked the same things.

"Bob," she said, "I hope I didn't offend you by asking you so many personal questions before we went for our swim."

"No, you didn't," I said, wondering if I had given the impression that I felt she was prying into my private life. I certainly did not want her to feel she was intruding.

"I ask only because you are so silent," she said.

"To tell you the truth, Nyura, there is little I wish to say. But there's much I'd like to know about you," I said. "I've been lying here wondering whether I should ask you certain personal questions."

"Please ask me anything you have in mind," she said. "I promise to answer you as best I can."

She seemed eager to share her life's story with me. There was nothing that I wanted to hear more. I wanted to know who she was, what she was like as a child (of course, she must have been sweet), what her parents were like, where she was educated, and then, the most important question and the one I was afraid to ask. Was she married?

"Tell me, who are you? What is your background?" I asked, looking straight into her eyes. "That you are not someone ordinary is something I feel deeply."

"Where do you want me to start?" she asked.

"Wherever you want to," I said, leaning on my elbow and waiting for her to begin.

"Well, both of my parents were born in Petrograd. My mother finished Gymnasium and my father graduated from the military academy. They were married in 1913, I was their third child, born in 1917. As soon as the revolution started I was sent with my mother and brothers to a town near Bessarabia, while my father fought on the side of the Bolsheviks.

"In 1925 our family went to Moscow, where my father became a navy pilot. From time to time he was sent on exploration missions to the North Pole. In 1936 he went on a mission from which he never returned. His plane crashed near the Pole and he and his crew were killed. The government awarded him the Order of Hero of the Soviet Union posthumously. My father was a great friend of Vodopianov, a very famous Arctic explorer. My mother was given a lifetime pension and three-room apartment at Government House, overlooking the Moscow River.

"In March of 1941 I graduated from medical school in Moscow and within two months' time I married a medical student. Five months later he was drafted into the army. About two-and-a-half years later I was informed that he was killed in action. He didn't live to see his daughter, who is now six. I am working in a children's hospital as a specialist and am doing fairly well. That's all I have to say, but if you have any special questions I'd be happy to answer them."

"I have a question," I said. "I'm a bit puzzled. Since your father was acclaimed a Hero of the Soviet Union, you would have a pass to stay free, including transportation, at either one of the two best sanitariums in the Soviet Union, yet you come to a second-rate one in Odessa."

Nyura was as taken aback by my question as I was surprised that I had asked it. But I was interminably analytical, and I had noticed an inconsistency in what she had said. I wanted to kick myself for asking such a dumb question. But Nyura was gracious in her response.

"I came to Odessa because I'd grown tired and bored with those two sanitariums you mentioned. It was a case of seeing the same people, all of them well-to-do, with their influential positions, all talking about the same things over and over again, year after year. One day while I was returning to Moscow on a train from the rest house in the Caucasus, I met a woman who told me about this sanitarium in Odessa, and what a wonderful time she had here. So I decided to try it. Because of my professional status I had to ask someone with political influence to purchase a pass for me to come here. I was able to get the pass, and I came incognito. You're the only person who knows what my background is. I hope you won't tell a soul."

After I assured her that I would not reveal her secret, she went on to say how much she was enjoying her stay in Odessa.

"It was wonderful that I was able to meet you, Bob, and learn so much about the plight of your people in America. I liked the opportunity to socialize with other, simpler people, and even to dance with them. I will go back to Moscow with fond memories."

"Are you sure you came here incognito?" I asked.

"You know, I have wondered about that, noticing people following us, but I haven't committed a crime, for from what I understand you have had a clean record for the past seventeen years in the Soviet Union."

She paused for a moment, as if studying her hands, and then asked, "You are not hiding anything from me, are you, Bob?"

"Nothing," I assured her.

"You know, the first time I met you I found you most interesting, but I did wonder about the wisdom of continuing to see you," she said. "I'm glad I didn't follow my cowardly instinct."

"So am I," I said.

Nyura looked at her watch. "It is time to leave; it's getting close to dinner time," she said.

As we rose to leave, we both instinctively turned to the left and then to the right, and together saw the same thing. Two of the three men who had been following us were sitting on a blanket about 150 feet away. We put on our clothes and walked back to the sanitarium, never once mentioning those two men who had seemed to drop out of the sky, in order to observe us enjoying one another's company on the beach.

I purposely avoided Nyura for the next four days. I knew that if I was with her continually I could easily lose control, and I could not afford for that to happen. She was unattached, probably wanting to marry again, and I felt there was something special, beautiful, yet dangerous for me, between us.

I saw her again the night before she left. She came to see me at supper time one evening to tell me she was leaving for Moscow the next day, and to ask me to escort her to the railroad station. I told her I would. Part of me wanted to hop on the train and head to Moscow with her. Bellah told me that she was leaving that same day and wondered if she could join us. Of course, we agreed. In a way this was good, since Bellah's presence provided a safeguard against the men who were following us constantly.

The next day, Nyura, Julia, Bellah, and I went to the beach together for the last time. Though we all dashed into the water together, we felt sad about our imminent parting. Julia and Bellah sensed that something deeper than friendship had developed between Nyura and me.

A few hours later, while waiting for the bus to take us to the railroad station, we all exchanged addresses and promised to write each other. Our promise was sincere at the moment, because our good times together were fresh in our minds. But once back home we would become immersed in our daily pattern of life and the desire to maintain the summer friendships would wane. After all of my vacations at homes of rest or sanitariums, I rarely received a letter from anyone I came to know, nor did I ever write one myself.

The railroad station was busy with people arriving to start their holiday, full of merry anticipation of the days ahead, carrying satchels and cardboard boxes tied with rope. Those departing were more subdued, except for the hundreds of Komsomols who had just finished twenty-four days at a Home of Rest outside Odessa. They were the apple of the Kremlin's eye, and they knew it. They were a confident group, enthusiastic about getting back to school or work, where they could demonstrate to their fellow countrymen the right way to help develop their nation into the greatest in the world. They behaved as if they owned the railroad station. No adult dared cross any of them.

When the railroad conductor signaled for all passengers to board the train, I shook Bellah's hand and bid her farewell, then turned to Nyura, who clasped my hand in hers. We stood there for a few seconds, searching each other's eyes for a special silent message that only people who care for each other deeply can convey.

"We must meet in Moscow," Nyura finally said.

"Yes, sure," I said. I could say no more. I was sure she knew how I felt. I stood there, as if riveted to the station platform, determined not to move until the train vanished beyond the horizon. Soon I noticed Nyura, her smiling face close to a window, waving to me. I waved back. As the train began to move, she continued to wave.

As I returned to the sanitarium, my mind was full of thoughts of Nyura, of the time we had spent together. I was oblivious to everyone and everything. I hoped that she would write, but doubted whether she would. With Nyura gone, the sanitarium seemed hollow. In fact, there were not many people around. A dining room that seated four hundred served only eighteen for supper. Three of them were the men who had been following Nyura and me wherever we went.

The next morning the men did not show up for breakfast. I tried to find out who they were by asking a registrar to tell me when they had arrived and when they had checked out.

"Comrade Robinson," she said, "we are forbidden to give out information about any of our guests to anyone, even to our staff. I am sorry, but I cannot help you."

Twelve days after Nyura left I received a letter from her. I was amazed. She must have written it upon returning home, for the trip to Moscow took about two days, and it would take four to five days to reach me, depending on whether it was censored. I opened the letter excitedly.

"Her feelings about me must be real," I thought. "Otherwise, people of her stature don't correspond with common people, in general, and with foreigners in particular."

In her letter she thanked me for being so kind to her during her holiday. She said the Komsomols whom she befriended on the train asked her questions about me, and that she enjoyed answering them. She also said that as soon as the got home she had told her mother and daughter all about me.

Two weeks later I answered her letter, trying to restrain my true feelings, because I knew that any serious involvement with her could lead to disaster for both of us. In a month, I received another letter from Nyura. This time she said her daughter was anxious to meet me, that she was continually asking when I was returning to Moscow. In a second letter, I told her that my return hinged on the completion of the film. Of course, I was delighted whenever I received one of her letters. I held onto them, and read and reread them time and time again, feeling pleasure just from looking at her handwriting.

When her next letter arrived it shocked me. She wrote, "I must be honest with you, for in doing so I hope you will be able to understand me better and see the logic of my decision. After carefully thinking over our distinct positions, outlook, habits, and customs, I know there is absolutely no possibility of my ever becoming your life companion. Therefore, that being so, there is no use to keep up a senseless correspondence."

I knew these were not her true feelings. I understood that the MVD had gotten to her. Her first letter had not been checked by the censors, but the second one had. No doubt she had been pressured to end our relationship, that people of her family background did not associate with foreigners, regardless of whether they were Soviet citizens.

My departure for Moscow was even more curious than were the original circumstances of my recruitment for the film. It was about a month after I received Nyura's third letter. Two days before my scheduled return to Moscow I had put in a full day at the studio. Tomorrow I would return for my final day. That night I went to bed at 11:00 P.M., anticipating a demanding final day. A short time later I woke up to the sound of pounding on my door. My landlady was calling out my name and shouting, "Wake up, there's a man here from the studio."

I opened the door. The man said, "Excuse me, but I have just been sent to tell you that a car will be here at five in the morning to take you to the airport for your flight back to Moscow."

"What? Who sent you?" I asked in amazement. From the way he spoke, I doubted his story.

He stammered in reply, "Er, I think it was the director of the film in the company of two other men. Anyway, be ready at five in the morning. Good-by."

I glanced at the landlady's clock. It was already past 12:30 A.M. I began to pack right away. I got very little sleep because the car arrived almost an hour early to take me to the airport.

Back in Moscow, my role in the film was completed. But I had not yet been given the ten thousand rubles due me. I was given 2,500 rubles while in Odessa and told that as soon as I returned home I would get the rest. When I went to collect the remaining amount, I was told of the money reform that had just gone into effect. The ruble was devalued ten to one, so I received only 750 rubles. As for the film? It was very well-received throughout the Soviet Union. In time it was regarded as a cinematic classic and shown at least twice annually on Soviet television.

CHAPTER 21

Attempts to Leave

TWO MONTHS AFTER THE GERMANS SURRENDERED, in July 1945, I filed for permission to visit my mother. She was getting older, and I longed to see her and my brother. I had to wait a year for a response from the Department of Visas and Registration of the Ministry of Foreign Affairs. At the end of that time, they rejected my request without explanation.

Now that the war was over, for the first time in years I could think about more than just my daily survival. I knew that I wanted out, and with the war over I decided to begin my quest. The country and system that at first had excited my curiosity—and offered me a higher wage and better job opportunities than I could expect in the United States—was thoroughly objectionable to me now. I had been living in Russia for sixteen years. I knew there was no way to cash in on the empty Soviet promise, given me when I inquired about citizenship, that I would not be held in the country against my will. I sensed that with every passing year my chances of returning to America were growing dimmer. After all, the Kremlin's propaganda apparatus had hailed Robert Robinson as an oppressed black American who had found refuge and freedom in the Soviet Union. They would be embarrassed if I were to tell the world outside the Soviet orbit that the facts were quite different. Rather than take any chances—despite my clean record of having never committed any counterrevolutionary act or criticized a Soviet official—the Ministry of Foreign Affairs was not taking any chances.

After the ministry rejected my request, I decided to appeal its decision in person. I quickly learned that there was no way to appeal. The clerks and officials I spoke with all said they did not know why my application had been rejected and there was nothing they, or anyone else, could do about it. They also asked me to sign a document stating that I had accepted voluntarily the ministry's decision not to approve my application. Between the final paragraph and the space for a signature was a blank area. Since I would not receive a copy of what I signed, they could type in later anything they wanted over my signature. This was a document I did not wish to sign. I was so angry and frustrated when the official presented it to me, that my first impulse was to slam my fist on his desk and throw his paperweight through the window. I wanted to rip the document to shreds and throw the pieces in his face. I wanted to cry; I wanted to protest. But to whom? No one really cared. At best, some bureaucrat would listen to my complaints, assure me that everything would be done to solve my problem, and then do nothing.

I somehow was able to control my temper. What held me back was knowing that in a matter of seconds I could eliminate any chance I might have of ever returning to America. They would brand me a potential counterrevolutionary and immediately increase MVD surveillance. I took the careful, cautious route: I signed the document, preserved my unblemished record, and went and applied all over again. I was restricted, however, by the rule that allowed only one request a year to visit a Western country. Beginning in 1945, a year never went by without my filing an application. In twenty-seven attempts over twenty-seven years, only once did I even come close to getting permission.

In 1953 I received a cablegram from my brother that my mother was critically ill; she wanted to see me immediately. I nearly panicked. This time, instead of approaching the usual agency and waiting months for the usual response, I composed a letter to the Supreme Soviet (the parliament of the Soviet Union) and headed for the reception center of the chairman of the Presidium, cablegram and letter in hand. I knew that nothing less than special consideration would allow me to leave to see my mother before she died. I approached the four-story brick building at the corner of Kalinin and Karl Marx streets feeling a combination of determination and foreboding. I opened the tall, heavy door and entered a small, empty hallway. In front of me was a white sign which read, "Entrance to the Chairman of the Presidium of the Supreme Soviet."

I opened the door slightly and heard such a commotion that I assumed I had ventured into the wrong place. I peered inside the large, high-ceilinged hall to see about two hundred people sitting on the floor. Some were crying loudly; others softly sobbed. A few were hysterical. All had papers in their hands and were on the right side of the hall. On the left side were two lines of about forty people each. Judging by their dress, they represented a cross section of Russian society. I walked in and stood at the back of one of these lines. In front of the line was a partition made of wood and opaque glass with several openings. I could see two women who were behind the openings. I watched them as they listened to each applicant, read the petition, and either rejected it on the spot or accepted it for consideration by giving the petitioner a receipt. At least those with receipts walked away with their hope still alive; for those who were rejected, this was the end of the road. It was a sad sight to hear the wails and see the hopelessness of those whose petitions were being rejected.

As I drew closer to the front of the line, I noticed that there was a third woman behind the partition, sitting comfortably drinking her tea. When she saw me in line she got up and beckoned to me to come and see her. Thinking that perhaps I was in the wrong place, she asked, "Can I help you?"

"Yes, please," I said, as I handed her the letter I had in my pocket. I had purposely addressed the envelope and written the letter in English.

"I can't read this," said the woman, as she handed the letter to the woman next to her. "Is the letter also written in English?"

When I told her it was, she pressed a button and in a few minutes a very large fellow appeared. She told him I had a letter for the Secretariat of the Presidium.

He told me to follow him, and led me up the stairs to the second floor, where we entered a large room where a man about thirty years old sat behind an impressive desk.

"What is it?" he demanded of my escort.

"This citizen has a letter to the secretary of the chairman of the Supreme Soviet," replied the large man.

The seated man looked at me for the first time, and I said, "Good morning, Comrade Secretary."

"Hello," he said abruptly. "I am the assistant secretary. What is it you came here for?"

"My mother is very ill," I said, "and I have come to ask the chairman of the Presidium of the Supreme Soviet to help me get an early visa to Jamaica." My mother had recently left New York and returned to the country of her youth.

The man smiled and said, "But the chairman does not issue visas."

I took the letter and cablegram out of my pocket and handed them to him. The assistant secretary and the other man began reading them. When they were fininshed, the assistant secretary said, "We'll see what can be done. I don't promise you anything definite. You'll be informed. That's all."

He then turned his attention to other business. I rose, said good-by, and left. No one answered my farewell.

Thirty days later a white postcard came in the mail with the printed statement, "Your application has been forwarded to the Ministry of Internal Affairs."

Nearly a month later a yellow postcard was delivered from the OVIR (Department of Visas and Registration), asking me to come to the OVIR office. I went the very next morning. Although I arrived before 9:00, there were still twenty people in line before me. When my turn came, I explained my predicament to a tall, stern-looking woman with blond hair. She listened impassively and said that for my application to be reviewed I would need to prepare an autobiography and bring a letter of recommendation from the factory committee, along with six head shot photographs. They also required a letter from the house committee in my apartment building, a group of tenants who took complaints and spied on everyone.

During the next three months I was interrogated by more than half of the twenty members of the house committee. The committee was extremely cautious; it was safer for the members to deny a request than to approve one. I finally received their half-page letter, but only because I pestered them constantly. I took my letters and photographs to the ministry and was told by a woman that they would inform me as soon as they received an answer from their superiors. I had still not heard from them almost one year later, when I received a letter from my brother saying that my mother had died.

A postcard from OVIR came in the mail two weeks later, asking me to come to the OVIR office. I wondered if the censors had opened and read the letter from my brother and told the ministry that my mother had died. The heavyset man assigned to interview me at the ministry said, "You had asked for permission for an exit visa. You see, we are so busy that it has not been possible to take up your case. Perhaps you have changed your mind and no longer wish to go?"

"My mother struggled against death because she wanted desperately to see me once more before dying," I told him. "Through no fault of my own I failed to reach her bedside. Although she is now dead, I want to visit her grave and seek her forgiveness. Yes, I still want to go."

The officer looked at me with cold, hard eyes and asked, "Are you sure you still want to go? I don't see the purpose."

"Yes," I told him emphatically, "I definitely want to go. I think it is a natural thing for a dedicated son to want to do."

"All right," he said. "As soon as we reach a decision, you will be informed. Without another word he stood up and walked out of the room.

In June 1956—three years after I had first filed an application—OVIR notified me to come and pick up my passport. But first, they required that I deposit 360 rubles ($72) at the state bank and bring my receipt, along with my internal passport, to their office with me. I went to the bank and then raced to the ministry. I was ecstatic, thinking about returning to Jamaica, my birthplace, after thirty-four years. I wondered if this could really be happening. I was shaking with anxiety when I reached the passport section. A pleasant clerk handed me my passport and said, "You have ten days to leave Moscow."

But there was a hitch. I learned the following day that the next ship leaving Leningrad for Britain—where I could catch a plane to Jamaica—was not for two weeks. At that time there was no commercial air travel out of Russia. I looked into the possibility of traveling into

Robinson being interviewed in his factory by William Worthy, an American journalist who tried to help him leave the Soviet Union.

western Europe, but I learned that special visas would be required to go through Poland and East Germany, which took at least thirty days to obtain.

I began to feel wretched. I considered taking a train anyway, and trying to get through the various checkpoints by showing my old Moscow Soviet mandate. But the dangers were too great; I might well end up deported to Siberia, imprisoned, or confined to a mental hospital for committing an anti-Soviet action.

I had clearance to leave, but there was no way out. I asked the ministry to extend my passport. All I needed was two more weeks and I could take the ship to England. A clerk advised me how to fill out the form and said I would have a reply in ten days. After ten days of enormous stress, I returned for an answer to my appeal. I was told that they did not have an answer and I should wait ten more days and then call them. I waited, and then called; still no answer. For the next three months I kept calling the same man, who kept telling me that a special committee was processing my appeal. Finally, one day, I lost my composure and challenged him, "Why are you denying me the extension?"

"You were issued a passport and refused to use it," he snapped back. "Blame yourself for still being here."

For the next few days I could only brood over my misfortune. Then one morning while at work I recalled a newspaper article I had read several months earlier that urged citizens to share their legitimate complaints with the chairman of the Supreme Soviet. For the next week I debated whether to go this route, recalling my previous, miserable experience there. Since I had no recourse, I decided to call on Comrade Voroshilov, the chairman.

When I arrived in the reception area, I went to the third window. Although there was no one there, there also was no long line of people waiting. Fortunately, the receptionist who had assisted me three and a half years earlier recognized me. She called me over to the front of one of the long lines and asked me what I wanted.

"I was here a couple of years ago with a letter to the chairman's secretary," I said, "and you allowed me to go up to see him."

"Yes, yes, of course; I remember," she said.

"Well, I am having difficulty over the same problem he helped me to solve," I said. "I have come to ask you to let me see him for just a few minutes."

The woman turned to speak with a colleague, then came and opened the low, swinging door to let me through. "Comrade Voroshilov's secretary is on the second floor," she said.

I bounded up the stairs and took several deep breaths in front of his office door, which was slightly ajar. I heard an incomprehensible response, much like a grunt, opened the door, and entered. Sitting behind a huge desk, in the middle of a large, carpeted room, was a heavyset, hulking man with long, thick fingers. He stared at me, his lips clenched tight, as if sealed.

"Comrade secretary," I said, "I have come to ask you the day and date when the chairman of the Supreme Soviet will be receiving personal petitions."

The man's face turned red. He rose from his upholstered chair and started walking menacingly toward me. "What! The devil f--- your mother!" he said. "Get the hell out of here or I'll have you sent away immediately!"

I fled. Even in the subway train I could not stop shaking. Such vile and vicious cursing—it was not only what he said but how he said it that was offensive. To my ears, the sound of Russian cursing is terrifying, more coarse and vicious than in the other languages I know. I was deeply offended; I had done nothing wrong. Citizens had been invited to submit their complaints; I was only following the rules. Obviously, I should have known better and assumed that the invitation to air complaints was just a typical Soviet paper promise.

Still, I did not lose hope. I knew I would not be leaving in 1956. Clearly, those who had decided to issue me the passport knew it was worthless. But I resolved to come up with another reason for leaving and try again.

My next attempt was in 1957. This time I went through Bulganin, who was now prime minister, the number two man in the Soviet hierarchy. I was not certain that he would respond to my letter but I had to give it my best shot. In my letter I reminded him of how we had met in 1935 when he was head of the Moscow Soviet, and that he had promised to help me if the need ever arose. I mentioned the awards and medals I had won through my work as a mechanical engineer and the production devices I had invented. When I went to the local post office to mail the letter, the clerk looked at it and said she could not accept it. When I asked to see the postmaster, the clerk said, "He is not in."

I next went downtown to the main post office on Gorky Street and again tried to send the letter by registered mail. But when I handed it to an elderly clerk, she saw Bulganin's name on the envelope and said, "It is impossible." She flung the letter back at me, then turned away and left without another word. As I walked away slowly, pondering whether to mail the letter without registering it, I noticed a clerk I used to deal with when my mother was alive and I was writing her once a month. She was a kindly, white-haired woman who enjoyed practicing her English on me. I explained that no one would register my letter to Bulganin.

"Yes, it is true," she said, "that you will not find anyone to do that for you. There could be consequences." Then she leaned toward me and whispered, "I know a place where letters to such important people are accepted and delivered. But I will tell you on one condition only, that you must not reveal how you learned about this place."

"You can trust me," I said.

"A few meters after you pass through the Kremlin's Trinity Tower entrance gates you will notice a small, unpainted door," she explained. "There is a sign above it in small letters which says, "Receiving point of mail to the Central Committee of the USSR."

I found the place easily, opened the door, and entered a long, well-lighted room with a wood and glass counter dividing it in the middle. I handed my letter to one of the two uniformed MVD men sitting behind the counter. He checked the name and address, read the return address, and then placed the letter on his palm and felt whether there were any strange objects inside. Satisfied, he assured me the letter would reach Bulganin.

I was astounded when I received a card from OVIR three weeks later asking me to come by their office. I went there, showed one of the MVD men my card, and then waited as he got up and went into another office. He came right out and told me to go in immediately, even though the large reception room was filled with people already waiting there. I entered the room and greeted the MVD officer who was sitting behind a desk piled high with paper. He pretended not to hear me and continued reading for a moment, then raised his head and motioned for me to sit down. Arranging the papers on his desk into a neat pile, he placed my card in the middle of the stack and then stared at me, with cruel, dull eyes. He picked up the card and said in a threatening voice, "Look, how long do you think we are going to let you continue writing and pestering our leaders with your constant complaints and grumbling? We gave you a passport but you did not accept it. Now you are indirectly blaming others instead of yourself. We want you to know that we are not prepared to tolerate your deviation any longer. Enough is enough!"

He continued his attack. "I hope you understand what I am saying, because we do not possess endless patience in the face of your constant objection to our collective decisions. We have here your last grumbling letter to the chairman of the Council of Ministers. It has been agreed that you be allowed to make another application for an exit visa. Make a list of the following items, which you must bring us before your application can be considered: six photos, an autobiography, recommendation letters from your factory and from your house committee, and forty rubles of special stamps. As soon as you have all these items, bring them to us. That is all. You are free to go."

I completed the application, gathered the items, and delivered everything in late spring, 1957. In early August an event was to occur that directly affected my chances of getting a visa. A program called the Festival of Youths and Students was held in Moscow from July 30 through August 14. Among the thirty thousand young people from around the world who took part was a group of about twenty-five blacks from Jamaica. On August 11 I received a telephone call from Rev. Marcus James, a member of the Jamaican delegation, who said he had read about me in Jamaica and wanted to meet me. He said he had been trying to locate me since he arrived and had just been given my telephone number by a British journalist. Although it was already late, I told him I would meet him that night in his hotel room.

When I arrived around 10:15 he greeted me warmly and said with enthusiasm, "I understand you are an important person in the Soviet Union. I have read so many good things about you and now I am honored to be able to meet you."

I felt embarrassed and said nothing, and the short, stocky man continued, "I understand you will soon be coming to Jamaica to help set up a Communist state," he said.

"That is nonsense," I replied.

"But that's what an English journalist has written in *The Gleaner*" (a daily newspaper in Jamaica), he said. "I read it myself. Surely it is true."

"Whoever wrote that article did not have accurate information," I said. "I am not a Communist. I believe in God and I am a Christian."

Rev. James was surprised. "If you are not a Communist, why have you lived so long in the Soviet Union?" he asked.

I did not feel like giving him the history of the past twenty-seven years, but I did say that I had been the victim of a set of circumstances that were beyond my control and that all my attempts to leave the Soviet Union since 1945 had been blocked. I was simply honest, and did not know how he would react, since at first it had seemed that this Christian minister was excited about the thought of communism coming to Jamaica.

Rev. James stood up from his chair and declared, "They have no right to keep you in this country against your will."

"Just three months ago I made another application to leave this country and I am still waiting for an answer," I told him.

"Why does it take so long to get a reply?" he asked. "I am going to go with my interpreter and speak with them about this. Who should I see? I will raise hell, just you see!"

"Exit visas are granted by the Ministry of Foreign Affairs," I told him, "but please don't go. You will only get me in trouble; it won't help."

The next evening, at the invitation of Rev. James, I met the other members of the Jamaican delegation. Perhaps I should not have gone, because inevitably the topic of my captivity came up. The Jamaicans were upset that I was being held against my will and said they wanted to send a delegation to OVIR to petition the authorities to grant me—their countryman—an exit visa immediately.

I strongly urged them not to do that. "This plan of yours will not work," I said, "and it could even cause the authorities to retaliate against me by dismissing my case for good."

Yet it seemed that the more I protested, the more determined they became to carry out their plan. They just could not understand how the Soviet system worked. I left for home feeling unsettled.

Rev. James called me the next day. "Come to my hotel room," he said, "I have some good news for you."

Against my better judgment I thought that maybe, by some miracle, he had succeeded. I could not wait to see him. When I met him at his hotel, he shook my hand energetically and said, "Man, I raised Cain with those people. I told them they must let poor Mr. Robinson go. I had the clerk quivering. He told me he was only a worker and directed me to his boss. I was very firm, and demanded they let you go. He assured me that he would talk it over with his colleagues."

Apparently Rev. James thought that my case was suffering from a lack of attention, and that all that was needed was for him to alert the authorities. This well-meaning man, ignorant of the ways of Soviet totalitarianism, could not have done more to ruin my chances of getting out if that had been his purpose. I did not even mention to him that the colleagues who would be alerted were officers of the KGB. I was so disheartened, all I wanted to do was leave. When I told him I would be leaving, he handed me a piece of paper and said, cheerfully, "Here is my London address. I feel assured that you will be visiting me there by early September. I pray that the man in the ministry will keep his promise."

"Thank you for your good intentions and concern," I said angrily, "but frankly, although you cannot understand it, you have done me a disservice."

I wondered how it was possible that educated people in the Western world could be duped so easily by Soviet officials, could be so ignorant of the reality of the Soviet system. I had never felt more miserable in my life. I received a card five days later from the Department of Visas and Registration, telling me to call them right away. When I called, a person on the other end of the phone said forcefully, "Comrade Robinson, your application has been rejected!"

I had been expecting the news, but when the blow actually came it was hard to take. However, at work I had to maintain a normal outward appearance because the KGB procedure was to inform the party secretary whenever the OVIR refused me an exit visa so that I could be placed under strict surveillance. I first learned about this practice in 1946, when a friend in the party approached me and said under his breath,

"Comrade Robinson, I was sorry to learn that your application for an exit visa was refused." I told him that it was disappointing, pretending that I already knew.

"You must try again," he said. "Don't give up the right to visit your parents and relatives. I know how you must feel. I have relatives only two hundred kilometers away, yet I yearn to visit with them, something which I am allowed to do only rarely."

"Yes, I will try again," I said. The post card from the OVIR telling me to phone them arrived the following evening.

My annual application for an exit visa continued to be turned down until 1973.

CHAPTER 22

The Death of Stalin

MARCH 5, 1953, was a dramatic day in the Soviet Union. At 9 A.M. we heard over the loudspeakers, "Attention! Attention! This is Moscow calling, beaming to all radio stations in the Soviet Union. Tass is authorized to inform the Soviet people, with deep sorrow, of the great loss sustained by the death of Comrade Joseph Vissarionovich Stalin."

I do not think anyone heard the rest of the announcement; we were all shocked. Nobody said a word. Some workers stood over their machines with their heads bowed, while others stared blankly into space. The foreman's weeping broke the silence and set off an avalanche of tears. Everyone began crying.

Stalin had been their leader for more than twenty-five years. However oppressive the circumstances, at least they had survived under him. Many called him Father Stalin; in a sense, their god had died. Whom could they believe in now? They saw Stalin as a person above and apart from the system that frustrated their lives, as an idealist who loved them, as much a victim of the system as they were. The workers in my shop began wailing like lost and desperate children.

The telephone rang and every head turned toward it. Perhaps the caller would say that the radio broadcast was a cruel hoax, that Stalin was alive. But when the foreman hung up he announced, with tears still streaming down his face, that a special meeting would be held in a few minutes and everyone must attend.

We walked down the stairs in silence to the auditorium on the floor below. By the time I arrived, the hall was nearly full, which meant about two thousand people were crammed in. I was about thirty feet from the stage. Everyone was standing and the men were all holding their caps against their hearts. Most of them were crying. Some of the women stood with their faces buried in their hands, weeping uncontrollably.

Our shop superintendent walked up to the microphones and said, "Dear comrades, as you all have heard, we lost our great leader, our beloved teacher and friend, the outstanding deliverer of mankind from fascism, our beloved Joseph Vissarionovich. Our loss is so great that it is impossible to express it in words. I have known no other leader in my life, and now . . .

He could not continue; he broke down sobbing. Two of his comrades helped him off the platform as the crowd's weeping reached a crescendo. Then a young woman, a Komsomol, climbed the stairs to the platform, walked over to the microphones, and cried out, "Comrades, it is very difficult for me to believe that our dear and great father is not alive. What are we going to do without him directing us? Life is not bearable without him." At that point she began to shake and sob. For the next thirty minutes speaker after speaker broke down in tears, unable to complete their speeches.

No one could do any work the rest of the day. Some people sat at their desks or workbenches either staring blankly ahead or crying; others paced back and forth. There was silence, except for the solemn music broadcast from Radio Moscow over the loudspeakers. Occasionally a solemn sounding newscaster broke the spell with an update of the sad news. After work the streets reflected the mood of our factory. Green mourning wreaths had been placed on the taxicabs and tram cars. Everyone was solemn.

Two days later most of the workers were still in a stupor. No work had been done, not even by the foreman. After lunch the solemn melodies were interrupted by an announcement. "Attention! Attention! This is Moscow calling. Tass is authorized to say that the body of our teacher and leader, Joseph Vissarionovich, will lay in state at the House of Trade Unions from 2 P.M. until late tonight to afford all toilers the chance to bid farewell to our deceased leader." Most of the workers left immediately, without waiting for the shift to end, so they could see Stalin's body lying in state.

I had no great desire to see Stalin's corpse, although I was interested in observing the people's reaction. It is just as well, because hundreds of people were crushed to death in a mob outside the Hall of Trade Unions. A man I knew, who was stationed there as a guard and witnessed the debacle, said it was worse than anything he had experienced in the war. He explained that rows of trucks had been placed about five hundred feet from the building as a security barrier, and that tens of thousands of people descending on the building from three directions formed a mighty wave that crushed the people in front against the trucks. Some people being pushed up against the barricade slipped to the ground to avoid being slammed against the trucks, only to be trampled to death. The more athletic ones leapt up onto the trucks on the backs of others, often knocking someone else off and on top of an injured person on the ground. The guards behind the barricades stood helplessly as people crushed against the vehicles, the blood pouring from broken bodies, screaming, "Save me! Save me!" Without an order from their commander, who was in a nearby building, the guards were not authorized to move the vehicles. This incident was not reported in the newspapers or on the radio.

The next day, on March 8, I received a call from Robert Ross, one of two other American blacks living in Moscow in 1953. At this time Ross was a willing and useful propagandist for the Soviet authorities, so he had some influence. He would be sent around the country to talk about the oppression of blacks in America, a country he incidentally had not seen since 1928. Ross invited me to join him to pay my last respects to Stalin. When I declined he said, "If I were in your place I would certainly come along. I am going and I think you should do likewise. If you decide to do so, we could meet at the Poli-Technical Museum between 3:45 and 4:15 in the afternoon. Hope to see you there."

I thought about what Ross had said and decided I had better put in an appearance at the Hall of Trade Unions, and that it had better be the Soviet way, which meant not to go alone. I was so tired of not being able to do something alone. Ever since I arrived in the Soviet Union I found myself doing practically everything with a group: going to the movies, picking berries, visiting museums. I was fed up with having to be part of a pack, and longed for the opportunity to do something without having to explain my feelings to others. I was tired of being diplomatic, constantly on guard for fear that I would say or do the wrong thing. I wanted desperately to experience my true feelings without having to compromise them for the sake of my survival. If I was going to view Stalin's body, I would have preferred doing it alone. But I knew better. To be branded a loner, or an individualist, could well mean that in a few weeks I would be given a notice to move to a remote village, which I could not leave except for annual visits to a home of rest. I already had a reputation for being too individualistic, and some people considered me arrogant. I had overheard people saying, "Comrade Robinson thinks he knows more than us because he lived in America. He has refused to see that we have almost caught up with the United States." I had enemies in the factory hierarchy such as Gromov who would have enjoyed the opportunity to help send me away.

So I showed up at 3:45, and Ross was there waiting. We joined the line, which was six people abreast, at a point so distant that we could barely even see the Hall of Trade Unions. It was 4 P.M., overcast, and a cold March wind soon penetrated into every bone in my body. I knew I could not stand for hours in that miserable weather. The line moved about fifteen feet in the first half-hour. When we reached the first checkpoint, I handed the guard my old Moscow Soviet mandate. When he saw it, he moved us up in the line so that by 5:30 were in front of the MVD Central Headquarters at Lubyanka Square, but still a long way from the hall. By now my feet were growing numb from the razor-sharp wind. I started tap-dancing to try and get my blood circulating, which embarrassed my friend and caused people in the line to laugh. Soon though, just about everybody was jumping or dancing in one way or another, trying to keep from turning numb.

After the second checkpoint, in front of the Bolshoi Theater, I noticed MVD men going in and out of what used to be an old movie theater. I told Ross that I had to go in there to get warm before my hands and feet fell off. Realizing that I was desperate, he followed me. As we left the line to walk toward the building, an MVD officer cried out to us, "It's impossible! It's impossible!" Ross pulled the officer aside, said something to him, and we were told to proceed. About thirty feet later we had to stop while a long procession of people passed, all dressed in black and carrying huge, green wreaths. Since we were out of line and thereby appeared suspicious, another MVD man ran over to us. Again Ross whispered something into the officer's ear, whereupon the MVD man walked into the street and held up the procession so that we could cross.

As soon as we opened the door we found ourselves staring into the eyes of a startled MVD officer. He was too shocked to say anything. Most likely the only blacks he had ever seen were in films. In fact, he was so frightened that he stammered when he asked us who we were. Ross smiled at the officer, showing his gleaming white teeth, and then opened his overcoat. When the officer saw his expensive white shirt, blue silk tie, and neatly tailored black suit, there was no need for him to ask for identification papers. He was certain that he was standing before someone important. Just then a door opened and a senior officer appeared; he took one look at Ross and asked us to follow him. As we approached a group of lesser-ranked officers they snapped to attention and saluted. The officer leading us saluted; to my surprise, so did Ross, and not knowing who he was, they saluted him back. I was too bewildered to do anything. I thought Ross' cunning was admirable, but dangerous.

After the senior officer had led us out of the entryway, he asked what we wanted. Ross explained that we wanted to view the body of "the revered Comrade Joseph Vissarionovich Stalin" and that we had come to the headquarters to warm ourselves because our feet were numb. The senior officer said he would provide us with a personal escort to the head of the line. I was amazed. Although two officers were assigned to us to push through the crowd to the head of the line, Ross and I were separated. When we were about a third of the way there, the crowd surged from behind and for about fifteen seconds I found myself being carried along in mid-air. Once I regained my feet I was some distance from Ross and our MVD escorts.

About an hour later, half-frozen, I stepped into the main floor of the hall. It was a gigantic room. The line of mourners was about ninety feet from the coffin, which was sitting on a high dais. Mounds of flowers separated the people from Stalin's body. The only sounds were the shuffling of feet and soft crying. We stood gazing at Stalin's peaceful-looking face for about twenty seconds and then a guard motioned us to move on. At 12:45 P.M. the following day, Stalin's body was placed next to Lenin's in the mausoleum overlooking Red Square. At that moment, in our factory and through the land, everything stopped as five minutes of silent mourning were observed.

Speculation began about who would succeed Stalin. Rumors circulated in our shop that the dreaded Beria would inherit Stalin's mantle as head of the Communist party and the Soviet government. After Malenkov, a leading member of the Poliburo, announced over the radio and in a front page article in *Pravda* that the Soviet people should not fear their government, people began to feel that Georgi Malenkov would be Stalin's successor. He was a plump man with a jolly face, somewhat like a Santa Claus. Some people reasoned that a person with Malenkov's looks could not orchestrate a purge. Then it was announced that Malenkov would succeed Stalin as the first secretary of the Central Committee of the Communist party.

Stalin loyalists and personal staff members were swept out of the capital. That they were neither killed nor exiled to Siberia seemed humane when compared to the purges. Members of Stalin's staff were sent far away—to different towns so that they could not organize themselves—and were prohibited from returning to Moscow. A friend of mine complained to me about how suddenly his brother-in-law, who was one of Stalin's chauffeurs, his wife and two children were shipped off to Astrakhan, a city on the Caspian Sea.

That spring, it seemed to Muscovites that they might gain a bit more freedom. One could see the sparkle reappear in people's eyes. Three months after Stalin's death, as I headed to a home of rest for vacation, I also sensed better days ahead. My rest site was in Klin, near the Tchaikovsky Museum, only eighty miles northwest of Moscow. On the day I arrived, the sun shone brightly in a cloudless sky. A huge garden of flowers in front of the main entrance was ablaze with color. Three rows of birch trees, spaced evenly apart, proudly displayed their young, yellow-green leaves.

A few mornings later we heard over Radio Moscow that the Central Committee of the Communist party had passed a resolution the night before, declaring that "all peasants are free to sell their personally grown agricultural products in the free market." The announcement said that the resolution had been signed by Malenkov. The Russian peasants were ecstatic. That night, as we were finishing dinner, we heard people singing in the distance. We went outside and saw more than two hundred peasants holding torches, dressed in prerevolutionary clothing, and heading our way. When they reached our building, several accordionists started playing music and peasants of all ages began dancing. Soon an elderly woman mounted the stairs, asked for quiet, and sang a song praising Malenkov as the savior of Russia.

It was obvious how much the peasants disliked collectivized farming. Years later a number of party members told me that nineteen million peasants had been banished from their lands as part of Stalin's efforts to enforce collectivized farming. Those who stayed on the land but refused to surrender all their animals to government ownership were subject to an additional tax-in-kind, (besides the regular tax-in-kind) which meant, for example, that for every hen they kept they owed the government eighty eggs a year. Keeping one pig meant giving up eighty-eight pounds of meat a year. A farmer with a cow was required to give the government eighty eight pounds of butter a year or sixty liters (15.6 gallons) of milk. Should a peasant fail to meet this quota through his own livestock, he would have to buy the products from a government agency and then give everything back to the government. This system would have been hard enough on the peasants if it had functioned properly, but it was controlled and corrupted by village Communist party bosses who often became rich through black marketeering. Malenkov's latest decree allowed the peasants a bit of free market enterprise, and reduced the tax in kind and the corrupt system it had bred.

After the old woman finished her song and walked down the stairs, the accordionists began to play a soulful Russian melody. In her wrinkled dress and high-top boots, the old woman glided gracefully in front of a young man who, in keeping with Russian custom, was now obliged to dance with her. They were both good dancers, and the crowd widened its circle to give them room to perform. Despite her age, the woman performed the acrobatics that are part of the Russian folk dance tradition as if she were a spry teenager. The musicians picked up the tempo and the dancers moved faster. The crowd was clapping and urging them on. Finally, the young man started to turn red and, sweating and breathing heavily, he stopped, while the elderly woman continued on by herself, appearing as graceful and effortless as a bird in flight. The peasants celebrated until around 10:30 P.M. that night and for the two nights that followed.

CHAPTER 23

Malenkov, Beria, and Khrushchev

THE PEASANTS' JUBILATION DID NOT LAST. Before long, without any public explanation, Georgi Malenkov was removed as first secretary of the Central Committee. Back in Moscow, there was speculation anew about political intrigue within the Politburo and fear that the harshness of Stalinist-type rule would return. The peasants feared that the tax in kind would be returned to its previous level and private farming would be abolished. During the time of uncertainty after Malenkov was demoted, a number of people in the factory—including *nachalniks*—sought me out to learn what the BBC and the Voice of America were saying about events in the Kremlin. Everyone was starved for information. Where was Beria? What was Beria doing? The questions were endless, and so were the rumors. One day it was Malenkov who had been murdered, the next day it seems he was arrested. Or it was Khrushchev, or Voroshilov, or Bulganin, and so on. I was extremely prudent in dispensing information because I had no way of distinguishing among those earnestly seeking information and the MVD informers.

The biggest fear was that if a power struggle was going on, Beria would win out. The efficient and ruthless MVD was in his hands; people imagined that if he also became head of the party, he would turn the country into an even greater police state of unimaginable proportions. However, we soon learned that Nikita Khrushchev had become the first secretary of the Central Committee. We knew little about him, except that he had been a faithful Stalin underling. All party members in the factory were summoned to a closed-door meeting during the lunch period, a few days after the announcement about Khrushchev. By the end of the day the most important information had been leaked to us nonparty members—Beria had been arrested and charged with being an imperialist agent. We were told that he would soon be brought to trial, a closed affair off limits to the people and the press. Soviet citizens, who become trained never to utter a political opinion in public, felt free to curse openly the hated Beria, now that he was in jail as an enemy of the state and facing certain execution.

Although the Soviet news media had been instructed not to report on Beria's trial, whether purposefully or not, bits of information leaked out now and then. Beria was a person for whom, in a campaign of vilification, additional sins need not be invented. I heard people saying Beria was amoral, but not until I overheard a young man in my factory saying to another, "I think Beria should be hanged by his testicles, after defiling so many of our girls," did I understand what was meant.

Several years earlier, in 1946, a friend of mine had come to me with a pitiful story. Leonid Nicolaevich was the father of a strikingly attractive Russian girl I had met in 1939 at a home of rest in Gagri, the Caucasus. At the time Lena was sixteen years old and was vacationing with her mother, who was a high school physics teacher in Moscow. Lena was of medium height, slightly plump, well-proportioned, and distinctively beautiful. She had probably never cut her reddish-auburn hair, which she wore in four long, braided tresses. Her eyes were large and brown, above a classical Grecian nose. When she smiled, her lips parted sensually and dimples appeared at either corner of her mouth. At that time Lena was studying English at the Moscow Institute of Foreign Languages. After meeting me, her mother asked me to help her daughter with her English pronunciation.

I continued seeing Lena and her family back in Moscow, until the autumn of 1943. At that time, when I came to visit, her mother and father simply said that Lena was not in. I visited three more times but each time they said Lena was out. Whereas before we had all been friendly, they were now abrupt with me and would barely look me in the face. Knowing that something was wrong, I stopped going after that. Perhaps Leonid Nicolaevich is receiving a career promotion, I thought, or the MVD had persuaded them to stop fraternizing with a foreigner. Whatever the case, I gradually forgot about the family. Then one evening in the fall of 1946, I answered my phone and whoever was on the other end hung up. About an hour and a half later I heard a knock on my door. Since I was not expecting company I first thought it might be the MVD. At the second knock I opened the door and, to my surprise, there stood Leonid Nicolaevich. Whereas before he was healthy, he now was bent over and had aged a great deal. His black hair had turned gray. After I took his coat and offered him a chair, he apologized for not seeing me for three years, and said I would understand after listening to his story.

"Comrade Robinson," he said, "my dear Lena suffered a terrible indignity for more than two years at the hands of one of the highest government officials. It began late in the afternoon in mid-August 1943. That will forever be a tragic day for me and my family. Lena was on her way to the institute, for extra studying because she had failed her examination the previous spring. To graduate in May 1944, she was required to pass that course before the end of the month. While walking on the circular boulevard not far from the Park of Culture Bridge, a small car drove up from behind and stopped just in front of her. Lena told me later that a tall, heavy-set man dressed in civilian clothes got out and greeted her politely. She kept walking, and he kept pace beside her.

"Then he told her that he was speaking to her on behalf of a very important government official. 'This man is interested in you,' he said, 'and invites you to his home tonight at 8:30. You will show up without fail.' He flashed his security badge and said, 'This person does not accept no for an answer. My advice to you is not to displease him.' He said he would wait for her and returned to his car. The man kept following her in his car as she walked on to the institute, crying all the way. My poor Lena knew she had no one to turn to, that anyone who might try to help her would be imprisoned, or worse. She knew that even her own loving parents would be helpless, and if she appealed to us she could even be risking our lives. After class she peeked out the window. When she saw the car still there with the security man inside, waiting for her, she thought about killing herself."

At this point Lena's father broke down in tears. He placed his head in his hands and said, "She had no choice. She had to go. My poor girl was raped that night. She had no choice."

The poor man started to wail. My attempts to comfort him were useless; I could only wait until he calmed down. He did not say, and I did not want to ask him, whether that was the end of it or if Lena had to submit herself again. When he finished weeping, Leonid Nicolaevich stood up and said that he had come to say good-by. Although he had lived in Moscow his entire life, he and his family had been ordered to leave within three days for Lithuania. The man had raped Lena to his heart's content and would now send her and her family away.

Now during Beria's trial I knew for certain what had seemed most probable, that the high official who had forced himself on Lena was the head of the secret police. Russians came to speculate that Beria had victimized hundreds of young women. It was said that during his fourteen-year stint as head of the MVD, he kept some as concubines, and replenished his supply at will. A long-time acquaintance of mine, who was well-connected to some members of the Soviet elite, told me that Beria was tortured as ruthlessly and thoroughly as his own victims; at times he not only cried and screamed but howled like an animal. His trial before a military tribunal lasted six months. In the final week of December 1953, the Soviet news reported that Beria had been found guilty of being an imperialist agent, sentenced to die, and executed.

During the time of Beria's trial, his immediate subordinates were swiftly arrested, tried, sentenced, and shot. All their property was confiscated and the surviving members of their families were sent far away, banished from Moscow for life. Others of a lesser rank in the MVD who had benefited from Beria or who were thought to be Beria loyalists, were arrested, tried, and if found guilty, expelled from the party and banished to labor camps in the far north or to the salt mines. We heard many accounts, by word-of-mouth, that the ruthless and sinister MVD was being shaken to its roots, and then restructured and reorganized, from top to bottom. It was during this time that the MVD, the Ministry of Internal Affairs, was split into the MVD and the KGB (the Committee for State Security).

There were many lucky, lower-grade MVD men who got off without being harmed. Thousands of them were sent to factories in Moscow and throughout the country, to work as superintendents and foremen, where they caused problems because of their lack of skills. All their lives they had been shuffling papers, jailing people, eavesdropping while standing in line at stores, sitting in cafes in order to overhear people's conversations, tailing suspects, riding the subway and buses while spying on people—and now they were suddenly supposed to become productive citizens.

One of these ex-MVD men was installed as superintendent of the department of precision castings in my shop. He replaced a very knowledgeable woman who had an engineering degree in metallurgy and ten years of experience in the field. The new superintendent, with no technical training, was paid 140 rubles a month, compared to the average worker's salary of 110 rubles. His salary was in fact equal to what I was receiving with my thirty years of toolmaking experience and sixteen years as a designer. He was distrusted and despised by everyone in the shop. One worker told me that he and the others regarded this ex-MVD man as a deadly foe. "It is bad enough to have the secret police disguised in our midst," he said, "but to work among us in the open is a tremendous affront. How many innocent people do you suppose suffered because of this man? For all I know he might still be spying on us for the secret police. He is a danger to our freedom and security!"

There was another ex-MVD man who was sent to my shop after Beria's execution. Simon Petrovich was a rough-looking, rustic fellow who stood six-and-a-half feet tall, was in his forties, and had small, constantly shifting, deep-set gray eyes. The rumor in the shop was that his job at the MVD had been to roam the city, listen to conversations, and report people who spoke carelessly, while at times also acting as an *agent provocateur* in order to entrap people. Although Petrovich had no professional training and only a seventh-grade education, the shop administration was required to find him an appropriate job, above the level of a machine or bench worker. They finally created a new position for him as the third assistant to the shop superintendent. This placed him on an equal footing with the production chief and the chief engineer, with a salary only slightly less than theirs. Anticipating that these other two assistants would resent Petrovich, the superintendent created a job for the former MVD man that would keep him off their turf—he was put in charge of the sweepers; the chip removers; a paymaster who also distributed soap, rags, and clean overalls to workers; and two men whose job was to repair the shop's wooden and glass roof constantly, which leaked whenever it rained or the snow melted in the spring. He was furnished with a desk and two chairs in a small four-and-a-half- by five-and-a-half-foot office.

Having been a functionary of the notorious MVD, this man was also hated from the first day he reported for duty. He had a peculiar way of walking, and during the first few months it was difficult not to laugh at him as he went on his rounds. He took very long, measured steps, with his head always set rigidly in place while his eyes constantly darted back and forth. His torso was out of sync with the rhythm of his steps and his arms did not swing naturally. He looked like a robot doing a version of the Nazi goose step. Watching him, workers sometimes would laugh until the tears flowed from their eyes.

A minor, but welcome benefit that occurred in 1953, after the death of Stalin, was the discontinuation of the tardiness law. In the early thirties, soon after I started work at the First State Ball Bearing Plant, the Central Committee of the party issued a disciplinary decree, designed to end the habitual tardiness of Russian workers. In my factory, very few workers, technicians, and office staff reported for work on time with any regularity. People frequently would arrive as much as a half-hour late, and sometimes leave before lunch. There was absolutely no discipline.

The disciplinary decree said: "Two days after publication, anyone who comes to work more than twenty minutes late is to be discharged and will evacuate the place where he or she lives, and will be banished from Moscow with no right to appeal."

On the first day the decree was in force, I woke up late, at 7:10. Even though I was an American citizen, I did not care to stand out as a violator of the new ordinance. I leapt out of bed, threw on my clothes, and ran down the stairs without tying my shoelaces, knotting my tie as I raced to work. I arrived ten minutes late. Scores of others were racing into the shop, out of breath and unkempt. A designer I knew dashed in unshaven, his hair a mess, wearing one black shoe and one brown one.

Whereas it was simply a matter of self-discipline for those of us living near the factory to arrive on time, those living at some distance, who had to rely on streetcars and commuter trains, were at a considerable disadvantage. Yet where matters of survival are at stake, Russians are masters.

For nearly a year after the enactment of the tardiness law, the number of arrests by the Moscow police department rose steeply and about three thousand rubles in fines were collected each day, from workers desperate to avoid conviction under the new law. People who were going to arrive late for work and needed an official excuse—to avoid being punished under the harsh tardiness decree—would get themselves arrested for a minor infraction. They smashed streetcar, train, and taxi windows; were taken to the police station; paid a fine; and received a precious receipt, which they could present at work to indicate that they had an acceptable excuse for being late.

We had one sad case in my machine shop where a man who lived just a five-minute walk from the factory arrived twenty-two minutes late for work—two minutes past the cut-off period. He was fired on the spot and told to vacate his apartment. He refused to leave, so a few days later his furniture was loaded onto a van and taken away, and he was locked out. Incidents such as this helped the workers to reorganize their lives so they could report to work on time, and the window-smashing greatly diminished after the first year.

In the spring of 1954 Khrushchev began an amnesty program to review the cases of people who had been arrested and deported during the purges of 1933 to 1938. Many innocent prisoners were freed, and others who had been declared enemies of the people and shot or who had died had their records posthumously rehabilitated. Khrushchev's amnesty committee often designated wives or children of a deceased husband or father to receive some form of compensation. A few months after this program began, I was startled to happen upon Marusya Kudinov in the GUM department store. It had been twenty-one years since her husband—the party secretary in the Stalingrad factory where I first worked—had been declared an enemy of the people and shot. Marusya had aged tremendously. Though only in her fifties, she looked twenty years older. I asked her how life had been for her.

"Comrade Robinson," she said, "after my husband was gone and I had to vacate my room, my relatives took me in, for I was not able to work because of rheumatism in my legs and feet. Then last spring my husband's case was reviewed, like thousands of others, and the evidence revealed that he had been the victim of informers. The amnesty committee called me to say that a grave error had been made and that they had found him to be totally innocent. He was given the Order of Merit posthumously."

Tears were welling up in her eyes as she continued. "Now I have been given a small, two-room apartment, and a pension of 140 rubles a month. Once a year I can go to one of the best curing sanatoriums in the country, for my rheumatism."

"Fortunately, your life has now become somewhat more comfortable," I said.

"Yes, that is true," she said, "but after those many long, lonely, tragic years, it is hard for me to feel grateful."

As the years went by, from time to time I was told other, similar stories. There was the Rouskin family; I first met Klara in 1953, nearly two months after Stalin's death. It was during a May Day celebration, and she was with three other women, friends who had graduated with her from the Moscow Art School. I was with some male friends, and when the evening was nearing a close the women invited us to visit the prestigious House of Artists with them the following day. As members, each of them was allowed to invite one guest. It was through my friendship with them that I was able to see many American films, and attend concerts that were unavailable to the general public.

One Sunday afternoon I bumped into Klara in a candy store on Stoleshnikov Pereulok. We walked down the street together, chatting, until she stopped in front of her home. Before parting, she asked me to come the following Sunday to help celebrate her mother's birthday. I told her I would be delighted to come.

Her mother, Evdokia Filipovna, appeared to be an affable woman in her early fifties. Hers was not a typical Russian face. They lived in a seventeen- by fifteen-foot room in an old log house on Pushkin Street, which was furnished with old pieces in the style reminiscent of the czarist intelligentsia. Immediately upon meeting the woman, I was impressed with her bearing and composure. There were twelve of us at her birthday party—four couples, her mother, her aunt, and Klara. When I was on my way out, Evdokia Filipovna held my hand firmly in hers and said, "Bob, I am so glad that you came. Please feel free to come whenever you wish. We will always be glad to see you." I became accustomed to visiting them now and then, until one day I dropped by to see them and Evdokia Filipovna did not seem to be her usual self. She had been crying, and I felt that I should not stay. As I was leaving I asked Klara to phone me as soon as possible. She called me several weeks later, and when we met a few days later she explained what the problem had been.

"When you last visited us my mother was very upset," she said. "It was seventeen years to the day since my father disappeared without a trace. I was nine years old when the tragedy occurred. Although I have been constantly on the go for the last six years—since my mother had to stop working because of her diabetes—I always try to be home on that day, because she needs to be comforted."

Toward the end of 1956 Klara and her mother received a post card requesting them to appear before the amnesty committee on a certain date and time. Klara later explained to me that she decided to go by herself because her mother was sick in bed. She found the building, entered a large room, and gave her card to a man behind one of several small windows. He looked the name up in a thick book and then asked, "Where is your mother?"

"She is sick in bed and could not come," said Klara.

"Tell me your father's full name and date of birth," he said. Klara told him. Then he asked for her mother's passport, which she handed to him, and told her that her father had been arrested, imprisoned, and died.

"He has now been found innocent of all charges," said the man. "The government has not only graciously exonerated him posthumously, but will compensate his nearest relatives."

The clerk asked Klara to sign her name next to her father's name, in his large book. Then he handed her a sealed envelope with the words, "Exonerated 1956. Stepan Nicholaevich Rouskin." Klara walked away and opened the envelope. There were eight new one hundred-ruble notes inside.

When Klara was telling me this story, her voice started trembling at this point. "Just think," she said indignantly, "my father's life is worth only eight hundred rubles! I can't even buy a good overcoat with that money."

I was astonished when she told me that it was such a paltry sum. I asked her, "Was your father a party member?"

"Yes," she said.

"Do you know what kind of work he did at the time of his arrest?" I asked.

"My mother told me that he was a foreman over two dozen workers in a small factory with a workforce of around 350 people," she answered.

I was comparing the amount of compensation they received with a number of other cases I knew of. It was becoming apparent to me that the government was awarding money based upon the victim's position at work. Her father had not been important enough to bring much money to his survivors.

Another woman I met, Nina, fared quite a bit better. We met one day in the post office on Gorky Street, where she was waiting in line with a good friend of mine, Katya. As the three of us were leaving the building together Katya said, "Do you know that Nina is one of the happiest women in the world today?"

"You must have just gotten married," I said.

"Not exactly," she answered, "but as things are in my life, this is even more than a marriage. A marriage can break up, but the cause of my happiness should last for a long time to come, providing I don't make a fool of myself and meddle in any way in politics."

Katya interrupted to say, "Let's make a long story short. Bob, a few weeks ago Nina and her mother received a one-room apartment with modern conveniences in a nineteen-story building on the New Arbat. Isn't that something to make a huge noise about?"

I agreed, and invited them to have a cup of tea with me in the restaurant at the nearby National Hotel. Katya accepted, and after assuring her friend that I could be trusted—that I was a Soviet citizen and had been working in one of the largest factories in the city for more than twenty-five years—Nina decided it was safe and agreed to come along also. As we entered the restaurant, my eyes caught those of a man who immediately caused me to feel cautious. I guided the women to a table some distance from him, and I sat down facing him, so that I could keep an eye on him. He was definitely keeping an eye on us. After we ordered tea and cake I spoke softly to Nina, "How fortunate you were to receive a new one-room apartment on one of the most celebrated streets in Moscow."

"Yes," she said, "I must admit there are moments when I think my mother and I were fortunate to get it. Yet at other times, when I think about the painful and terrible price that was extricated from us in advance, and for such a long time, it simply does not make sense to me. At such moments I am not quite able to erase from my memory the suffering, humiliation, helplessness, and despair that my mother and I had to bear alone for twenty years. I was six when it all happened, and my mother was forty-two."

Nina paused, and I cautioned her in a low voice to speak quietly. She understood what I meant; we were all accustomed to living with the omnipresent secret police. I asked if she would not mind confiding in me the reasons why she and her mother had suffered for such a long time. She looked up at Katya for reassurance and then began to speak slowly and softly.

"My father was twenty-two years old in 1917, when he became a member of the party," she said. "He left medical college in his third year to go and fight at the front for the Bolshevik cause. He was there for three years, and then was appointed assistant commissar at one of the garrisons near Moscow soon after peace was restored. Later he was made commandant of the garrison in the Kremlin, and was given a five hundred-square-foot, two-room apartment on the third floor of a nice brick building. Two years after I was born, he was allowed to build a two-room summer cottage about fifty kilometers from Moscow. He built it by himself, over a period of two years, working on his days off. He was arrested in 1937, and we never heard from him again. We were forced out of our two-room apartment and given a thirteen-and-a-half- by fourteen-foot room in a one-story log house without any inside conveniences. A few weeks later the summer house was confiscated. We wrote everywhere and to everyone in high office, but never received an answer. We settled into a life of misery and want.

"Then in 1950 I got married and went to live with my husband and his mother in one room. But my mother was ill frequently and I felt a sense of duty to help her whenever necessary. At first my husband did not object when I would go off and stay with my mother, but the day came when he told me that he could not live with a woman who spent more time with her mother than with him. We were divorced less than three years after we were married.

"Now, in 1957, as if from nowhere, the amnesty committee

sent for me and Mother and told us that my father was to be freed. In the next breath they told us that, unfortunately, he was dead, but that he is awarded posthumously the Order of Merit, and we would receive a seventeen-and-a-half- by seventeen-and-a-half-foot apartment worth fifty thousand rubles.

"When my mother saw the apartment, tears flowed down her face as she remembered all that she had been through after the loss of my father. First everything was taken away from her, and now she is rewarded with a luxurious room for all her past miseries. The real tragedy now lies in the fact that my mother is a very sick, old woman, with failing vision and barely able to walk. Can you understand what a terrible price we have paid?"

I nodded as I saw the grief expressed in Nina's eyes. "By the way," she said, "I forgot to tell you, my mother is to receive a pension of 160 rubles a month, starting next month. Now she will be able to see a private doctor, also on pension, who will be more interested in helping her than the district clinic doctors."

I said a few words of comfort, and then Katya mentioned that she had to go to a lecture. As we were getting up to leave, I noticed that the suspicious-looking man was still there, pretending to read a book, which more than likely was a notebook that contained his daily reports for the KGB. He caught me looking at him, and quickly averted his glance.

PART III

The Khrushchev Era

CHAPTER 24

A Space Era Begins

THE CRUSHING OF THE 1956 Hungarian revolt put the Russian workers into a deep depression, which was finally lifted by the electrifying news of October 4, 1957. I heard the first announcement over the radio, while I was at work: "Attention! Attention! This is Radio Moscow, broadcasting all over the Soviet Union. Tass is authorized to inform the Soviet people that the USSR has placed an artificial satellite in space, and it is orbiting the earth every ninety minutes."

All the workers stopped what they were doing and began talking about the announcement. As they began to understand the meaning of what their nation's space scientists had done, workers began to clap, slap each other on the back, cheer, and even dance in jubilation. Many people stole glances at me to see how an American would react to the news that the Soviet Union had catapulted ahead of the United States. Sergei, a Komsomol, climbed onto a workbench and asked for silence. "Comrades," he said, "I know one thing. America, with all of its supposedly superior science and technology, was not able to accomplish what we have done today. Who can deny such a thing?"

Before the workers could cheer the telephone rang, with the message from the factory director that everyone was to report to the conference hall for a celebration. People in the conference hall were exultant. The factory hierarchy, consisting of the director, the district party secretary, the shop's party secretary, the head of the Komsomols, the head of the trade unions, shop superintendents, chief engineers, production managers, as well as eight model workers, were standing on the platform in front. At the side of the platform a group of workers was holding a large, hastily made banner which proclaimed the USSR as the world's leader in science. Party members and Komsomols in the crowd were holding up placards with slogans such as, "There's no question about the superiority of Socialism over Capitalism," "Soviet people, be proud of your progress and achievements," and "Hurrah for our Motherland." We were supplied the usual parade of speakers, who praised the government and the party and hailed the Soviet space achievement as the greatest scientific feat of the century. The workers became intoxicated with nationalism, and swiftly substituted a brazen attitude of superiority for their usual mood of brooding inferiority to the United States.

One of the model workers advanced to the rostrum and read a prepared speech into the microphone: "Comrades," she said, "as of today we are no longer competing with, but we are ahead of the USA. Why is this? It is because of our system, because we are better organized. Now that we are ahead, this is no time to relax. I therefore challenge all our Komsomol workers to a Socialist competition. We must increase our productivity, eliminate spoiled products by 20 percent, and our output must be excellent." Everybody applauded.

The factory director, in his closing remarks, urged workers to double their efforts in order to quicken the pace of Soviet technological development and ensure even more wonderful scientific breakthroughs. For the rest of the day the thirty or so middle-aged coatroom attendants enjoyed a lucrative sale of unaged rye vodka and *vobla* (the flat, bony, salty, dried fish).

After work, out on the streets, on the tram, and in the housing complexes, people were speaking about only one thing—*Sputnik I*. When I arrived at work the next morning, my shop was transformed. The factory's slogan artists had worked through the night. Wherever I turned I found a slogan glaring at me, proclaiming the Soviet victory in space. I could only imagine how many millions of yards of cloth, gallons of paint and paint remover, and thousands of miles of cord are manufactured in the USSR in order to sustain similar propaganda efforts in factories throughout the country.

In the afternoon, it was announced over the radio that Muscovites could see *Sputnik I* sometime between 6:30 and 7 P.M. That night, along with thousands of others, I went out into the street and waited with the festive crowd for the satellite to pass overhead. "It's coming! It's coming," someone yelled. We all looked to the sky. At first I did not see anything, but then in a few seconds I could hear at short intervals a strange sound much like the pulsing sound of an ambulance siren. Just then a silvery object appeared, streaking across the sky. The crowd began cheering and cheering, and did not stop until the satellite was well out of sight. After this spectacular experience I stayed around in the crowd for a few more minutes, then returned to my room. I chose not to celebrate through the night, although I knew many others would.

The next morning at work Sergei, the Komsomol in my department, walked past and said, "Beep, beep," as if he was speaking to no one in particular. I must have heard that from him twenty more times during the day. That night, on my way to visit my good friend, Jorge Abramovich, I encountered a *Sputnik* celebration a few blocks from the subway station. The area had been closed off to traffic and was filled with people dancing under the glare of floodlights to the music of a large brass band. I had never before seen Russians so happy, not even on the day the Nazi surrender was announced. Once again, banners were everywhere—in the subway stations, in the trams, hanging from buildings. I wanted to shut my eyes and plug my ears to the nationalistic chest-beating, and thought that I could find refuge with my friend Jorge. In the midst of the current, widespread, government-sanctioned anti-Semitism I did not expect Jorge, a Jew, to be celebrating.

Jorge greeted me at the door, hugged me, and patted me on the back. Although I had known him for twenty years, I had never seen him this upbeat. He had also caught *Sputnik* fever. "We have put the first artificial satellite in space," he said. "This is a technological feat—and a humanitarian accomplishment—far better than the United States, which only tries to create more powerful bombs." Jorge's wife and children shared his enthusiasm. That night the Abramoviches were proud to be Soviet citizens, even though their internal passports listed their nationality as "Jewish" instead of "Russian."

When Jorge grabbed my shoulder affectionately and asked me what I thought of the USSR's fantastic scientific achievement, I hesitated before answering. This kind of question was uncharacteristic of him. I felt a sudden sense of alarm. Could he have been spying on me all these years? I had been programmed to distrust everyone and never to let my guard down fully, even with a friend of twenty years. But I decided Jorge was safe. I decided he was just caught up with enthusiasm over *Sputnik*, but I was nevertheless cautious in answering his question, simply saying that I was impressed with the accomplishment. I chose not to explain how obnoxious I found the chauvinistic reaction of the Soviet government and people.

On the way home, *Sputnik* mania trapped me in the subway. As two drunks at the other end of the train bellowed out songs praising their Motherland, two other Russians staggered into the train and sat down on either side of me. I felt trapped. One of them leaned over, looked me right in the eye, and asked if I spoke Russian. I shook my head no. He started talking to me anyway. First came the obvious question, "What do you think of the Soviet Union's great *Sputnik* achievement?" I played dumb. They both kept talking to me, simultaneously, until one of them gave up and slumped over in his seat. The other one took this moment to proclaim loudly to his captive audience of passengers, "We the people of the Soviet Union have overtaken the United States in science and technology. From now on we are going to lead the world, and the US will be second best!"

The other fellow arose from his stupor and began beating his chest wildly. He shouted, "Long live Russia, our Motherland! Hurrah! We have surpassed the United States. Hurrah, comrades, hurrah!" I couldn't take it anymore. I decided I would transfer to a different train, and I got off at the next stop. As I was walking down a corridor in the subway station I heard some Russians singing a song that had died out during the purges, but which Paul Robeson, the black American singer, had revived recently during his first concert in Moscow. They were singing, "I do not know where there is such a country in the world in which a person can breathe so freely." I soon saw that the singing was coming from a group of teenagers—most likely Komsomols—followed by a larger group of adults, all walking toward me.

I sized up the crowd and approached one of the more sensitive looking youngsters. "Where are you coming from?" I asked. He didn't answer but stopped and looked at me with a mixture of suspicion and hostility. Three other young people joined him and he told them what I had asked.

"You must have heard about our wonderful success in putting *Sputnik I* in space," said one of them. "We are coming from a youth gathering where we were acquainted with the worldwide significance of our *Sputnik.*" I thanked him for the information. As I walked away the group stopped singing and broke into a unison chorus of "beep beep" until I was nearly out of sight. For the entire next month the radio and newspapers were filled with news of *Sputnik I,* promises of greater accomplishments in the future, and assurances that the United States would never catch up. Special meetings were called at the factory to hear Kremlin propagandists talk about the Soviet Union's superior technology and its pursuit of peaceful scientific endeavors. The number of monitors in my shop alone was increased from four to seventeen so that everyone would hear the daily readings from *Pravda* and *Izvestia* in praise of Soviet science and technology. As one who was looked upon as a foreigner, I was additionally hounded by little "beep beeps" wherever I went in Moscow. The "beep beeps" were clearly part of a cute little campaign, conceived by some Kremlin leader or propaganda committee, to remind foreigners of the Soviet Union's preeminence in the field of science. Throughout the country, there were twenty million Komsomols to put their plan into action.

The following year, the Soviet bubble burst. Not much was said over Radio Moscow when the United States launched its first satellite; there were only a few lines buried in a newscast. But the Soviet people were stunned. The official propaganda had led them to believe that it would take the US six, eight, or even ten years to duplicate what Soviet scientists had done, and by that time the Soviet space program would have embarked on more sophisticated extraterrestrial exploration.

The day we heard of America's *Explorer I,* the workers in my shop were like a people in mourning. I was amazed at how suddenly and thoroughly their mood could change. Minutes after we heard the news, their cockiness disappeared and they became listless, and were almost in tears. No more "beep beeps" from this group, I figured. A few diehard party members valiantly tried to lift their comrades' spirits by circulating a rumor that the American space claim was a hoax, but the rumor did not catch on. One party member, who held a high rank in the factory hierarchy, approached me, looked over his shoulder, and whispered, "Comrade Robinson, I just cannot understand why they lied to us so grossly."

Just after lunch another party member sought me out and said, "You know, it just doesn't make sense. We were assured of one thing, and here we are witnessing the opposite. The Americans were only a few months behind us all the time." He shook his head and paused, perhaps to gain courage, and added, "Why do they treat us like that?"

Three days later, when I arrived at work, it seemed as if the Kremlin had adjusted its propaganda message successfully to reflect this new development. I noticed that the workers were no longer downcast. Three party members almost pounced on me when they saw me enter the shop and said, loudly enough for everyone to hear, "Comrade Robinson, how was it possible for a country like the United States to send a tiny orange into space and fool the whole world into believing that it, too, had accomplished what we had done three months ago? As tricky as they are, the United States can't fool us, the Soviet people."

I was unprepared for this new tact. Hours earlier I had been trying to lift their spirits by reassuring them that America's success in no way diminished their country's accomplishment. Now they were treating me as the opposition, a test case for their newly-gained sense of hopefulness. I blurted out, "Comrades, I think that you are being unjust toward me. I've been among you for more than twenty-five years. I even labored, went hungry, and slept in wooden shelters with you during the second world war. I never left the Soviet Union except to visit my mother one time in the 1930s. Why do you want to attack me for what the United States does or doesn't do?"

Since they usually found me to be very compliant, my retort was unexpected and left them speechless. I went on to say, "Most of you standing there, trying to start a debate on the merits of the US space mission, are originally from the villages, but you haven't been back there for at least twenty-five years. Would it be fair for me to hold you responsible for something that happened in your village a week ago?"

The more seasoned of the three Communists who had confronted me responded, "Comrade Robinson, we agree that you have been among us for a long time, but we have not forgotten—and we are sure you have not either—that you are not Russian and were not born here. I think it is natural that you should feel closer to the United States than to us."

It made no difference that I was a citizen of their country, paid taxes, was a fellow union member, and had never spoken harshly of the Soviet Union nor highly praised of the United States. To them I not only remained a foreigner—who by custom and instinct must be distrusted—but I also represented the United States. Because they were envious of America, they were envious of me. If I had stayed to respond to them, which in any case would have been foolhardy, I would have been late reporting to my desk. That would have given the shop party secretary an excuse to write an editorial in the factory newspaper deploring my tardiness and lack of discipline, so I hurried off. It was more important to keep my work record clean than to try and win an argument.

After I reached my desk and started to work, I noticed that the people in my shop seemed rather cheerful. The Kremlin's strategy was working. A party member came over to me and said with derision, "Hah! America's tiny orange in space! Just think of it; we not only can't see it, but it's silent. We can't even hear it."

He laughed scornfully.

Two or three days later, an editorial in the factory newspaper carried the Kremlin's explanation. "How can such a highly developed country like the United States put into space such a tiny object and want the whole world to believe that it's a real satellite, when it is only make believe?" read the account. The workers had been so programmed to view Americans as lying, scheming, treacherous people, that this propaganda scheme actually succeeded. Those who thought the US satellite might actually be real solved their problem by deciding that if it was, it must surely be vastly inferior to the *Sputnik*. Unfortunately, the Kremlin's success meant that I was once again tormented by a revival of the "beep beeps."

Years later I was told by a reliable source that when Khrushchev was briefed about the US satellite launch, and was told it was a small object, he laughed and exclaimed, "Oh, but it is no larger than an *apelsinchik*" (tiny orange). Khrushchev's remarks were shared with the government's propaganda office, which in turn passed them on to Moscow's twenty-three district party secretaries, who then instructed the party secretaries of every factory and collective farm to make sure that every worker understood what the premier had said about the US space effort. From Moscow the word was passed on to party secretaries throughout the country, reaching into the smallest villages in the most remote spots. It was a remarkable demonstration of the ability of the Soviet apparatus to change the reality of more than 200 million people in just three days. I found it nearly inconceivable—although I saw it happening—and somewhat frightening.

Tiny orange jokes were created. Cartoons appeared in the factory newspapers. *Sputnik I* had lifted the spirits of the people, and the Kremlin leadership was loathe to see the people become demoralized. A brooding, pessimistic people would be less productive and more susceptible to counter-revolutionary thinking. Therefore, the American space effort was made to appear as a meaningless, inconsequential challenge to the Soviet effort.

Imagine, therefore, the excitement on April 12, 1961, when Radio Moscow announced that a Russian pilot, Yuri Gagarin, had just become the first man ever to journey into outer space. No one could work in my shop. The workers exploded with joy. They jumped on each other, hugged each other, laughed, cried, and danced around their machines. Throughout the day people went up to one another and said, "Comrade, I congratulate you on our success," to which the proper response was, "I congratulate you, too."

Workers were trained to feel—and at moments such as this did feel—that their labors played a part in national achievements. This was usually plausible, because we rarely knew how the parts were to be used. A typical example was the two thousand metal links we made in 1934. This project, like most, was considered a secret; the drawings had no name, only numbers and letters. It was not until after the war that I happened to discover that the links were connected together and formed the chain that attached to the stairs of the metro escalator. There is no doubt that my shop and factory did make small ball bearings for the Gagarin space venture.

Following the announcement of Gagarin's feat, we were called to the usual meetings, to hear the usual speeches extolling the virtues of the Soviet system and the death of capitalism. Banners appeared everywhere and Russians got drunk. Khrushchev boasted in a radio broadcast, "We are in the lead in space, and we are determined to stay in that position. Whenever the Americans land on the moon, we shall already be there first. We will welcome them, and according to our ancient custom, will be pleased to offer them bread and salt."

About a month later, in May 1961, America launched Alan Shepard into space. Although the Kremlin issued a few official words of praise, the average Russian ridiculed the American accomplishment. After all, Shepard had not circled the earth like Gagarin. My fellow workers believed that the US was a very long way behind the Soviet space program and doubted whether they could ever catch up. I regretted that I happened not to be in my shop on the day we were told that two US astronauts had landed on the moon.

That ultimate day of reckoning came on July 21, 1969. I was vacationing at a home of rest thirty-eight miles from Moscow. We were gathered for a 9 A.M. breakfast on a beautiful, sunny morning, when the director of the home of rest entered the dining hall, cleared his throat loudly, and asked for everyone's attention. He looked downcast, so I expected bad news. Perhaps a member of the Politburo had died. Instead he announced, "Comrades, I have an important announcement to make. Two American cosmonauts have landed on the moon, and are still there. A special film, which has been beamed from the moon by communications satellite, will be shown in the winter concert hall at 10:30 A.M." Tears were welling up in his eyes. He quickly left without speaking to anyone.

All 270-odd guests were dumbstruck. They sat without moving; no one said a thing. Everyone's porridge, bread and butter, and coffee was untouched. Three women at my table began to cry. The silence was broken by the man to my left, who whispered, "The devil take it!" A man at a nearby table asked, rhetorically, "But how could that have happened?" The man sitting across from me swore in anger: "Son-of-a-b----; it's difficult to believe!" In a stupor, people put down their utensils, got up, and left. Instead of the usual socializing, people went to their rooms. I arrived at the concert hall early, took a seat in the far corner, and began to read. I was eager to see the film but wary of being the only foreigner there, and an American at that. Fifteen minutes before the film began, every seat and all of the standing room was taken by guests, staff, and people from the nearby village.

What a sight! We all watched, transfixed, as Neil Armstrong and Buzz Aldrin stepped onto the moon. At that instant, when you might normally expect to hear applause, people in the room burst into tears. Some began to sob uncontrollably. Once the brief film clip ended and the lights were turned on, people stayed in their seats for a few minutes before beginning to file out quietly. Many were still crying softly as they left. I was one of the last to leave, because I wanted to avoid an encounter with an emotionally crushed Russian. When I came out, I saw all of the men, and many of the women, moving slowly down the road, much like mourners in a funeral procession. My curiosity got the best of me, so I followed them at a distance to find out where they were heading. Their destination turned out to be a rural store, about a twenty-minute walk down the road, where they intended to drown their misery in vodka.

People lined up outside the store, waiting their turn to go in and buy bottles of vodka and pickled cucumbers. They sat on the grass outside the store, eating and drinking in silence. After awhile, a short, fat, bald-headed man stood up and addressed the crowd. He was followed by several other people, whose basic message was that the moon landing was a fluke and the Soviet Union would catch up, if indeed she was not still ahead. After about an hour I returned to the home of rest. Amazingly, during the next week, no one pestered me with questions about being a foreigner, or with boastful, patriotic pronouncements about the superiority of the Russian people and the Soviet way of life.

All of our regularly scheduled events—except meals—were cancelled, such as the basketball competition, the dance contest, and a trip to Palekh, a nearby village where beautiful souvenir boxes were still being made in the same manner as during the time of Peter the Great. For the most part, guests were on their own, and the main topic of conversation was the US moon landing. One conversation I overheard was among five men drinking vodka under a tree. "Vit, you know what," said one man, "that scoundrel Khrushchev is to blame for the slowdown plan that prevented us from being the first to land on the moon."

"How can you say that?" asked another man. "It has been over five years since he went on pension."

"Maybe," said the first, "but you see, after he left office, it took that new Politburo a long time to overcome all the mistakes he had made.

Now all of the bourgeois capitalists are very happy that they beat us to the moon. The devil take it!"

Added another man, philosophically, "It is true I have been totally shaken by this news, but I am now forcing myself to see the reality of it all. I advise you to do the same. Let us drink, for what happened cannot be helped."

When I returned to Moscow, the city seemed even grayer and more solemn than usual. Banners hailing the USSR as the leader in space technology had been taken down. In fact, the only banners remaining in my shop were the ones imploring workers to work harder, to avoid waste, to be more disciplined, and to strive to meet our production goals before the October Revolution celebrations. No one in my shop mentioned the US moon landing, and I certainly was not going to bring it up. It was as if the event had never taken place. I wondered how the workers had reacted, and about a week after my return, a man I trusted, and who was privy to the party thinking in the factory, came up to me at lunch and brought up the subject.

"Bob, everyone was totally shocked at the news," he said. "They simply could not believe it, because we had been told by our leadership that we were far ahead of the Americans in space technology. Remember that Khrushchev had predicted that we would reach the moon first. People believed him, and we were not prepared for what happened. This is a terrible blow to all of us."

CHAPTER 25

Racism in Russia

KREMLIN PROPAGANDISTS HAVE WORKED HARD over the years to advance the myth that the Soviet Union is the most socially harmonious country in the world. Both to their own people and abroad, they labor to present their nation as a paradise of equality. Officially, the Soviet Union does not have a racial problem. The reality, however, is quite different.

During my early days in Stalingrad, I was not very aware of the extent of Soviet racism because I was absorbed with the American contract workers' campaign to get rid of me. Also, in the early thirties, the government was welcoming foreigners; it was several years before every foreigner became suspect as untrustworthy and a potential saboteur. Then came the postwar strategy to glorify the Russians as the most superior people in the world. Old prejudices were dusted off and used to advantage. Anti-Semitism spread swiftly; the Jew—or "Yid," as they are called with derision—was once again spat upon in Russian society. Non-Jewish Russians who married Jews were ridiculed by their friends and relatives for lowering themselves. Under the burden of constant social pressure, many of these mixed marriages ended in divorce. By the late fifties Jews were being denied entrance into the leading professional academies, and most of those already established in their careers were stripped of any political or military power.

The bias against non-Russian ethnic groups and nationalities held blacks and orientals at the bottom. I learned about the bigotry against Soviet citizens from the eastern part of the country during the second year of the war. Thousands of these yellow-skinned men were sent to my factory from places like Uzbekia and Kazakhstan, to replace workers who had been drafted. The army had turned down these men of oriental lineage because they already had enough of them for the construction battalions. They were not trusted to carry weapons, only picks and shovels. Their job was to move boulders, cut through forests, and build roads; they were the Red Army's chain gang.

Workers in my shop were disgusted when they learned that these men were coming to work with us. They said that they were stupid and lazy, that they smelled, that they could not be trusted, that they were sneaky. When they arrived into such an alien and hostile environment, I found their behavior modest and quiet. They were not without their problems, however. They struggled with the Russian language, lacked technical experience, and were not accustomed to big city living. Life for them was hell. They were ridiculed and insulted continually by their Russian co-workers. If anything went wrong, a finger would be pointed at some yellow-skinned worker. I was amused to see how the Russian workers derided the Uzbeks and Kazakhs for wearing a coat in the summertime, not understanding that it acted as an insulator against the heat, keeping them far cooler than the red-faced, sweating Russians. After months of persecution, the easterners reacted in concert, through a work slowdown. In a few days every one of them was shipped back to his native republic. I expect the only reason they were not shot on the spot was because their muscle power was needed elsewhere; Russia experienced a serious shortage of civilian unskilled laborers during the war.

Russians regard the Chinese, Japanese, and Koreans as strange and deceitful people. No sensible Russian would consider marrying one. I witnessed many instances of prejudice against these nationalities. One typical example occurred while I was at a second class home of rest during the summer of 1953, a time when the North Koreans were highly regarded because they had fought against the Americans in the Korean War. Many students from North Korea began coming to the Soviet Union for technical training unavailable to them in their own country. One of them, named Chiang, an aviator who had flown a number of combat missions against American jet fighters, was vacationing at the same time.

During the first night, which according to custom was a get-acquainted evening, an attractive young woman asked Chiang to dance. He danced very well, with grace and ease, and during the next few days these two were seen together frequently; she was helping him with his Russian language studies during the day, and they would dance together during the evening social hour. One evening I overheard the conversation of a cluster of Russian men who were watching the dancing. "That girl's parents should not let her associate with that Asian man," said one. Another man announced, "I am going to warn her parents. Otherwise we're going to end up with a slanted-eyed, yellow baby. We helped them win the war against the Americans, but that is no reason for us to let them overrun us with yellow babies. After all, their culture is inferior to ours."

The couple sat down near me, obviously enchanted with each other. The Korean leaned over and whispered something to the young Russian woman that made her laugh. Their mood of familiarity upset one of the men sitting behind me. He walked up to the woman and said, "Valya, be careful; otherwise, you'll be scattering a lot of little Korean Chiangs around here. Take my advice, and watch what you are doing."

The couple was too stunned to respond. Finally Valya stood up abruptly, grabbed her partner's hand, and the two of them walked out of the room together.

By the time the decade of the fifties was coming to an end, the government had cultivated Russian biases so successfully that their pride was scarcely bearable to me, a black and a non-Russian. By the end of 1962, race prejudice against blacks had reached a fever pitch. By this time, all blacks were treated as second-class human beings. It seemed as if the days of the simple, warm, and friendly Russian were gone forever. By this time, the effect of prejudice against blacks in the Soviet Union was worse than anything I recalled in the United States during the 1920s, and without question, a great deal worse than in the United States after the decade of the 1950s.

For one thing, in America, at least most people—blacks and whites—do recognize the presence of racial prejudice and institutional racism. Groups, institutions, and individual leaders are working to combat the problem. However, in the Soviet Union, Russians refuse to accept that prejudice against blacks, or any other races, nationalities, or ethnic groups, exists. To make such a confession would be to violate the façade of equality and brotherly love which they have created. Many American blacks, attracted by Communist propaganda, came to the Soviet Union believing that they had been delivered to the land of freedom and opportunity. Then they would let their defenses down, move eagerly into Soviet society, and get rejected. Eventually they not only were humiliated, but disillusioned as well. At least in the United States they understood and could adjust to the official and unofficial social ground rules, while trying to resist at the same time.

I did not go to the Soviet Union believing I was about to enter paradise, as did most other American blacks. But I too was inflicted with the pain of racism in Russia. With my professional record, if I had been white, I would have received career promotions. After the 1930s, the Soviet government and Russian people did not want to admit officially that a person with black skin could be as capable as, or more capable than, a white. I was never allowed to go on foreign or domestic technical missions, while other designers—Russians, of course—with much less experience than I were sent. Often they would return with new ideas that they could not implement on the drawing board, so they would turn to me to figure out how to make their borrowed concepts work.

Every American black I knew who settled in the Soviet Union became painfully aware of Soviet racism. Henry Scott, a tall dancer from New York City, and Robert Ross, a big, strapping fellow from Montana who had no professional skill and became a propagandist, are two cases in point. Like other western Young Communist League members, when they first came to the Soviet Union searching for social equality and political enlightenment, they were enrolled at the Communist University for Theoretical Training. This initial experience was difficult for them, for reasons having nothing to do with racism in Russia. Neither of them had finished high school in the United States and neither had academic exposure to political theory. In their classes, they were competing with young British Communists who were graduates of Oxford and Cambridge, and American whites who were college-educated. Along with the African students, who likewise lacked much formal education, they failed the courses. A clique that excluded the blacks developed among the students. There was an implicit understanding at the university that in any case, blacks were genetically inferior. Ross and Scott tried hard, but to no avail. After two years of study, every black student—American and African—was expelled. The Africans returned home, but the Americans stayed, because they were unable to return as a failure and face the people in America who had sponsored their trip to the Soviet Union. For the Kremlin propagandists, it was by no means a waste of rubles to have blacks studying at the theoretical university, regardless of how they were treated or how they performed. The important thing was the pictures. They could spread the image around the world of Soviet society as a place where blacks and whites studied Marxist-Leninist doctrine together in harmony.

Henry Scott readily found a job after his university experience was ended. He was hired by Tfasman, a Jewish pianist and leader of Moscow's best jazz band. He featured Scott as his top dancer. A short time later Scott married a pretty young woman, who was a recent graduate of the Institute of Foreign Languages' English department. Because they were unable to find an apartment, it was a year before they actually lived together. Scott continued to sleep in the corner of one of the band leader's rooms, and his wife, Valya, lived with her grandmother, who detested Scott. Although he tried everything he could to win her over, she viewed him as an abhorrent alien who was using her granddaughter to gain entry into Moscow's more prominent social circles. She would not even allow Scott to enter her apartment. During warm weather he and his wife would meet in a park, where they would often stay until the guards ordered them to leave at closing time. In wintertime they would rendezvous at museums or restaurants. Finally, they were able to rent a tiny room, seven feet square, just large enough for a bed, a chair, and a dresser. Scott was ecstatic nine months later when his daughter, Marjorie, was born. He loved being with the baby, holding her, playing with her, talking to her.

However, to survive, the Scotts needed more money, so Valya took a job as an interpreter, which meant placing the baby with her great-grandmother during the day. Scott resisted this plan at first, but ultimately relented to his wife's wishes because it seemed the only practical thing they could do. Work and mothering soon became such a strain on Valya that her grandmother insisted on keeping the baby during the week and only giving her up to Valya one day a week, on Valya's day off. Scott rejected this plan, and told Valya that he would find someone else to take care of the baby during the week. But no one wanted to mind a mulatto, Valya's mother got her way, and in time Scott's worst fears were realized. The grandmother succeeded in turning his child against him. As the months passed, the child began to avoid him, and would cry out in fear for her great-grandmother whenever Scott would try to pick her up. Scott tried again to find a different babysitting arrangement, but without success. He and his wife fought over this issue and became estranged from each other, and then divorced. Scott married a young Russian woman, and in 1938 they left Moscow for the United States. A few years later we learned that Scott was poisoned at a banquet where he had given a speech about his experiences in Russia.

Marjorie grew up to be her father's daughter in more ways than one. As a child, she showed considerable promise as a dancer, and when she was eight years old, her great-grandmother used her influence to enroll Marjorie in the choreographic school of the Bolshoi Ballet. Marjorie was an immediate star, and in two years was ready to perform professionally. Her greatest wish was to dance on stage before a packed auditorium and to represent her country abroad as a ballet dancer. But time and again she was denied the opportunity to dance outside the Soviet Union, while dancers with less ability and less standing than she had were chosen. By this time Marjorie's mother had remarried, to Ralph Parker, a British journalist who was sympathetic to the Soviet system. Marjorie asked her mother and stepfather to take her case to the Central Committee of the Communist party. Her mother took this daring step, and wrote a long letter to the Central Committee, pointing out her daughter's recognized talent and noting the times she had been passed over when the Bolshoi was forming ballet teams to perform abroad. Although the mother never received a direct answer to her letter, a few months later Marjorie was selected to go to Egypt, and later went to the United States where she danced in New York and several other cities. Marjorie told me that she knew it was the color of her skin and the texture of her hair that had kept her from being selected.

After he was expelled from the university, Robert Ross was given a job in the foreign department of the Moscow postal office, with the aid of an American who was in Moscow helping the Soviet Union reorganize its postal system. Those of us who knew Ross suspected that he had been hired to censor English-language mail, although I never confronted him with my suspicion. He eventually married a Russian girl whose apartment he had been living in for about a year. Seven years into his marriage he discovered that his wife was an MVD agent, a source of anger and frustration that led him to divorce her in 1944. With their two children, they had been evacuated to Tashkent, the capital of the Uzbek Republic in the southeastern part of the Soviet Union, during the war. When I first saw him after his return to Moscow in 1948, he was more mature, and had more self-confidence, a new wife, and an eight-year-old stepdaughter.

He also had a new job, which brought him a degree of security he had not known in the thirties. Back then, he was always hustling, trying to survive. But now, as a Kremlin propagandist, he had a modern seventeen-foot by seventeen-foot apartment with an alcove large enough for a bed, a small table, and a chair. After spending a month away from Moscow lecturing, he would come home with twelve thousand to fourteen thousand rubles, baskets of fruit that were unavailable in most Moscow stores, and cases of wine. He was the Kremlin's expert lecturer on social conditions in the United States. He of course gave particular emphasis to the plight of blacks, and made use of a slide show that had been prepared for him. When he was on tour, he would average three lectures a day to factory workers, students of all ages, guests at sanatoriums, homes of rest, and so forth. Although Ross was always friendly to me, and sometimes gave me gifts of fruit, I never confided in him, nor do I believe did other blacks in Moscow. For a life of material comfort he had agreed to spread a distorted picture of America throughout the Soviet Union.

He was also used to host visiting American blacks. He would organize lavish parties and serve delicacies that the average Russian could only hope to see in his dreams. Ross' superiors always made sure the parties included a nice racial mix. Ross would invite blacks he knew and his superiors would supply native Russians. He would also escort visiting Americans to the best concerts and museums, and was instructed to treat them like dignitaries. These visitors obviously gained no understanding at all of what life was like for the average non-Russian in Soviet society.

One day in the mid-fifties, Ross noticed me in the central telegraph office on Gorky Street and insisted that we go somewhere to talk. I declined his offer of lunch, so we went to a nearby park. His big, exciting news was that he was going to get an automobile, a luxury reserved only for top bureaucrats, politicians, military leaders, directors of factories, and people in particular favor and with special influence. Ross confided in me that he needed a car because his wife refused to travel with him on public transportation. It seems that they had encountered a drunk on a subway train one night, who cursed Robert's wife for being married to a black. The man spit on the floor of the train and called her a prostitute.

Four months later Ross called me up and asked if he could visit. Ten minutes later the doorbell rang. There was Robert Ross, standing as tall and proud as I had evern seen him, grinning from ear to ear. His wife was with him, and after they came inside and we were sipping tea, he told me that he had the automobile, which he had specially ordered at a cost of thirty thousand rubles. The car was outside, and he urged me to come have a look. It was brand new, flawlessly painted, and elegant well beyond the average car one sees on Moscow's roads. Ross was particularly proud that his car had more horsepower than most of the others available at that time.

About a year later Ross phoned to invite me to a film festival at the Lenin Arena. We agreed that he would pick me up at the National Hotel, and when I approached our meeting place, I encountered a large crowd of well over a hundred people. As I came closer, I saw that they were attracted by Ross' impressive-looking black and white car. But when they got closer to the car and saw the letters G.A.3 on the front of the hood, they turned away in disappointment. "Oh well, it's nothing special after all, but only one of ours," they said, when they realized it had been manufactured in the Gorky Auto Factory. Ross was nevertheless in his element, choosing not to notice their disappointment. "I say, man, do you see how the people flocked to see my car?" he asked with pride.

This incident illustrates the peculiar ability of the Russian people to deceive themselves. On the one hand, they maintain with enormous pride and arrogance that anything made in Russia is better than anything made elsewhere; on the other hand, they will fall all over themselves to obtain foreign-made goods. I found it risky to wear western-style clothes, because invariably a Russian would say, "I like that shirt you are wearing; sell it to me." It was the same with shoes, raincoats, argyle socks, and colorful ties. At the last home of rest I stayed at before I escaped, I was wearing an attractive pair of French socks given to me by a student from Senegal. On two occasions on the first day I wore them, Russian men struck up a conversation with me and then after a few minutes mentioned what remarkable-looking socks I was wearing. One of them first checked to make sure that I had not bought them in a Russian store, and then bluntly offered to buy them from me for fifty rubles ($55). The other man used a different approach. "You know," he said, "your socks remind me of a pair that was stolen from me about two years ago. Please sell them to me when your stay here ends, since I miss mine so badly."

Perhaps Ross eventually realized that a Russian-made car was not nearly as impressive to Russians as a foreign import, because he sought desperately to buy a sleek, chrome-plated Chevrolet, which he heard Marjorie Scott's stepfather was selling. This was a real luxury car in the Soviet Union. Even though Ross knew it was a crime for the average Soviet citizen to sell or buy cars privately, he still began scheming to get that car. He knew some black marketeers—a group of Georgians—who were willing to pay him fifty thousand rubles for his car, which would give him enough money to buy the Chevy. In order to avoid getting into trouble, he told some of his influential friends what he wanted to do, and in a few weeks he was driving around Moscow in his shiny new, eight-cylinder, American-made Chevrolet.

By mid-1967, Ross' good fortune began to fade. He had begun lecturing less, and a year later he was told that the section of the propaganda program that he was assigned to was being disbanded. His source of money was gone. He ordinarily would have been old enough for a pension, but they told him a propagandist was not considered a worker, and denied his application. None of his influential friends were able to help him now. A few months later he grew ill and was hospitalized. He was diagnosed as having terminal cancer, and the hospital administrator told him to go home, that there was nothing they could do to help. Ross's wife was desperate to find a hospital that would take him, because she did not want to have to care for him. She finally succeeded in finding a place to take the emaciated Ross, who died two days later.

His wife skipped his funeral, saying she was too distraught, and sent her daughter and son-in-law to represent her. However, Ross' first wife and two daughters came to pay their respects. His funeral was sadder than most I had attended. I thought of his last, lonely days when, reduced to a pauper, he was rejected by his Russian wife of twenty-six years and his Russian friends. He had let himself be used to the fullest. When they were done with him, they threw him away like a piece of garbage.

During my years in the Soviet Union, I came to know sixteen children who were the result of mixed marriages. They were all the brunt of racist pranks and taunts during their school years. Some were flunked by bigoted teachers even though they turned in excellent exam papers. One student made it into college but had to quit and take his degree via a correspondence course because of the racism he encountered. Only five of the sixteen managed to hang on long enough to get a college degree, and then when they graduated they were not offered jobs for which they were trained. One student, who had prepared for a career teaching at the college or high school level, was given a job in an elementary school. A young woman who majored in African and black history was given a job as a receptionist at the Soviet Society for African Studies. Those who did not enter college received low-level or menial jobs.

These mulatto children had difficulty marrying. One very attractive young woman whose parents were both Americans—her father was a black cotton specialist and her mother was white and Jewish—became the tennis champion in the Uzbek Republic. Linda, who was also a pianist, came to Moscow in 1952 to study at Lomonosov University. She and a Russian who was studying music at the conservatory soon met and fell in love. They wanted desperately to get married, but his parents and relatives were bitterly opposed. They told him that they would beat him if he tried to bring her to the apartment, and if he stooped so low as to marry her, he would be disowned.

He married her anyway, and for awhile they met in the parks or just walked the streets together. Fortunately, she soon passed her entrance exams to the university and was given an eight- by seven-and-a-half-foot room. A student normally was not allowed to live with a spouse in a university room, but they asked Robert Ross if he would appeal to someone influential on their behalf and, as a result, the university administration had to let the couple live together. They were there until she graduated four years later, and then were forced to move out in a week.

They were back in the same predicament, meeting in parks and walking the streets. In desperation, her husband pleaded with his parents to change their minds, but to no avail. Linda came to think the situation was hopeless and talked to her husband about breaking off their marriage. A month later, at a student party, her husband drank all night long, then drove his friend's car over a railing and down a steep embankment. He was killed instantly. His parents and brothers blamed his death on "that mulatto girl, Linda."

Linda encountered other problems because of her skin color. She was bypassed for a goodwill mission being organized for model Komsomols, to which she belonged. When she tried to join a second group, an official from the cultural ministry told her she could not go.

"But why not?" she asked. "Aren't I in the same category as the Komsomols who were chosen?"

"All right, I'll tell you," the man said, turning red. "If we send you, who are you going to represent? What kind of message do you think we want to give about our country?"

After Linda's father died, her mother came to live with her, giving up a two-room apartment in Tashkent to share Linda's small room in Moscow. Linda fruitlessly tried to obtain a larger room. After a time she fell in love with an African student from Zanzibar, and wrote the authorities asking for a two-room apartment so they could get married. Her efforts were fruitless; she never heard from anyone. She married anyway, and a few months later Zanzibar and Tanganyika merged to form Tanzania, and her husband was called home immediately. A few weeks later she received word that her husband had been appointed minister of energy and transport. I doubted whether he would come back for her, even though she had given birth to a baby girl during his absence.

One day while she was at work she received a call from the Moscow Housing Trust to come over immediately. When she arrived, she was congratulated and given an order for a separate two-room apartment in a new, multi-story building. Linda was dumfounded. They told her to move in immediately, along with her mother, and that she would be assisted financially in buying new furniture and other items. She was even given artificial flowers in beautifully designed vases and new kitchen appliances. Linda and her mother were amazed and confused, until a few days later notice came from her husband that he would be arriving in Moscow within a week. Clearly, the authorities had already intercepted his letter and wanted him to carry a glowing report of Soviet life back to

Tanzania. After her husband's visit, Linda applied for a visa to travel to Tanzania. To her amazement, she was told within two weeks that the passport was ready. Unfortunately, however, Linda never made it to Africa. About a week before her scheduled departure, she was reading a Tanzanian newspaper and saw a picture of a wedding ceremony: it was her husband, with his new wife.

Children of mixed marriages had a little less difficulty finding spouses once the newly independent African states opened embassies in Moscow. Male staff members often found these mulatto women attractive. At one point in the early sixties there was a rash of marriages. Although these women hoped they would find a better way of life once they left the Soviet Union, they faced a difficult path. One young woman I knew, after accompanying her husband back to his native country in Africa, later fled back to the Soviet Union. She could not adapt to freedom. All her life she had been told what she could and could not do. She was accustomed to having most of her important decisions made for her by the authorities. And she was overwhelmed by the need to manage a large household with many servants.

One day, while her husband was at work and her child was being cared for by servants, in desperation she headed out to the airport, boarded a plane, and returned to Moscow. But returning was not so easy, either. She was detained and interrogated for three and a half hours at the Moscow airport, because she had returned without first getting permission from the Soviet embassy. She was finally released and returned to her mother's apartment, where she broke down in hysterical weeping, and secluded herself for several weeks.

News of her experience reached some of the other Soviet women who were living in African countries; nevertheless, three others I knew fled for Moscow. They chose to be humiliated at the airport, face life as a spinster, live in crammed quarters with relatives, and wait in long lines whenever they ventured out to buy something, rather than cope with the uncertainties of freedom.

CHAPTER 26

Paul Robeson, Langston Hughes, and Others

WHEN PAUL ROBESON FIRST ARRIVED IN MOSCOW IN 1934, he was hailed as a brilliant international artist who possessed one of the greatest voices in the world. I received an invitation to attend a reception given in his honor by the prestigious All Union Society for Cultural Relations with Foreign Countries. This official correspondence, as usual, was addressed to "Negro Robert Robinson."

The reception excelled by far anything I had attended thus far in the Soviet Union. Men were dressed in tuxedos and women wore evening gowns. The food was exquisite and the entertainment more than I expected. We not only heard Robeson sing, we also were treated to performances by several outstanding Soviet singers and musicians.

After the entertainment, I tried to go backstage to congratulate Robeson on his stirring performance, but I was stopped by two men in plainclothes who rudely demanded to see a pass, which I did not possess. Because I strongly wanted to meet Robeson, I went to his hotel the next day and succeeded in making my way to his suite, where I saw him surrounded by leading Russian artists, writers, and journalists. His wife noticed me, walked over, told me she was Eslanda Robeson, and asked me who I was. After I told her my name and the reason for my being in the Soviet Union, she said, “My husband cannot see you now. Call us tomorrow and we will be able to tell you when you can drop by.”

When I finally met Robeson two days later, he seemed preoccupied. I had hoped to talk to him about my experiences in the Soviet Union, but he did not allow me the opportunity, and our meeting was superficial. He told me, “I am happy to learn that you are making a contribution to the building of socialism. You are doing a great thing. I wish you success in your work.”

I thanked him, and told him how much I had enjoyed his performance. “You know, he said, “I have never faced an audience like the one the other night. They really know how to listen to music here, especially folk music.”

I told him that the Russian people, and most other Soviet people, have been exposed to folk music for much of their lives, and that there is much in common between Russian and black American songs of suffering. At that point Eslanda asked, “Mr. Robinson, how long have you been here?”

“I arrived in July 1930,” I told her.

“Where did you learn your profession and where are you from?” she asked.

I told her, “I was born in the Caribbean, on the island of Jamaica. When I was five, my parents travelled to Cuba and that is where I learned my profession.”

“Then I suppose you speak Spanish fluently?” she asked.

“I used to,” I said, “but that was eleven years ago.”

“I’ve always like Spanish,” she said. “I thought I detected a Spanish strain in your features, when I first saw you enter the concert hall with your husband.”

“Yes, a number of Spanish-speaking people have told me the same thing,” she replied with a hint of vanity, clearly pleased to think of herself as having a discernible resemblance to a European people. At that point Robeson rose and said, “Robinson, we are happy you came over to see us, so that we could learn that you, a black man, are taking part in the development of this great new social order. Keep in touch.”

With that, he reached out and shook my hand with a hand so large and a grip so powerful that, had he pressed slightly harder, he would have broken my bones.

The evening newspaper the previous day had strung together about a dozen superlatives in praise of Robeson's performance. Both the press and the radio urged him to return. And he did. I met him again when he came back to Moscow in 1936 and enrolled his son in a Soviet school. Robeson was an idealist, and he thought that the social climate in Russia was better than in the United States. By bringing his child to Moscow, he wanted to remove him from the experience of racial prejudice. The Kremlin of course knew of Robeson's idealistic view of Soviet society, and worked successfully to shield him from the harsh realities of Soviet life and mold him into a totally committed Marxist-Leninist.

In 1939 Robeson returned again, but this time it was to remove his son from the Moscow school he was attending. War had broken out in much of Europe and he did not want his son trapped in Moscow. When Robeson came again ten years later, in 1949, the press proclaimed him a hero for his work during the Spanish civil war. Media accounts said that he had risked his life to entertain the International Brigade. Robeson performed three concerts in Moscow with Lawrence Brown, his famous accompanist, at the piano, and then toured other cities in the Soviet Union.

Three years before this visit by Robeson, in 1946, I had met Ethiopia's ambassador to the Kremlin. After I told him about my situation, he invited me to go to Addis Ababa to help at their newly-opened technical school. I told him, "Since the age of twenty, when I heard Marcus Garvey speak about the duty of every conscientious black man—especially those trained in a profession—to return to Africa and help build those nations, I have longed to do just that."

Although the ambassador later told me, in August 1948, that he was going on vacation and would press my case with the highest officials of his government, I learned five weeks later that, unfortunately, he had died while in surgery. Yet he had planted the thought in me that I would be welcomed in Addis Ababa, if I could only get out. Therefore, when Robeson was still in Moscow in 1949, I went to see him in his hotel suite the day after his first concert, and asked if he would intercede with the Soviet authorities to allow me to go to Ethiopia, where I could pass on my technical knowledge. He listened attentatively and said, "Robinson, I understand what you have said, but I cannot give you an answer now. I will let you know soon."

Four days later he performed at the cultural club at the giant Zil Auto Factory. After the concert, I went backstage and told him how delighted I was to hear him sing again. He thanked me for the compliment and said, "Robinson, I have not had time to think over my answer to your request, but I'll do so soon." I assured him that I had only come to hear him sing, not to press him for an answer.

A week later I went to see him again at his hotel. Another of his accompanists, a black man named Stevens, opened the door for me, and said, "Paul is not in." With his index finger, he indicated I should sit down in a chair. Then he blurted out, angrily, "What are you thinking of doing, Robinson, running away from here? You must stay right where you are. You belong here for the good of the cause. Or maybe you're trying to tarnish Paul's reputation, by getting him involved in your attempt to leave. That is all I have to say to you. You may go now!" I was crushed. Stevens was telling me what I already suspected but had refused to accept—that Robeson had been so thoroughly won over by Soviet flattery and attention, that he would not help me.

When Robeson returned to the United States after his triumphant tour of the Soviet Union, US authorities invalidated his passport for having made what were considered to be anti-American statements. At one of his concerts he had said in Russian, "I was, I am, and I will always be, a friend of the Soviet Union." As an encore, he regularly sang a famous Soviet propaganda song, "I don't know of another country where a human being can breathe so freely."

At Robert Ross' invitation, I attended a birthday party held for Robeson, *in absentia,* in the large House of Trade Unions building. When we arrived, Ross and I were escorted to the presidium, where we sat with thirteen others during the festivities. This was clearly for propaganda purposes—to get a couple of black faces into the crowd—as evidenced by the pictures in the following day's newspapers of us sitting alongside others. The caption under the photo read, "Two prominent blacks in Moscow condemned Robeson's illegal detention in the U.S.A." During the birthday celebration, speakers hailed Robeson as a great son of his people, and attacked the US for taking away his right to travel. Following

Robinson with Paul Robeson (left), after Robeson's concert at the First State Ball Bearing Factory.

Robinson arranged for Paul Robeson to perform in his factory in July 1961. Above, seated left to right, chief engineer of the machine shop; assistant director of the factory; Robeson; assistant party secretary. Standing left to right, trade union secretary, machine shop party secretary, Robinson, an assistant party secretary, machine shop superintendent.

the speeches, the fifteen of us were invited for refreshments, and then a concert followed, for which I did not stay.

In the early 1950s, Eslanda came to Moscow, on her way to China. I received a call from her interpreter saying she wanted to see me. When I visited her the next day, after the usual greetings, she asked me to go with her to a food store and help her buy some provisions to take on her trip to China. On the way back to the hotel she became quite pensive. After a while she said, "Robinson, you asked Paul to help you go to Ethiopia. We have thought about your request, and he has decided that he cannot help you. You see, we do not really know you well enough, to know what is in your mind. Suppose he were to help you leave, and then when you arrived in Ethiopia, you decided to turn anti-Soviet. We would find ourselves in trouble with the authorities here."

Even though I was not surprised, Robeson's refusal to help still hurt me deeply, especially in light of his frequent references to "My fatherland, Africa." With his international stature and his connections with the highest Soviet officials, he could have made my dream come true. His reluctance to help revealed that he was far from being a free man. Part of the price he had paid for his fame was to lose the ability to act purely out of conscience.

Paul Robeson returned to Moscow in the late fifties, where he performed to a standing-room-only crowd at the branch of the Bolshoi Theater. A week later, thirteen thousand people crammed into the Lenin Arena to hear him. Robert Ross and I were disappointed when neither the police nor the arena manager would let us backstage to see Robeson, even though we assured them that he knew us well and would be eager to visit with old friends.

When Robeson came back in 1961, I asked him to give a concert for workers in my shop. He agreed, and I told the factory authorities about it a month before the concert date. It was not until the day of the concert, two and a half hours before he was scheduled to arrive, that a factory-wide announcement was made over the public address system. I quickly helped to build a platform and move in a piano and four chairs and then, as more than five thousand workers began to squeeze into our shop, I dashed to the party secretary's office to await Robeson's arrival. Robeson arrived in his chauffeur-driven car with a pianist, an interpreter, and two tall, powerfully built security men. As soon as we entered the shop, the workers broke into thunderous applause. I intended to slip into the audience, but the assistant director of the shop trade union committee told me that I must sit on the platform.

"Why is it necessary for me to sit up there?" I whispered. "I am no one special; I belong in the audience with everyone else."

"You don't understand," he said. "Your compatriot will feel better if he sees you close by."

I knew I was not going to persuade him otherwise, so I moved toward the platform but not up onto it. Robeson started speaking in Russian and, looking at me, he said, "Comrades, my dear friend Robert Robinson, who has worked with you for decades, invited me to your factory. I am very happy to meet with you face-to-face. I want to sing a few songs for you, which I hope you will like."

Robeson captivated the workers with his voice and his personal magnetism. He seemed to be able to reach into the spiritual core of everyone there. After singing several songs, Robeson began another one that startled me. It was a song I was familiar with, a mournful song out of the Jewish tradition that decried their persecution through the centuries. I knew this song would alienate party officials in the audience. I wondered whether Robeson, who was so determined to see only good in the Soviet system, was even aware of Soviet anti-Semitism. I decided that he must be, and that perhaps he knew what he was doing. As he sang, there was a cry in his voice, a plea to end the beating, berating, and killing of Jews. Although he sang in Yiddish, I was certain that even those in the audience who did not know the song would understand the spirit of what he was conveying. Everyone was riveted to his pleading face marked with sorrow, his trembling lips and mournful voice. He created a spiritual bond with an audience that could reach into its own past and touch the depths of sorrow. I believe he struck a chord that lies buried deep within the Russian character—their profoundly religious nature. Robeson finished his performance with this song, leaving the workers pensive as they filed out of the shop and returned to their workplaces.

A week or so later, the press reported that Robeson was resting and visiting children's camps in the summer resorts to the south. Soon after that a rumor about Robeson began to spread in my factory and throughout Moscow, to the effect that he had had an unpleasant confrontation with Khrushchev. As I heard the story from three different party members, Khrushchev was vacationing in the same region as Robeson and invited the singer to his villa. Robeson asked Khrushchev whether stories he had read in the western press about Soviet anti-Semitism were true. A party man whose integrity I believed in told me, "Being such an unpredictable person, Khrushchev reacted with vehemence and accused Robeson of meddling in our country's internal affairs." Robeson was so shocked by Khrushchev's fury that he left the next day for East Gemany where, according to East German radio, he was placed under medical care.

I was anxious to try and test the truthfulness of these rumors. A few months later I met the interpreter who had accompanied Robeson to my factory and I asked her whether Robeson had sung the Jewish song at any of his other concerts in Moscow. She told me that he had. I wondered, was Robeson singing it deliberately? Had he decided that he had been hoodwinked by the Soviets, and were his eyes beginning to open to the realities of Soviet oppression? These were questions I would never have answered, but it did become apparent that Robeson fell quickly out of favor. Ever since his first postwar concert in Moscow, in 1949, his music was aired twice a week throughout the country, including a half-hour every Sunday. I used to listen to his music regularly; I would pick up the broadcast that was relayed from the radio station Mayak (the Beacon) to Soviet commercial ships all over the world. But as soon as the rumors of Robeson's controversy with Khrushchev arose, the broadcasts of his music ceased. I never again heard his voice over Radio Moscow, and never read another word about him in the Soviet press. He was erased from the collective memory of a nation he had admired. Robeson was the darling of the Soviets as long as he blindly towed their ideological line, but was made a non-person when he questioned Soviet domestic policies.

I learned through foreign visitors that Robeson's health declined quickly after his encounter with Khruschev, and he remained sick until his death. He never again visited the Soviet Union; we were never treated to the long-promised production of *Othello,* with Robeson in the lead, which had been talked about for years. It seems that the poor man died of a broken heart.

* * *

I first met Langston Hughes in 1932, two days after he arrived in Moscow. Although only thirty years old at the time, he was already a well-known poet and writer, out of Harlem, and was president of the League for Struggle for Negro Rights (a Communist party creation that was later transformed into the National Negro Congress). He and twenty-one other black Americans had been brought to the Soviet Union to make a Soviet-sponsored epic film about Negro life in Harlem, Mississippi, and Georgia. The project eventually was scrapped, either because of pressure from the US government, or from white American businessmen who enjoyed lucrative contracts with the Soviets, or both. During their stay in Moscow, as so-called official representatives of black America, the artists and intellectuals were given the red carpet treatment. Their Soviet hosts escorted them around town to showcase the positive changes in the lives of Soviet people that had resulted from the revolution.

The entire group was housed at the Grand Hotel in Moscow, and that is where I first met Hughes. I visited Hughes, and other members of the group, several times a week during the many months they stayed in Russia. As a fellow black American who was living inside the Russian system, I felt my advice and assistance would be helpful. From my first meeting with Hughes, I was impressed with his zest for life and love of people. He was as easygoing and charming, perceptive and intelligent in person as was the best of his poetry. He enjoyed a good time, and if he could not find one, he would make one on the spot, with his hearty, infectious laughter. He had been hired to write the screenplay for the film, but because the project was trapped in a maze of bureaucratic red tape, he was in Moscow several weeks before he even got a look at the script he was to rewrite.

One afternoon I took Hughes to a store near the hotel, so he could purchase a supply of paper and pencils. An attractive young woman who waited on us smiled pleasantly at Hughes as she helped us with our purchase. When she handed him the parcel she said to me, "Tell your friend to come again." When we reached the street I noticed that Hughes had become pensive, and asked him if anything was wrong. He did not respond, but when we came to a small park in front of the Bolshoi Theater he said, "Bob, if you don't mind, let's sit in the park for awhile."

As we sat down on a bench he said, "I'm glad you came today and rescued me from our interpreter." I asked him what he meant, and he explained, "We have been here almost two months, and every day she takes us somewhere whether we want to go or not."

"I suppose they are trying to be good hosts," I said. "They want to keep you busy so you won't become lonely or bored." Then I asked him, "Langston, what do you think about this new, socialist country, now that you've been here a few weeks?"

His open, handsome face brightened. Suddenly animated, he said, "I have not come to any final conclusions yet, because I haven't seen enough. But there are some things that the US could copy, to its benefit. The main thing I have noticed is a definite lack of hatred against me as a black man. Take the woman in that store. That kind of experience is rare, to be treated with courtesy and friendliness by a white woman. In France and Italy, racism is supposedly nonexistent, but when I was in those countries a few years ago, I felt that I was merely tolerated. I never felt as I did today, that my skin color was unimportant. When we left the store I was silent for awhile because I was thinking about how the two races should be able to live in peace in America. If white, brown, dark and yellow skins can live in peace and without ethnic friction in this country, where there are more than 150 nationalities, could not the same principle be applied in the US, too?"

His face was a mixture of sadness, perplexity, and hope. I asked, "What do you think is the answer for us blacks in America?"

"To be honest with you," he said, "the struggle before us will be long and torturous. What we need now is a really knowledgeable and farsighted leader, someone with the gift to organize all of us, not only in the US but throughout the world. We must have a common global goal, because without it, many people will fail to keep their eyes on the ultimate goal of freedom and justice for all people.

We sat in the park much of the afternoon, trading impressions of the United States and Russia, and also getting to know each other better. I had never met a writer before. At this time, and in all my subsequent visits with him, I found in Hughes the same compassion and lack of affectation. He took his craft, his art of writing, very seriously, but he was too good-natured and down-to-earth to become arrogant about his special gift.

* * *

Coretta Arle-Titzs, the black American singer who introduced me to the Bermins in 1933, came to Russia in 1912 with a traveling theater group. She fell in love with a Russian intellectual, decided to stay, and five months later they were married. However, the young man's family and friends ostracized him because he had married a black woman. The pressure grew heavy on him and he spent more and more time away from home; when he returned, she would quiz him on his whereabouts. They argued and fought, and eventually Coretta left him. By then she was enrolled at the Imperial Conservatoire—an opportunity for formal musical training which was unavailable to her in America—and she stayed in St. Petersburg to complete her studies and gain her diploma. Coretta's dream was to return to America and open a singing school for young children. But by the time she graduated, it was two years after the revolution, the US had recalled its ambassador, her passport was no longer valid, and there was no transportation to the West. With no immediate way to get back home, Coretta acceded to the wishes of a persistent Russian suitor, and remarried.

She had met Boris Arle-Titzs during her third year at the conservatory. He was a student there, a reserved and very polite young pianist who asked her to marry him after a year-and-a-half-long friendship. Coretta told me, "I turned him down about four times. When he would not give up, I finally told him everything about my first marriage. He just said that I should not think that all men were alike, that he would never allow anyone to interfere with his private life, and that the color of a person's skin color had nothing to do with the color of one's spirit. He said he loved me as a woman and that my race was irrelevant."

To strengthen his argument, Boris warned Coretta that she would face anti-Red prejudice if she returned to America, and that establishing her school might be more difficult than she thought. After their marriage, Coretta was accepted by his family and friends but she never heard back from her parents in America after she wrote them about her marriage. Despite the circumstances of Soviet life, their life together was a good one, revolving around their pursuits, and friends, in the arts. They were friends with Maxim Gorki, Hippolito-Ivanov (a talented and popular opera composer), and many others. Although Coretta lived under communism for thirty years, until her death in 1951, she never told me what she thought of the Soviet system, as much as I subtly sought to pry.

* * *

John Sutton was another black American friend of mine. Sutton had studied at Tuskegee Institute, Drake University, the Massachusetts Agricultural College (now part of the University of Massachusetts), and had a master's degree from Columbia University. Early in 1930 the Soviet Union invited George Washington Carver, of Tuskegee Institute, to help them develop their agricultural industry. Rather than going himself, he recommended Sutton, who then arrived in Moscow in 1932 as one of a group of eight black American specialists in agriculture, poultry, and cotton. From Moscow they journeyed to Central Asia and other parts of the Soviet Union to advise Soviet farmers on ways to improve crop and poultry production.

Sutton stayed in the Soviet Union, and in the mid-thirties he invented a sturdy new type of rope made from rice straw, a development that enabled the Soviets to establish a new industry. Before Sutton's invention, Soviet rope was weak and often broke apart. But because of his work, Russia could stop importing jute and hemp and became a major exporter of string twine. I asked Sutton what he received for his invention. He smiled and said, "My organization gave me a couple of hundred rubles."

One day, after Sutton had returned temporarily to Moscow from the Uzbek Republic in Central Asia, I asked him what life was like for him, professionally. "To tell you the truth, Bob," he replied, "life in Uzbekia is far from simple. I meet resistance every step of the way when I try to introduce new methods of technology. People are so accustomed to doing things the old way, they really do not want to change. Our efforts also suffer from a great shortage of equipment.

"I talked to my boss," he said. "I have written to Moscow. I receive promises from everywhere that the situation will be looked into, but nothing has changed. I just give in and do the job the way the people want it done and keep my innovations to myself. But then I feel guilty, because the result is just the opposite of what I was brought here to do. But how is it for you, in the factory?"

"Resistance to change is not as great, or as direct, as it was when I first arrived," I told him. "My proposals are rejected, ignored, or accepted, but then I am not allowed to implement them. I solve the problem by working after hours, and then inviting the superintendent, the chief engineer, the department foreman, and party secretary to a demonstration of how a job can be done more efficiently and in less time. At that point, and with all of them there, they cannot very well sabotage the already-completed project."

"You make it sound almost easy," he laughed.

"Well, as we both know, it's not easy. There is still a great deal of red tape, but this usually works for me." Sutton said he might try a similar strategy when he returned to Central Asia.

* * *

George Tynes was an agriculturist with a degree from Wilberforce University. He was an expert in poultry and fish husbandry, but could not find work in his field in the States, so he taught English in a Negro school in the South and later worked as a longshoreman in New York. He was recruited, along with fourteen other blacks, by a trade union activist. Immediately upon arriving in Moscow in 1932, this group was sent to Uzbekia to help salvage their foundering duck industry. They gave Tynes the novel title of zoo technician. His work was instrumental in helping the Soviet Union produce more and healthier ducks. From Central Asia, he was transferred to Simferopol in the Crimea. After the war, he landed on an experimental farm a few miles outside of Moscow, where I was able to see him on occasion. His wife was Ukranian, and their three children were pleasant and outgoing, like George.

He was a powerfully-built, broad-shouldered man, over six feet tall, with powerful hands and fingers. In all the years he spent in the Soviet poultry and fish industry, Tynes never received a promotion, even though he was an exemplary worker who usually knew more than his superiors. Because of him, the Soviet poultry exhibition won first prize in an international fair held in Belgium in the mid-fifties. However, it was his supervisor who received the medals and was acclaimed as an industrial hero in Soviet newspaper and radio accounts. Tynes was simply listed in the fair's program as a technician. Although he had become a Soviet citizen, he was a black, non-native, and the Kremlin was obsessed with impressing the world with the superiority of Russia's own people. Once back in Moscow, George was given two of the medals awarded in the competition. Even though he was denied full recognition for his efforts, Tynes was nevertheless proud of his medals and wore them whenever he came into Moscow. He particularly enjoyed seeing the startled reaction of many Russians, who were unprepared to see evidence of a black man succeeding professionally in Russia.

CHAPTER 27

My Longest Friendship

JORGE AMBRAMOVICH WAS NOT THE TYPE of fellow to attract your attention. He was a quiet person, who listened attentively before answering. He was about five and a half feet tall, clean-shaven, well-groomed, and a bit pudgy around the middle. We first met in 1937, when we were fellow students at the engineering institute. Jorge was a serious student, with an inquisitive and well-disciplined mind.

We soon became friends, and when I was invited to his home for dinner I had my first direct experience with Moscow's much lamented communal living. Jorge and his wife lived with his mother and father in a single large, partitioned room. Eleven families shared the same kitchen and bathroom. In the kitchen, each family had its own hissing kerosene stove; thus, an hour and a half before dinner, eleven women could be found bent over their stoves in a room filled with the aroma of *borscht* and cabbage soup. The Abramovitch family woke up each morning at 4 A.M. in order to use the toilet before the line started forming at 5:30. They would then go back to bed for another ninety minutes of sleep.

Jorge's parents—well-educated, cultivated people—were both teachers. They were interesting to talk with, as was his wife. She was also Jewish, was a good painter and, though a quiet person, had an alert and creative mind. I frequently joined Jorge at his home, where we would study together. I was startled when a few months before the war, I learned that Jorge's wife had left him and was living with her sisters. When his father died and the family lost his income, Jorge was forced to drop out of the institute and work a second job. Near the end of the war, when the institute reopened, Jorge resumed his studies through correspondence courses, receiving his mechanical engineering certificate in 1947. A few months later, at the age of twenty-nine, he was made the director of a mechanical designing bureau with a staff of sixteen. About six months later he married Lena Solomonova, a lovely black-haired, brown-eyed Jewish engineer on his staff, and she moved in with Jorge and his mother.

I visited Jorge about once a week in the late forties. He was obviously in love, always talking fondly about Lena, sharing with me his deepest feelings toward her. Nearly every time I visited, Lena's mother was also there. She would always leave to catch the 10:30 P.M. bus, and insisted that Jorge and her daughter walk her to the bus stop and wait until her ride appeared. Within a year, Lena gave birth to a daughter. Now it seemed as if her mother was always there, and she and Lena would talk continually, nearly to the exclusion of Jorge. My friend confided in me that it had come to the point where sometimes the only time he could speak to his wife was when they were in bed, and by that time he was usually too upset with her mother, and too tired to say much of anything.

Jorge asked my advice, but I am afraid I was not able to be much help. I told him that I needed time to get to know his mother-in-law. Perhaps then I could understand why she was so possessive of her daughter, and suggest a solution. It took a long time, about two years, before I won enough of her trust so that she would share with me the story of her past and her feelings. I ended up amazed that either she or her daughter was still alive, so turbulent and painful had been their battle for survival.

Maria Solomonova was born in Kiev in 1901, and at the age of eighteen she moved to Leningrad where she met and married her husband, a young Communist idealist and filmmaker. Lena was born in 1921. Although food was scarce and they were living in tiny, cramped quarters, their confidence in the future helped them to endure present hardships. Their buoyancy changed as soon as Kirov was assassinated and the purges gathered steam. Terror swept through the city. Friends and neighbors of theirs were being rounded up and shot. Despite her husband's membership in the party, they knew he could be next. Every night for more than five years they went to bed, afraid that the secret police would come knocking on their door. Fortunately, her husband was never arrested.

However, life during the war years was even more grim, and a more desperate struggle for survival, than before. By the winter of 1941, the German army had surrounded Leningrad and was shelling the city daily. The Soviet army's one supply line was in range of the enemy's heavy artillery, so very little food made its way to the civilian population in the city. To keep from starving to death became as important as avoiding Nazi bombs and bullets. Maria's husband, who by now was an assistant director of the Leningrad Film Studio, joined the army in order to fight the Nazis who were at the city's gates.

Maria and Lena were left alone in the middle of winter, with very little money. To keep warm, they chopped up their furniture and burned it in their stove. When they had used up all the wood in their apartment, they would sleep with several layers of winter clothing, to keep from freezing to death. For food, they hunted dogs, cats, and rats. When they could not find any animals by themselves, they would go to the butcher shops, in hopes of obtaining a bit of rat or cat meat. Maria told me that the following winter of 1943-44 was even more desperate.

"The Germans were still shelling us," she said. "My Lena had gone to try to get our portions of black bread—16.7 ounces for each of us. One day, while waiting in line, an elderly woman whom we loved and trusted told Lena that a ring of black marketeers had been discovered the day before. They were selling human flesh as horse and cow meat. Soldiers on patrol had discovered two men in a basement. One of them was standing over a warm corpse with a bloodied axe in his hand. It was like an animal slaughterhouse, except that it was a human being on the ground, who was missing the flesh from his buttocks. Hunks of flesh were hanging from hooks on the wall. The old lady told Lena that the soldiers shot the two men on the spot."

Maria paused while telling me this story, and then said, "Two days earlier Lena and I were thrilled to have purchased a pound of meat. And we ate it. After hearing this story, we were sick for days."

Maria explained that many of her friends and neighbors died from the bitter cold and lack of food. "We were determined to survive.

Lena and I would hug each other for an hour at a time, to keep warm," she said. "We ate things unimaginable. We even boiled my husband's old films. The celluloid turned into a jelly-like substance, which we ate with black bread. One day, when we had been without bread for some time, we decided to follow a tip that an old man had given Lena; we boiled an old shoe. After two hours the leather had softened, but still was not edible. So then we put the shoe through our meat grinder and stuck it back into the boiling water. The water turned brown and a substance thickened on the surface of the water. After it cooled off, Lena tasted it. She declared that it was no worse than the film jelly, so I decided to try it too. Soon enough, we had eaten all of our old shoes, and then we began rummaging in the streets and alleyways for more. Lena and I grew so close that we became almost like one person. It was as if she was I, and I was she. We each felt as the other felt, and encouraged each other to keep going."

Jorge already knew some, but not all, of this story. Once Maria unburdened herself to me, I was a better sounding board for my friend. In his mind, he understood and could accept the reasons for his wife and her mother being so close. But the fact remained that their relationship was starving him emotionally. He was doing everything within his power to obtain a two-room apartment with a private bathroom and kitchen. At the time, he, his wife, his daughter, and his mother-in-law were living in two small rooms in a communal apartment complex, whereas his mother was living alone in a room in a different part of the city.

Finally in 1962, six years after he applied, he was assigned a small, modern, two-room private apartment. He was a happy man, because now his family could have its privacy while his mother-in-law could stay where she was. Unfortunately, Maria sabotaged his plan. She was home alone when the housing commission inspectors came to visit, before giving final approval to his move. She told the men that she, too, would be moving with her daughter's family to their new apartment. As a result, they had to give up their existing apartment, and the occupancy papers for the new apartment listed four people instead of the three he had originally asked for.

His housewarming party was therefore a bittersweet affair. In fact, it was the first time in twenty-five years I had seen Jorge drunk. When I saw him a few days later he said, "The situation has worsened.

I am so upset with her, I can't even talk. And Lena is spending even more time with the old woman. I come home from work feeling so lonely, if I didn't have my daughter to talk to, I think I would lose my mind. When I tell Lena of my anguish, she reminds me of what she and her mother endured during the war, says they need each other, and that their bond will never be broken."

Poor man, what could I say? He was aging quickly, and looked more and more like his father did before he died. Although it was not something he could ever mention to me directly, I knew that if he had the chance, Jorge would choose to leave the Soviet Union. All he wanted out of life was to be free and have a normal family life, and he could have neither.

A little while later, his troubles grew worse, and this time I was unfortunately the cause. I was at the central Moscow post office one day, registering a complaint because I had not received the last three issues of *Ebony*. (Over a year before, I had met a black judge and his wife who were visiting Moscow as tourists. When they returned to the US, they bought me a one-year subscription to *Ebony*, for which I was very grateful, because it told me something about the social and economic circumstances of American blacks. His name was George Crockett, and he now represents Michigan's thirteenth district in Congress). I decided to ring up Jorge, whose office was only two blocks away, and he suggested I come over and visit him as soon as I was done. I got to his office a little after 5 P.M. Most of his staff had left for home, and he was alone with a designer, whose drawing he was correcting. As he introduced me to the woman, who was the department's electrical circuit specialist, I noticed two men sitting in an office to my right, looking intently at the three of us. I felt certain that one of them would be the department's party secretary, while the other one was probably the superintendent. While talking to Jorge and his designer, I glanced in their direction a couple of times. I felt uneasy that they were still looking at us, and I knew I must leave as soon as possible. In their eyes I was a foreigner; by fraternizing with me, Jorge could be accused of breaking the socialist code of behavior. When I told Jorge I had to leave, he urged me to stay another half-an-hour, not suspecting that his bosses would view his association with me as a crime.

Unfortunately, my suspicions turned out to be well-founded. I did not receive Jorge's customary phone call the following week or the week after. When a month had passed, I called him. An unfamiliar voice answered the phone, and asked who was calling, which was a precaution his family had never taken before. I was told that Jorge was not home, which I took as a signal to leave him alone.

I did not hear a word from him, or about him, for almost two years. Then, one Sunday afternoon I received a call from Lena, who said that her family missed seeing me and wondered if I would be home the following Saturday. I said yes, and six days later heard a knock on my door and I jumped up to let them in. When I opened the door, there was Jorge, standing alone, looking like an old man. My dear, dear friend, this caged bird who wanted desperately to fly away, clearly had suffered a great deal since I last saw him. I invited him in, served him tea, and turned on the record player, while we said how much we had missed each other. I was sure he had a heavy load to get off his chest, and thought that I might make it easier on him if he could renew his relationship with me gradually. I asked him to help me solve a tricky designing problem, which we wrestled with for the next two hours until it was solved. At this point he seemed more at ease, and I asked him about his family. Although the relationship between his wife and her mother was the same, in discussing it he seemed to have become more accepting.

"Jorge, how are things in general?" I asked. He put down his teacup, walked over and turned up the volume on the record player, then returned to his chair and began to explain. "First of all," he said, "I purposely came to see you so that I could explain why I stopped calling you and visiting with you during the past two years. The day after you visited my office, I was summoned into the party secretary's office and interrogated about my relationship with you. They grilled me for more than thirty minutes. They assumed that there was a sinister reason for you to visit me, and they wanted me to confess. All I could tell them was the truth, but that was not what they wanted to hear.

"Then later in the day the party secretary called a special meeting of the entire staff, and announced that a prominent member of the collective had violated the secret moral code of socialist interest. He pointed me out as the perpetrator, and said that the party could not tolerate such brazen violators, and that I was a menace to the nation. He told everyone about my crime—that I had brought a foreigner to our workplace and had thereby exposed what we were doing to our enemies.

"Then a rank-and-file designer, a party member, asked to say a few words. He stood up and began reading aloud from a prepared statement that he pulled out of his pocket. 'Comrades, you have heard of the criminal action of Comrade Abramovich, who brought an enemy to inspect what we're doing here,' he read. 'Great harm has been done, and we cannot allow such damaging behavior to continue. I urge everyone to think seriously about this matter.'

"After the young man sat down, the party secretary stood up and said, 'All those in favor of not having Comrade Abramovitch in our midst, raise your hands.' Of course, everyone raised his hand.

"Even though I had told the party secretary that you and I had been classmates at the engineering institute, that you had been a Soviet citizen for more than a quarter-century, and that you were an engineer in good standing at the First State Ball Bearing Plant, he discharged me. He had already decided what he would do, regardless of the truth.

"The reason for my dismissal was written out in my workbook the next day, which was my last. It said: 'Dismissed for negligence about socialist collective security and a complete lack of vigilance regarding foreigners.' Because of this, I could not get a job in another designing collective—or anywhere else, for that matter.

"Fortunately, about nine months after I was fired, I met a man I had known in secondary school, who by now was a high-ranking party member. When he asked how life was treating me, I told him how I had been fired. He was incensed at the injustice, and he found me a job as a designer in one of the largest collectives in Moscow. I was on probation, and was being watched closely. After three months on the job, my former schoolmate called me and said that I was doing well, and to continue the good work. A while later I was made supervisor of several designers, and three months after that I was appointed as the director of the entire collective."

Jorge became quite emotional and said, "I hope you are not holding anything against me for avoiding you during the past two years. I think you can understand that I was in a difficult position. I want very badly to resume our friendship." I assured him that I understood, and that I assumed our friendship had never ended.

Jorge took the news of my leaving Soviet Russia hard. Two weeks before I left, he came to my apartment, obviously distraught, for there was no one else in his life he could share his true feelings with. Our walks in the park—one of the only safe places one could converse freely—would come to an end. He'd have to shrink back into the gray mass of humans called Soviet citizens, stepping in unison to an oppressive cadence. Jorge's last words to me were whispered: "I wish I could do as you have." And extending his hand and in a sad voice, said: "Good-bye dear friend!"

CHAPTER 28

Reflections on My Private Life

DURING MY YEARS IN THE SOVIET UNION, my friendships with women occurred under the same cloud of surveillance and suspicion as all of my other activities. Traps commonly are set by the authorities by orchestrating sexual encounters or dangling in front of a man the possibility of an affair. They probe your weaknesses, to learn how to control you, and to establish a case against you so that—should they desire—they can blackmail, punish, or entrap you more seriously in the future.

The first time the government tried to assign a woman to entrap me was in Stalingrad, after the Louis and Brown incident. An attractive young Russian woman walked up to me one day, handed me a note, and walked away. I could not read much Russian yet, so I took her note to one of the Russian-Americans to translate. She had written that I was in the Soviet Union, that I should feel free, I had friends everywhere, and she was one of them. I did not think the note required an answer, and I soon forgot about it.

About a week later I was surprised to find the same woman downstairs in my apartment building. She asked if she could visit me. Although I preferred to send her away, I did not want to be impolite, so I invited her in. After about a half-hour she asked me to get her some clothing and a pair of shoes in the store reserved for foreigners. I immediately felt a sense of foreboding, not knowing whether she merely wanted these things for herself, or whether she had been sent to entice me into dealing on the black market, a criminal offense. I told her I could not help her, because what she was asking me to do was illegal.

Despite my refusal, she visited me a few more times. She was a married woman, and I did not do anything to encourage her. However, one day she came over very determined to get me. After about fifteen minutes she became very aggressive. She grabbed me, trying to hug and kiss me, and trying to arouse me in other ways. I virtually had to fight her off. I was not interested; she was not my type, and besides, I was fairly certain that she was not acting on her own. I told her I was not planning to get married in Russia because I had a girlfriend back home in New York. After that failed attempt she never returned.

My next test occurred soon after I started working at the First State Ball Bearing Plant in Moscow. One day I heard a knock on my door. I opened it and saw a young, beautiful, well-dressed woman standing there. "Are you Robinson?" she asked.

I told her I was. "I am from *Pravda,*" she said. "May I come in? I was given the assignment to come and have a little chat with you because we want to write about you."

I invited her in and asked, "What do you want to know?"

"Let us not begin by talking about journalism," she said. "First, I would like us to get acquainted." We talked, she asked me where I had learned my profession, and the conversation proceeded aimlessly. Finally, I asked her when she was going to begin the interview. She told me not to be in a hurry. Then a few minutes later she started to come after me; she soon had me virtually cornered, and was trying to kiss me and embrace me. I was not interested in this woman anyway. I distrusted her motives, and she was too aggressive. A woman has to please me mentally and physically; I cannot treat an affair as if it is two dogs meeting in an alley, doing their thing, and then going on their way. So I was not in the mood, even though this woman was attractive, well-dressed, and shapely. I told her right away, "Listen, if I get entangled with you, the next thing you will want is to marry me. I am not planning to marry anybody in this country, so you might as well leave me alone. I cannot do anything with you."

She was upset, and said with an air of wounded pride, "Well! You are the first man who ever ignored me." It took me another two hours to get rid of her. She kept trying; perhaps now she considered me a challenge. She exposed everything there was to expose. Practically the only thing she did not do was undress herself completely. Finally, when she saw it was useless to keep trying, she left. Russians believe that black men cannot resist white women. In fact, although the word Russians use for a black man—*chornamazi*—literally means "swarthy," the notion behind the word is that the African's skin turned black because of extreme excitement during the sexual act. From some comments this woman made, I expect she was sent to test this belief in the uncontrollable sexuality of black men, to find out my vulnerabilities.

About a year later I met a nice young woman while I was waiting for the tram. Our encounter was seemingly accidental—not arranged by her—and her interest in me eventually became genuine, whether or not she was put up to it by someone else. She walked over to me after we had been standing a few minutes and asked if I was Comrade Robinson. I told her I was, and she said, "I work near your plant, at a factory where we make tires. I have noticed you before, and heard a lot about you, from other workers and in the newspaper. I am glad to meet you."

She introduced herself—her name was Lena—continued chatting, and when the streetcar came we sat next to each other until she got off a stop or two before mine. Before leaving she said she would like to see me again, since I seemed like a nice person and she had enjoyed our conversation. She asked for my telephone number. I answered, "That would be fine, but I cannot remember my phone number, so we will wait until we meet again. As it happened, we did see each other again three months later. I thought I should not evade her any longer, so I told her my number. When I walked in the door of my room a short time later, the phone was ringing. It was Lena. "When can I visit you?" she asked.

"I'm very busy right now," I told her, "because I had learned that Russian women can be very demanding, imposing on your time in every way they can think of. But when she called again I decided I might as well deal with her now as later, and we arranged a time for her to visit. She arrived on time, and stayed for a couple of hours. We talked about all sorts of things and then, as I suspected, she wanted to arrange time for another visit before leaving.

I did enjoy her company well enough, even though I was trying to avoid any entanglement. Lena was a pleasant girl, and over the next few months she visited occasionally. Although she knew I was from America, she was curious about my earlier origins, and one day she asked me, "Are you an American, actually, or an African, or what?"

"What do you mean?" I asked.

"You don't act the way I expected a Negro to act," she said. I asked her to explain what she meant, and she said, "I have been told that black men are so attracted to white women that they are powerless to resist them. But I've been coming here for the last nine months, and you haven't even tried to touch me."

"I am of African descent," I told her, "but perhaps your concept is wrong. On the other hand, perhaps I am just different. You can decide."

Lena continued to visit and, regrettably, she fell in love with me. One day when she came to my apartment, I could see she had been crying. I asked her what was wrong, and she answered, "At my factory they called me in for questioning and threatened me. They wanted to know why I was seeing you so frequently. They knew I have been coming here once a week, and they asked me for details about our relationship. I said we were acquaintances, that's all. But now, they told me that I must stop coming here or I will be fired."

"What are you going to do?" I asked.

"I don't know exactly," she said. "But one thing I do know is that I can't give you up. I have to think about it." I told her to let me know once she reached a decision, but I frankly did not see any rational course except for her to stay away. For that reason, I told her to call me with her decision rather than risk visiting again. However, she did come back to tell me that she was going to stay with me in spite of the threat that she might lose her job.

Again I cautioned her, "Please don't think that I am going to marry you just because you are being threatened." She said she didn't. We talked a while, for what turned out to be the last time for three years. For her crime against the state—developing a relationship of which it disapproved—she was banished from Moscow. One day, three years later, she showed up at my apartment, and told me that she had been sent away and had not been allowed to return or to correspond with anyone in Moscow. Now, however, her exile was over, and she was allowed to return and live with her mother and sister. I told her not to come to see me anymore. "I must see you," she objected. "I cannot resist." I told her no emphatically, saying that she might get me in trouble, and if she came to see me again, I was sorry but I would not let her in.

I met another young woman during my vacation at the Mis-Mor Home of Rest in the Crimea, in June 1934. The friend of a dancer I knew slightly from Moscow, Valya was fascinated to meet a genuine black man. Until meeting me, she had only seen photographs, and could not understand how people could have black skin. A few days before I was due to return to Moscow, Valya told me that she was going to be in Moscow for ten days with the Leningrad Ballet and Opera Company, en route to Leningrad.

She called me from the Grand Hotel in Moscow, and I met her there that evening. She invited me up to her room to talk, and while we were there she told me more about herself. She told me that she was Jewish, that her husband had been Jewish but she was now divorced. She was explaining what life was like in the ballet company when there was a knock at the door and then, without waiting for an answer, a man barged in. He was with the hotel and was carrying a pad and pencil. He asked Valya, "May I take your order for supper tonight?"

"I did not order any supper. What are you doing here?" she responded curtly.

He said, "Somebody told me you ordered supper; what would you like?" ignoring her question.

"Please leave, I do not want supper now. I have company," she told him, and he left.

It was a good thing we were only talking when this fellow, obviously sent to find out what we were doing, burst into the room. Valya and I visited awhile longer that evening, and then I went home. When she returned to Leningrad she sent me a letter, inviting me to come and spend a week with her.

This woman was not trying to entrap me; she was just stupid. Imagine thinking that I could just leave my job for a week and go where I pleased! I would have been followed wherever I went. I sent her a pleasant reply, telling her that the demands at work were such that I would not be able to get away. I saw her a few more times when she came through Moscow with her company, but it was always up to her to get in touch with me. We never had enough time together, our visits were only for a couple of hours at a time, and eventually I no longer heard from her.

In 1947 I met a woman at a home of rest who interested me. Her name was Dalia, and her French grandfather had come to Russia with Napoleon. I noticed her the first day I arrived. She was a tall, attractive, vibrant woman, and when she first caught my eye I noticed that she had the particularly French habit of speaking with her hands. That evening I was standing with some people I had met when, to my surprise, Dalia came up to one of the women in the group, whom she recognized as an old acquaintance. They hugged one another and each carried on about how the other looked. They exclaimed how long it had been since they had last seen each other, while I continued talking with the men in the group. Dalia's friend introduced her to all of us.

The next day Dalia approached me and asked me if I wanted to go for a walk with a group. I went and, although we were with a group, she stayed close to me the entire time. That night at supper, Dalia arranged with the woman in charge of the dining hall for us to sit at the same table. We talked and talked, and after the meal we went to the cinema together. Our friendship grew, until the day before I was scheduled to leave, when Dalia said she was going to return to Moscow with me, even though she had three more days left. Before we parted company in Moscow, she asked for my telephone number. The minute I got home, the phone rang. It was Dalia, wanting to know when she could see me again. And so it went, but nothing ever happened between the two of us, because the authorities intervened.

The next week, she invited me to go to the opera with her, and the week after we went to the cinema. After the movie, I noticed that she was acting cold and detached, which was not her usual nature. She was a warm and friendly person, not only with me, but with everyone. I concluded that, for some reason, our friendship was over. When we neared her home she said she wanted me to call her on the following Wednesday, at 4:00 P.M. "Dalia," I said, "why do you want me to call you? And why at such a precise time? You have never even asked me to call you on any specific day before." All she said was that I would find out when I called.

I was still trying to figure out what had gone wrong when I called her at the appointed time. There was no answer. I hung up and called a second time, but again, no one answered. I tried a third time, saying to myself that if no one picked up, I would not try again. But this time, just as I was about to hang up, somebody answered the phone and said hello. I recognized Dalia's voice. From the shakiness in her voice I could tell she had been crying. She said, in a loud voice, "I want to ask you to please never call me again because we cannot meet anymore."

Clearly, she was under instructions, and either someone was there with her or was listening in on the line. So I said, "All right, all right," and hung up. That was the end of Dalia, until one day in 1969 my phone rang. It was Dalia, and she said—as if it were twenty-two hours later and not twenty-two years: "Hello, this is Dalia. I was thinking of you because today is Paul Robeson's birthday, so I decided to call."

"What a surprise to hear from you," I said, "but tell me, how did you get my number?" I had a different number then, and she would have had difficulty finding it out. To hear from her this way after the manner in which she had ended our friendship aroused my suspicion. She told me not to worry, that she just wanted to visit me, and she would explain everything when she saw me. I told her to come by, because I was curious to learn what had happened to her in 1947. When she visited a few days later, I did not recognize her at first. She was much heavier, and it seemed that the intervening years of Soviet life had etched themselves unattractively into her features.

After she was settled on my couch with a cup of tea, I asked her directly, "Why did you act the way you did, years ago."

She looked down, and said, "I was forced to. That's enough. Don't ask anymore." And then she began to cry.

"Why are you crying?" I asked.

"Because I have had such pain in my life," she said, "and to see you reminds me of the time when life seemed simpler and full of promise. I was forced to stop seeing you, and then later there was a man I wanted to marry, but I ended up married to another. This was not my doing. I was not able to control my own life. I am sure you know what I mean."

I believed her story, and at the same time I thought, "If the MVD forced its way into her life back then, and even though she may be sincere in her desire to see me, it is likely that she is either an agreeable or an unwitting pawn of theirs. She told me a little about herself, and explained that she had a twenty-one-year-old daughter. She only stayed forty-five minutes and then said she had to leave. I walked her to the bus and said good-by.

About a week later, she called again and said she wanted to come and talk with me. Thinking that she had something new to relate to me, I told her to come. When she arrived I was surprised that she had brought her daughter. I was the first black person the young woman had ever seen, and she gazed intently at me during their entire visit. We drank tea and ate cookies, talked for about an hour and a half, and then they left.

The next day Dalia called again and said, "We had a nice visit, but you cannot imagine the effect you had on my daughter. She is mesmerized by you. She has talked of nothing but you since the moment we left. Although I would like to continue our friendship I don't think I can bring my daughter again. She speaks as if you are the man of her dreams, even though I pointed out that compared to her, you are in fact an old man. She said that doesn't matter to her."

Although Dalia visited me four more times, and seemed hopeful of renewing a relationship that might have been—but wasn't—over twenty years earlier, I never touched her nor let her make advances to me. And she left her daughter at home.

There was another woman I met, in 1972, who asked for my phone number, and later called to see if she could visit me at my apartment. It was just after her visit that a number of my precious documents, including my old Jamaican passport, were missing. There was a period of about ten minutes when the record player was on and I was in the kitchen making tea, when she could have found them. I realized later that my wardrobe trunk had not been locked at the time. It could have been that instead of her, the KGB had sent someone into my room, when I was at work, to take the papers. But regardless of who got them, I believe she was sent. Her purpose may have just been to see how things were laid out in my apartment, so the break-in artist could operate swiftly and efficiently. The KGB agents did not find what they wanted, which was the passport permitting me to leave for vacation in Uganda.

The last woman I met before leaving the country was a doctor who lived in the center of Moscow near the office of the Central Committee. On my first visit to her home, I noticed KGB people around the place. As I entered her home I could see, reflected off my eyeglasses, two agents watching me. I enjoyed the evening I spent with this woman, Zina, and her mother and grandmother. However, when I left, I noticed that the KGB were still outside, watching me leave. The next time I visited, it was the same way.

I was attracted to Zina, but we never got a chance to become close friends. The first time she visited me in my apartment, she said she could only stay forty minutes. The second time, she brought her mother with her. By this time I had learned that the mother herself was with the KGB. A short time later Zina called me and told me not to call her anymore, which I knew was either her mother's doing, or the other KGB people telling her she could not meet with me. I told her I understood—there was nothing else I could say—and hung up.

One day, about three months later, Zina called, started telling me how sorry she was that she had to do what she did, and said she wanted to see me. I told her that, given her situation, it was useless. Just as she was about to answer me, she let out a yell as someone snatched the phone from her. That was the last I heard from her.

My personal life in Soviet Russia was very difficult because, as a religious person, I was familiar with—and sought to live by—the Biblical rule against having pre-marital sexual relations. Attempts to form deep, lasting friendships with Russian women would in any case have been doomed. Soviet life is so regulated. I was not free, and neither were they.

CHAPTER 29

The Sixties

WHEN I FIRST ARRIVED IN THE SOVIET UNION, I was too naive to understand that I was being watched by the secret police. I was in awe of my new surroundings, and I spent most of my time and energy soaking up the intriguing experiences that greeted me daily. Because I was apolitical—neither for or against the Soviet system for ideological reasons—I never considered that I might be under constant observation by the secret police. The beginning of the purges alerted me to some realities of life in the Soviet system; as time passed I came to understand that as long as I was in Russia I would be living under surveillance. However, it was not until 1965 that I encountered another unpleasant aspect of life in the Soviet police state that seemed to threaten any chance of ever getting out.

As I entered my fourth decade of life in the Soviet Union, I was more determined than ever to escape. Every year I had been applying for visas to visit either the United States or Jamaica, for legitimate reasons that would not leave me open to attack. I had always served the state well; from participating as a member of the Moscow Soviet, to having an exemplary record as a toolmaker, designer, and engineer. I was an obedient citizen with medals and certificates of honor; I had never criticized the Soviet state and never committed a crime—or for that matter, been accused of or sentenced for a noncrime. I was watched all the time, my incoming and outgoing mail was opened and read, numerous neighbors were informing on me, yet still my record was spotless.

The secret police (KGB) could know whatever it pleased about me when I went to bed, who my friends were, what I did and said at work, what I ate, and which shoe I put on first. But I made certain they did not know my fundamental secret. Nobody in Russia, no friend however close, and especially not the secret police, could know that I yearned to get out. At least, until 1965, that is what I thought.

My secret became exposed as a result of an attempt I made to get out through President Sékou Touré of Guinea. *Pravda* ran a long article about the newly-independent Republic of Guinea, and mentioned that the president of this African nation would soon visit Moscow. The article, which was predictably anti-colonialist in tone, explained that France had stripped the fledgling nation of all its technological equipment, even removing telephones, electric light bulbs, and flush toilets, before leaving its former colony to its own devices. I thought about this article for a couple of days, and hoped that, although I was not being allowed to visit the United States or Jamaica, maybe I could obtain an invitation to Guinea. I knew I could be useful to them; I was still fluent in French, could teach mechanical engineering to students, and could help the nation in other ways to industrialize. I wrote a letter to Touré, offering my services. Now the only trick was getting it to him.

Obviously I could not mail the letter, lest it be read by the censors. I decided that I had to get it to him during his visit to Moscow. But how? Who could I trust, who would have some chance of getting close enough to Touré to hand him my letter? The best person I could think of was an Australian journalist I knew. We had met several years earlier, when he sought me out for an interview a few weeks after he first arrived in Moscow. He had read about me in the *Soviet Journal* while still in Australia. I had been impressed with him right from the start; soon after he invited me to meet his family, and we became good friends. I visited my friend and explained that I had a letter for Touré that was too sensitive to mail. I asked if he could try to deliver it for me. As I expected, he was eager to help me.

Touré came for his visit, and as soon as he left, I wanted to dash over to see if my friend had succeeded. I decided to wait a day and give him a chance to contact me, but when I didn't hear from him by the second day, I went by his apartment. By the warm, enthusiastic way he and his wife greeted me at the door, I thought he had succeeded. But after I was seated, he went into his bedroom, returned with my letter, and handed it to me. My heart sank—another failure!

"Bob, I tried to get the letter to the president," he said. "I attended every one of his official functions in an effort to get close enough to him. But the KGB agents were practically glued to him. If I had tried to get through them, I would not be standing here talking to you. I'm very sorry."

What could I say? Disconsolate, I thanked him for trying and assured him that I understood the problem and appreciated his efforts to help me. I returned home, opened my wardrobe trunk, and placed the sealed letter in the upper drawer. I locked all four drawers, shut the trunk, and locked it.

When I learned two years later that President Kwame Nkrumah of Ghana was going to visit Moscow soon, I decided to attempt the same strategy with him as before, with Touré. Rather than write a new letter from scratch, I figured I could copy what I had written earlier. I went to the upper drawer of my trunk, but the letter was missing! I had seen it there just two weeks earlier, when I was getting something else out of the trunk. Where could it be? Maybe I inadvertently put it in with the pictures in the drawer. I searched there, but without success. I looked among the handkerchiefs; it was not there, either. I got down on my hands and knees and looked around. Perhaps it had fallen out. I got up and looked through the entire trunk. I looked through every drawer, and then looked again and again, probably searching the same place a dozen times before I gave up in frustration. Where could that letter be? I knew I had not removed it from my trunk.

Every day after work for the next week I renewed my search. I came up empty-handed. Two days before Nkrumah was scheduled to arrive, I decided to write him a new letter—that was no problem—but where was my original letter? I had no idea. This time, I decided to try and deliver the letter myself. Fortunately I was able to meet Nkrumah's press secretary at the Leningradskaya Hotel, and I asked him to deliver the letter to the president. He said he would, though I had no idea whether he kept his promise, since I never received a reply. It did occur to me that, seeking good relations with the Soviets, even if Nkrumah got my letter he might be unwilling to do something that the Soviets might view as meddling in their internal affairs. As for my missing letter, I never stopped looking for it. A year later, I understood what had probably happened to it; several years later I learned that my suspicion was well-founded.

My enlightenment came in 1965, while I was at the Zavidova Home of Rest about ninety-five miles from Moscow. One evening, while I was watching couples dancing, a rather plump woman who seemed to be in her mid-forties said to me, "Comrade, I have noticed that you are always by yourself. Why don't you dance also? I am sure you are an excellent dancer. Am I right?"

I responded lightly, "Yes, years ago I used to be pretty good, but my knees are not well-oiled anymore, and I fear that my joints squeak. I can't get my legs to obey my orders, anymore." The next day after lunch, the same woman approached me and asked if I had any plans. I told her that after lunch it was my custom to go for a walk in the woods or find a spot on the wharf and read. She asked if she could come with me. As we walked along, she introduced herself as Lydia Stephanovna. From her speech and her attire she was clearly from an educated, sophisticated background. We returned from our walk, went our separate ways, and agreed to meet again for a stroll the next day, after lunch. It was then that she told me that she was a party member, that her husband—also a party member—had disappeared in 1952, that she had a married daughter, and that she was a well-established Moscow economist. As she explained her background to me, she suddenly became silent and appeared preoccupied, as if she were gazing intently into her past. After awhile she turned to look at me with sad eyes and asked, "I wonder if you could be trusted? You see, you are the first foreigner I have met on such a simple and friendly level. Most foreigners I meet are big shots in their country, and I deal with them on official business."

Immediately my guard went up. I wondered if she was a KGB agent, trying to trap me. After all, the entire initiative in our relationship had been from her. I answered cautiously, "I don't know what you have in mind, about trusting me."

"I just feel you are the kind of person who will listen to my concerns," she said.

"Rest assured that if you feel like telling me anything that's on your mind," I said, "feel free to do so. Anything said here will remain between you and me."

She began, "You know, I have been a Communist for over twenty-five years. I have made many sacrifices—as did my husband, before he disappeared. But I don't see any rewards. Since the twentieth party congress [in 1956], I find I no longer am able to hold the ideals of the party sacred. Many of my friends feel the same way—gloomy, distrustful, and convinced that our system has deceived us. We think there will never be any real communism in our country."

"Wow!" I thought. "Is she ever candid! If this is a trap, it sure is a big one." I had no intention of saying anything in response that could be construed as agreement. I simply gazed at the ground, pretending to reflect on what she had said. She wanted me to respond.

"Don't you think it is going too far for a system that you served for so long and well to be suspicious of you?" she asked.

"In what way are you treated with suspicion?" I asked, while I thought how uncanny it was that she was expressing the very feeling I had about my life in the Soviet Union.

"You wouldn't believe it," she said.

"Maybe yes, maybe no," I said. "It all depends."

"Well, for your information," she said, "suppose for the last four years, while you were away on vacation, your room was opened and explored for documents that would incriminate you as someone disloyal to the Soviet Union. Suppose that those documents were taken and photographed, and later returned, but in such a way that it was obvious to you that someone had been snooping around in your personal things. If that happened to you, wouldn't you feel disgusted with and outraged by the system?"

"Oh, my God!" I thought. "My missing letter to President Touré. How stupid of me not to realize! It is probably in the hands of the KGB. This means they know my secret. They know I'm trying to get out." Undoubtedly this woman was checking me out. She was working for the KGB, she had been briefed about my letter, and was trying to draw me into making the kind of anti-Soviet statement that would destine me for a labor camp in Siberia. Although I was extremely upset to find out that my desire to leave had been exposed, I said to her without a trace of emotion, "Why not report the matter to the police, and then when you are about to leave for your vacation inform them so that they'll keep an eye on your apartment?"

"No, no, that wouldn't do," she said. "You don't understand how our system works. It has an infinite ability to interfere in everyone's life, but complaining about it to anyone only makes things worse. There is no such thing in our country as an honest court system; a citizen who tries to address a real grievance will get into serious trouble."

Now I was a little puzzled. From her response, I thought that she might be sincere after all. Was I misjudging her? Or was she extremely crafty? Whatever the case, I was not going to take any chances. I continued talking with her in a very noncommittal manner, and then we walked back to the home of rest. After my vacation was over and I returned to Moscow, one of the first things I did when I got home was check my trunk again. There it was! The missing letter had mysteriously returned, still sealed—or rather, I should say, resealed. It was buried in the middle of the same upper drawer, though in a different spot from where I had placed it three years earlier.

Now I could understand, without a doubt, why officials in my factory had instituted a new policy, about three years earlier, of keeping me away from all foreign visitors. They were afraid that I would develop a link with an outsider, someone who might be able to help me break loose from the Soviet embrace.

Several years later, upon returning from another vacation trip, I discovered that some other precious documents were missing. They were never returned. Clearly, the KGB was sending a locksmith to my room, who was able to open the American combination padlock on the outside of my trunk, and look carefully through my belongings for anything that might be interesting.

The secret police were even more present from the mid-sixties on, than they had been in recent years, as a result of Leonid Brezhnev succeeding the ousted Khrushchev as General Secretary of the Communist Party, in October 1964. Khrushchev had not been as repressive as Stalin, but Brezhnev turned out to be worse than Khrushchev and more sophisticated than Stalin. Soon after he gained power, Brezhnev reinstated a nineteenth-century Russian practice of declaring mentally unfit, and incarcerating, those people who would dare to speak out against the regime.

I soon learned that nobody liked Brezhnev, not even in the party. He was a binge drinker and it was said that at times he completely lost his mind and did not know what he was doing. I had every reason to consider myself in as much—or more—danger as I had ever been.

PART IV

Brezhnev to Gorbachev

CHAPTER 30

Entrapment Again

IN THE SUMMER OF 1967 I traveled overnight to a home of rest located between Moscow and Leningrad, an eight-hour train ride away. We reached Vyishny Volochov around 7 A.M., boarded one of the waiting buses, and rode thirty minutes to our destination. After the usual registration procedures, I went outside for a walk to see what the surrounding countryside was like. I arrived back at the home of rest, and went to the dining hall long enough before mealtime to ensure that my assigned seat was not taken by someone else.

At the first meal at a home of rest, the Russians have a simple custom whereby each guest at a table introduces himself to the person beside him, until everyone at the table becomes acquainted. Beginning in 1951, when Soviet citizens were sternly warned against having anything to do with foreigners, I was ignored both during these initial greetings and also at the first evening's get-acquainted dance. Because the propaganda against foreigners failed to distinguish between an actual foreigner and a person like me, who had been a loyal citizen for many years, the Soviet people treated all non-natives with the same degree of rudeness and suspicion. There were many times, for example, when I would be riding in an overcrowded subway with two empty seats—one on either side of me. At this particular meal, as I was seated before other guests arrived, when they came and sat down, although I said hello to them, they greeted one another but ignored me.

About a week into my vacation, Radio Moscow announced that a war had suddenly erupted between Israel and the Arabs. The announcement said that the Arabs were defending themselves valiantly. On the morning of the sixth day it was reported that the Israelis had occupied a large portion of Arab territory because of massive supplies given them by the United States. From this report, we could understand that the Israelis had won. Although a vicious barrage of anti-Israeli propaganda was launched over the radio, I was surprised to learn from general conversation that it was not taking hold. Although the prevailing attitude of the Soviet people had been anti-Semitic since the retreat from Moscow on October 16, 1941, compared to the non-white Arabs, the Jews were coming up smelling like roses. It became apparent to me that the Russian rank-and-file—this was a third-class home of rest where, incidentally, there were no Jewish guests—did not like Arabs any more than they liked blacks. The night Israel's victory was announced, my four roommates, in opposition to official pro-Arab, anti-Israeli policy, shamelessly raised their glasses and drank to the Jewish victory. When I returned to Moscow I encountered the same anti-Arab, pro-Israeli attitude.

A few days after Israel's victory in the Six-Day War, a young man in his mid- to late-twenties and wearing an army uniform, approached me. Although we had never spoken to one another, I had noticed during the first few days that he was usually alone, and then later I saw him strolling with a young woman. He greeted me after breakfast, asked how I liked the weather and then, before I could respond, questioned, "But you speak Russian fluently. How long have you been in the Soviet Union?"

"More than a decade," I said, not wanting to explain my entire past to him.

"You mean you have been able to learn our language so well in just a decade," he said. "By the way, my name is Piotr, but you can call me Petya [a more familial term]. What is yours?"

"My name is Bob," I said, noticing that he had a pilot's insignia on his shoulder.

"Where are you headed?" he asked. I told him that I was going to get a book and find a spot in the woods to read. He asked if he could come along, and I told him that would be fine. During our walk to the woods he asked me the usual questions that most Russians ask anyone they think is a foreigner: where did I come from, how did I come to the Soviet Union, why had I come, was I studying in Moscow, how old was I, was I married, and so forth.

When I told him that I had been invited by the Soviet government to teach precision toolmaking to young Soviet workers, he was surprised. "To teach what?" he asked.

"To teach toolmaking," I repeated. He stopped walking and stared at me with wide-open eyes. "But how can that be?" he asked. "We have always been told that people of your race in the United States are not allowed to become literate. Now you are telling me that our government invited you to come and teach our young people. I don't understand."

"Excuse me, please," I said, "but do I seem illiterate?"

"No, of course not. That is just the point," he said. "I assumed that you got your education here, since you've been here for a number of years and, moreover, you speak Russian. But you're telling me that you were already a professional worker when you came here."

He was silent for a moment and then asked, searchingly, "Then do you mean to say that our government has not been telling us the truth?"

"I never said you have not been told the truth. Perhaps the teacher who was instructing you forgot to explain a few important things, that's all," I said.

Petya was very curious about the United States and fired a number of questions at me. I told him what I knew, always explaining that I was talking about an America nearly forty years ago. I could not speak about what America was like today. Over the next several days he came over after most meals to visit with me and ask me more questions about America. One evening after dinner he was waiting for me outside the entrance to the dining hall. "I would like to talk to you very much," he said. "Could we go someplace where it is quiet?"

I said that would be fine, and as we began walking together I asked him a number of questions about himself. He explained that he had been born in a village not far from the provincial city of Kalinin—midway between Moscow and Leningrad—and that he was a pilot who flew a route between Kalinin and Odessa three times a week. He lived in Kalinin, was married, and had a five-year-old son. Then he surprised me by saying, "As you must pass through Kalinin on your way back to Moscow, I would like you to visit me and my family there. We have four trains daily from Kalinin to Moscow, so you can come early in the day, stay with us a few hours, and then I'll take you to the eight or ten o'clock train. I'll help you to change your ticket from the day train to a night train. You must come, by all means. Here, write down my address."

I was noncommittal, and after walking a few more minutes we came across a large, fallen tree. Petya suggested that we sit for awhile. He glanced around, as if to see if anyone was nearby, looked down at the ground and then said in a low, measured tone, "Bob, for the last few days I have been wrestling with two questions, and have been unable to understand the answers to either. As you are aware, we are deeply involved in the struggle in the Middle East. We have been supplying Egypt with arms, and have been training her army on their use, for over four years. On the other hand, the United States has armed and helped to train the Israelis. Now the Israelis have soundly defeated the Egyptian army and gained some territory in the process.

"What disturbs me is the prospect that we shall continue to arm the Egyptians and might end up confronting the Americans ourselves. Maybe I am too pessimistic, but I think that if this happens it would be a disaster for us. You were born and lived abroad, and now you have the experience of living here. Please tell me, am I right in thinking that we might become impossibly tangled up with the Americans in a fight over someone else's business? I don't think it is worth it for us to continue aiding the Arabs. What do you think?"

Before I could say anything, Petya began to explain his second concern. "Bob, look also at the growing power of the Chinese. Do they not present a real future danger to Russia, even more so than at the beginning of the eighteenth century? There are nearly four Chinese to every one of us. Couldn't they defeat us just by swarming over the country like ants? In the event of a war with China, do you think the US would support us or the Chinese? I think they should support us because regardless of our present differences, we come from the same root. We are more in common because we are both white."

While speaking, Petya had remained staring at the ground.

Now he lifted his head up, looked me in the eye and said, "I don't know why, Bob, but I sensed from the first time I saw you that I could trust you. This is my reason for being so open. So now, please tell me what is your honest opinion about what I have confided in you and no one else?"

I thanked Petya for his trust and confidence, but as usual in such circumstances I was on my guard, wondering whether I was facing a subtle and suave *agent provocateur*. I answered him in my well-practiced, noncommittal way, trying to confine my statements to known and accepted facts, without straying from the government's official positions. Petya kept stressing his points, trying—if indeed he was laying a trap—to get me to support what he was saying. We soon finished our conversation and walked back to the main building.

As Petya's pass was only for twelve days, he was scheduled to leave before me. He had asked if I would accompany him to the train station. We arrived at the station and waited for the train to arrive. As it neared the station and began slowing down, the people on the platform suddenly dashed toward it and pushed and pulled at each other in an effort to board. It was the sort of frenzied scramble I had witnessed countless times; they feared that if they waited for the train to stop before hopping on board, they might miss it. As I was watching, Petya suddenly gave me a huge hug and dashed past down the platform to a coach that had a smaller crowd trying to board. He managed to leap onto the steps of the coach and, as the still-moving train passed me, he shouted, "I will get in touch." The train finally did stop, for about ten seconds, and then it pulled out again without any announcement or signal.

A few days later I received a telegram from Petya reminding me to stop at Kalinin on my way home, and to let him know my departure time from the home of rest. He reminded me to wait for him at the station in Kalinin if he was not there when I arrived. At Vyishny Volochov he had already told me that there was a bench, under a tall tree, in an empty lot behind the station, where I should wait.

I did just that when I got off at the station in Kalinin, because Petya was not there. He arrived soon after and greeted me with his usual enthusiasm. Kalinin was a medical center, with a large number of foreign medical students, so I asked Petya if he knew whether there was a foreign bookstore in the city. He said there was, and just as I was about to tell him that I would like to go there before going to his home, a tall, impressive looking man who was also a pilot in uniform suddenly appeared as if out of nowhere. He stood stiffly and spoke authoritatively to my acquaintance, "Piotr Aleksandrovich, you are wanted immediately by the commanding officer. Report to his office at once!"

Petya snapped to attention and said, "Let it be so, Comrade Captain." Then as the captain left, Petya turned to me and said perfunctorily, "Bob, sorry, but I must go. Anyone can direct you to the foreign bookstore. Good-by." He ran off at full speed toward the officer, and once he caught up with him, they walked together until they were out of sight.

I stood, dumfounded, wondering what in the world this mysterious incident was all about. I wondered if it was something designed by the authorities; but if so, for what purpose? I stood there like a statue, tormented, unable to make any sense at all out of things. When I finally came to myself, I realized that I would have to change my train ticket before I did anything else. I walked back to the train station and went up to the ticket counter, where a dull-eyed clerk grunted in response to my request for a change in my train ticket. She looked at my ticket and asked, "Where are you coming from?" When I told her, she looked at me and asked in a suspicious tone, "If you were traveling to Moscow, why did you stop here?"

"I stopped to see an acquaintance of mine who was also a guest at the same home of rest," I answered.

"Show me your home of rest pass stubs," she demanded. I had the stubs on me, since they need to be presented to one's place of work upon returning, as a way of determining whether a person really went on vacation where he was supposed to have gone. But after showing the woman my pass stubs, she wanted my passport also.

"Why aren't my stubs enough identification?" I asked her.

"If you will not give me your passport I will have to call in the militia," she said. Sensing that she was in a nasty mood, I quickly handed her my passport. She carefully compared the name in the passport with that on the stubs, and then checked the date when the passport was issued, the code number, and my Moscow address. Only then did she decide to change my ticket to a train leaving late that afternoon. Realizing that I was not up to anything dangerous or devious, and that she was not in danger of getting into trouble by changing my ticket, the woman now became hospitable.

"How did you like our home of rest?" she asked.

"Quite well," I replied.

"Was it the first time you have been to one?" she asked.

"No," I replied.

"Tell me, where are you from?" she asked. I told her, and then asked if she knew where the foreign bookstore was. She told me she did, sketched out a map on a piece of paper, and then came out of the ticket office and walked me to the end of the platform so she could point me in the right direction.

As I headed off to the foreign bookstore, I thought how this was representative of the nature of Russian people. One minute she is ready to turn me over to the KGB; the next she is going out of her way to be helpful. I passed off her crudeness, and the crudeness of Russians when dealing with foreigners, as a product of their desire to feel important. When Russians deal with foreigners, the encounters usually alternate between an initial cordiality, a period of gruffness, and then, if the foreigner is patient and does not become distracted or annoyed, the Russian often will return to his former reasonable self.

Later that afternoon I boarded the train and headed back to Moscow, wondering if I had seen the last of Piotr Aleksandrovich. One evening in late August, nine weeks later, I had my answer. I was returning to my room after work, and as I reached the bottom stair of the third floor where I lived, I saw a man and a woman sitting at the very top of the stairs. "We greet you, Bob," said the man. "I greet you too," said the woman beside him. I looked more closely and was surprised to notice Petya, wearing his flier's suit and cap, with his woman friend Lucya, from the home of rest. I returned his greeting and then asked him, "How did you find my address?" for I had not given it to him.

"I got it from an information booth downtown," he said. But that could not have been true. A number of people had told me that they had tried to obtain my address this way but were told, "We don't give that number to anyone." I knew Petya was lying, but I saw no choice but to invite the two of them in. He behaved as if he were an inspector, first checking out my room, and then looking into the kitchen, the bathroom, and the small balcony. They made themselves at home, and behaved as if the three of us were old friends. After about an hour, Petya went out and soon came back with seven bottles of beer, a large chunk of boiled sausage, half a dozen green cucumbers, and a large loaf of black bread. He went straight into the kitchen with his bounty, and called to me for dishes, a knife, and eating utensils. He prepared the food, opened three bottles of beer, and then proposed a toast to our friendship. The two of them guzzled their beer without pausing, whereas I did not touch mine. When Petya asked why, I explained that I did not drink.

"What, you don't drink!" he exclaimed. "How can that be? Here, there is a time to begin everything."

When I politely refused, he acted as if I had just insulted him, and then opened two more bottles and handed one to Lucya. They spent the next hour drinking beer, as I nibbled on the sausage, bread, and cucumber. At one point Petya asked if I would put on a record so that he and Lucya could dance. I did so and they began to dance; after a few steps Lucya closed her eyes and rested her head on his shoulder. After the song was over they went and stood for awhile on the balcony, then came back in for more eating, drinking, and music. About 11 P.M. Petya asked me to go into the kitchen with him. Once inside, he closed the door, placed his arm around my neck, and said, "Bob, I am going to ask a great favor. Let us stay in your room for the night. Please do not refuse us."

I had anticipated his question, and answered, "Petya, you know very well that if I were to do such a thing, and be discovered, I would face a year in prison and possibly banishment from Moscow."

"But you are a foreigner," he said, "and such measures will not apply to you. Besides, we shall leave early in the morning." He was asking me to violate a law which forbids any Moscow resident from letting someone stay in his room overnight without first obtaining permission from the local district police. This law was first announced during Germany's invasion of Moscow. It was relaxed for awhile after Stalin's death, but now it was again before enforced strictly, something everybody was well aware of.

"Listen," I told him, "it is useless for you to try and convince me. I intend to live within the law."

I opened the kitchen door and went back into my room. In a

few minutes Petya came in, walked over to Lucya at the balcony, and said, "Sorry, Lucya, but we have to go." Petya picked up the remaining two beer bottles and, without saying a word, he and Lucya left.

This unannounced visit clearly was designed to get me in trouble. I still could not understand the strategy behind the peculiar incident in Kalinin, but Petya's mission with me was clear enough. I guessed that the main strategy was to catch me in a trap that would enable the authorities to banish me from Moscow, so that I could no longer contact foreign black tourists, or continue my attempts to obtain an exit visa.

I had ample reason to fear the possibility of banishment. I had not forgotten the fate of two blacks I knew who were banished during the purges. One of them, Lovett Whiteman, came from Chicago and by 1936 had been teaching English for several years at the Anglo-American school in Moscow. He offered some criticism of a book by Langston Hughes, *The Ways of White Folks,* during a discussion at the Foreign Club. A black lawyer from the upper echelon of the Community Party USA was in the audience, and he stated during the evening that Whiteman's criticism of the book was counter-revolutionary. About three weeks later, Whiteman was summoned to NKVD headquarters and told that he was a counter-revolutionary and was to be banished from Moscow. He was ordered to be in a certain town on a specific date, and immediately on arrival to report to the local police. None of us ever heard from Whiteman. However, in 1959, I heard news of Whiteman's fate. A Russian who had been banished to the same town as Whiteman was rehabilitated by Khrushchev and allowed to return to his family in Moscow. This man told a friend of mine that Whiteman was assigned to his group of laborers, and was severely beaten many times when he failed to meet the norm. He died of starvation, or malnutrition, a broken man, whose teeth had been knocked out.

Another black exiled from Moscow fared no better. Originally from the Belgian Congo, he had been living in Belgium before coming to Moscow as a tourist and deciding to stay. He became a very popular dancer with the Tfasman orchestra, but after about a year he was arrested and charged with having an illicit affair with a teenager; he and a seventeen-year-old girl had been living together. He was convicted and sent to the Arctic region. A year later an investigation showed that he was innocent of the charges—because of the girl's age and her willingness—and an order was sent for his release. However, he died two days before the order arrived.

Although I never saw Petya again, I knew the possible consequences if I let down my guard for even a moment.

CHAPTER 31

A Passport at Last

IN 1966 I TURNED SIXTY YEARS OLD and was still in Russia. As I thought about it, I could scarcely believe that I was still here. I did not feel old, and I was always looking ahead, rather than back at my life, as many elderly people do. In fact, I had petitioned my factory successfully to keep working, even though I had reached retirement age, would receive a pension, and no longer had to work to support myself. Facing new designing challenges at work was what made life bearable. I was not the sort of person who could spend my day in the park, playing chess or feeding the pigeons. The last thing I wanted was to have time to reflect on the greatest frustration of my life—my inability to leave the Soviet Union.

By now I had spent so much time in the Soviet Union that I thought in Russian rather than in English. Although at times I purposely would act like a Russian in order to minimize people's fears and suspicions that they were in the presence of a foreigner, there were also times when I used Russian mannerisms without realizing it. I tried not to feel like a Russian, because I did not want to give up my sense of individuality, my connection to my own roots, or my hope of escaping. I believed that giving in to the Soviet system, surrendering my sense of my uniqueness, would be the first and fundamental step that would have made me a spiritual captive of the Soviet system that had made me a physical captive. Reading the Bible and remembering God every day gave me the strength that kept me from going the way of Wayland Rudd, Robert Ross, Henry Scott, and other blacks who desperately sought something they could never get from the Soviet Union—acceptance as an equal. I understood that I had four strikes against me: being a foreigner; being black; being not just any foreigner, but an American; and being at the mercy of the Soviet system, which treats everyone capriciously. I knew I could not expect to be valued as a human being in a system based on an ideology that hates the notion of a loving God, and promotes the concept that people are only valued for what they produce for the state. I did not like any of these things. I was often stung emotionally. But I understood and adapted to reality in order to survive, without compromising my sense of integrity, while continuing to think and plan how to leave the Soviet Union and find a place where I could breathe freely, without fear.

My regular efforts to befriend African students in Moscow afforded me the first step in realizing my dream. I sought Africans as companions because I felt more at ease in their company than with most Russians. But in the back of my mind I also sensed that some association, at some point, might lead me to freedom. That very process began, without my knowledge, in the summer of 1961. I was on my way to one of the few churches that was still open. A church closer to my district had been shut down by the government after the revolution. The trip took an hour and a half and involved three buses. When I entered the last bus, I noticed a young black man sitting next to the window, so I sat down beside him. We shook hands, chatted, and eventually exchanged names and addresses. He was an Ugandan in his late twenties, well-mannered and well-dressed, and spoke English, French, Arabic, his native tongue, and some Russian. His name was Ibrahim Mukibi, and we grew to be friends. He and his Russian girlfriend, whom he later married (despite her parents' vehement opposition and government harassment), became frequent visitors to my apartment. Through him I came to know many other Africans who were in Moscow pursuing university degrees. Financially, this was an excellent opportunity for them, because not only was tuition free, but they also received a monthly stipend that they could live on. However, my friend eventually got into trouble with the authorities.

It was understood that as part of the deal, the African students would make anti-West speeches. When he decided to stop making speeches, his professors began flunking him in his courses. He appealed unsuccessfully to the dean, and finally was expelled. He went to Yugoslavia, but the Russians intervened and had him kicked out of there also.

Before leaving the Soviet Union, he introduced me to another Ugandan who was studying in Moscow, named Kizito, who is now a physician in Uganda. This man came from a prosperous, well-connected family in Kampala, and had been studying in England while preparing to compete in the Helsinki Olympics. It was in Helsinki that the Soviets recruited him to come to the USSR and study. Through Kizito, I was able to meet a number of officials in the Ugandan embassy, including the ambassador and his American wife.

In 1971, ten years after I first met Mukibi on the bus, I received a dinner invitation from the newly-arrived Ugandan ambassador to the Soviet Union, Mathias Lubega, and his American wife, Patricia. I was delighted at the thought of sharing an evening in the company of this couple, but I had some reservations since I knew that all the embassies were watched carefully by the KGB. I considered the damage that being photographed entering the embassy would do to my continuing efforts to get a passport to travel abroad. Finally, my hunger for new experience and good conversation got the best of me, and I decided to take a chance. The KGB agents and I noticed each other as I entered the embassy grounds. I acted as if I were on a routine visit in order to avoid arousing their suspicion.

The evening was everything I had hoped it would be, and it was the beginning of a close friendship with the Lubegas. During their year in Moscow we spent several evenings together, and on one occasion, they and their children visited me in my apartment, staying for about five hours and feeling very much at home. On my last visit to the embassy before the ambassador was due to depart, he asked me to come to his country to share my engineering knowledge. He said they had need of me at the technical college in Kampala. He was surprised when I told him that it would be virtually impossible. He wondered why, stating that it seemed perfectly logical for Russia to send a black engineer who knew English and French to help an African country.

I explained, "Mr. Ambassador, logic has nothing to do with it.

People with less experience and skill than I, who don't speak English or French, have been sent to Zambia and to the Congo, instead of me. Since I also speak Spanish, I volunteered to go to Cuba, but I was turned down for this, also."

He understood, without my saying it directly, that I was the victim of racism. Later in the evening he walked up to me and guided me into a room where we were alone. He said, quietly, "Once I reach home, I will try to help you get out of this jail you are in."

I thanked him for his concern, but in my heart I knew that he lacked the power to carry out his promise. I felt that he was also aware of this, and that he was simply trying to inject hope into what he knew to be the dull, spiritless, mundane life of a Soviet citizen. I was astonished eight months later when I received a letter from him reminding me that he had not forgotten his promise. At that time, having already served at the United Nations and in Moscow, he was about to become Uganda's ambassador to the Organization of African Unity (OAU). Because of his letter, I allowed the faint flicker of hope within me to grow into a steady flame, though it was still far from being a roaring fire.

A few months later, in early 1972, I received another letter from Ambassador Lubega. This one was an official invitation, stamped with the ambassador's coat-of-arms and bearing his signature. He wanted me to spend my annual vacation with him and his family in Uganda. The next day I went to the Soviet Visas and Registration Office to ask what I had to do to visit Uganda. After waiting an hour for a response, a receptionist returned to me with the letter and explained that it was not a valid document.

"What makes it invalid?" I asked.

"The letter must be endorsed by the Soviet ambassador to Ethiopia," she said.

"Ethiopia!" I exclaimed. "But the man is from Uganda."

"But the letter is from Addis Ababa, Ethiopia," she said sternly.

And so it was. I had forgotten that my friend was at the OAU, which was in Addis Ababa. I went home and wrote to him, explaining my problem. I decided that I was destined to spend my vacation at another home of rest. However, seven weeks later I received another letter from the ambassador, and this one contained a signed endorsement from the Soviet ambassador in Addis Ababa.

This meant that I was officially eligible to apply to go to Africa for my vacation. But I knew that eligibility was one thing, and actually getting on an airplane traveling out of the country was something quite different. I was already very familiar with the unbelievable amount of red tape involved in trying to secure foreign ministry approval to travel abroad. First there was the autobiography, then the recommendation from my factory, the references from my house committee, the long, complicated application, the six new photographs, and forty rubles worth of postage stamps.

Five weeks after I submitted my application to my factory, I was called before the six-man shop party commission that was the first barrier to acceptance. The chairman read the group's recommendation aloud. Without letting me comment, he asked for those who approved to raise their hands. Six hands went into the air; it was unanimous. But I did not like something I had heard. As they were about to leave I said, "Comrades, please, wait a minute. Could you change the last paragraph, the one that reads, 'However, the party committee of the machine shop is of the opinion that the climate in Africa will have a harmful effect on his health after living in the Soviet Union for so long.' This will discourage the people in the visa office from approving my application."

What I wanted to add was that if I could survive the Russian winters, I could survive anywhere. But instead I reasoned, "Comrades, I want you to know that I was brought up in the tropical climate of Jamaica and Cuba, which is the same kind of climate as Uganda. I am positive the warm weather will not bother me. Please delete that last paragraph."

They knew what they had done. It was a typical, dirty trick. In response to my plea, the chairman said that they would think it over.

I heard nothing for three weeks, and then was told to report to the office of the secretary of the factory's party committee after work. There were six other people there, all applicants for travel abroad to Eastern Bloc countries. Of these, only East Berlin was out of bounds. We entered a hall where more than one hundred party members were gathered to rule on our applications. I knew many of them: there were the extremely ambitious ones who constantly sought more power and status, and there were the less aggressive ones who nevertheless had to be alert enough to maintain their current status, with its benefits and influence. I also noticed some of the known shop informers, who would sell their souls or wives to get ahead politically. There were also a few men whom I respected, not because of their political views, but because they were genuine idealists who still believed that communism could make the world a saner, more peaceful place.

The audience seemed serious. These party representatives had been gathered from every section of the factory to decide the fate of our seven travel recommendations. Mine was to be considered last, so I sat waiting, wondering, praying, and watching what the other applicants had to go through. Any representative was given the opportunity to question the applicants. The only questions asked were why they wanted to go and what they intended to do there. Then a vote was taken. Each applicant was approved, and left with a smile on his face. I was not sure my experience would be as pleasant.

When my turn came, I was bombarded with questions, some of them cruel, some of them filled with suspicion. One man who had been working in the factory since he was demobilized in 1948, and was known by many as a party watchdog and informer, stood up and asked me in a surly manner, "Comrade Robinson, suppose we were to let you go to Africa. How can we be sure that as soon as you get there your old bourgeois feelings would not return and take hold of you?"

"Oh boy, would they ever," I thought. At the same time I told myself to stay calm and be firm. I looked directly at the questioner and said, "Comrade, you know as well as I do that your question does not have any valid foundation, so far as I am concerned. Had you made such a statement thirty-five years ago, perhaps then there would have been a cause for concern. But it cannot be so now; after all, I have lived in the Soviet Union for more than two-thirds of my life. I have reached the stage where I think like a Russian and even talk to myself in Russian."

I paused at this point, but kept staring at the man, never once looking away. I added, "I cannot understand how you can entertain such a thought. Do you now know that people living abroad at my age are out of work, while here I am allowed to work even though I am on pension? Where else could I have such an arrangement?" I looked at the man for a few more seconds, and then sat down.

The chairman asked if there were any more questions, but no one raised his hand. Then he called for a vote. I could not bear to watch; I closed my eyes, opening them only when I heard the chairman an-

About our contribution to the factory

Маршрут продолжается

Ветеранов завода, особенно тех, кто создавал его и рос с ним, всегда тянет к месту, где прошли молодые годы, где вместе с товарищами разделялась радость побед и горечь утрат. Исключительно велико это влечение в памятные даты. Завод отсчитывал последние дни сорокового года своей жизни, когда в родных для меня стенах инструментального цеха я встретился с триумвиратом старых товарищей.

В. Котерев, Р. Робинсон, Н. Селезнев — ветераны, с которыми начинал грызть гранит «инструментальной науки». Совместно перелистываем страницы жизни родного цеха. В памяти всплывают приборы «КОН», индикаторы, копиры «мастер-пляйты». В создании перечисленного инструмента первых лет работы цеха каждый из тройки вносил толику своей творческой мысли, энергии, труда. Позже предметом волнений и тревог стал штамп для одновременной пробивки отверстий в конических сепараторах. То была заметная веха в процессе развития прогрессивной технологии.

Вспоминали мы сохранившуюся и сегодня готовность инструментального словно по боевой тревоге откликаться на требования времени. Оборонные задания, сельское хозяйство, метро, все, помимо основного производства, находило отклик в бурно пульсирующей жизни цеха.

Инженер Робинсон сконструировал барабаны для шлифовки бочкообразных роликов на проход. С его авторством связана задняя бабка к токарному станку для сверления глубоких отверстий с механической подачей. Механизм для шлифовки калибрующих кулачков стоил Робинсону немало бессонных ночей. Все увенчалось успехом благодаря коллегиальности в стиле работы и чувству товарищеского локтя, свойственного тт. Котереву, Селезневу и Робинсону.

Трудно в газетных строках перечислить все этапы большого пути, пройденного тройкой ветеранов в когорте славных инструментальщиков. Сегодня же у них направление главного удара нацелено на участок электрофизической обработки твердосплавного инструмента.

Закончена беседа с товарищами-однополчанами. Расстаешься полный ощущения бодрости, почерпнутой из воспоминаний о боевых делах и днях родного цеха. В памяти же фиксируется постоянная готовность Котерева помочь словом и делом рабочей братии; не забывается терпеливый инструктаж Селезнева о методе работы на «мастер-пляйтах», а за четким силуэтом Робинсона просматривается созданный им первый в цехе индикатор и 36 обученных квалифицированных шлифовщиков.

Маршрут цеха продолжается. Вместе с ним в поступательном движении ветераны Котерев, Робинсон и Селезнев, готовые к овладению новыми техническими высотами.

А. ЦЫН.

На снимке: Н. Селезнев, Р. Робинсон, В. Котерев.

An article in an Estonian newspaper, Youth Principles, *reports the contributions made over a forty-year span by the author and two of his associates at the First State Ball Bearing Plant. Pictured are (from left) N. Seleznev, senior designer; Robinson, senior designer; and V. Kotorev, technologist. The article reports that they are "the veterans who struggled to make tool-making science possible. It is to them we must look forward to a continued supply of precision measuring tools."*

nounce, "The recommendation for Comrade Robinson has been approved." I later learned that I made it by only five votes, whereas the other applicants had been approved with near unanimity.

The next step was to send the recommendation to the visa division of the ministry. No one except a special courier was trusted for this task. My recommendation was delivered nine days later. By now it was early June 1973. Five weeks later I received a card from the visa division, ordering me to report to them immediately. I rushed down there the next day after lunch, full of expectation mixed with apprehension. As I approached the receptionist, I noticed my application on her desk. She looked up and said, "Unless your factory agrees to eliminate the paragraph about the party committee's opinion that you will not be able to take the African climate, you will not be granted a visa."

I was speechless. I thought they had deleted that section. I told her I would take the recommendation back to the party committee, but she told me that the applicant was not allowed to do that. I rode the bus back to the factory more angry than discouraged. I was determined to straighten things out, to spring myself from their trap. I went immediately to the factory assistant party secretary, who could tell that I meant business. Russians respect firmness, and on that day I think my resolve was like granite. After telling him what I had just gone through, he assured me that he would take care of the matter first thing in the morning.

When I called his receptionist the next day, I was surprised to learn that he had gone to the visa division personally, brought back the recommendation, and removed the damaging paragraph. However, she explained, the recommendation could not be delivered because the special courier was ill and was not expected back for another week. Before hanging up, I insisted on seeing the receptionist after work. I do not know what was possessing me, but I was determined that I would not be intimidated, bullied, or otherwise prevented from getting the recommendation to the visa division. I did not even think about the possibility of being sent to jail for my behavior, or banished to Siberia. When I saw the receptionist I said, "Nina, don't you think it would be a good idea for me to come here tomorrow morning at 9:30, take the document by taxi to the visa division, turn it in, return immediately, and report directly to you?"

She thought for a moment and said, "Yes, that is a good idea. Come here in the morning, and I will have everything ready."

I left hoping I had not scared her into agreeing with me, because then she might not do as she had said. She was a party member, and their promises often were not kept. However, when I arrived the next morning she had everything ready for me. With difficulty, I restrained myself from sprinting to the street to hail a taxi. The last thing I needed was to alarm the factory's security people. Once I arrived at the visa division I had to avoid the receptionist I had dealt with before. Fortunately, she was not there, and I gave the papers to another woman who did not bother to check whether I was an authorized courier.

By this time, back in the factory, word of my request to go to Uganda had spread. All sorts of people were coming up to me and asking whether it was true. When I acknowledged that it was, they asked such questions as, "Do you think the authorities will really let you go?" My response, of course, was always noncommittal. I would usually say, "I am prepared for any eventuality."

Others said such things as, "There is one thing that all of us are sure of, that if you are permitted to go you'll never come back." What they actually meant by this was that I was insulting them, that I did not like their country, that I was unappreciative of all that the Soviet Union had done for me, and that I was abandoning them. This kind of statement, coming from them, was really a form of accusation. Some of my closer friends and associates tried to dissuade me from visiting Africa. They could not bear the thought that I might want to leave their country. They started calling me two, three, or four times a week, with new reasons why I should not leave. Some came to my apartment to reason with me. When I told them that all I was doing was going on vacation, the universal answer I received was that there were places in the Soviet Union I had not seen that I would find more enjoyable than Africa. They all felt that I was betraying them and their country.

On December 18, 1973, a bitterly cold day, I came home from the factory and found a post-card in my apartment mailbox. It was from the visa division, ordering me to report to their office as soon as possible with my internal passport, and to deposit 360 rubles ($400) in a bank in the name of the Office of Visas and Immigration Registration, and to bring them the deposit slip. Everything seemed to be going smoothly, though of course, unbearably slowly. The next morning the shop superintendent readily granted me permission to leave work and attend to these errands. I headed from the bank to the visa division office and joined a line of seven people. After thirty minutes my turn came. The receptionist, with an air of obvious, painful boredom, reached for my post-card and asked for my internal passport and bank receipt. Then he started to search through a big file box until he came to the letter "R". He kept looking in this section of the box, but could not find whatever he was looking for. I thought, "Oh no, now they've probably lost my application." I was feeling extremely anxious as I waited and watched him look once, and then start looking again.

Finally, he pulled out a red passport. What a relief! My trip to Africa suddenly became more concrete in my mind. The receptionist opened the passport and slowly and methodically checked the information inside against my internal passport. Then he looked up and said, "Congratulations. Comrade Robinson, we are giving you a passport valid for forty-five days to the Republic of Uganda. I hope you will enjoy your trip there." He picked up the passport and continued, "But before handing you this, there are certain rules that you must agree to follow while overseas. They are: you must always uphold the integrity of the Soviet Union; you must be presentable at all times—always sober; you must shave daily; and you must not allow yourself to be in doubtful company. If you agree to these requirements, please read them again as they are written on this card, and then sign your name."

I did as he instructed, actually signing two cards. One he kept, and the other one he slipped into the passport. "One other thing," he said. "You can only take with you the following items: two suits, three shirts, three sets of underwear, three pairs of socks, three ties, four handkerchiefs, and two pairs of shoes. I must warn you, if you take along more possessions than you are allowed, they will be confiscated." He shoved another card toward me, with these restrictions on it, and I signed it. Then he placed two slips of green paper, with a series of code numbers on them, into the passport, and said, "Those papers should be given to our bank and you will receive enough foreign currency to last you during your stay in Uganda. Also, all citizens must be vaccinated before going abroad. Here is your vaccination coupon. Try to report to the address on this card at 10:00 in the morning. After you've done all these things, take your passport and vaccination papers to the Aeroflot agency at the Metropole Hotel, where you are to purchase your plane tickets." He handed me the passport and other papers and said, "I wish you a safe voyage, pleasant stay, and return."

I was numb and unaware of my surroundings, as I walked out of the visa division. Although I still had a few more hours left in my workday, I went home to my apartment instead of going back to the factory. Once inside, I locked the door, took the passport out of my suit jacket pocket, and sat gazing at it. For years and years I had kept my emotions at an even pitch, not only fighting low feelings, but denying feelings of excitement, exhilaration, and joy as well. This was important to my survival, both to avoid pain and as a caution against acting foolishly, which would be more likely if I were depressed or exuberant. But now I could feel an emotion I had suppressed for years growing inside of me. The sensation was exquisite; I let it come. It rolled over me. It was joy, pure joy! I wanted to jump, dance, cry, and whirl around my room, to leap in the air and click my heels together, to shout and cry and scream. In my hands was my ticket to freedom, which I had been struggling to obtain for more than twenty-eight years. I fell on my knees and thanked God. Robert Robinson, single and alone, an obscure black man, defenseless and helpless, had won his battle with the mighty colossus, the greatest state monopoly that had ever existed.

But I had to get out, I told myself. "You aren't actually out, yet," I said aloud. I calmed myself down, and reminded myself that I was still in the Soviet Union, in the land of the omnipresent KGB. I began thinking how, once I set foot on African soil, I would try everything within my power to keep from returning to the Soviet Union. I knew I meant *everything*, even to the point of death. Then I started to search for a safe place to hide the passport, where no KGB intruder could find it while I was at work. I could just imagine the scene at the visa office, if I returned and said my passport was missing. "Comrade Robinson, this is the second time you have played games with us. First, we granted you a passport and you chose not to go; now we graciously and kindly give you another one, and you say that you have lost it. There is nothing we can do in the face of these contradictions. Your case is closed! Go away!"

I drew the extra heavy, dark red curtains so that no one in a facing apartment could see what I was doing. It took me an hour to find a safe hiding place. I carefully unglued a small section of wallpaper, down at the baseboard behind my sofa. I placed the passport inside and then glued the wallpaper back in place. The only thing left now was to take care of the rest of the business that needed to be done before I could leave, and to count the days.

CHAPTER 32

Freedom!

WHEN I REPORTED TO WORK THE NEXT MORNING, I was told to see my foreman. He seemed very cordial as he reached out to shake my hand and said, "Congratulations on being allowed to go abroad." It was uncharacteristic of him to treat me in a civil fashion. I wondered what he had on his mind. He added, "But I must tell you that I cannot let you go until you finish the job on your drawing board."

It was a complicated job. I was designing an attachment for a cylindrical grinding machine, so that it could grind widely-spaced but unevenly-pitched threads on huge round drums, that would form the conical ends on small-sized rollers for precision roller bearings. I had to design 162 parts, giving the dimensions and tolerances for each one. And that was not all. My foreman said that before I could leave, every design and set of dimensions and tolerances had to be checked and approved by the senior designer. Only then would the shop superintendent sign a form releasing me for fifty-two days of vacation time. The Communist party of the entire factory had met to approve my vacation, I had obtained a passport, but my factory still had the power to block my trip.

I set to work feverishly, working during and after hours until I finished the project, while in the few hours I spent at home I was busy putting together the things I needed for the trip. Clothes were no problem, but I spent a great deal of time sorting through my technical books, trying to decide which ones I should take with me, in case I really did end up teaching at the technical college in Kampala. Of course, I had to be careful not to take too much; it could not appear that I was bringing things out of the country because I had in mind a permanent stay.

One evening after I had made my choice and placed the books I wanted in a suitcase, I decided to check through my valuable papers, which I kept in my wardrobe. I knew I would want to take some of them with me, also. I noticed right away that an envelope containing some important documents was missing from the shelf where I always kept it. In it was a letter I had received from Marcus Garvey while he was in jail in Atlanta, my Soviet mandate, my old British passport, a treasured letter from a mulatto woman who was born in the Soviet Union, and a clipping from a western newspaper about blacks living in the Soviet Union in the 1930s. I looked everywhere for that envelope, that night and every night for the rest of the week. I looked on every shelf, in every corner, in every cup and glass, in every pocket of every jacket; I even went through every book I owned—and there were hundreds of them—but the envelope was gone. No doubt it went the way of my letter to President Touré.

In the meantime, I drew up a list and went about accomplishing all the things I needed to do before leaving. I had no problem at the vaccination center. I was given my shots and all the right papers were signed. At the bank, I handed a clerk the green slips of paper, and after waiting a few minutes, I was given and signed for $176, the amount of money they determined I was to have for my forty-five day stay in Uganda. Obviously, it was just barely enough to subsist on, and too little to enable me to extend my stay past the approved number of days, without going broke. However, even if I had been given $10, I would have gone. I regretted that by fleeing the USSR, I would forfeit my $133 a month pension, the 1,020 rubles I had in the bank, and my few—but highly prized—belongings. I had learned that rewards do not come without some sacrifice, so I accepted my losses. If I succeeded in staying in Uganda, I would gladly give up everything I had for my freedom. I doubted, with sadness, that I would ever be able to return to the United States, but anyplace outside the Soviet orbit of influence would be infinitely better than life inside the Soviet prison.

I went to the Metropole Hotel and purchased my ticket from Aeroflot, the Soviet airline. They first checked my passport and my vaccination receipt, then asked for 840 rubles ($924). It hurt to have to pay for a round trip ticket when I had no intention of returning. There was only one flight a week to Uganda, and the next one was several days away. Departure time was February 13, at 10 P.M. As I walked out of the hotel I said to myself, "That will be a date to remember."

The next day I had the pleasant chore of going to the Ugandan embassy to pick up an entry visa. Once inside the embassy building, I could feel layers of tension falling away. It took only a few minutes to get the document. While I was talking with the chargé d'affaires, another Ugandan came up and said the embassy would like me to come for dinner on the day of my departure. That was nice; it felt good to be among people, in an environment where they could express their care and friendship freely. I felt that I was being weaned from forty-four years of a life based on fear.

On February 12, the day before my departure, I called the embassy to be sure the dinner was still scheduled. I was not totally weaned from caution and fear, because I dared not call from my apartment. For years I had assumed that my phone was tapped, so I called from a nearby telephone booth. The people at the embassy were surprised to hear from me. They said that of course, nothing had changed, and they were looking forward to seeing me the next evening.

I was happy. I was really, genuinely, without compromise or hesitation, happy. It felt good to let my feelings loose, without restraint, without working to convince myself that my hope would soon be frozen in the cold of the Soviet police state, so better not to let the feeling blossom. For the first time, I felt assured that I was leaving. I had everything that was required—a passport, airline tickets, a vaccination receipt, and all of the other documents I needed to pass through customs without trouble. I thought, "This simple, lovely feeling of happiness must be what free people feel."

I wanted to share my happiness with someone, so I called on one of my neighbors, a nice old lady whom I knew had been recruited by the KGB to spy on me. One night, a few years earlier, when her son was drunk, he told me of her activity. I did not hold it against her, because I understood that she had had no choice but to do what the secret police demanded. When she opened the door, she seemed happy enough to see me, and invited me in. When I told her that I was leaving on vacation for Africa the following day, it appeared from her response that she had already been informed. She wished me well, but also said, "Before coming back, please don't forget to bring me one of those beautiful African dresses and a nice pair of shoes." She went across the room to get a pencil and piece of paper. She wrote down her dress and shoe sizes and handed me the paper, admonishing me, "Now don't forget, Comrade Robinson."

I told her I would not, knowing full well that if my plan worked out, I would never see her again. I felt sad after saying good-by to her, as I thought about the woman and how limited her understanding of life must be. I thought that she must have her moments when she realizes her situation is hopeless. But on the other hand, I thought, like most Russians she is a hearty person, a survivor, with an uncanny ability for shoving unpleasantness out of her mind. As far as I knew, happiness for her was when her son came home sober. He would be escorted home often, sometimes even carried, by friends or by the police.

That night, I do not think I slept more than four hours. I lay awake imagining, alternately, scenes of myself walking on non-Soviet soil, and then other thoughts of being met at the airport in Kampala by a corps of husky KGB agents, who would then haul me back onto the Soviet plane and escort me back to Moscow. The next day went by exceedingly slowly. At 4:30 P.M., I called for a taxi to pick me at up 6:00. Although I was not due at the embassy until 7:00, I had planned a round-about route because, if I were being following by the KGB, I would prefer to try to lose them on the way. First I took a cab to the Taganka subway station, then I walked a block to a taxi stand and took another cab two blocks past the embassy, where I got out and walked back. This was quite an ordeal, carrying two medium-sized suitcases, one of which was filled with books. I preferred to strain myself physically than to take any chances of being intercepted. Years later I would laugh, recalling what I had done to get to the embassy, but at the time I was deadly serious.

A Soviet guard outside the embassy checked me over carefully as I approached, but did not say a word. Once inside the embassy, I felt relieved. Two Ugandans, who were waiting for me in the foyer, escorted me to the apartment of the chargé d'affaires, where an elegant meal awaited us. The food was exquisite, and after the meal the chargé assigned two Ugandans to drive me to the airport in their car and wait until I was on the plane. I was very grateful for this arrangement, because I still had to get through the lines and pass the scrutiny of the personnel and police at the airport.

Once we got to the airport and made our way to the international flight section, the first person I dealt with was a woman who asked to see my passport. She directed me to a line where people were waiting to have their luggage weighed. When my turn came, a tall, powerfully-built KGB officer asked to see my passport. As he looked through my passport, he kept glancing up at me. I realized I might be in for trouble. He could not believe that this black man was a Soviet citizen. Still puzzled, he asked me to show him my foreign currency and my customs clearance receipt. He inspected everything, even checking the quality of the paper. He went through every piece of currency, counting it twice. Then he asked to see my vaccination papers. Satisfied that they were in order, he asked me how much Soviet currency I had. I told him that I was carrying ten rubles, in order to pay for my taxi ride home from the airport when I returned. He asked to see the rubles; I showed them to him. Then he just stood there and stared at me as if I were a freak, looking me up and down.

Finally, he came out from behind the counter and demanded, "Where are your belongings?" It was then that I realized just how huge he was; he must have weighed nearly three hundred pounds. He looked through one suitcase, put it aside, and then began looking through the other. I looked over to where the first suitcase had been a moment before and discovered, to my horror, that it was gone! The woman behind me in line saw the look of terror in my eyes. She quietly motioned to me that my suitcase was on the conveyor belt. I had not noticed the baggage clerk pick it up and place it there. Then she gestured with her hand for me to calm down. At this point, the KGB agent had stuffed my tape recorder back into my suitcase and asked, "Is this all?"

"Yes," I said, shaken by my momentary fright over my suitcase. I was still uneasy, because I had not seen my suitcase on the belt. And what if I misunderstood what the woman was trying to tell me? What if the KGB had grabbed it, and was trying to provoke me into making a scene? I bit my tongue. I decided that to get to Kampala with no luggage was still a great deal better than not getting there at all. The colossus behind the counter, who continued looking at me as if I were a creature from a different world, asked to see my tickets. Those he only glanced at, handed them back to me with a boarding pass, and pointed me and my companions to a nearby waiting room.

"It is really happening," I thought. "I'm really going to leave." Having the boarding pass in hand made it that much more real. Everything was in order! No snags! Only my missing suitcase. My two African companions began reminiscing about what it was like back home. It was good to hear; it all sounded so wholesome. My heart leapt into my throat when I heard the announcement over the public address system: "Passengers bound for Odessa, Khartoum, Kampala, and Nairobi, it is time to embark, please!" Chills swept over my entire body. The two Ugandans embraced me, wishing me well, and I left them to join the excited, chattering crowd that was heading outside to the runway. By the time I was outside, people in front of me were already piling onto a waiting bus. In about a minute another bus arrived for the rest of us.

A hostess kept urging everyone to move faster, to hurry up and board the bus. I was at the door to the bus, and as I was lifting my foot about to enter, I heard, "Robinson! Comrade Robinson!" Someone was calling my name. I turned around and saw a female inspector running toward me. My heart sank. I climbed into the bus and took a seat. The inspector came to the door and called out my name again. I did not budge; I thought, let them think that I was on the first bus. Finally, the bus driver said, "Will Robinson please get off the bus." I decided I had better respond, that the bus was not going to move, and in a moment they would call in the police.

As soon as I stepped off the bus, it drove away to the waiting plane. They were heading for Uganda. I was still here! I pleaded with the inspector. "I'm going to miss my flight. What are you doing? Why are you keeping me from getting on that plane?"

She showed me my vaccination permit saying, "You need to be vaccinated again. What they did was wrong."

I did not believe her, but I knew it was no use to argue. She was standing here in the freezing cold without a coat on. Clearly, someone had suddenly told her to race out and intercept me before I left on the plane. I walked back with her to the terminal, too stunned to say anything, to cry, or even to think. As I entered the building, I saw my two Ugandan friends, as shocked as I was. They hurried toward me and, keeping their distance, followed us to the inspector's desk.

As I was walking along, I thought, "A decision came from above to stop me. If the Ugandans had not stayed to see me off, I think this would have been the end—they would have scooped me up and sent me a thousand miles from Moscow." I believed that since the KGB had failed to find my passport when they searched my room a week before my departure date, their next step would have been simply to whisk me away. Thank God for the Ugandans.

When we reached the inspector's desk, she asked for my passport and tickets and stamped the word, "Annulled," over the words, "Departure 13th February." Without saying a word or looking at me, she moved away from her desk and motioned for me to follow. I turned around; the Ugandans were still there, keeping pace with me. When the inspector and I reached a small room away from the rush of passengers, she motioned for me to enter. Inside sat a large, fat man, his eyes trained on a magazine spread on his desk before him. Without lifting his head to look at me he grunted, "What do you want?"

"Excuse me," I said, "but my passage was cancelled because of an error made on my vaccination papers." He turned the page of his magazine, without responding. "Can you tell me where I can have the papers corrected?" I asked. With his eyes still on his magazine, he reached for a piece of paper, wrote something on it, and handed it to me. It said, "For proper vaccination." He still had not so much as glanced at me. And he was done. That was it. I had pressed a button, and this blubbery robot of a man reacted in the precise way he no doubt responded to hundreds of other people each month.

The inspector was waiting for me outside the office, and she escorted me to the terminal exit. Not only had I been prevented from leaving Russia, but I was leaving with only one suitcase. I assumed the other one was lost forever. If it had not been for the Ugandans, who rushed to me as soon as the inspector left, I would have collapsed. Never in my life had I felt so defeated. How I had tried, over the years, to keep from building up false hopes. But when I was handed the boarding pass, I had let my guard down. As a result, I was so overcome with disappointment that I wanted to cry. My African friends each placed a hand on my shoulder, and helped guide me to the embassy car. I had no words.

On the way back to the city, I turned my face toward the window and gazed out unseeingly. All I could remember was how, for a few moments, I had felt. Like a Russian peasant, in the face of my despair I turned numb; otherwise I might have gone out of my mind. As the car reached the center of Moscow, the bright lights drew me out of my stupor. I thanked my companions for all they had done and suggested they leave me off at the Mayakovsky subway station. From there I could take a train directly to my neighborhood. It was a good thing that one of them asked if I had enough money for the fare, because when I checked my wallet, I discovered that the ten ruble note was gone. It had probably fallen out at some point while my documents were being inspected at the airport. One of the students gave me a ruble. I thanked him, and asked that they tell the chargé d'affaires what had happened.

I arrived home long after midnight. I lay in bed, unable to sleep. I thought through my entire life. I knew that all I could do was try again in the morning, and I drifted off to sleep. When I awoke and got out of bed, it was still dark. One of the first things I did was check the slip of paper the fat man had given me for the address of the vaccination center. It was a different location than where I had previously gone. I wondered if another set of vaccinations, just a week apart, would be harmful, but I knew whatever the case, it was worth the risk.

I made my way to the address I was given, and found a modern, clean building in the center of town. A tall, middle-aged man dressed in a uniform, and with a carefully trimmed beard, greeted me cordially and opened the door. I noticed a sign inside that said this area was for foreigners. Just as I was realizing that I was in the wrong place, a man came up to me, smiling and courteous, and asked if he could help me. I handed him the slip of paper I had been given at the airport. He asked for my passport. As soon as he saw it was a Soviet passport, that I was not a foreigner, his expression changed to a scowl. He nearly threw my documents at the girl next to him and walked away. He was upset that he had mistakenly put on his courteous face for a mere Soviet citizen. The young woman informed me that I had come to the wrong place. She wrote down a different address and explained how to get there by bus. When I reached the exit, the doorman opened the door, bowed, and said, "I wish you all the best."

I smiled to myself when I got off the bus and realized I was back where I had started. This was the same one-story wooden building, badly in need of a paint job, where I had come the week before. This place was for Soviets, not foreigners; there was no doorman here, only a line eight people deep and no vacant seats. I knew from my earlier experience that each person would take about a half-hour so I prepared myself for a three- or four-hour wait. About fifteen minutes after I arrived a nurse came out of the examination room and asked, "Who is next?" Then she noticed me leaning against the wall. Ignoring everyone else, she came over to me and asked, "Why, you were here just a few days ago; why are you back again?" When I explained what had happened, she told me she would be right back, and ducked back into the examination room.

She reappeared a moment later and called me inside. The same doctor who had vaccinated me earlier was there. She was disturbed by what I had gone through and muttered, "What negligence. I vaccinated you. What more do they need? Let's do it this way. If I vaccinate you again it could make you seriously ill. I will simply put a new stamp on your papers."

As I walked out of the medical clinic, another one of those paranoid yet plausible thoughts came to my mind. Perhaps it was part of the strategy to prevent me from getting out of the country, that I would get sick from a double dose of vaccine and be unable to leave. I suddenly realized that I was very tired, so I bought enough food for a few days and went home. As I approached my apartment building I noticed something unusual—no one was sitting on one of the benches near the entrance. In my thirteen years in that building, residents, pensioners, and party spies had always been sitting there. But now there was no one. Since I was officially gone, there was no need to sit there and watch me.

After a good night's sleep, I awoke the next morning with more energy. In fact, I felt good. I went to the Aeroflot office to see when I could book another flight. I was told the next one was in four days, on February 20. I said I wanted a seat on the plane, and ten minutes later, after inquiring at their central office, she said there was space available. She asked to see my passport and vaccination papers. I gave her my documents, plus my cancelled tickets. She processed everything in about fifteen minutes. I walked away with a new set of tickets, went to the first phone booth I spotted, and called my friends at the Uganda embassy.

They were overjoyed to hear from me and again invited me to the embassy and said we would leave much earlier for the airport, in case customs tried to stall me and force me to miss the plane.

I spent the next four days in my apartment. I continued searching for the missing envelope—futilely, of course—and watched Soviet television, something I rarely did, in order to pass the time. For four days I was captive to the agonizing thought that I would run into another barrier and still be stuck in the Soviet Union. On the day I was to leave I went outside to a phone booth, called for a taxi, and then telephoned my Ugandan friends. I told them the route I would be taking to the embassy.

I got off two blocks from the embassy. After walking back half a block I saw the same two Ugandans walking toward me, beaming. My heart jumped; as soon as I saw them I forgot my troubles. I walked faster until we met, and as we walked back to their embassy, they told me some good news. My missing suitcase had arrived in Kampala and was waiting for me at the Ugandan foreign ministry. They also explained that when I did not arrive with the suitcase, Ugandan authorities in Kampala cabled the embassy in Moscow to ask what had happened. Just hearing that transformed me. I asked them to tell me everything, all over again, so I could savor the news. "There really is a world out there that wants me," I thought. "If my suitcase can escape to freedom, then by golly, so can I!"

Gazing at my friends, and feeling their affection, I almost totally relaxed. I felt a lightness and hope that I had never experienced before. I thanked God for these people. I thanked Him for the protection that had enabled me to endure for so long in a system that viewed me as an enemy. I told Him that He was in control of my destiny, and I was putting my life in His hands. I suddenly felt totally confident that this time I would fly out of Moscow, out of Russia, and out of a world that distrusted me as much as I had grown to fear and distrust it.

In less than thirty minutes we left for the airport, and arrived there more than three hours before my departure time. The guard at the terminal gate said, sarcastically, "I see the three of you are back again," but none of us responded. I hesitated a moment when we entered the terminal. It was not just the noise that affected me, or travelers rushing about; it was all the dead-looking, compassionless men and women in uniform and the line of offices along the wall that troubled me. I did not know if I could stand to get so close again, only to fail, and to end up once again with the fat man reading the magazine. But I moved forward, catching up with the Ugandans who were three or four steps ahead.

I joined one of the lines, and my companions stood by my side, watching. I wondered if they realized how much their presence meant to me. Without them, I thought, I might turn back. At that point I heard an inner voice saying to me, "No!" I thought of the agreement I had made with God just a short time before. "Well, here is my first test," I thought, and I moved forward in the line. As I came closer to the counter I noticed there was a different inspector there this time, who looked less severe. When my turn came, all of my papers seemed to be in order, except for the money clearance receipt. He said that my carbon copy was not sufficient. When I told the inspector that I had to give the original receipt away the last time I was here, he expressed surprise. Then I had to tell him what had happened the week before, which of course meant that he had to go check with someone else about my case. He left for one of the offices along the wall. He returned ten minutes later with the original receipt, and asked to see the foreign currency I was carrying. He counted it, stamped the date of departure on my tickets, and told me to go to the line where passports were being checked. The Ugandans followed me.

I was soon facing a stocky, stern-looking KGB agent, who asked for my passport. From the look on his face, I sensed that he thought I was a fraud. Of course, I also knew he was trained to have a look that said to everyone, "You are a fraud." He examined every page of my passport. When he came to my picture, he studied it and then gazed at me for the longest time. "Where did you get this passport?" he snapped. I was not going to let him intimidate me; firmly, I told him the truth. "Excuse me, citizen," I said, "the administration of the factory where I work, the First State Ball Bearing Plant in Moscow, named after the great leader, Vladimir Ilich Lenin, made an official request together with party recommendations to the Visas and Registration Office that I be granted a passport to visit my friends in Uganda."

The KGB agent checked the passport again, slapped it against his palm, and said, "I'll be right back." He headed for one of the offices along the wall. I checked my watch.

About ten minutes later the door to the office opened and the man came out with someone else, who appeared to be his boss. They stood there staring at me. I stared back. In the meantime, the line behind me had grown considerably. My resolve was growing even stronger, and when the passport inspector walked back to his station, I never took my eyes off him. He stepped inside his booth, handed me my approved passport and boarding pass. I thanked him and he lifted the crossbar to let my companions and me through to the waiting room.

They sat on either side of me in the waiting room. One of them smiled and said, "It was a good thing we left early. Otherwise you might have missed your plane."

I checked my watch and said, "There's no question about that." It was strange, but I was relaxed. It was not like the last time; it was as if the three of us were in an invisible capsule. My flight was announced, but I did not rush to the gate with the two hundred or more other passengers; I felt content to move along slowly behind. My friends were with me and the younger one pointed ahead and said, "There's an African couple." He pressed through the crowd, caught up with them, and talked to them briefly.

He made his way back to us and said, excitedly, "They're Tanzanians." We were glad to know there would be other blacks on the flight. When we reached the gate where we were to wait for the bus, the Ugandan spotted another black person, and left us to go see who it was. It turned out to be a fellow Ugandan, who was returning to Kampala after studying in Moscow for several years.

"This is God's protection," I thought. "I'm not going to the land of my forefathers alone." My Ugandan friend went over to his countryman again, and returned with him so he could introduce us and suggest that we sit together. I gave each of my friends a big embrace, and they urged me to wire the embassy as soon as I arrived in Kampala. With my latest Ugandan acquaintance, I walked through the open gate and onto the waiting bus.

I boarded the plane and found my seat. The Ugandan was seated next to me and to my delight, I noticed the Tanzanian couple only three rows back. I buckled my seat belt, closed my eyes, and leaned my head back. The pilot fired the engines. I waited. No one called out my name. The plane rolled down the runway and lifted off. I was in the air! I thanked God with such intensity and emotion, that I wept silently.

When I opened my eyes I could tell that my new friend was

concerned about me. He asked if I was sick. I told him no, that I was doing fine. To have really told him how I felt would have taken twenty flights around the world.

About an hour after takeoff, I did begin to feel ill. The Ugandan sensed my discomfort and asked if I had ever flown before. I told him I had, and that I had never become sick. But my last flight had been many years earlier, and I was older now. I thought a sip of the cognac the stewardess was serving might settle my stomach, so I took a glass and sipped slowly. The plane stopped over in Odessa, and then took off again. I thought, with relief, that we would now be leaving Soviet air space, and then suddenly I began to feel better. We were flying over a vast body of water, which I figured was either the Black Sea or the Mediterranean. Ten hours later our landing flaps and wheels came down, and I looked out into brilliant sunshine burning on a dry, parched land. "Khartoum," the stewardess announced.

"This is Africa," I thought, a place I have heard and read so much about but have never seen. I felt a sense of reverence, as if I were on a pilgrimage to the land of my ancestors. When the plane landed, we were allowed to disembark for twenty minutes. When I stepped onto Sudanese soil I felt I was returning from the dead. The people looked so beautiful, so open, so warm, so friendly. I wanted to kiss everyone I saw. Freedom, freedom! I wanted to shout about it, revel in it, absorb every bit of it, all at once. I was intoxicated! I wanted to leap, and dance, and sing!

Back on the plane, the stewardess announced that we would be arriving at Entebbe Airport, in Uganda, in about three hours. At that moment, forty-four years of injustice and hardship in the Soviet Union passed before me: the racism; the KGB; the perpetual gloom, the loss of friends through imprisonment, banishment, and execution; the open and disguised contempt, the impediments to romance, the isolation—I could do nothing to stop the thoughts, the memories, the feelings. I was surprised that I did not feel angry, because of all the nights when I was cooped up in my tiny apartment and nearly consumed by anger. But as the plane started its descent, my heart was at ease, and I felt good.

As the plane's wheels touched down, I looked out the window. The lushness of the land took my breath away. Flowers blooming in February? I wondered if this wasn't a touch of heaven. I was excited

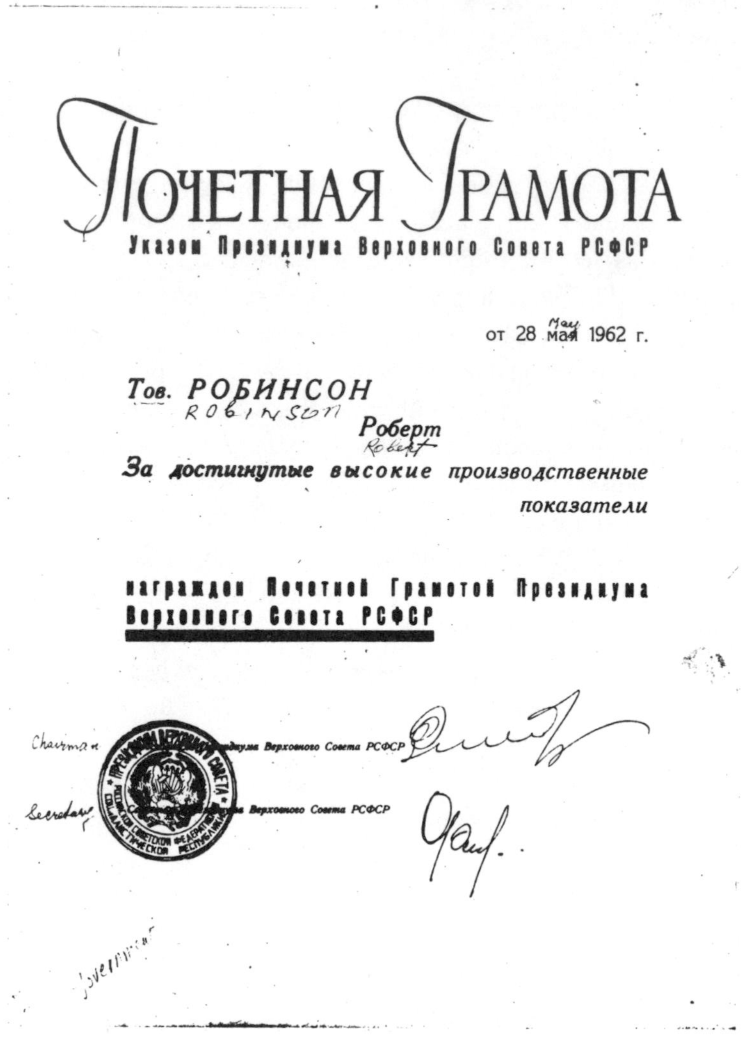

Почетная Грамота

Указом Президиума Верховного Совета РСФСР

от 28 мая 1962 г.

Тов. РОБИНСОН

Роберт

За достигнутые высокие производственные показатели

награжден Почетной Грамотой Президиума Верховного Совета РСФСР

Chairman ...идиума Верховного Совета РСФСР

Secretary ...а Верховного Совета РСФСР

A copy of the inside title page of an honorary diploma awarded to Robinson on May 28, 1962. It reads: "For achieving high and overall production index" Robert Robinson "is awarded with an Honorary Diploma from the Presidium of the Supreme Soviets, RSFSR." When the factory director, Gromov, awarded the diploma to Robinson, he also handed him a meager bonus of five rubles, as an insult. When Robinson left the Soviet Union in 1974, he took the rubles with him to serve as a reminder of the years of humiliation he endured.

Soviet rubles that Robinson received along with an honorary diploma for overall production output on May 28, 1962.

beyond measure, unsure whether I had the self-control to restrain myself. I wanted to dash out and kiss the ground. The engine shut off and the passengers were removing their belongings from the compartments above the seats. The stewardess opened the front door and people began to deplane. My student companion signaled me to go ahead of him.

I walked up the aisle to the top of the mobile stairs. I looked out, and felt embraced by the warm sun. I remembered my first boat ride on the Volga, and my surprise at the way the Russians nearly worshiped the sun. Forty-three Russian winters later, I felt the same way. I grabbed hold of both railings, for I was shaking, and I started walking down the steps.

"Mr. Robinson, Mr. Robinson! I am here!" I heard someone calling my name, in a pleasant voice. I noticed a man below, on the runway. It was my friend, Oseku, whom I knew from the Ugandan embassy in Moscow. He ran toward me, still calling, "Mr. Robinson, Mr. Robinson." He reached me just as I was about to step off the stairs onto the runway. His face aglow, he gave me a big hug and said four exquisitely beautiful words: "Welcome to our country!"

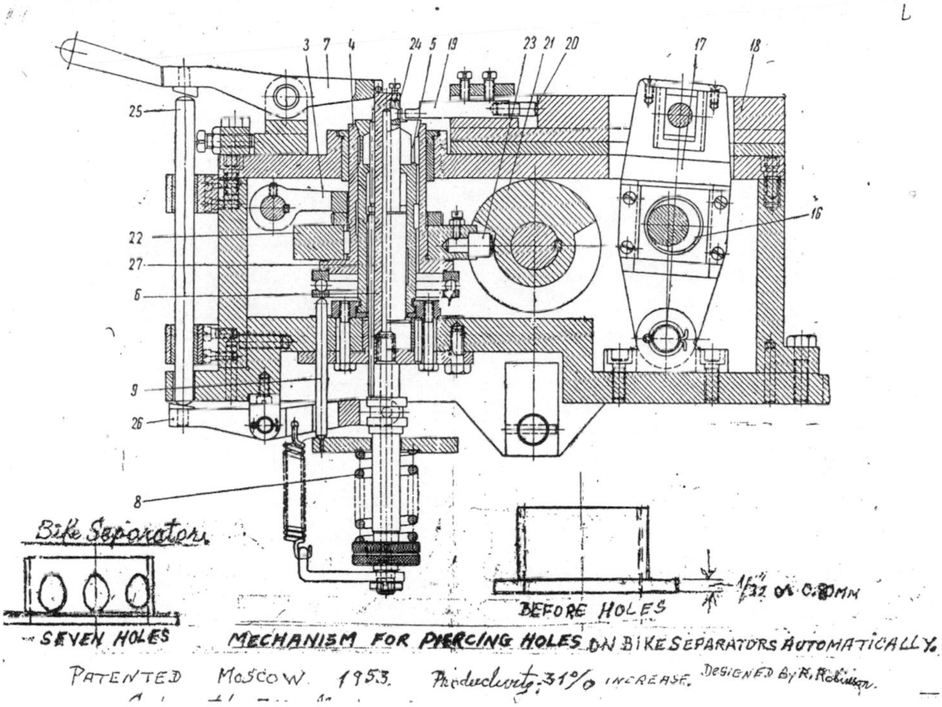

The "mechanism for piercing holes for bike separators" (above) was one of many industrial inventions Robinson designed for the Soviet Union. He designed this one-ton mechanism to replace a sixty-ton press that was being used to produce a separator 1/64 of an inch thick. The factory director asked Robinson and the chief designer to work on this project. Robinson completed it after hours, at home, in two weeks. After submitting it to the chief designer, the designer made an effort to redesign it and claim the invention as his own. Robinson applied for and received a patent for his invention in 1953, for which he was paid 390 rubles (worth $396 by the official exchange rate at the time, or $68.40 on the Vienna black market). He increased factory production by 31 percent, and cut down on electricity usage. The invention was also useful to the Soviet Union's fifteen other ball bearing factories, as well. No one ever thanked Robinson for his invention, nor did he receive any compensation.

Top factory administrators and Communist Party leaders appeared at a reception given to honor Robinson in 1957, on the occasion of his twenty-fifth year at the factory. Left to right, A. Gromov, factory director; B. Victorov, factory's party secretary; A. Brodsky, machine shop superintendent; and Robinson.

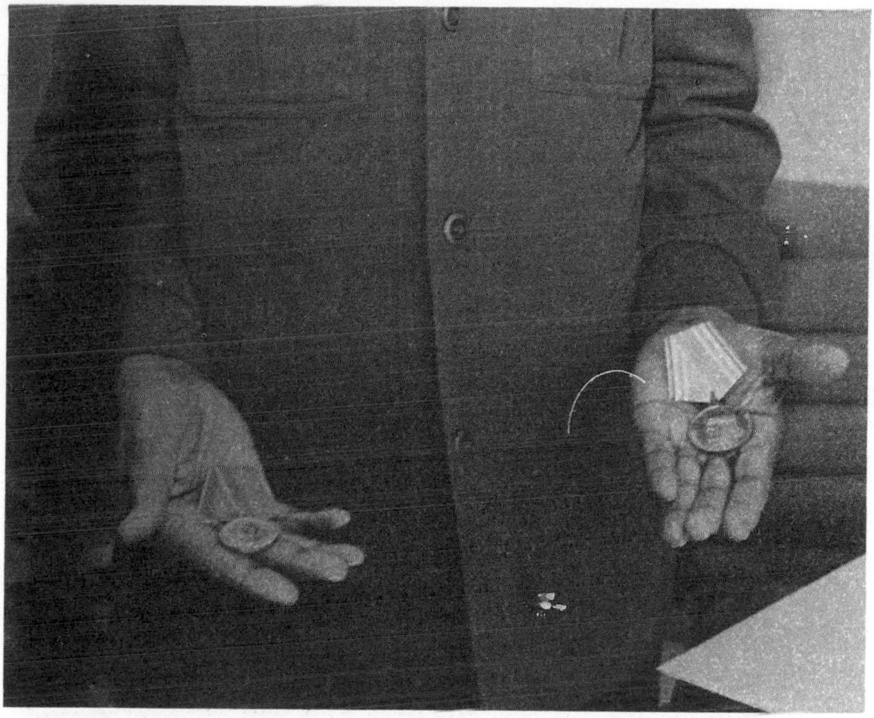

Among the numerous citations Robinson received for his skill and productivity on the job are these two medals (above right), for excellent production output during World War II, and (above left) for consecutively high productivity.

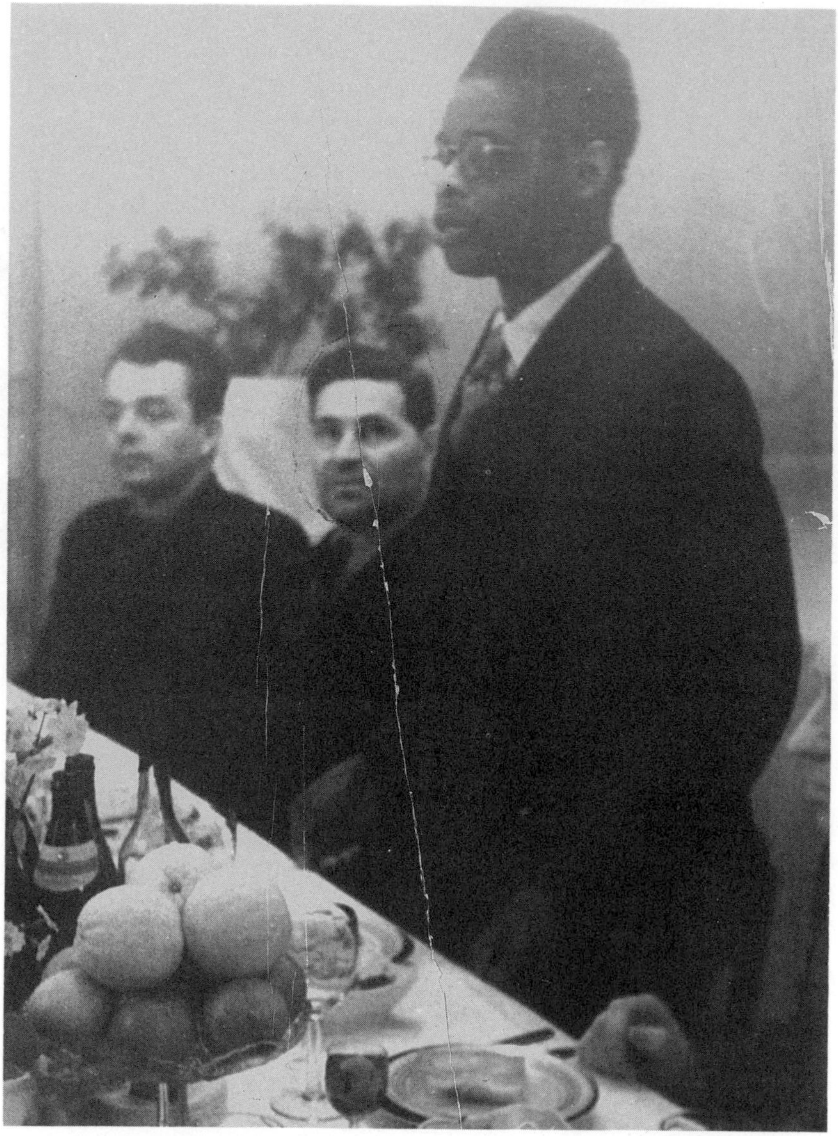

Robinson delivers a speech at a reception in his honor, on his twenty-fifth anniversary at the First State Ball Bearing Plant. From left, Nazarov, secretary of trade unions, and Gromov, factory director.

Robinson recognizes Victor Hoshlushin, a classmate of his at technical college, during remarks at his twenty-fifth anniversary reception. From left, Hoshlushin; his wife Olga; Brodsky, the machine shop superintendent; Navarov, secretary of the House of Trade Unions; and Victorov, the factory's party secretary.

1 мая 1949 г., № 38 (3095) СТАЛИНСКИЙ ПРИЗЫВ

„Я другой такой страны не знаю, где так вольно дышит человек!"

За время работы на нашем заводе Роберт Робинсон обучил шлифовальному делу около 40 человек.
На снимке: Р. Робинсон (в центре) среди своих учеников — В. Папкевича (центральная лаборатория), И. Жильцова, В. Звонова и Н. Грицова (инструментальный цех).
Фото М. КРИМЕРА.

Семьсот белых и один негр

Робинсон едет в СССР

Первое открытие Робинсона

Последующие открытия

Робинсон остается в СССР

Р. Робинсон за работой в техническом отделе инструментального цеха.
Фото В. НИКОЛЬСКОГО.

И. ИРОШНИКОВА.

An article about Robinson appeared in the May 1, 1949, issue of Stalin's Call. *The caption for the photo at top reads: "During his work in our factory, Robert Robinson has taught precision grinding to almost forty persons." In the photo are (left to right) V. Papkevich (Polish), I. Jilson (Russian), Robinson, V. Zvonov (Ukrainian), and N. Gridsov (gypsy). Photo caption below: "R. Robinson at work at the technical library of the factory."*

CHAPTER 33

Under the Wing of Idi Amin

WHEN I FILLED OUT AN APPLICATION for an exit visa I determined that if I succeeded in getting out I would never return to the Soviet Union. Now I was in Uganda on a forty-five day pass and with a worthless return ticket to Moscow, which I had to buy in order not to alert the Soviet authorities that I had no intention of returning. The Soviets had allowed me to bring just enough money with me—the equivalent of $174—to subsist for forty-five days, but no longer.

Fortunately, upon my arrival I was taken to a hotel where the manager was told that I was the personal guest of President Idi Amin. I stayed there for six weeks, eating three meals a day, without having to pay a cent. Two days after checking in, I received a phone call telling me that a car would be sent to take me to see Idi Amin. Soon after I entered his office, the Ugandan president began asking me many questions about my life in the Soviet Union. He was particularly interested in my professional career. Based on this interview, and the information he had gotten about me from Mathias Lubega, Amin said, "I am prepared to give you citizenship if you want it, because I like black people. I don't care where they came from, they began in Africa." He also offered me a teaching job at Uganda Technical College, located in Kyambogo, about seven miles outside Kampala.

I politely declined his offer of citizenship, saying I needed time to think it over. Having just escaped from a Communist country, I had no intention of trapping myself in a dictatorship. I was two days out of the Soviet Union, after forty-four years there. I had no idea what was in store for me, but my ultimate goal was to return to the West, although I doubted that I would ever regain American citizenship. Sitting in Idi Amin's office, I also knew that it would take time for me to adjust psychologically after a lifetime of being constantly on guard because of Soviet tyranny and racism. I knew I should proceed slowly and cautiously. As kind as he was being to me, I believed that if I put myself under Amin's power, he could decide to send me back to Russia at any time. I told Amin, "If I could teach whites in Europe, I see no reason why I cannot teach blacks in Africa. I am very pleased to accept your kind job offer."

A reporter covering our meeting wrote an article that appeared in the February 23, 1974, issue of the main newspaper in Kampala. It said:

> President Amin has received a black Soviet citizen, Bob Robinson, who was born in Jamaica and has lived and worked in the Soviet Union for the last 43 years.
>
> The President assured Mr. Robinson that he will do everything possible for him and asked him to feel at home while in Uganda. General Amin told him that he loves all black people all over the world, whether they are Ugandan citizens or not, because Uganda is their home.
>
> Thanking him for coming to Uganda, President Amin told Mr. Robinson that arrangements will be made for him to stay here by the various government authorities, so that he can help his brothers in Uganda in his profession. In this connection, the President said he will be at the Uganda Technical College.
>
> Thanking the President, Mr. Robinson told Mr. Amin that he is willing to give everything in the line of knowledge to Africans. He added that the President's offer is timely and if he was of service to Europeans, why should he not be of service to Africans, who are his forebears.

> Mr. Robinson told President Amin that his aim of coming to Africa began since his childhood and that he has always wanted to be of service to fellow black people. He also took the opportunity to brief the President on his profession and duties in the Soviet Union.

I could not have asked for more. The president of the country was taking personal care of me. I now had a reason for staying, a means of supporting myself, and the opportunity to put my knowledge and experience to good use. Yet I was still concerned that the Soviets might try to force me onto an Aeroflot jet and take me back to Moscow.

When I discussed my fears with Lubega a few days later, he told me there was no cause to worry. He said, "President Amin has already told his Minister of Foreign Affairs to advise the Soviet ambassador to Uganda that you will be staying here to teach."

This was at a time when the Soviet Union was intent on maintaining its excellent ties with Uganda, and Lubega was certain the Soviets would accede to Amin's request. I began to relax. After about a month, I began to thaw out enough to start to feel the real me again. Years of accumulated tension were falling away in waves. It took six months until my body felt at peace. I was not afraid during the daytime, even though I could not break the habit of looking to see if the KGB was behind me. At the slightest noise, I would startle and look back. At night, I would become gripped by fear and unable to sleep. Frequently, I would stir from a fitful attempt at slumber, jump up and run to the window, and check whether I was really in Uganda.

After two months I was asked to report to the Ministry of Technology, where they told me that they had received word from the president that I should be employed. However, they added, I would still have to follow their official procedures and satisfy members of Uganda's Public Service Commission that I was qualified for the job. Four people sat on the commission—two were British and two were African. They asked me technical questions for over an hour. Then they declared themselves satisfied with my answers and said that I was hired as a Lecturer in Mechanical Engineering in the School of Mechanical and Production Engineering, part of the college. A few days later I received word that I

Top, Robert Robinson, age twenty-three, in a photo taken in Detroit before he left for the Soviet Union. Bottom, Robinson, age sixty-eight, shortly after his arrival in Uganda in 1974.

was to leave the hotel, and that Amin was providing me with a fully furnished, two-room house.

My first day of teaching, May 2, 1974, was somewhat complicated, because all of the other lecturers at the college were either British or from India or Bangladesh. They were accustomed to lecturers being from abroad, and not black, with the British dominating, since Uganda was formerly their colony. It took me a few days to gain the respect of the students, who were initially skeptical of me, because of their colonial experience. They had grown accustomed to thinking—often subconsciously—that blacks were not as capable as people of other races. It was two weeks before a man the commission had assigned to observe my teaching—under the pretext of being a student—apparently felt satisfied that I was competent, and left. During my time there, I taught mechanical engineering, design, and toolmaking. I learned that although the British and Indian lecturers were well-equipped with theoretical knowledge, they were unable to help the students produce on the machine what they had designed on paper. I was pleased that because of my combined theoretical and practical training, I was able to be of particular help to the students.

Here I was, teaching at a college in Uganda, after forty-four years in the Soviet Union. I was free! What an incredible feeling! I could go anywhere I wanted, whenever I wanted. There was no more surveillance. In Moscow, every morning at 5:00 A.M. my telephone would ring faintly. Three little jingles told me that a new shift was beginning. Once when I picked up the phone, the person at the other end said, "You son-of-a-b----, put the receiver down!" In Kampala, my phone never jingled.

The friendliness of the people in Kampala greatly helped my mental and spiritual rehabilitation. Word got out that I was there, and people I had known in Moscow came to visit. Other, new acquaintances came by, and they were all warm and sympathetic. Although I was no longer young, I still thought and felt like a young person. How I enjoyed the friendly, open faces of the African women. In order to survive in the Soviet Union, I had put a padlock on my feelings toward both men and women, but I especially had to protect myself against falling in love with a Russian woman. In Kampala, my heart began to open.

I had to be so strict with myself in Russia. I never once told a

Russian woman, "I like you," or ever took the initiative with any of them. Nevertheless, now and then, a charming woman would appear to tantalize me. On such occasions, I sought to demonstrate that there were many ways in which a man and woman could enjoy each other's company without entering upon the sacred intimacy of sex. I denied myself the normal human need for warmth and affection from a person of the opposite sex. I could not afford to let myself go. This devastated me, because I sometimes felt as if I were a dog. Only a few Soviet women broke through my barrier. I was often depressed from having to live this way. It felt so wrong and was so contradictory to my true nature. But I knew I must deny the human part of a relationship for fear that, if I did not, I would end up trapped for life.

Now that I was in Africa, I thought about some of the African students I knew who had come to Moscow in the early sixties. They were showered with praise and attention when they first arrived. Russian women would greet them with flowers, hugs, and kisses. These African boys had never seen a white woman so close, and instead of these women running away from them, they were chasing after them. The African boys did not understand Soviet society, did not know just how the Soviets were plotting to use them. Some of them got married, only to discover that their Russian wives were spies and were compelled to report on them to the secret police. Fortunately, they still had their passports and could leave.

In the Soviet Union, as a single man, I was asked constantly, "How have you been able to live in Russia for so long? We have so many beautiful Russian girls. Is it possible that none of them appeals to you? Why haven't you found someone you wished to marry? Don't you like our women?"

I could never tell anyone that I intended to leave. But even if I had not intended to, I could not imagine taking the risk of finding out some day that my wife of twenty years had been reporting my every word, thought, and feeling to the secret police. Furthermore, my Christian faith was such that I could not share my life with a non-believer, and all the Soviet women I knew were either atheists or agnostics. And I knew that if I allowed myself to fall in love with a Russian woman and marry her, and then have children, my attachment to my family would make it impossible for me to abandon them to an uncertain fate, if I were to get out myself.

Two additional Russian characteristics influence my feelings. First, Russian nature tends to be arrogant. I found their deep-rooted conceit, that Russian ideas, culture, history, and accomplishments are superior to the rest of the world, to be very distasteful. Second, there is an aspect of Russian behavior that is maddeningly unpredictable, which I think may be the result of their brutally cold winters. Some days you just could not understand what was wrong with a Russian woman or, for that matter, with a Russian man. When the temperature would drop to thirty-two to thirty-five degrees below zero, I knew I would begin to witness aberrant behavior. I often saw women suddenly stop what they were doing, look vacantly into space, begin weeping, and become short-tempered. Friends of mine sometimes complained to me that their wives were acting strangely, and they could not figure out what was wrong.

Men would become easily provoked, and would start yelling at each other over slight misunderstandings. The men in my shop who were normally talkative would come to work and refuse to speak all day, except when it was absolutely necessary to clarify some aspect of a job. When I would say good morning to a fellow worker during one of his moods, it was not unusual for him to ignore me altogether.

The moodiness, unpredictability, and frequent rudeness of the Russian people are common traits that became apparent to those few foreigners who live among them for many years. These characteristics are typically unrecognized by the outside world because, during short periods of contact, the Russian people are able to restrain themselves. After my first decade in the Soviet Union I had seen enough to believe that, if I were to marry a Russian woman, I might end up as perplexed by her behavior as a number of my foreign friends were about their wives. In Kampala I could mingle freely. I did not have to fear that women were instruments of the KGB's constant efforts to intrude upon my personal life.

I could also worship God openly, as I chose, without fear of being declared an enemy of the state. As the months passed, I began to feel a little more distant from my life in the Soviet Union. I reflected how every year had been an enormous struggle. With my constant preoccupation with staying alive, the years had taken their toll on me emotionally. In spite of my best efforts, the system, the climate, and the people wore on me, and just like the Russians I lived and worked with, I became suspicious, distrustful of strangers, and at times paranoid. I was not strong enough to stay really alive, in a spiritual sense. I fought against becoming preoccupied with acquiring food, shelter, and warm clothing, but I often felt I was losing the battle.

As a Christian, I knew the importance of becoming detached from worldly things. More importantly, I knew that without constantly working to develop trustworthiness, kindliness, selflessness, and love, I would be little more than a beast. I confess that there were times in Russia when I felt that I was no better than a caged animal, as I cowered in my tiny room, afraid to go out, constantly checking the bread box, and making sure my door was securely locked. I would become completely self-absorbed. I knew this was wrong, but I was not strong enough to fight it. I would long for freedom and lament that I was allowing the rigors of life in the Soviet police state to overwhelm whatever virtues I may have possessed when I came. I prayed every day, but during my periods of despondency, I could do little better than to ask God why He had placed me in such a wretched place. I believe that one thing carried me through: however miserable I felt, I never stopped praying. I never accused God of abandoning me, and I never gave up on Him. And when these periods of depression ended, I always asked God for forgiveness.

I found it painfully difficult to counteract the ever present and powerful forces that sought to destroy religious faith. While America was debating the constitutionality of prayer in the public schools, I was living in a society where the only permissible mention of God was to denounce Him. Spiritual concerns were never even discussed when I was with friends I had known for years. Practicing religion was a lonely experience. It was painful to me because I had no one with whom to share my feelings about God, except God. In many ways, the ache in my soul was worse than the hunger pains in my stomach. Food could relieve my physical agony but my spiritual hunger persisted until I escaped.

I attended a Catholic church in Moscow every Sunday, even during the war. I was not a Catholic, but form and doctrine mattered less to me than the opportunity for fellowship with others. The church, which was attended mostly by foreign diplomats, was in the center of town across the street from KGB headquarters. I saw men looking out their windows when I arrived and departed. I was so accustomed to being routinely followed, as I was frequently under surveillance, that a little more spying made no difference. In fact, on one level, I liked it, because I felt that since they were going to spy on me anyway, I might as well let them know I was religious, as a way of testifying to God, and as a means of rebelling against the spiritual and emotional poverty that sought to grind me up.

In the late thirties, when my four-year term on the Moscow Soviet was about to expire, a delegation from my factory came to question me about my political and religious views, under the pretense of a social visit. When they asked if I believed in God, I honestly and without fear told them that I did. Subsequently, my appointment to the Soviet was not renewed.

For me, to have denied my faith would have meant that I had lost everything. I never let go of my faith in God, and I am sure that as a result He never lifted His protecting hand from me. I survived the purges, unbearable cold, hunger, the loss of friends, serious illness, the war, the Soviet bureaucracy, and the secret police. Just to have survived the purges was evidence to me of His presence.

In Uganda, I could worship openly. I also learned how to breathe freely, and alter the suspicious and distrustful nature I had developed in Russia. I finally stopped looking over my shoulder for the KGB, and began to feel alive again. There was even one time when I was walking by the side of the road, on my way to visit a friend, and a limousine drove past me, stopped, and the driver honked. The Soviet consul got out and asked, "Mr. Robinson, where are you going?" I told him I was visiting a friend and he said he wanted to give me a ride. I got in his car, for two reasons. First, the Soviets had given their word to Amin that I could stay and I felt confident that they would not do anything that might jeopardize their relationship with him, just to try and get me back. I also felt that I had to show the Soviet consul that I was not afraid. I had learned in Russia that the minute you show the slightest bit of fear—that whenever they sense a vulnerability—they will begin to poke and probe and never leave you alone until they have exploited that weakness to the fullest extent. Life was a constant, daily, spiritual war.

CHAPTER 34

Marriage and Departure

NEARLY A YEAR AFTER ARRIVING IN UGANDA, I met the lady who was to become my wife. Zylpha Mapp was the Senior Lecturer in the Department of Educational Psychology at Uganda's National Teachers' College, the sister college to Uganda Technical College. Our campuses were adjoining, and I first noticed her in the dining hall used by educators at the colleges.

She had heard me give a short speech in December 1975, at a private reception on the occasion of a book exhibition mounted by the National Spiritual Assembly of the Bahá'ís of Uganda, and thereafter she said hello when she noticed me in the dining hall. One day I invited her to join me at my table. Our friendship gradually developed over the next few months. We discovered that we had many interests in common, and I would invite her to my house on Sunday afternoons to share our love for classical music. We would often go for walks together, and talk about our goals in life. She was an American with a master's degree in education and a Certificate of Advanced Graduate Study in Guidance and Counseling from the University of Massachusetts. She had come to Uganda in 1970, as a member of the Bahá'í faith, to offer her talents for the sake of the country's social and economic development.

During the time Zylpha and I were becoming acquainted, a high official in the People's National Party of Jamaica was in Uganda. Dudley Thompson was then Jamaica's foreign minister, and I received word one day at work that he wanted to see me. When I arrived in his quarters at the Jamaican embassy, he said that he had only recently heard about me and would like to know my story first-hand. He startled me when he said, "Mr. Robinson, at present my time is limited, so if it is possible, I would like you to come with me tomorrow to Jamaica."

"Excuse me, Mr. Thompson," I said, "but I am under contract. This country has given me hospitality and I could not just pick up and leave tomorrow. I am sorry, because I appreciate your offer. But if it is possible, I will come next year when I have my vacation."

He agreed to this plan, and told me to contact him before I applied for a visa, since I had a Soviet passport, so that he could arrange everything for me. I was delighted by this development. Although my dream was to return to the United States, I thought my chances of actually doing so were extremely limited. I had only been a naturalized citizen, and from my encounter with Ambassador Bullitt nearly forty years earlier, I assumed that my files with the State Department or the Immigration and Naturalization Service contained damaging statements that would block my chances with the U.S. government. I had only one contact in the U.S.—Bill Davis, a career diplomat with the United States Information Agency, whom I had first met when he was in Moscow in 1959. Whenever he returned to Moscow subsequently, he always looked me up. I wrote him immediately after I escaped to Uganda, since he was such a good friend, to let him know I was out, and in the hope that he might be able to help me get back to the U.S. However, I considered my chances extremely remote. I thought it was far more likely that I could become a citizen of Jamaica, the country of my birth.

By the time my vacation arrived, I had made the necessary arrangements through Thompson, and flew to Jamaica. Once there, I told them that I would like to become a Jamaican citizen, and filled out all the papers. I wrote to my American friend, Bill Davis, to let him know about this development. Then I waited, but after two months the Jamaican government still had not come to a decision. I believe the problem was the same article in the *Gleaner* that the Jamaican minister who visited me in Moscow years earlier had read. This article described me as a black

Robinson tried to obtain a Jamaican passport, on the grounds that Jamaica was the country of his birth. While he was waiting for his passport application to be approved, he was given a permit allowing him to enter and leave Jamaica freely for a two-year period from August 15, 1975, until August 14, 1977.

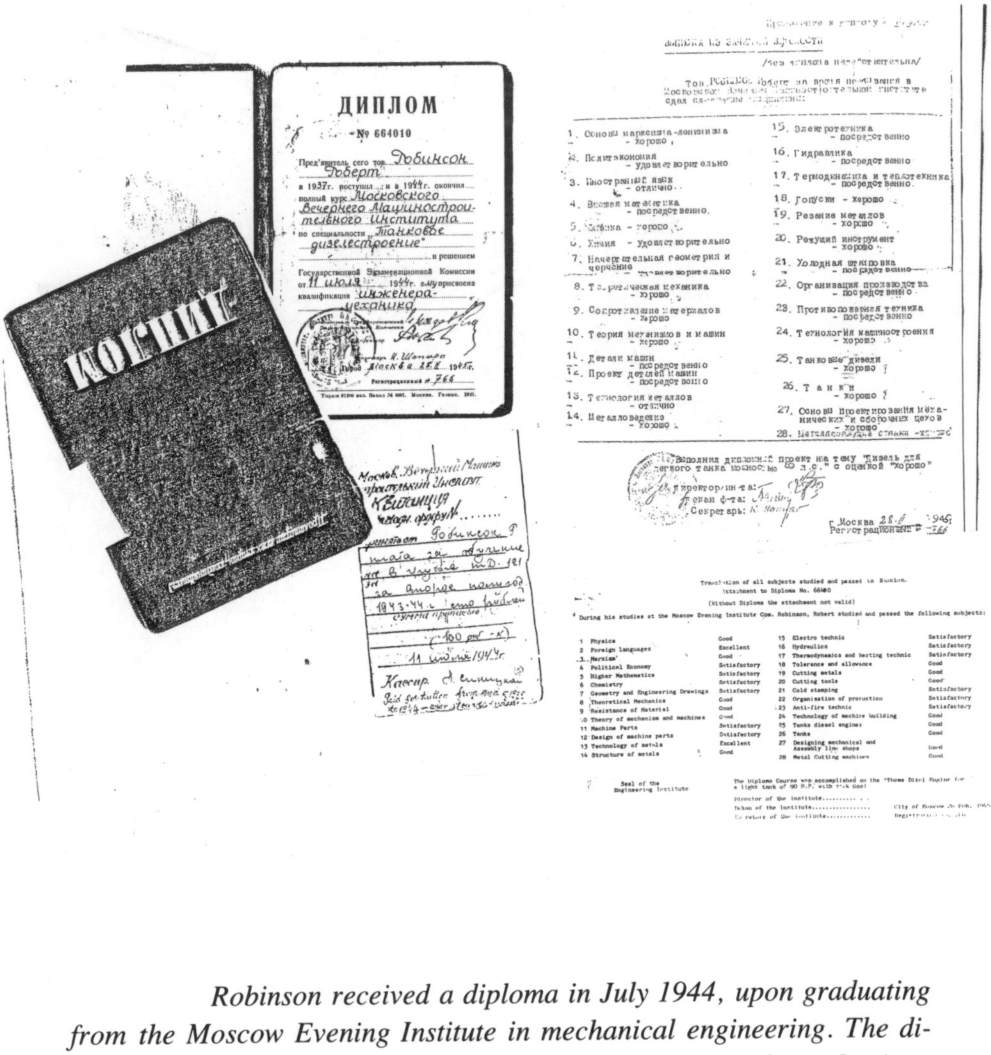

ДИПЛОМ

№ 664010

Пред'явитель сего тов. Робинсон Роберт в 1937г. поступил и в 1944г. окончил полный курс Московского Вечернего Машиностроительного Института по специальности "Танковое дизелестроение" и решением Государственной Экзаменационной Комиссии от 11 июля 1944г. ему присвоена квалификация инженера-механика.

Москва 28 II 1945г.

Регистрационный № 766

Translation of all subjects studied and passed in Russian.

Attachment to Diploma No. 66410

(Without Diploma the attachment not valid)

During his studies at the Moscow Evening Institute Com. Robinson, Robert studied and passed the following subjects:

1	Physics	Good	15	Electro technic	Satisfactory
2	Foreign languages	Excellent	16	Hydraulics	Satisfactory
3	Marxism	Good	17	Thermodynamics and heating technic	Satisfactory
4	Political Economy	Satisfactory	18	Tolerance and allowance	Good
5	Higher Mathematics	Satisfactory	19	Cutting metals	Good
6	Chemistry	Satisfactory	20	Cutting tools	Good
7	Geometry and Engineering Drawings	Satisfactory	21	Cold stamping	Satisfactory
8	Theoretical Mechanics	Good	22	Organisation of production	Satisfactory
9	Resistance of Materiel	Good	23	Anti-fire technic	Satisfactory
10	Theory of mechanism and machines	Good	24	Technology of machine building	Good
11	Machine Parts	Satisfactory	25	Tanks diesel engines	Good
12	Design of machine parts	Satisfactory	26	Tanks	Good
13	Technology of metals	Excellent	27	Designing mechanical and Assembly line shops	Good
14	Structure of metals	Good	28	Metal Cutting machines	Good

Seal of the Engineering Institute

Director of the Institute...........

Robinson received a diploma in July 1944, upon graduating from the Moscow Evening Institute in mechanical engineering. The diploma reads: "The bearer Com. Robinson, Robert, entered M.E. Institute in 1937 and finished in 1944 the entire course of "Tank Diesel Construction" at the Moscow Evening Institute of Mechanical Engineering, and by the decision of the State Examination Commission of July 1944, he is duly qualified as a Mechanical Engineer. Below, a list of the subjects he studied in Russian. Whenever asked, a graduate had to display the diploma and the list of subjects for the diploma to be recognized as valid.

Jamaican who wanted to return to Jamaica and start a Communist revolution.

Finally, after eight weeks, I told Thompson, who was still the Minister of Foreign Affairs, that I could not wait any longer and I was going to return to Uganda. He told me to get my photograph taken. When I returned with the photos, I was presented with a temporary document that permitted me to return to Jamaica. They said that if I would come back the next year, they would give me a passport.

I returned to Uganda, and went back to Jamaica the following year for a passport, but all they would give me was another temporary travel document. When I went back the third time, the Jamaicans continued to play the same old game, and refused to give me a passport. However, this visit was eventful for other reasons. My friend Zylpha Mapp was vacationing in New York at the same time I was in Jamaica. One afternoon I received a telegram from her saying she would be visiting Jamaica before returning to Uganda, and asked me to locate the Bahá'í Center in Kingston for her. It was during her stay that Zylpha became my wife, on December 28, 1976.

I was still in Jamaica when I received a letter from Bill Davis, who told me that he was making arrangements for me to get a visa to come to the United States, and to visit him at the National War College. Davis arranged for someone in the American embassy to pick me up at my hotel and bring me into the embassy, bypassing the long lines outside. The person to whom I was directed inside was annoyed at me. He asked, tersely, "Who are you? We were instructed to give you an entry visa."

I told him, "I don't know; somebody must have done it for U.S. government reasons."

Then he asked to see my passport. I told him that I could not give it to him, and he demanded to know why. I told him, "I think your instructions are to give me an entry visa to the United States and they do not include presenting my passport."

He said he could do that, but that he must look at whatever documents I had, to be sure that I was not asking him to fill out a visa under a false name. So I showed him my passport, and he exclaimed. "But, this is a Soviet passport!"

"Yes, it is," I said.

"How is it that you are a Soviet?" he asked. I told him that it

NIV- 20784

0/6185

VISA

KINGSTON

B-2 1 APR 1977

1 JUL 1977

ONE

ROBERT D. ROBINSON

DESCRIPTION:

xx Male ☐ Female

Height 5 ft. 7½ in.

Born on June 22, 1906

at Kingston Jamaica

Issued in accordance with 22 CFR. 41: ~~(2)(b)~~ 112(4)

UNITED STATES OF AMERICA

Tariff Item No. 22

Fee Paid $ nil

Local Cy equiv.

On April 1, 1977, Robinson was given a visa on a plain piece of paper valid for three months, by a member of the US State Department in Kingston, Jamaica, who was operating on orders from Washington, D.C.

was a long story and that I would have to wait to tell him another time. He gave me a visa on a plain piece of paper, so that I could make it into the country without being turned back. Zylpha returned to Uganda, and I caught a plane for New York, with connections through Miami. I had last visited Miami forty-seven years earlier, on my way back from visiting my mother in Cuba. I reflected on that visit, and my fateful decision to go to the Soviet Union, as the plane's wheels touched down on the runway. I continued on to New York to see my brother, who was living in Harlem. I did not give him any advance warning; I just showed up. He was shocked, and could not believe his eyes. He had not thought he would ever see me again, although he knew I was out, because I had written him from Uganda. He was trembling when we hugged each other. When I looked at him, tears began rolling down my cheeks. I had prepared myself to be emotionally collected when I saw him, but we were both so happy, I just let go. He took me to dinner that evening, and we had a wonderful time.

He told me about how in 1945 he had traveled to Washington to talk with officials at the State Department, in an effort to get me out of the Soviet Union. He was preparing to send me an official invitation, in accordance with procedures, until someone at the State Department told him not to waste his time, because the Soviet embassy had told them that I did not want to leave. When I had last seen my brother in the thirties, he was married, but now he and his wife were divorced, and he was single and living alone. I asked him what had happened, but he did not want to tell me.

Manhattan was different than I had imagined, and I was especially saddened to see how much Harlem had deteriorated. I had expected it to be better than it had been in 1933, not worse. We walked down 125th Street, and Seventh Avenue, which used to be full of well-dressed high rollers. But now it was a dump, and when I saw the condition of the people, I asked my brother when it had started happening. I had been told that blacks were politically, economically, and socially better off in the United States, so I had expected something much better.

I flew to Washington, D.C., and was met by Bill Davis. He drove me to 1600 Pennsylvania Avenue and took a picture of me standing in front of the White House. I told him my entire story, in more detail than I had been able to relate to him through letters and phone conversa-

Uganda Technical College

P.O.Box 7181, Kampala, Uganda.

Principal: N.B. Balyamujura, Dip. Eng., M.A.S.E.E. (U.K.) M.I.E.E.E. (U.K.), Dip. Educ., Dip. Admin.

Your Ref.

Our Ref. UTC/70 21st March, 1985. Telephone 65211-3
Telegrams: Technical, Kampala

TO WHOM IT MAY CONCERN

MR. R. ROBINSON

The above-named was appointed by the Public Service Commission as Lecturer in Mechnical Engineering in the School of Mechanical and Production Engineering at this College with effect from 2nd May, 1974. He taught both Ordinary and Higher Diploma students. He left the College on medical grounds in 1978.

Mr. Robinson was a very good teacher, efficient, keen and interested in his work and I have no hesitation in recommending him for employment.

(Christopher Ntambi)
AG. PRINCIPAL

Principal
UGANDA TECHNICAL COLLEGE

At age seventy-nine, the author requested and received a reference from Uganda Technical College to aid him in looking for a job in the United States. The acting principal of Uganda Technical College writes, "Mr. Robinson was a very good teacher, efficient, keen and interested in his work and I have no hesitation in recommending him for employment."

tions. He encouraged me to believe that I could get permanent resident status. He asked me to leave some photographs and, without going into detail, he said he would see what he could do. I returned to Kampala to finish my contract, hoping that Davis' efforts would be successful.

Before long I heard from him. Because there was no American embassy in Kampala, I was to go to Nairobi, Kenya, to pick up a sealed package with my name on it, which would contain documents enabling me to return to the United States. I learned later that Davis had spent more than an hour explaining my case to the district commissioner of the Immigration and Naturalization Service in Baltimore, Maryland. He showed the commissioner my documents and correspondence, and persuaded him to give me advance parole so that I could enter the United States unencumbered.

Very excited, I went to the American embassy in Nairobi, but when I told the woman in charge of the consulate section that I was there to pick up a package with my name on it, she said they had not received it. She was going to send me away, but I insisted that she check with her superior. Seeing my stubbornness, she told me to wait a minute, and then she returned with the package, saying that she had not been aware that it had arrived. But she said that she needed more instructions because some forms were not properly filled out, and she could not give me the package at that time. I tried arguing with her, but it was useless.

I returned to Kampala and phoned Bill Davis in the United States, to tell him what had happened. I learned later that he called Barbara Watson, the Assistant Secretary of State for Consular and Security Affairs, and told her what had happened to me in Nairobi. Watson told him that she would cable the woman in the Nairobi embassy to meet her in the Seychelles Islands and explain why she had not handed over the documents.

Several weeks later Davis called me to say that I should go to Nairobi again to pick up the package. I went, and when I encountered the same woman, she asked me, "Mr. Robinson, please tell me, who do you know in Washington? I was reprimanded for not giving you the documents when you first came here." She was very pleasant and helpful, and after three days of processing documents, she gave me the package containing the proper documents.

I told her that I really did not know that I knew anyone in

original

Предъявитель сего, граждан ин/ка СОЮЗА СОВЕТСКИХ СОЦИАЛИСТИЧЕСКИХ РЕСПУБЛИК

РОБИНСОН
(фамилия)

РОБЕРТ
(имя и отчество)

1906 г.р. г. Кингстон
(дата и место рождения—date et lieu de naissance)

ROBINSON
(nom)

ROBERT
(et prénoms)

отправляется за границу.
se rend à l'étranger.

ЧАСТНАЯ ПОЕЗДКА

Лица, внесенные в паспорт
Personnes inscrites dans le passeport

Выдан 19 . декабря 19 73.
Délivré le

Паспорт действителен до 19/XII 75
Ce passeport est valable pour ... 19 ... г.

Подпись

Robinson photocopied a page from his Soviet passport, before mailing it to the Soviet embassy in Jamica by registered mail on December 14, 1980. Along with the passport he sent a letter renouncing his Soviet citizenship. (See page 418).

particular, and I was sorry if she had gotten into trouble. I went back to Kampala, documents in hand, and my wife and I prepared to move to the United States. I had been having some medical problems; almost every day for a year I would have a fainting spell. Neither a battery of doctors in Uganda, nor a specialist I had visited in England, could find anything wrong with me. I finally saw a Ugandan doctor who discovered that I had probably had a minor stroke. He prescribed some medication, and things got better, but as a result I was able to leave Uganda Technical College in 1978 on medical grounds. I obtained a letter from the acting principal of the college, which stated that I was "a very good teacher– efficient, keen, and interested in my work," and recommended me for employment elsewhere.

Zylpha and I packed our few belongings and flew to America. Uganda was getting hot for both of us, anyway, because of its war with Tanzania. Either way, foreigners were at risk. We were in potential danger because of the nationalistic fervor of the Ugandan army and we might well have found ourselves trapped in a war zone. So we left. When we arrived in Washington, D.C., I was overwhelmed when Bill Davis met us. He had my green card waiting for me, and presented it with a flourish.

"I now declare that Robert Robinson is a legal resident of the United States of America," he said. He had already prepared a place for us to stay. I began writing my memoirs, while keeping a low profile. Even though on December 14, 1980, I had sent a letter to the Soviet embassy in Jamaica renouncing my Soviet citizenship, and then returned my Soviet passport to them, the Soviet government could still technically have claimed me as a Soviet citizen. They could have picked me up anywhere, at any time. I did not want to become visible, because if they had gotten me inside a Soviet embassy, I would have been in Soviet territory. Finally, on December 6, 1986, my dream of forty years came true. I became an American citizen once again.

Cross Roads,
P.O. Box 35,
Kingston 5, Jamaica W.I.

DECLARATION OF INTENT

DATED the ......14th...... day of December, 1980.

To the Consul General of the United States of Soviet Russia,
Kingston, Jamaica, West Indies.

I, ROBERT ROBINSON, heretofore a Soviet Citizen, do solemnly declare that from the date hereof I shall cease to be a citizen of the U.S.S.R., and thereby renounce allegiance to the flag, the government, its laws and all regulations thereof.

This Declaration of renunciation is deemed absolutely necessary because of the fact that I have regained my previous Jamaican Citizenship, wherein I was born, and in addition to that is the factor of my advanced age.

I am therefore returning to the Soviet Government, through you, my present Soviet Passport No. OK 671989,** which was granted to me in Kampala, the Republic of Uganda, East Africa, in exchange for the first Passport No. OM-Z-179476 issued to me in Moscow in December, 1973.

With my respects to the Soviet Government and you,

Sincerely yours

Robert Robinson
ROBERT ROBINSON

from 1978 - 1983

Receipt of registered letter to Soviet Embassy
REGN No. 0158 CERTIFICATE OF POSTING
REGISTERED ARTICLE
...SSED TO:
Embassy of the Union of Soviet Socialist ...
REGISTRATION FEE PAID
Receiving Officer's signature (or initials)

Robinson sent a letter "To the Consul General of the United States of Soviet Russia," in Kingston, Jamaica, renouncing his Soviet citizenship, which he mailed on Dec. 14, 1980.

CHAPTER 35

Perestroika

EVER SINCE I ESCAPED FROM THE SOVIET UNION in 1974, I have kept up my observations from the outside. Whatever I could find about the Soviet Union, I have read. I observed the Soviets operating in Africa, and I have followed developments in US-Soviet relations. When I believed it was safe, I have spoken with Russian emigrés and dissidents. I have thought a great deal about America, and its responsibility in the world.

Looking back now, in March 1988, I must admit that my feelings were mixed when I arrived in America and was handed a green card. My dream to return home and enjoy a life of personal freedom was coming true. However, I have not been able to relax. I know the Russian mind and I know the Soviet system. I realize, painfully, that most Americans understand neither. Herein lies my problem. I am well-advanced in years. I should be content to pass the time in a rocking chair, but instead, I worry about the survival of the Free World.

I am burdened by my knowledge that Soviet communist party members believe it is their country's destiny to dominate the world. The message is everywhere. It is drummed into the heads of party members five-days-a-week, at meetings after work which they *must* attend, and which non-party members who want to gain favor from the officials in charge of their jobs, *should* attend. Children are influenced from an early age. They learn in school, in meetings of the Young Pioneers, and as members of the Komsomol, that it is Soviet destiny to defeat America and dominate the world.

In the absence of any competing point of view, the indoctrination works. I can say without fear of contradiction, after living in the Soviet Union for forty-four years, that it is as natural for a Soviet citizen to believe that they should dominate the world as it is for an American to believe that the democratic system offers the best way of life. The Russian people are willing to endure almost *any* sacrifice to achieve this goal. They boast about their ability to tighten their belts and do whatever is necessary to bring down America.

The nation is obsessed with the need to be superior to America. They adjust their tactics, but their eyes do not waver from their goal. It does not matter whether it is *détente* or peaceful coexistence in foreign affairs, or *glasnost* or *perestroika* domestically, these are tactics. Their goal remains constant. Americans are not very good at distinguishing between Soviet tactics and Soviet goals.

From inside the Soviet Union, I deeply regretted that toward the end of World War II, American leaders did not act in a way that reflected a deep understanding of their adversary. Americans could have prevented Soviet adventurism then, because America was much stronger than the Soviet Union. But America misconstrued the threat, and thereby lacked the will.

In 1972, when the Soviet economy was clearly going downhill, America should have let them keep sliding, but instead Americans publicly and privately stepped in to help the Soviets. I was still there when the Soviets first began buying American grain. The Russian people had no idea where the grain was coming from. When I left in 1974, Soviet factories were still using machinery imported during the 1930s. After three shifts a day, seven days a week for forty years, the machines were in bad shape. They were breaking down and needed repair, but the Soviets would not take the time to repair them adequately, since they were making war material, which was in constant demand.

In my factory, they were having difficulty making precision ball bearings. The Russians never officially addressed the rumor circulating in Moscow that they were using Swedish and American bearings in their airplanes instead of their own because the Russian-made bearings would crack when heated. The Soviets also make their own machines, but during the time I was in the Soviet Union, these were of poor quality. As a result of problems in their manufacturing sector, many products were being hand-tooled. Soviet steel, after it has been treated and worked, often cracks on the inside.

How is America to deal with the Soviet Union today? In most cases, butter is better than bullets, and in every case, peace is better than war, provided territorial integrity and personal freedom and dignity remain intact.

Can America persuade the Soviet Union to change its quest for world domination? Should America encourage, or attempt to prevent, increased trade between the two countries? What steps can be taken to create trust and diminish suspicion between these superpowers? What do the Soviets need from America today, and what should be America's response?

I see clearly that the Soviet Union urgently needs three things: time, machinery and technology. They need enough time so that they can catch up with the level of Western economic development, they need to retool their factories with new machinery, and they need to scrap the piecework system if they wish to match the quality of consumer products in Western countries.

Their technological processes are woefully out-of-date. They borrowed and adapted various ideas from the West—such as the piecework system—to their own use and called it their own. Assigning production quotas and paying according to what is produced does not lead to production efficiencies. It is quite the reverse. The Soviet system is structured so that the only way an ordinary person can make a living is through deception and corruption. Workers, factory administrators, and the members of the Soviet administrative elite—the *nomenklatura*—are all co-conspirators in filing and covering up for falsified production reports. From top to bottom the system is corrupt: the *nomenklatura* make their living through corruption; inspectors who are sent to reconcile reports on paper with actual productivity are invariably bribed by factory administrators. Everybody cooperates to insure that the factory will receive its monthly bonus for meeting or surpassing its quota.

I doubt whether the Soviets leaders can ever restructure their industrial system in a fundamental way. They are trapped on both sides. Most people are stuck in their ways and would fight to preserve what they have against signs of change. Others will seize upon new opportunities and push zealously for more. From both directions the leaders will risk undermining their entire political system. They must delicately balance their need to improve the economy with their need to control people. What they can address is the necessity to modernize their plants. For this purpose, the Soviets have set aside a huge amount for capital investments in their 1988 budget. Whereas they usually budget at least 20 percent (and were over 30 percent during the rapid industrialization in the 1930s) they have pushed their capital investment figure up to 30 percent for 1988. General Secretary Mikhail Gorbachev and members of the politburo are not capable of simply declaring reforms into existence.

They are walking a fine line with their current domestic policies. Yet one must remember that the Soviet people have no freedoms which the Soviet leaders are bound to respect. If the system itself begins to be threatened, the state's police apparatus will be turned on the people overnight, who are as helpless as lame chickens being stalked by a wolf.

Gorbachev visited the US for the December 1987 summit meeting with President Reagan, for more reasons than to conclude negotiations on a nuclear arms treaty. He and his associates came begging for opportunities to acquire American technology, and to increase their trade with American companies. Members of the Soviet team unabashedly contacted government officials who had nothing to do with the treaty to discuss these economic issues, and they held a meeting with American businessmen where Gorbachev made a personal pitch for more American trade.

Soviet officials desperately want to achieve most favored nation status with the United States. At every opportunity, they appeal to American businessmen to take their appeal to Congress and the executive branch. They have a strategy with American business leaders. They produce a list of products they would like to export to the United States, and complain that US regulations do not allow them to do so. They then seek to entice these businessmen with the idea of developing joint ventures between the private American company and the Soviet government.

However, the Soviet idea of a joint venture is to gain most of the benefit while sharing little of the risk. In most cases, the Soviets would have the American company furnish them with capital, technology, and management skills, while the Soviets provide only the raw products and the labor. The Soviets want to manufacture the products in the Soviet Union for export to the West, so that the American company will end up competing with itself in Western markets. The Soviets also propose that there are some products they will market in the Soviet Union, and will repatriate a good portion of the American capital at an honest rate of exchange.

Opportunities in West Germany interest them even more than in the US. The Soviets currently have about 350 joint operating proposals on the table to West German companies.

Gorbachev is working to soften Western attitudes toward the Soviet Union, in order to obtain what they need. He has caught the imagination of people in America and in other Western countries. He knows how to handle public relations. But whether or not he wears a fedora, he does not have a Western mind. Gorbachev is a product of the Soviet system and has a deeply emotional attachment to the Russian soil. He was the protégé of Yuri Andropov, the former director of the KGB, who later became general secretary of the Communist Party. Gorbachev is doing what his mentors in the Politburo permit him to do. He cannot act without their consent. If he goes too far or too fast, without proper consultation with his older colleagues, he may suffer the same fate as Khrushchev.

As long as the Politburo can use Gorbachev to gain favor and credibility in the West, it will continue to do so. The situation inside the Soviet Union is delicate. Gorbachev appears to be brash in extending and encouraging *glasnost* (openness) in Soviet society. For the time being, the result is good for the Soviet people. They are now free to criticize the bureaucrats in the system, although under no circumstances may the ordinary people criticize the system itself. It is probable that *glasnost* will not last, because it is difficult for the people to exercise restraint. They will most likely push too hard. A free press, for example, cannot become *too* free without endangering the system, and it is a cardinal rule in Soviet society that the system itself cannot be wrong.

When Boris Yeltsin, former Moscow party chief, startled his colleagues with his criticism of the rate of speed with which *perestroika* (restructuring) was taking place under Gorbachev, he touched the tender nerve. He was criticizing the system and not the leadership of Gorbachev. Perhaps this was a calculated move. We may never know, but what we do know is the outcome. Although Yeltsin supported Gorbachev personally and was considered a good friend of the general secretary, first he was thrown out as Moscow party chief, and then a few weeks later he was removed from his seat on the Politburo. The limits to *glasnost* were communicated loudly and clearly to the Soviet people: "You may castigate a bureaucrat, but don't attack the system!"

It should be understood that through *glasnost* and *perestroika*, the Soviet leaders are trying to strengthen the country's economy and military might. They are seeking to invigorate the people, and in the process position the country to achieve what they believe is its historical destiny.

They are not interested in raising the standard of living as an end in itself, but are doing what they feel is necessary to obtain rapid industrial growth. An invigorated people will be better able to help accomplish what Soviet policymakers believe is the country's historical destiny. Although *glasnost* may be short-lived, some form of economic reform must continue even if *perestroika* as currently conceived is adjusted. Early indications are that the economic reforms are not going well. Performance figures for 1987 show at least twenty-one industries operating below the level of 1986. We should not expect the Soviets to reduce their military budget. Total expenditures on defense are still about one-third of the 1988 budget, and one-fifth of the gross national product.

One of the fundamental new rules under the system of *perestroika* is to prohibit the drinking of alcohol in offices. Gorbachev apparently recognized that the high rate of consumption of vodka results in public drunkenness, lost production, and shoddy products. He called for a halt to the practice of serving vodka and cognac in offices during working hours. It had been traditional for Soviet officials to offer visitors alcoholic drinks, coffee or tea, and chocolates in their offices even before noon. As a result, visitors were encouraged and always welcome. Although Soviet vodka is exported to the US in bottles with screw-on tops, the bottles of vodka sold to Soviet people at home are sealed only with a piece of aluminum foil. Once the seal is broken, there is no readily available way to close the bottle. As a result, a bottle once opened is usually consumed in its entirety.

Social and economic reforms are not new in the history of the Soviet system. They have come, and they have gone. Lenin introduced the New Economic Policy in 1921, in an effort to revive a depressed economy. Under Lenin's policy of War Communism, from 1918 to 1920, the nation underwent extremely fast socialization while in the midst of a civil war. Beginning in 1921, Lenin reduced peasant taxes and permitted small private stores and manufacturing in the cities. According to both Western and Soviet eyewitnesses, consumer goods were cheap and easily available.

Stalin continued Lenin's New Economic Policy while he worked to consolidate his power. In 1928, Stalin began his first Five-Year Plan. He closed the small private stores and workshops and forcibly collectivized the peasant private farms. There were immediate shortages of food and consumer goods. No Soviet leader has had the courage to destroy the collectivization system, which created the agricultural mess in which the Soviet Union still finds itself today. Instead, following Stalin, each leader in his turn has tried to achieve incremental improvements within the system of collectivization.

While closely watching the changes underway in the Soviet Union, Americans should not become prematurely euphoric about the prospects of concluding a successful treaty or series of treaties with the Soviets. It would be well for us to understand better the people with whom we are dealing. A Russian is capable of telling you one thing today and, when you bring the same issue up the next day, he will say that you are mistaken. He will say that you misunderstood him. This is what the Soviet Union does in the international sphere, with treaties. For them, a treaty is just a piece of paper, which they can throw away when it suits them.

In trying to decide what steps to take, in dealing with our formidable adversary, we must avoid the trap of trying to see the Soviets as mirror images of ourselves. Soviets and Americans are different. They have a different set of needs, values, and desires from those of the West. Their decision-making process is different from ours. We have an open and democratic system, but we do not have to expose ourselves to our enemy. We must not reveal projects that have military implications. We must not allow the Soviets to have even a peephole through which to see what we are doing. We make it easy for them to steal our manufacturing and technological knowledge. America must revise its methods for keeping information classified.

There are two things which the Soviets understand thoroughly: power and reciprocity. If we have power and demonstrate the courage to use it, they will respect us. If we have the power but lack the will to use it—or if we allow ourselves to become weaker and weaker—the Soviets will use their power against us *unless* we can convince them that neither side would gain anything and both sides would take unacceptable losses.

There are a few things we can require from the Soviets as demonstrations of goodwill, which would help them to earn our trust and respect, just as we seek theirs.

The Soviet Union should:

1. Permit freedom of travel for its citizens out of and back into the USSR.
2. Stop provocations and disinformation programs.
3. Diminish its programmed hatred for America.
4. Be completely truthful to its own people.

The United States should:

1. Learn how to be patient in negotiations with Soviets. The Soviets might be operating on a different timetable. We need to care more about the substance of the agreement than about any deadline to reach it.
2. Recognize that the Truman Doctrine of containment is no longer valid.
3. Whenever possible, encourage exchange visits by Soviet and American citizens so they can communicate on a person-to-person basis.
4. Encourage the study of the Russian language in the early stages of school in America, so our new leaders will have a better understanding of what our adversaries are all about, and our ordinary citizens will be better equipped to carry the message of freedom and democracy directly to Soviet citizens.

I lived as an American citizen during my early adult years. For the next forty-four years, I lived and worked in the Soviet Union, side-by-side with its people. Having now been blessed with the opportunity to live out the rest of my life as an American citizen once again, I have written this account so that anyone who wishes may learn what life in the Soviet Union is really like.

Afterword

ON A PLEASANT AUGUST DAY IN 1959, I was in the geodesic dome of the American exhibition at Sokolniki Park in Moscow explaining the functions of the IBM high-speed electronic computer in Russian. As usual, a large group of Soviet citizens were gathered around listening to my commentary and poised to ask questions not about the computer, but about the price I paid for my shoes or my suit, how much salary I earned, and "How many meters do you have?" By law, each Soviet citizen is guaranteed (at least on paper) a designated number of square meters of housing space. The acute housing shortage in the USSR nearly always prevented that guarantee from being met.

That day, there was something unusual about the crowd. I spotted a black man in the group and wondered who he was and why he was there. I later learned that he wondered the same things about me. After the demonstration of the computer, which printed out answers to a list of one thousand keyed questions that could be requested by the audience, the crowd asked me a lot of personal questions and then moved on to the next exhibit stand.

However, the black man remained behind. He stood ramrod straight. Unlike most Soviet men who wore open collar shirts and no jackets, the black man wore both a necktie and a complete suit.

He approached and looked at me quizzically. Finally, in polite but crisp Russian language, he said, "Hello." I responded in Russian. He then asked where I was from. I replied, "Detroit." The serious expression that had been on his face gave way to a smile. He said we had something in common because he too was from Detroit. At that point, we both switched to English.

The black man was Robert Robinson. He asked if we could talk privately later. I agreed and asked how I could get in touch with him. He gave me his telephone number. That was the beginning of a friendship that has lasted now for twenty-nine years.

In such privacy as we could find, walking along the streets of Moscow and through the parks, he told me how he came to the Soviet Union in 1930, and how he had been repeatedly denied permission to leave since the end of World War II. We never discussed anything serious inside a room in any building. He was taking a chance in sharing his story with me and placing confidence in me. I respected his confidence and admittedly was shocked by his plight. The more I heard, the more determined I became to help him to return to America—which is what he said he wanted to do.

Numerous attempts were made to help him get out of the USSR legitimately. All efforts failed. I returned to the USSR on business some years later and found that Robinson was still desperately trying to find a way out of that country. Still, there was nothing more that I could legitimately do to get him out. I was not going to try anything that would violate Soviet laws.

In 1974, Robinson got out of the USSR through a ruse to take a vacation in Uganda and made contact with me in the United States. Now that he was safely out, I began working through contacts in the White House, and the US Immigration and Naturalization Service (INS) to arrange for Robinson to return to the United States as a resident alien. At that time, he was still a Soviet citizen.

I was successful in arranging for Robinson to enter the United States legitimately as a resident alien. I acquired a green card (alien registration) for him from the INS. Furthermore, I provided a place for him and his newly-wed American wife to live for a year and insisted that he spend as much time as possible in writing his memoirs. He began immediately and produced over one thousand pages of typed manuscript. He wrote everything in longhand. His wife transcribed it with the typewriter. Obviously, the manuscript had to be cut considerably in order to be published. Forty-four years of his experiences in the USSR could fill several books.

What you have read in this book is only part of an extraordinary account of the trials and tribulations of one black man against the world's leading communist government. It reveals the determination and faith of one man to overcome an entire governmental apparatus to stifle his quest for personal freedom.

Robinson won that battle, but he had to keep a low profile until he could regain his American citizenship. Although he had renounced his Soviet citizenship in a letter to the Soviet Ambassador in Jamaica, he feared each day and night that until he regained his American citizenship, he might be picked up by KGB agents, forced onto Soviet diplomatic property, and informed that he was still regarded as a Soviet citizen, subject to Soviet laws.

Even now, armed with an American passport, Robinson constantly looks over his shoulder to avoid pushing his luck too far. Inasmuch as he knows the workings of the Soviet government so well, fear is likely to be with him for the rest of his life.

William B. Davis

Epilogue

For writing this book, I am certain that I shall be attacked without mercy by those people whose specific duty is to defend the Soviet system from criticism at all costs. Truth disturbs the leaders of that country.

It is fair to speculate that I will be denounced. Efforts will be made to discredit my account. Perhaps false documents will be presented, or recordings purporting to be of my voice will be produced. Soviet disinformation and propaganda can be skillfully done. By simply writing the truth about my forty-four years in the Soviet Union, I will now be considered by the government as an irrevocable enemy.

Yet all that I have written happened. I saw it all, experienced it all, and heard almost all. Many party members and nonparty members alike, holding responsible jobs and whose integrity I learned to respect, revealed a great deal to me under the pledge of strictest secrecy. If some of my account seems unusual or even bizarre, remember that this book deals with an unusual country that uses extraordinary methods to control its people.

My purpose has been to acquaint you with the life of the Soviet people as it really is for them, and as it was for me, a black. My only regret is that there are omissions. I could have written a thousand pages but, of course, space was limited. I sought to be candid, objective, and descriptive, without grinding axes, without vindictiveness. I have done my best to be as balanced as possible.

Hopefully, my years of struggle in the Soviet Union will provide many people with valuable insight on the realities of life in that country, where good and decent people live and die in frustration under a system of government that views freedom as a threat to its existence.

Index